Software Engineering Education

Software Engineering Education
The Educational Needs of the Software Community

Edited by
Norman E. Gibbs and Richard E. Fairley

With 31 Illustrations

Springer Science+Business Media, LLC

Norman E. Gibbs
Software Engineering Institute
Carnegie-Mellon University
Pittsburgh, PA 15213
USA

Richard E. Fairley
Wang Institute of Graduate Studies
Tyngsboro, MA 01879
USA

The Software Engineering Institute is operated by Carnegie-Mellon University under contract with the Department of Defense.

The views and conclusions contained in these proceedings are those of the authors and should not be interpreted as representing official policies, either expressed or implied, of the Software Engineering Institute, Carnegie-Mellon University, Wang Institute of Graduate Studies, the Department of Defense, or the U.S. Government.

Library of Congress Cataloging in Publication Data
The Educational needs of the software community.
  Papers presented at the Software Engineering
Education Workshop, held at the Carnegie-Mellon
University Software Engineering Institute,
Feb. 27–28, 1986, sponsored by Software Engineering
Institute and Wang Institute of Graduate Studies.
  Bibliography: p.
  1. Computer software—Study and teaching
(Higher)—United States—Congresses. I. Gibbs,
Norman E. (Norman Edgar). II. Fairley,
R. E. (Richard E.). III. Software
Engineering Education Workshop (1986:Carnegie-
Mellon University Software Engineering Institute)
IV. Carnegie-Mellon University. Software Engineering
Institute. V. Wang Institute of Graduate Studies.
QA76.751.E38   1987   005.1'07'1173   86-29757

© 1987 by Springer Science+Business Media New York
Originally published by Springer-Verlag New York, Inc. in 1987
Softcover reprint of the hardcover 1st edition 1987
All rights reserved. This work may not be translated or copied in whole or in part without the written permission of the publisher (Springer Science+Business Media, LLC),
                    except for brief excerpts in connection with reviews or scholarly analysis. Use in connection with any form of information storage and retrieval, electronic adaptation, computer software, or by similar or dissimilar methodology now known or hereafter developed is forbidden.
The use of general descriptive names, trade names, trademarks, etc. in this publication, even if the former are not especially identified, is not to be taken as a sign that such names, as understood by the Trade Marks and Merchandise Marks Act, may accordingly be used freely by anyone.

9 8 7 6 5 4 3 2 1

ISBN 978-1-4612-9129-9   ISBN 978-1-4612-4720-3 (eBook)
DOI 10.1007/978-1-4612-4720-3

Foreword

Participants in the Software Engineering Education Workshop included 25 invited persons from academia, industry, and government, and 10 members of the SEI technical staff. Invited participants were asked to write position papers; suggested topics were: Intellectual Foundations and Fundamental Concepts of Software Engineering, Current Practice and Needs Assessment, Current State of Software Engineering Education, Technology Transition, and Evolution of Software Engineering. Based on the abstracts received, the chairmen with the help of the SEI Education Division staff partitioned the papers into four categories:

- Software Engineering Principles
- Current Software Engineering Curricula
- Experiences with Existing Courses
- Future of Software Engineering Education

Working groups were formed by the organizers to address issues in almost the same four categories. Discussion questions were prepared with the goal of focusing the working groups on issues the SEI should address as part of its educational mission. Three weeks before the meeting all participants received the position papers, working group assignments, working group questions, and the material included in the appendices to these proceedings.

The opening session included welcomes from the workshop chairmen and a keynote address delivered by Professor Frederick P. Brooks, Jr., Kenan Professor of Computer Science, University of North Carolina at Chapel Hill, and author of the classic book, *The Mythical Man-Month*. Professor Mary Shaw, SEI Chief Scientist, discussed the scientific aspects of software engineering based on ideas from the position papers and her experience as a leading software engineering educator. Professor James Collofello, Arizona State University, summarized the papers that discussed current software engineering curricula. After these presentations at the opening session, Professor Nico Habermann of Carnegie-Mellon University moderated a discussion that included the three speakers as panelists. The purpose of the panel was to give all the participants an opportunity to comment on the position papers and the questions to the working groups prior to the smaller group meetings.

The working groups met during Thursday afternoon and Friday morning. They made brief reports to the entire group the first afternoon and final reports were given at the closing session Friday afternoon.

The proceedings are arranged into four major sections. The first includes a transcription of the keynote address and the panel discussion moderated by Nico Habermann. The next section includes all the working papers submitted by the participants. Allison Brunvand of the SEI Education Division placed them into a consistent format under the guidance of Susan Dunkle and Purvis Jackson of the SEI Documentation Services. Any mistakes in the transcription and editing of the papers are solely the responsibility of the SEI and not the authors. The bibliographies of all papers were arranged into a single bibliography for these proceedings. Because this bibliography may be useful to people intending to start new programs, it is included immediately following the papers and additional copies may be obtained from the Education Division, Software Engineering Institute, Carnegie-Mellon University, Pittsburgh, Pennsylvania 15213.

The third section is a summary of working group activity. It includes the questions given to the working groups as their charge, a list of group members, and transcriptions of final group reports. The SEI arranged for a transcription service to record the keynote address, the panel charging the working groups, and the reports of the working groups. The reader must keep in mind that text presented orally will not appear as polished as written text.

The last section includes two papers which were mailed to all participants in advance of the workshop. Appendix 1 is an SEI draft curriculum that played a central role in the deliberations of all the working groups. Appendix 2 is an SEI report on the educational needs of the software community.

Preface

The 1986 Workshop, *Software Engineering Education: The Educational Needs of the Software Community*, was held at the Carnegie-Mellon University Software Engineering Institute (SEI) on February 27 and 28, 1986. The workshop was jointly sponsored by the SEI and the Wang Institute of Graduate Studies. Norm Gibbs of the SEI was general chair and Dick Fairley of Wang Institute was program chair. The primary focus was on master's level education in software engineering, although there was some discussion of undergraduate and doctoral level issues.

The 1986 workshop was held almost exactly 10 years after the Interface Workshop, *Software Engineering Education: Needs and Objectives*, was held at the University of California, Irvine on February 9, 1976. The main purpose of the 1976 workshop was to provide a forum in which educators and people from industry could explore needs and objectives in software engineering education. In contrast to 1976, the 1986 participants were mostly educators with considerable experience in teaching software engineering in academic and industrial settings. Four persons who attended the 1976 workshop were also present at the 1986 workshop.

In 1976 few educators had extensive experience in software engineering education, but by 1986 a great deal of progress had been made. In 1986 many universities were routinely offering one or more software engineering courses and at least three United States institutions: Wang Institute, Seattle University, and Texas Christian University, were offering Master's programs in software engineering. In addition, numerous governmental and industrial organizations were offering a wide variety of programs in software engineering, ranging from short training courses to prolonged and intensive educational programs.

It seemed timely and appropriate to convene a limited attendance workshop in which software engineering educators from academia, industry, and government were invited to assess the current state of software engineering education and recommend future directions. It also seemed appropriate that it be sponsored by both the Software Engineering Institute and Wang Institute. The SEI is a federally funded research and development center established by the United States Department of Defense to improve the state of software technology. The Education Division of SEI, headed by Norm Gibbs, is charged with influencing software engineering curricula development throughout the education community. It has undertaken the task of working with educators through the SEI affiliates' programs to design, develop, insert and support a graduate curriculum in software engineering. Wang Institute of Graduate Studies was founded and endowed by the An Wang family as a non-profit, autonomous institution of higher learning; Wang Institute is not affiliated with Wang Laboratories. The primary goals of the School of Information Technology of Wang Institute, chaired by Dick Fairley, are to provide graduate level education in software engineering and to offer other professionally oriented programs that meet the needs of industry.

We were gratified by the time and effort that the participants devoted to their position papers, and by the level of enthusiasm and quality of participation they exhibited during the sessions. We believe that these proceedings are a genuine contribution to the emerging discipline of software engineering, and to software engineering education in particular. The quality of this contribution is a direct result of their efforts, and we thank them. Of course, we take full responsibility for any errors that have been made in transcribing and editing their contributions.

We also thank the support staffs of the SEI and Wang Institute. Their collective expertise and cheerful competence in handling logistics, local arrangements, and emergencies made chairing of the workshop and editing of these proceedings pleasant and rewarding experiences. In particular, we thank Allison Brunvand and Albert Johnson of the SEI Education Division, Susan Dunkle, Purvis Jackson, and Carol Biesecker of SEI Documentation Services, and Sue Hovey of Wang Institute for their efforts.

The preface to the 1976 workshop on software engineering education, which was edited by Peter Freeman and Tony Wasserman, and also published by Springer-Verlag, contains the following paragraph. We think it is as appropriate to this 1986 proceedings as it was to the 1976 proceedings:

> "We believe that these proceedings will be of interest to all persons involved in developing computer science and software engineering curricula, not only in universities, but also in industry. Furthermore, we hope that these proceedings can serve as the starting point for additional work in the development of coherent software engineering curricula."

Richard E. Fairley
Wang Institute of Graduate Studies

Norman E. Gibbs
Software Engineering Institute

June 1, 1986

Contents

Contents

SECTION IV APPENDIX

List of Participants

Dr. Bruce H. Barnes
NSF
Computer Research
Washington, D.C. 20550

Professor Victor R. Basili
Department of Computer Science
University of Maryland
College Park, MD 20742

Dr. Jon Louis Bentley
AT&T Bell Labs
Room 2C-317
Murray Hill, N.J. 07974

Professor Gordon H. Bradley
Department of Computer Science
U.S. Naval Postgraduate School
Monterey, CA 93943

Dr. Frederick P. Brooks, Jr.
Department of Computer Science
University of North Carolina
New West Hall 035 A
Chapel Hill, N.C. 27514

Professor David Budgen
Department of Computing Science
University of Stirling
Stirling FK9 4LA Scotland

Professor James S. Collofello
Department of Computer Science
Arizona State University
Tempe, AZ 85287

Professor James R. Comer
Department of Computer Science
Texas Christian University
P.O. Box 32886
Fort Worth, TX 76129

Dr. Richard E. Fairley
Wang Institute of Graduate Studies
Tyng Road
Tyngsboro, MA 01879

Dr. Gary A. Ford
Software Engineering Institute
Carnegie-Mellon University
Pittsburgh, PA 15213

Professor Peter Freeman
Department of Computer Science
University of California, Irvine
Irvine, CA 92717

Dr. Susan L. Gerhart
MCC
Software Technology Programs
9430 Research Blvd
Echelon Building One
Austin, TX 78759-6509

Dr. Norman E. Gibbs
Software Engineering Institute
Carnegie-Mellon University
Pittsburgh, PA 15213

Professor Robert L. Glass
Software Engineering Program
Seattle University
P.O. Box 22012
Seattle, WA 98122

Professor Nico Habermann, Chair.
Department of Computer Science
Carnegie-Mellon University
Pittsburgh, PA 15213

Professor M. M. Lehman
Department of Computing
Imperial College
180 Queen's Gate
London SW7 2B7 England

Dr. William McKeeman
Wang Institute of Graduate Studies
Tyng Road
Tyngsboro, MA 01879

Professor Everald E. Mills
Software Engineering Program
Seattle University
900 Broadway Ave.
Seattle, WA 98122

Mr. Al Pietrasanta
IBM Corporate Technical Institutes
Systems Research Institute
500 Columbus Ave.
Thornwood, N.Y. 10594

Major William E. Richardson
Department of Computer Science
U.S. Air Force Academy
Colorado Springs, CO 80840

Dr. William E. Riddle
rMise
P.O. Box 3521
Boulder, CO 80303

LCDR George F. Rowland, Jr.
Department of Computer Science
Ward Hall
U.S. Naval Academy
Annapolis, MD 21402

Lt. Col. Walter D. Seward
Air Force Institute of Technology
WPAFB, OH 45433

Dr. Mary Shaw
Software Engineering Institute
Carnegie-Mellon University
Pittsburgh, PA 15213

Dr. S. E. Smith
IBM Corporate Technical Institutes
Software Engineering Institute
500 Columbus Ave.
Thornwood, N.Y. 10594

Professor Richard H. Thayer
Department of Computer Science
California State University
Sacramento, CA 95819

Dr. James E. Tomayko
Software Engineering Institute
Carnegie-Mellon University
Pittsburgh, PA 15213

Professor David B. Wortman
Computer Research Center
University of Toronto
Ontario M5S 1A4 Canada

Dr. William A. Wulf
Tartan Laboratories
477 Melwood Ave.
Pittsburgh, PA 15213

Software Engineering Institute
Carnegie-Mellon University
Pittsburgh, PA 15213

Observers:

Dr. Mario Barbacci
Dr. Peter Feiler
Mr. Albert Johnson
Mr. John R. Nestor
Dr. Joseph A. Newcomer
Mr. Charles Weinstock
Mr. William Wood

Mr. Karl Shingler
U.S. Air Force
SEI Joint Program Office

Section I

Keynote Speech
and
Opening Discussion

People Are Our Most Important Product

Frederick P. Brooks, Jr.
University of North Carolina at Chapel Hill

Introduction

The function of a keynote speech (if any) should be to give perspective. Coming from outside the software engineering research field, but from within the computer field, I would like to offer an outsider's perspective on some current software engineering curricula proposals.

Let me start with a disclaimer. Since writing *The Mythical Man-Month*, I have not worked in software engineering management nor in software engineering research. Everyone here is more current in the field than I. I am a lifetime fan of computers and of software engineering; I teach a course in the subject, and I try to stay up-to-date in the field. But I am not really working in it.

The peak year in sales for *The Mythical Man-Month* was only two years ago. Yet the book was written in 1975, about an experience in 1963-65. The fact that it has the slightest relevance now is a sad comment on the progress of the discipline.

Wave After Wave

In the some 40 years since I first became interested in computers, we have seen seven revolutions, the first of which is the computer revolution represented by the Harvard Mark I. I was 13 when the Mark I was introduced, and watching with big eyes. That was the first I had ever heard of the idea of a computer. I decided that it was the exciting thing, and I started heading that way.

Second, came electronic computers and the invention of assemblers and interpreters. In 1952, I had a chance to learn to program (in octal absolute) on the not-quite-delivered, vacuum-tube-based IBM 701. That experience was a major milestone for me.

The third revolution was brought by the transistor and Fortran — for me, that meant three years helping design Stretch. The System/360 was another major milestone for me. It represented the fourth revolution — integrated circuits and mandatory operating systems.

The fifth revolution brought minicomputers and the concurrent development of communications as an inherent part of most computer systems. The most recent revolution involves microcomputers and — one of the most important factors today — the mass marketability of microcomputer software and its corollary, packaged application programs.

Hardware	Software
1. Computers	
2. Electronics	Assemblers
3. Transitors	Compilers
4. Integrated Circuits	Operating Systems
5. Minicomputers	Communications
6. Microprocessors	Programming Environments
7. Mass-Market PCs	Packaged Applications

Figure 1. Revolutions

Twenty Tries at a Software Project Course

One of the things I did as soon as I got to Chapel Hill, was to start the kind of one-semester, small-team, classical project course that Jon Bentley, who is a member of the technical staff at A.T.& T. Bell Laboratories says in his paper is not the right way to do it. I think everyone agrees it would be better as a two-semester project course.

Except for two years on sabbatical, I have taught that course every year for 22 years. Twice I have team-taught it with David Parnas, which was phenomenally exciting. One year, I taught it with Bernard Witt, of IBM's Federal Systems Division, and another year with Constance Smith, who taught at Duke. The evolution of the course has been interesting.

I am teaching the software engineering project course this term, as for the last two years, over our statewide television network. I can see the students at the remote sites, and they can see me. That has an unexpected advantage: although I would normally be teaching live over the network, I can give them a videotaped lecture. That is what I am doing there this afternoon.

One of the laymen at the Microelectronics Center of North Carolina at Research Triangle Park, which serves six member institutions, had been watching a lecture on a monitor installed in the lobby. He said, "You don't seem to be teaching. You seem to be preaching." Indeed so. There are two reasons why. One is we do not really know that much to teach. Gordon Bradley, who is a member of the Computer Science Department, Naval Postgraduate School, Monterey, California and Mary Shaw, who is the Chief Scientist at the Software Engineering Institute, speak in their papers about the lack of identification of principles. Second, we are trying to teach practices that we believe — and this is an article of faith — involve short-run pain for long-run benefit. Preaching always involves persuading people to undergo short-run discipline for long-run benefit. That is what preaching is all about. So it is no accident that a great deal of what we do when we teach software engineering is, in fact, exhortation. We are trying to motivate the will of the students, rather than merely to inform the mind. I expect some element of exhortation to be necessary forever. The conversion of our students' long-run ambitions into daily motivation is always an important function of the teacher.

Today, I want to talk about the state of software engineering as I understand it, and some opinions on the curricula issues that are before us. The viewpoint, I fear, will be that of the leper at the feast. After reading the pre-distributed position papers, I find I am in fundamental disagreement with a good deal of what is proposed, described, and practiced.

On Software Engineering

Engineering

I will start with my definition of software engineering. I like to distinguish four things: a program, a programming system, a programming product, and a programming system product. Software engineering is concerned with building programming products and programming system products. In other words, it is proper to call it software *engineering*. It is indeed an engineering discipline — it focuses on building.

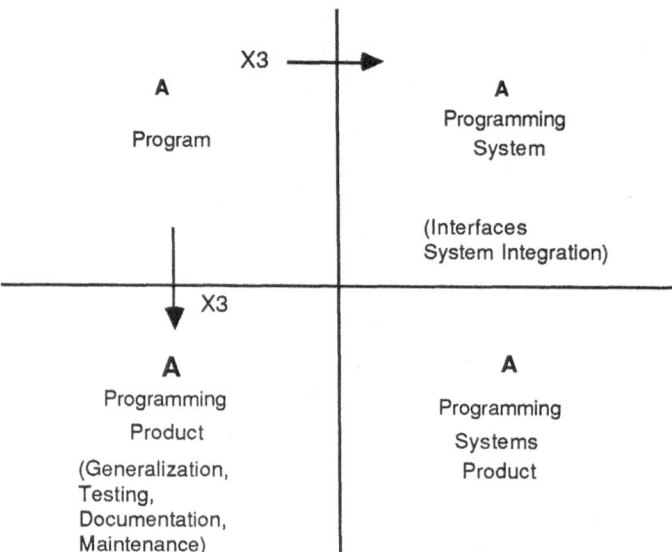

Figure 2. Evolution of the Programming Systems Product©[1]

In graduate school I roomed with a high-energy physicist. He spent a year building the electronic apparatus for his experiments. He then spent two weeks at Brookhaven National Laboratory taking pictures of events in a cloud chamber, then a year looking at his 100,000 pictures. If you looked at the way he spent his time, you would have said he was doing engineering. On the other hand, I have known engineers who

---

[1]Frederick P. Brooks, Jr., "The Mythical Man-Month," © 1975, Addison-Wesley Publishing Company, Inc., Reading, Massachusetts. Pg. 5, Fig. 1.1. Reprinted with permission.

seem to spend most of their time taking measurements about hitherto unknown phenomena. If you were asked what he was, judging by how he spends his time, you might say, "He looks like a physicist."

The difference lies in the *motivation* and not in the *activity*. **The scientist builds in order to learn; the engineer learns in order to build**. We can accurately use this distinction to characterize software engineering. As an engineering discipline, it is concerned with quality, effectiveness, cost, and schedule — concepts that, if not alien, are at least of little concern to the underlying science.

Arbitrary Complexity

What is peculiar about the engineering of computer software objects? How does it differ from the classical disciplines? It differs in an important way from two of the supporting disciplines, mathematics and physics, from which electrical engineering derives. Most mathematicians and physicists dislike real-world computer science problems. The reason is that our problems are characterized by what I call *arbitrary complexity*. Anyone who has wrestled with an operating system and had to interface 44 different kinds of input-output devices; or a payroll system and had to deal with the income tax for 50 states, plus the federal government, plus innumerable cities that have peculiar income tax laws; or wrestled with the other forms of artifact that we have to build and the environments into which we have to build them, will recognize this as a common characteristic.

Mathematicians and physicists dislike this for different reasons. The mathematician dislikes complexity, and the mathematician's fundamental attack on complexity is to abstract. One forms an abstract model of the problem, solves the abstract model, and then applies the solution back to the original problem. That paradigm has been phenomenally successful. The history of applied mathematics, intertwined with the physical sciences for more than two centuries, is one of the rich results produced by that model. Increasingly, however, as one comes up against intrinsic complexity, we find that smooth models of classical mathematics do not work. So we come to fractal mathematics for describing or abstracting roughness. We continually have to invent new mathematics to deal with deeper levels of complexity.

On the other hand, physicists dislike the arbitrariness. They are no strangers to complexity. Anyone with 26 elementary particles recognizes that the world is complex. What they dislike is that it is arbitrary, because physicists, no matter how atheistic, are fundamentally convinced that there are *not* 26 elementary *anythings*; that there is a fundamental, unified theory to be found. It is that faith that keeps the physicist going forward.

No such faith comforts the computer scientist. Our complexities are arbitrary, because they are the fruits of many independent minds acting independently. Consider the task of interfacing to an operating system 44 different input-output devices, each designed by a different engineering team. Unless there was a pre-existing interface, there is no reason to believe those designers acted under any unifying principle at all. This arbitrary complexity of interfaces characterizes much of what we do. It is a reason why we had to develop a new science, with approaches and techniques different from those of the classical disciplines.

What About Software Makes Its Engineering Hard?

A natural question is, "Does it have to be this hard?" Is it not just that we have not yet found the key to unlock the door? Studying the nature of these arbitrary complexities, we see that the essence in building software products involves the complexity of the conceptual structures we are working with, rather than the labor of representing them. This complexity is compounded by the necessity to conform to an external environment that is *arbitrary*, *unadaptable*, and *ever-changing*.

All we ask ourselves, "How have the big gains in productivity and effectiveness in software engineering come in the past," I think we will see those gains — in high-level languages, time-sharing, unified programming environments — all broke major artificial roadblocks to *expressing* the complexities of our solutions and our problems. The high-level languages remove the artificial roadblock of coding programs in machine-level instructions in zeroes and ones. Time-sharing removed the artificial roadblock of limited access to hardware. The unified programming environments remove the artificial roadblocks that were caused by a lack of common file formats and command philosophies.

We will make progress by continuing to remove these artificial roadblocks, via workstations, better languages, richer programming environments, etc. I think, however, that fundamental progress can only come by really attacking the underlying complexity, not the difficulties of expression. There are many promising attacks, as Figure 3 suggests. I will not take the time to talk about them, because I really want to go on to curriculum. But I must remark that we vastly underestimate the work, the difficulty, and the error-proneness of setting system requirements in the first place.

- Top-down design — N. Wirth
- Outside-in design, system architecture — G. Blaauw
- Incremental growing on an executable driver — H. Mills
- Information-hiding modules — D. Parnas
- Chief Programmer teams — H. Mills
- Verification — E. Dijkstra, Floyd, Hoare
  useful, but limited by costliness
- GOTO-less programming — E. Dijkstra
  structure, yes; avoiding GOTO, no.
- Structured walk-throughs

Figure 3. Key Ideas

Iterative Development is Crucial

I like Christopher Alexander's maxim in *Notes on the Synthesis of Form*: "The only way to define fit, is as the absence of misfit." If one wants to grind a steel plate flat, one takes an optically flat standard plate, paint the whole works with purple goo, slap it up against the plate one is going to grind, then grind all the purple places. Then one paints the optical flat with goo again, slap the two together again, and grind the places that are still purple with a finer wheel until, finally, instead of *none* of it being purple, *all* of it is purple. So, the only operational way to define this optically flat plate, is having no *bulges* or *valleys*. Correspondingly, I believe the process of dealing with arbitrary complexity, in terms of the user's requirements, is iterative: we build prototypes, put purple paint on them, slap them up against real users, and grind the places that are still purple — in the products, not in the users.

Iteration on a programming product specification is an inherent, proper part of the professional's job. We cannot stand back and gripe that the user didn't know what he wanted. We must take it as given that the user does not and cannot know what he wants about artifacts as complex as those we now build. The mind of man cannot imagine all the ramifications of such artifacts. There must be an iterative cycle in which the professional works with the user to define the requirements; demonstrates their consequences in human factors, cost, and performance; then in a prototyping phase iterates with the user to develop a product that is, in fact, satisfactory.

The Failure of the "Standard Software Development Process"

Let me offer a discouraging observation on the state of the art. I did a little mental study in which I wrote down a set of what I call "exciting software products." These are ones that have avid fan clubs, ones that people are crazy about. You can add names to this list, shown in Figure 3. We typically call the fans *bigots*: *APL bigots*, for instance. I think the ancestral group should be Fortran's. Those of us who work with physicists and chemists today, recognize that there are still Fortran bigots about! Each of these exciting products has such a group. I put Visicalc as the latest, but not the last.

I put a different set of things, which you can call the "work horses" of the field, in another category. This group is made up of things that are immensely useful, in many cases immensely successful, and have made major contributions to getting work done. People appreciate some of their successful characteristics and don't appreciate others, but it is very hard to find bigots, excited fans, about any of them.

Outside Product Houses	From Product Houses
Fortran	
APL	OS/360
	COBOL
Pascal	Algol
LISP	DEC's VMS
C	PL/1
UNIX	Ada
Tenex	IMS
Visicalc	
VM-CMS	
System R	

Figure 4. Exciting Software Products

I have trouble finding any exciting software product — one that arouses passion on the part of its users — that was developed inside a normal product process. What does that tell us about the normal product process? About the state of the art? About the importance of teaching the normal product process? I think it tells us something about software products and designs in general: the thing that makes exciting software products is conceptual integrity, and conceptual integrity comes from individuals.

One can elaborate a little bit. Committee design is a minimax strategy. It limits the losses and goofs. It also limits the upper reach of quality, elegance, function, and speed. This is true of bridges, cars, movies, novels, paintings, music, etc. So the theorem I would leave you with, because I can't prove it, is that a product that *surely* excites *somebody* is more likely to excite a lot of people than a product that *more or less* suits *everybody*. The "work horses" I referred to, the ones that do not have fan clubs, can be characterized as having "homogenized designs," and the ones with bigots, "idiosyncratic designs." The homogenized design process is aimed at producing products that more or less suit everybody. You may want to propose other candidates, and you might challenge some of my choices of candidates, but I think that the thrust of those two sets is unmistakable.

- Limits losses and goofs
- Also limits the **upper** reach of
  quality/elegance; function; speed
- Bridges, cars, movies, novels, theorems, paintings, music
- Idiosyncratic vs. Homogenized
  A product that **surely** excites somebody is more likely to excite a lot of people than one that **more or less** suits everybody.
- True of software system
- Of software engineering curricula, too.

Figure 5. Committee Design is a Minimax Strategy

On Software Engineering Curriculum

Standard vs. Individualistic

I think this theorem is also true of curricula. We may be richer, in the process of evolving a generally accepted software engineering curriculum, if we have a *lot* of places forming a *lot* of curricula and publishing them, than if we move too rapidly toward any kind of *standard* curriculum. If you look in many different college catalogs, you will see that there has developed a great deal of standardization among undergraduate physics curricula, for example. In the middle two years of undergraduate physics, one takes the same courses anywhere one goes, and one may take them from the same text books. Is this done through standard curriculum development by the American Physical Society? No. The similarity exists because the importance of the subject matter is self-evident: there is a consensus in the field of what the principles are. I suggest that a standard curriculum be grown organically by developing a set of principles. That is the only way to make it durable, important, and portable.

Does that mean it is not useful to develop model curricula? Of course it is useful. In any branch of art, the people who went through it first, and learned what not to do, can be of great service to those who come on the scene by explaining where the pitfalls and minefields are. Sharing experience with curriculum development saves people from making the same mistakes again.

The most important principle to teach a software engineer is, "Don't build software (if you can help it)." It is almost always cheaper to buy it if you can, and it is almost always cheaper to buy it even if its price is about the same as your estimated cost for you to build it. That is, one generally underestimates the effort required to build product-quality software. Even by buying it, you may not get product-quality software, but your odds are much better.

Permanent vs. Transient Truths

From the perspective of looking at seven computer revolutions over the past 40 years, the first thing that strikes me is that one has happened about every six years. Second, most of what we learned and talked about in the 1950's, we would not think of teaching today. Much of what we taught is no longer true, or if true, no longer relevant. Are we training people for an initial job or educating them for a career? If we are educating for a career, I wholeheartedly support Mary Shaw's identification from the Carnegie Plan of what is involved in professional education for a career. We need to teach them to think like software engineers, rather than to train them in 27 programming languages, 15 methodologies, and 30 tools. That means they will have to be exposed to some methodologies, some tools, and some programming languages. But those are not our *objectives*. Our objective is to shape ways of thinking, and, by experience at wielding some tools, to develop and facilitate the implementation of new tools in the field.

That brings me to the points about which I would argue. It seems to me that all the central questions about software engineering curricula can be summarized by a set of dichotomies, as in Figure 6.

Standard	vs.	Individualistic
Transient	vs.	Permanent
Fat	vs.	Thin
Narrow	vs.	Solid
B.S.	vs.	M.S.
Science	vs.	Design
Projects	vs.	Exercises

Figure 6. Software Engineering Curricula

Thin vs. Fat

Let me put forth another theorem: if you do not know what to teach in a software engineering curriculum and, if in putting one together, you find a lot of modules that are short on principles — where one can teach only tools or methodologies, or today's practices — instead of most of those modules, teach nothing at all. Instead, encourage students to spend those hours learning something such as physics, mathematics, or accounting, which they *do* know what to teach. One of the most valuable courses I had as an undergraduate, and today use regularly, was a one-semester course in accounting for non-accountants.

I would not offer an undergraduate software engineering curriculum at all. I would offer a two-semester software engineering course, as part of a computer science curriculum. Young people come to me and say, "I want to be a computer professional." I reply, "Do you want to go to graduate school, and become a real professional?" If they say "yes," I say, "Do not take a computer science major as your undergraduate. Get educated."

Our oldest son fell into that fiery passion for computers which often strikes in the teen years. It is very much like being engaged and being married. You want to experience and enjoy that initial passion, but you would like to grow out of it into a more mature relationship, one that will always be fired with moments of the passion. I encouraged each of our children to do that with the computer passion while they were in high school, because it can ruin a college year if it first strikes then.

When that son got ready to go to college, he wanted to study computer science. I said "Well, if you really want to work with computers, do a physics major. Study all of the sciences. Do not fall into this one just because it is handy." (He had been exposed to a lot of computers during his life.) "Then, when you are a senior, if you still want to become a computer scientist, I will quit hindering and start helping. But first, sample all of the sciences to see if your infatuation with computers comes merely from that propinquity." The summer after his junior year we were walking on the beach and I said, "Well, son, what do you think? Which subject interests you most?" And he said, "You go into a room, and you look around, and you say, 'Look at all the pretty girls.' Then you say, 'But *this* is the one I love.'" I said, "I quit." He is now in a PhD program in computer science at Stanford.

Look at your undergraduate college experience. Which parts do you retain as most valuable? For me, it is a Shakespeare course, a French literature course, a lot of experience in public speaking, a lot of training — extracurricular and curricular — in how to run meetings, writing training, an accounting course, and especially some courses in electricity and magnetism. Those experiences are still very useful to me. I can tell you lots of things I spent hours on that I have not used. Some of them were in the liberal arts, but many others were in the major.

In like manner, we must train professionals who have been educated to be citizens, leaders, and communicators. The software product today consists of more documentation than code, and the good software product today includes *good* documentation. How will you learn to write if you have not studied the good models of writing and practiced the techniques? Do we want to displace a broad and useful undergraduate education with training in software engineering tools and methods? Surely not!

Broad vs. Narrow

At the graduate level means I would recommend a particularized *software engineering* curriculum only to practitioners who have had field experience and are coming for career upgrade education, who know they are getting a specialized, technical training, not graduate education. For all new software engineers, I would recommend a master's in computer science, with several courses in software engineering, but not a software engineering curriculum. Why? Because much of what we teach today will not be true ten years from now, and a great deal of the rest will not be relevant. More important, they will *need* the broader knowledge.

Can anyone in the software-building business really operate without understanding simple accounting? Can anyone in software engineering really operate without understanding the principles of at least the first course in numerical analysis: concepts, error propagation, and the vagaries of floating point?

Most curricula being put forth for software engineering — and there are exceptions in the Proceedings — give a one-course, at most, discussion of computing machines. Undergraduate exposure, which typically is one course in machine architecture, is assumed for the graduate courses — and those may include another one. Are we going to build all of this software without understanding the engines with which it will run, the trends shaping those engines, and the ability to project the corresponding advances for hardware that will revolutionize the kind of software we have to build? So, I would argue very strongly for broad versus narrow.

Solid vs. Hollow

All the university departments I know want to create a lot of courses that address topics at the very forefront of the field. Why? Because that is what the faculty wants to teach. So we construct, particularly at the graduate level, what I call "hollow curriculum"; in football terms, no blocking, no tackling, but Statue-of-Liberty plays all over the place. We shuffle the core curriculum courses off to the most junior faculty members to teach, and we elders teach the advanced ones. A solid curriculum is one in which those intermediate-level things that seem like old hat to us, but are not old hat to the students, fill in the interior. These are the established principles represented by algorithms, data structures, operating systems, languages, machines, and compilers.

Design vs. Science

The science vs. design debate rages in engineering schools everywhere, all the time. I think the papers in the Proceedings properly emphasize that if the motivation is to build, we have to teach the art of design and not merely the supporting sciences. It is in this respect that software engineering courses differ from many of the underlying computer science courses. We must teach people to design. The only way to teach people to design is to have them design, criticize, have them redesign, and then to have them build the designs.

Projects vs. Exercise

What they design brings us to the exercises vs. projects question: How little and how big? I think the answer is you really want to do some of both. The real issue is the precise balance between exercises and projects.

Great Designers

Now one more thought: If we go back to the list of great software products, exciting ones, we observe that they have a conceptual integrity that comes from very small design teams: Fortran with half a dozen people, APL with two people, and so on. These design teams are not only small, but also comprise really first class minds.

Let me suggest one more principle: **great designs come from great designers**. Good designs, as distinguished from bad designs, can be produced by teaching people good principles and proper methods. We take the step from good designs to great designs, however, by finding the people who have the talent to do the great designs.

Look over the whole body of classical music. How much has survived? On any classical music station you can hear obscure selections from the 16th to the 19th centuries. When you listen to them, you know why they are obscure. You can count on your ten fingers the great composers in each century. Indeed, even they have written some losers, but there really is a qualitative difference between the great and the obscure.

Opening Discussion

A. Nico Habermann, Moderator

Nico Habermann: This discussion will focus on the work to be done by the task forces, laying some common ground. To begin, I have summarized four of the major points from the papers in the conference proceedings and from the presentations this morning. We have heard provoking words by Fred Brooks, Mary Shaw discussed the scientific aspects of software engineering, and Jim Collofello remarked on the current practice. So we will use this discussion hour to direct the task forces to their particular tasks.

My four observations from the papers are:
1. The nature of software engineering.
2. The difference between small and LARGE.
3. Evolution vs. Revolution: No particular methodology or technology will emerge that will radically change software production.
4. Software engineering must grow with changing technology.

First, it is clear from what we have read in the conference proceedings that people are concerned about the nature of software engineering: exactly where it fits in, how it has been developed up to this point, and our responsibility. Software engineering should be based on principles, and I think we can all agree on this. We are not talking about a large number of tools or technologies, or even a large number of methodologies. We must look for those things that have a long-term value, not just for the things that are a "quick fix."

The second thing that is clear from the papers is that people are also concerned about the distinction between small and large and how we use small projects and exercises to show the complexity of the large systems.

Third, we don't expect to find, all of a sudden, the cornerstone for solving all of the software production problems through education. Touching place that have changed the field dramatically. But the educational process has not gone through these large revolutions. It is questionable whether we can even spot the revolutions in the software engineering discipline. And no one actually expects a sudden, major breakthrough in software engineering that will help solve the problems of software production.

Fred challenged this point very strongly. Is it, indeed, the right approach to go with joint design? Is it, indeed, right to form these committees and say, "Let the committee write a proposal for a master's degree in software engineering curriculum?" If that is not the right approach, how should it be modified?

Finally, the point has been emphasized several times today that the field is growing very fast and education must keep pace. It cannot be static. It must evolve over time. This point comes out in many of the papers: if we look for a basis for software engineering, then we look for related disciplines. No one seriously proposes to start software engineering before such a basis has been laid. That actually is the foundation for software engineering.

Sometimes I think methodologies, as Bill Wulf points out in his paper, are overemphasized. If we don't have one, single methodology, it doesn't mean that we are lost. Just looking at the development right now, we have lots of tools and techniques available.

We do agree, and this is clear from the papers, that there must be some form of experimentation. Jon Bentley argued against the project idea, but I think that, nevertheless, the experimentation idea is among all of us. And Fred Brooks has argued strongly that experience should be gained by practice, by being exposed to working on large systems, and then come back to what is narrow education and training at the master's degree level. I think that some form of actual experimentation, included in this type of software engineering education, is something we can all agree upon.

So, let's open the floor and use these four points as a basis for our discussion.

Manny Lehman: I think the critical issue — and the thing that is wrong with many of the curricula in the proceedings — is that software engineering is not yet based on principles of science and engineering. At present, what software engineering requires, to a large extent, is the identification of principles by the development of models, and the creation of engineering discipline. All we have now are lots of isolated methods, tools, techniques, languages, and so forth. As software engineers, we need to train our students to be able to observe, to think and to perform; to be familiar with what exists but also to understand the theory and principles that lie behind what exists and unite it into a coherent discipline.

For example, to develop an integrated support environment involves an understanding of what the programming process is all about. We have to be able to develop theories of the process and to understand the context in which particular objects are created. A civil engineer doesn't design the repeated picks and shovels; whenever possible he uses the available picks and shovels to create a road, a bridge, or a large building. Software engineering has an integrated discipline that we and our students are going to *create* in the future from the primitive concepts that exist at the present time. Thus we have to educate students to be familiar with much more than presently available methods and tools.

I liked Fred's distinction between scientists and engineers: that scientists build in order to learn and engineers learn in order to build. We are still in the learning phase. The prime duty and responsibility and challenge to the software engineer — and to the software engineers we will be training in the next decade — is to learn intelligently and to extend and apply what is learned to the world at large — to the system developers.

Nico Habermann: Thank you for your observation. I think that in order to be able to build some theories, you also have to learn the technique itself. And that is something you can learn at the undergraduate level.

Dick Thayer: The argument that we don't have a science to base engineering on in the software area bothers me very little. We had medicine long before we had a medical science. I think that we are at the stage in software engineering where we have to find ways of developing software whether or not the principles are defined. The science can evolve on its own — let's first worry about how we go about developing software.

Mary Shaw: I would like to reply to Dick. A colleague of mine commented to me not long ago that even the purest of the sciences, mathematics, has withstood fundamental changes in its foundation on a number of different occasions without destroying the edifice that rests upon that foundation. So those of us who feel an instinct to build the foundation before starting to erect the edifice should take heed. Even in the field in which you would find that most unlikely, progress can be made in the absence of absolute certainty about the foundation.

Peter Freeman: I have not seen the relationship between software engineering and systems engineering addressed, and I would like to get the task forces' comments on it. By systems engineering I am not referring to the purely mathematical, narrow definition, but to the very real activity that goes on — where a large software system is being engineered. As we automate factories, for instance, there is a large cadre who are concerned with systems engineering, but it includes a lot of things that are not software. What do you think is or should be the relationship between software engineering — however we define it and teach it — and that larger activity?

Fred Brooks: I get the impression that engineering discipline is in so bad a shape, with respect to lack of principles, as we are. But, this is a different "art." Even though there are books and curricula, the hard task is to distill out the common part. We should be in conversation with the professional systems engineers, watching closely what they are doing in their education, but not necessarily hitching our cart to that horse.

Bill McKeeman: I think Fred pointed out the danger of committee work. Maybe the SEI can use this more as a vehicle for getting creative people the time and opportunity to produce those wonderful artifacts, in the discipline or the field itself, to do what we want to do. But there is an issue I would also like to see addressed on this: there is a difference between the order in which something can be learned by a novice and the order in which we would want to present it as the science. There isn't one big tome called "physics" that, when handed to students, suddenly lets them assimilate the knowledge of the physical world. Instead, they do simple experiments and work from examples to generalize that knowledge. So, the bottom up and top down approaches probably have to be mixed; I would hate to see us dictate a top down approach. It might kill our youngsters' urges to learn.

Mary Shaw: I agree with Bill. The effective way to teach theory is in the context of examples. The best principles we can find, in the context of the best current practice, provides not only comprehensive skills, but a set of tangible examples that can be used to appreciate the theory as it comes.

Fred Brooks: A self-describing principle is: We learn inductively and teach deductively.

Bill Wulf: In response to Bill's comments, it strikes me that physics is taught by a succession of increasingly accurate lies. We have simple models — and a series of progressively more accurate ones, which gives us a couple of nice properties. First, it is fairly easy to comprehend the simple models and, second, it implicitly teaches the student to be suspicious of any theory, which is just right when you are describing physical work.

But the real point is that we talk about principles and we talk about things like methodologies and tools. Somewhere in there is missing the notation of facts — our transition from being a producer of computer sciences to being a consumer of them. It strikes me that the younger kids coming out of bachelor's programs simply don't have a lot of the factual information I would expect them to have. They lack the factual information to make good engineering decisions, and that is kind of missed in the distinctions.

Nico Habermann: I tried to point that out in my paper. One principle I listed was that the body of knowledge and the facts have to be relied upon in teaching the discipline.

Dick Fairley: Although I agree with most of what Fred Brooks said, there is an elitist view expressed there. It is elitist on two counts. One count is on fundamentals vs. techniques, and the second is how you deal with the unwashed masses — you are still dealing with 1960's technology. The issue I want to raise is the balance between fundamentals and techniques for training vs. education. I think it is incumbent on us to produce graduates who grasp the fundamentals and can continue to learn and evolve with the passing of time. But, people also have to know how to do something useful and practical.

Fred Brooks: Harlan Mills remarked once that, in trying to inculcate new programming methodologies throughout the IBM Federal Systems Division, the most effective thing they have done is to mix new graduates in with the old timers. The old timers understand the applications, and the new graduates understand the new methodologies. This is, of course, following the university model, where the faculty learns each new development from the graduate students.

But in terms of washing the masses, the masses among software practitioners are already selected to be rather bright — and by now are rather stuck in their ways. Part of the washing, then, is to expose them to another generation.

Dick Fairley: The other thing I hear in your remarks is an industry responsibility, as well as the university responsibility.

Mary Shaw: When a position is criticized as being elitist, there is often hidden behind the criticism a suggestion that some of the students can't handle the material. I think we need to recognize that there are hard problems in the world — and that those problems require people with certain sets of skills to solve them.

We need to attack this by thinking a little more carefully than we have in the past about the collection of job descriptions that exist within the software field. Not everybody who deals with software needs to be a software engineer. There is an increasing set of requirements on the performance, reliability, and functionality of the software we are being asked to produce. I think we are getting very close to the point that just wanting to be a software engineer and having a lot of experience pro-gramming is not necessarily a set of adequate qualifications — anymore than liking bridges makes you qualified to be a civil engineer. If we can identify the job descriptions within the domain, and the real require-ments for each of those descriptions, then the argument about elitism is blunted because we can identify positions for which a software en-gineering education is required.

Bob Glass: Are there any disciplines we could incorporate in our cur-riculum that would help people learn to grasp the complexity and ar-bitrariness that Fred Brooks talks about?

Mary Shaw: We do have a set of abstraction techniques, as math-ematicians do.

Bill McKeeman: That takes care of the complexity. How about a course in political science for the arbitrary factor?

Peter Freeman: It is important to keep in mind what Fred said about applying the liberal education approach, but not everybody thinks that way, learns the fastest that way, or becomes successful that way. It seems to me that we also have to keep in mind, as educators, that people have different learning styles and different capabilities. The real issue is to be able to provide appropriate diversity in the educational experience.

Joe Newcomer: The *scientific* discipline is one that I see lacking in many so-called software engineers. In the simple task of measuring the system, it is not enough to just run the time command. You need to understand what you are measuring, the accuracy of your tools, and the methodology for validating what you have done in order to be able to apply it. As we go more toward the scientific discipline of software en-gineering, we need to have a bit more of this fundamental, basic, scien-tific training so people who come from diverse backgrounds — not necessarily scientific ones — have some exposure to this piece of methodology. I have noticed that computer scientists who come from different backgrounds — mathematics, physics, economics, philosophy — approach certain classes of problems differently. There is a distinct gap there.

David Wortman: I have two comments. First, in spite of our best intentions, it is often difficult to direct students to take the broadening courses we would like them to take. Unless you have a heavily mandated curriculum, the students can find countermeasures to avoid courses.

Second, many of the proposed curriculums don't calibrate well against where we traditionally think the effort goes in large software systems. Statistics show that, in large systems, half the effort is spent in maintenance, yet most curricula are light on maintenance. Similarly, a lot of effort is dependent on documentation, but curricula are light on documentation. And in many systems a lot of effort is spent on interface design — often half the code is the input and the output interface. That involves not only computer graphics, but also a lot of human factors in order to understand the interface. It's something that isn't covered very comprehensively in the curricula we are examining.

Mary Shaw: I will reply to David's first comment. Strong advising is needed. An advisor who is looking out for the student and exercising an advisor's responsibilities knows when a formal logic course in the Philosophy Department is being used to finesse a breadth requirement. And as for Peter's related remark about some students really digging in their heels, some really do learn better and others just dig in their heels because they don't think they like it.

Ed Smith: Underlying the discussion is an assumption that, somehow, engineers producing hardware are doing a much better job today than engineers or programmers producing software. Is there a difference in curiosity level? What is it that, after four years in a bachelor's program in electrical engineering, for example, that produces someone who has a set of attributes different from someone enrolled in a software engineering program? Can we assume that hardware engineers do a better job than software engineers?

Fred Brooks: When I moved from the engineering half of a project to the software half of the same project, I found that the underlying building disciplines were radically different. There was an engineering discipline in place whereby a prototype computing machine could be debugged on a four-shift, around-the-week basis, with a 10-minute handover between successive shifts. The new shift could pick right up and continue with the debugging right where it was. How many software project teams can do that?

Ed Smith: That may be the visibility.

Fred Brooks: Yes, but it also has to do with having an established set of engineering disciplines. Moreover, there is a difference in the experience of the practitioners. If you look at the hardware shops, the average age of the professionals is greater from that in programming shops.

Jim Collofello: I think another part of the problem is the complexity of the effort given to it.

Ed Smith: You must reach a point where you feel as though you have intellectual control over what you are doing. There is a certain decomposition process that has to take place in either one.

Jim Tomayko: I was talking the other day with a civil engineer who is teaching a graduate-level, computer-based course at Carnegie-Mellon. He told me that the bachelor's graduates are very good at designing modules, but they can't produce the larger product. It made me ask myself how they learn to design bridges. So, I think Ed's point is a good one in the sense that the hardware engineers not only have a more mature discipline, they also have more mature people hanging around to learn from and work with. When you think about it, the oldest software engineers are now the youngest executive vice presidents of software engineering consulting firms — and there isn't the same kind of continuity in that.

Dick Fairley: I have both a bachelor's and master's degree in electrical engineering and my greatest disillusionment in electrical engineering is that none of the theories ever worked in practice. Electrical engineers have their problems, too.

Mary Shaw: To follow up on Jim's comments, my impression is that, by and large, most civil engineers don't design bridges. The few very singular, very conspicuous bridges are designed by the very few bridge experts and the rest are routine modifications of standard designs. In Pennsylvania we have a recognized, generic definition for bridge designs in which you select a dozen or so parameters for things like the number of lanes of traffic, elevations, traffic flows, and so on. The bridge design is then cranked out automatically, but it is hedged about with requirements that the design be signed off by a registered engineer.

This simplifies the search of the design space so you can rapidly generate acceptable designs and select from among them based on your criteria. The effect is that the engineers in the bridge business don't design bridges from scratch. They design them by very substantial reuse of prior designs. Design information and the knowledge about good, adequate, functional — but not great — design is systematically encoded for reuse. That is a lesson we should attend to carefully.

Dick Thayer: The other day a colleague of mine pointed out that when we teach software engineering, we preach that software should be developed and managed like hardware. Yet when we asked the hardware (i.e., electrician) engineering teachers how they teach hardware engineering, the subjects of life-cycle development, project management, and analysis before design are not mentioned.

Dick Fairley: But your students don't know that. As Bill Wulf said, you are telling the perfect lie.

Mary Shaw: What do the academic engineers in the engineering departments tell their students about mill practice?

Dick Thayer: I don't know the answer to that one, but I know we spend a lot of time with the little pieces and parts.

Mary Shaw: It is my impression that, in practice, civil engineers do a reasonable amount of advance performance layout and material analysis and the collection of things that we preach.

Gordon Bradley: We ought to separate what people do in education from what people do on the outside. In getting my undergraduate engineering degree, I took only one design course; the rest of the time was spent in doing mechanics. We were not expected to design something immediately. An architect doesn't get to design a building the first year out.

Civil engineering or architecture isn't a field like software engineering where you declare yourself a software engineer with no academic background. We hear the complaints that when students go out, they don't know how to work in teams. They don't know how to design. They don't know the politics. We shouldn't expect 22-year-olds to know those things. Universities teach hard things, integrated things, very well.

I absolutely agree with Fred. We want an integrated view of things in the curriculum. Wang Institute does this. But the notion of modules in an academic, intellectual curriculum is what I could call a category error. You can put a thing called curriculums into the category of things that can be reduced to modules. However, we cannot modularize education. We cannot modularize the core. We want to teach people how to think like software engineers — and that is a long, integrated process that cannot be broken up into one-day modules or pieces.

Mary Shaw: The role of design in undergraduate engineering education has a long and mixed history that varies from university to university. In the 50's or thereabout, when engineering education was substantially revamped, Carnegie-Mellon added a significant design component to the curriculum in conformance with the Carnegie Plan. It was well received, both by students and by employers, because it was backed by a large collection of courses that seemed reasonably effective. Those courses proceeded as an architecture studio might proceed: you present the problem, looking over the shoulder of the students as they attempt to solve it. But, it came across to the engineering community as a soft discipline. As engineering proceeded, more and more factual things, with equations behind them, came into practice, and there was increasing pressure to add these to the curriculum.

The effect of this has been a gradual erosion of the design component. I suspect that there is some version of that history at each of your schools. I don't take that as an indication that we should omit or neglect design. A substantial part of what software engineers do is design. In software engineering they probably do it earlier than in electrical engineering, and, therefore, the need is greater.

Gordon Bradley: It's possible that it went away because a lot of the experience was a single individual at a single university.

Mary Shaw: When the great designer stops teaching the course, it is hard to transmit that course to another instructor.

Gordon Bradley: That's right. When the Frank Lloyd Wrights go away, the idea of teaching architecture goes back to the tried and true. Universities do know how to teach some things very well. We only seem to be able to teach design with great designers.

Fred Brooks: We should at least teach it with experienced designers. My chemical engineering chairman friend says, "We do not hire green Ph.D's to this faculty. They must have worked in a chemical engineering industrial environment before we would consider them as teachers at all." I would propose that for a software engineering program, as well.

Dick Fairley: I think in the university, the analytical will always drive out the synthetic. Analysis will always drive out design. And in the long scheme of the history of what universities are about, that is probably appropriate. The point is that you need to distinguish between the goals of professional graduate education and those of the universities. Given the goals of universities, professional graduate education may not be possible unless you have a separate school for software engineering — someplace where that can happen apart from the normal reward structure of the university, in the same way that medical and law schools are set apart.

Nico Habermann: Drawing to a close, I think we can conclude that we have many thoughts and opinions about our discipline. It isn't clear what will emerge, but these discussions are useful. There is still a lot of room for different opinions and we welcome the possibility to influence each other's thoughts on this subject.

Section II
Part 1
Software Engineering Principles

The papers in this section generally present a broad view of software engineering and of software engineering education. They offer fundamental parts of or structures for a software engineering curriculum.

Gordon Bradley, Dick Fairley, Peter Freeman, Walt Seward, and Ed Smith present particular perspectives of the goals and organization of a software engineering program. Bob Glass describes software engineering by contrasting it with computer science. Bill Richardson categorizes the important problems in software engineering that a curriculum must address.

Vic Basili, Nico Habermann, and Bill Riddle identify specific aspects of software engineering that they consider essential: experimentation, environments, and technology selection. Bill Wulf presents a case for breadth in the curriculum, rather than concentrating on a few specific methods.

The Experimental Aspects of a
Professional Degree in Software Engineering

Victor R. Basili
University of Maryland

Abstract. Software engineering needs a support mechanism to aid in the transition of research results into practice. Such a mechanism for providing education, training and practical experience in software engineering could be provided by a special degree program: a Master of Software Engineering (MSE). The key to such a curriculum is the establishment of the equivalent of a teaching hospital through various software development organizations: a teaching software engineering laboratory. Combining classroom education with skill development, the professional software development laboratory will use the latest techniques and tools, and the practitioner will have the opportunity to gain experience in using them under the supervision of experts.

Research results must be organized in a systematic way using well defined methods and tools before they can be applied in a practical way. Practitioners must be educated, trained, and have experience in applying these techniques if they are to be used effectively. Thus educational programs must act as the bridge between these research advances and their successful transition to the wider audiences that can make use of those results. The educational process should include an understanding of the underlying theory of the discipline, the training in the use of the associated methods or tools, and the opportunity to develop skills in their use. Without these three components, the technology cannot be transposed into competent, standardized practices [110].

Software engineering is in desperate need of a support mechanism to aid in the transition of the research results into practice. There is too much ineffective and inconsistent use of the methods and tools available, too little evaluation of their effects, and too little refinement and adaptation of the techniques themselves.

These methods and tools of software engineering must be studied, applied in a laboratory setting, and skills developed until the practitioner becomes expert in their application.

A mechanism for providing the education, training and practical experience in software engineering could be provided by a special degree program, a Master of Software Engineering. There are a few programs with similar aims already in existence, e.g., the program at Imperial College in London, the program at Wang Institute of Graduate Studies, and the program at Seattle University.

It is important for the educational needs of the software community that a new, standardized professional degree be created; a Master of Software Engineering, along with the specification for a certificate for support roles in software engineering. These degrees and certificates should represent the structure of a new profession of software engineering. The key to such a program is access to experimentation with the methods and tools that must be provided the participants in order to gain proficiency in their application for different problem domains in different environments.

The medical profession provides a useful analogy for this kind of education. Software engineering stands where medicine stood years ago, on the threshold of university education. Today the profession of medicine has a structure of position and practices that permits many educational institutions to participate in training personnel for the profession, not for individual organizations. For example, a surgical team is put together from people educated at different institutions in different specialties, of surgery, anesthesiology, nursing, radiology, etc. Such terms are defined by the profession, not by the individual hospitals, with a high degree of interchangeability among personnel of the same speciality.

In contrast, software teams today are universally 'home grown,' their activities are defined by their organizations, often by their team leaders. As a result, there are few real standards of proficiency. It is well known that people holding comparable jobs in software differ in productivity by a factor of ten. It is less well known that software teams with comparable assignments also differ in productivity by a factor of ten. The advent of university education in software education will create standards of proficiency which will permit organizations to recruit or procure professionals of more certain productivity.

The foundation of the medical profession is the medical degree — a professional, not a research degree. Although medical research goes on, it is the function of specialists, typically PhDs, not MDs.

In the same way the foundation for software engineering will be a professional, not a research degree, the MSE. The MS and PhD in computer science will still be the basis for computer science research. But the MSE will be the basis for the practice of software engineering.

The MSE has quite a different purpose than the MS and PhD in computer science. The objective of the MSE is consistent, competent practice in software engineering — software development in all its phases, usually in multiperson, possibly multiorganization, arrangements.

The key to such a software engineering curriculum would be the establishment of the equivalent of the teaching hospital through various software development organizations, a teaching software engineering laboratory. Such organizations need to provide a form of prototype laboratory setting for the use and refinement of software techniques where software engineering students can have the opportunity to learn and apply the studied methods and tools, measure and evaluate their effect, and refine them for the particular applications at hand.

These organizations might be supported by industry or government. Candidates might be such existing organizations as the Software Engineering Institute or the Software Productivity Consortium, or any organization whose charter involves the development of quality software and the advancement of the field of software engineering. Such an organization, in affiliation with the computer science department of some major university, can create a teaching software engineering laboratory that will provide MSE degrees. One of the constraints is that the results of the efforts must be available for public consumption and admission must be open to the public.

Results of the various practice activities, e.g., designs for certain classes of problems in a particular design language, the statements of the requirements for some applications, or the mechanisms for software evaluation and assessment, need to be recorded and taught in the curriculum. They can become standardized and passed on to new generations of software engineers to be further refined. The existing body of knowledge at any time can be recorded and used in the training process.

As an example of a program, the degree might be based on a two year program, consisting of a mix of courses in the first year and professional experience and skill development in the second year at the affiliated organization. The course requirements would be twenty-four credits of course work in the department consisting of twelve credits in general computer science courses (e.g., Programming Languages, Systems, Artificial Intelligence, Data Bases) and twelve credits in software engineering specialization (e.g., Requirements and Specification, Design and Development Technology, Software Management, Models and Metrics for Software Management and Engineering). The professional experience and skill development would involve working in the software development laboratory, and managing, developing and evaluating software projects under the tutelage of one of the professional software engineers employed by the teaching software engineering laboratory and associated with the university.

The curriculum will clearly evolve and change as the technology evolves and changes so that it will always keep current with the latest and best ideas. This would be the advantage of associating the program with a University. The program can also evolve to a variety of specialities in the various aspects of the discipline, e.g., management, requirements.

The goal of the program would be to combine classroom education with skill development. Since much of software engineering expertise must be learned actively and skills developed by experience, a professional software development laboratory will be an ideal place to practice those skills. It will be using the latest techniques and tools, and the practitioner will have the opportunity to gain experience in using these techniques and tools under the supervision of experts. The students will be able to fine tune their skills and become experts themselves. At the same time the teaching software engineering laboratory will gain from the use of these bright and capable students in the development of the various tools and prototype systems.

The program will create a set of highly qualified software engineers who will become key managers and developers of software. It is in this way the needs of the software community can best be served since the degree deals with the long range solution to technology transfer.

Acknowledgement: The idea of a professional Master's degree in Software Engineering was first brought to my attention by Professor Harlan Mills, and many of the ideas presented here have been influenced by his vision of such a program.

Cognitive Science View of Software Engineering

Gordon H. Bradley
Naval Postgraduate School

Abstract. The present foundations of software engineering are reviewed and found to be inadequate for an effective theory of software engineering. The properties that a foundation (or theory) of software engineering should have are developed. The present and possible future relationships between cognitive science and software engineering are explored. A cognitive based perspective on software engineering is outlined that offers the possibility of a coherent foundation for the field that will allow an ambitious and effective research agenda.

Background

In all the years that I have taught software engineering, I have never hidden from my students or my colleagues my low opinion about the body of knowledge called software engineering. I don't think that the software engineering literature provides a vocabulary or organization to adequately describe the existing software processes much less provide a basis to think about the field or to improve the state of the practice. The most serious problem that results from this inadequate intellectual foundation is that we have not been able to define a clear research agenda nor identify an effective research methodology to advance our state of knowledge [note 2].

In these years, I have learned much about the art, science and practice of software development and maintenance and have become even more enthusiastic about the production of software. Developing software is great fun, and I have become more productive as I have continued to read, teach and struggle with the software engineering literature. However, despite the fact that I have become more knowledgeable about and more effective developing software, the field of software engineering has not provided an adequate let alone inspired framework to organize my knowledge, experience and thoughts about the software process. It is not an effective body of knowledge to identify and evaluate effective mechanisms to advance the state of the practice or to teach students about software production.

In my lover's quarrel with the software engineering field, I have struggled with the question of how we could develop an adequate and precise vocabulary, a viewpoint, a framework and ultimately a foundation that would help us to identify researchable questions and to inspire us to resolve them. I have tried to identify what attributes such a result must have. I believe that such a view will incorporate into its core assumptions the quantities of what Simon [89] called the "sciences of the artificial." Our research paradigm will reflect that we study objects that are synthesized to attain goals and to function — objects that are as they are because they have been chosen rather than as they must be to satisfy natural laws. As such we will be more like one of the social sciences than one of the natural sciences. Notice that I decided this without reference to the fact that current development of software is mainly human based. The changing division of labor between man and machine is based primarily on economic considerations, but this division of labor does not change in any way the property that software is synthetic rather than natural.

The present software engineering literature is almost totally descriptive. That is, it documents the state of the practice by describing how software is now developed. This approach allows only a limited perspective on how the process could be changed. I do not believe that it will be possible to induce general results with a bottom-up atheoretical research approach [note 3]. This is not only because the processes are so complicated and so detailed that they can not be effectively studied, but more fundamentally because a study of synthetic objects by bottom-up approaches will be incapable of distinguishing among what must be, what is because of choice (design), and what is accidental (as it is because it had to be something). I believe that like other sciences in their formative stages, progress in software engineering will result from a top down strategy to build theories (or models) that abstract properties of the complex reality. This approach will admit (indeed require) positing goals and intentions. In this approach, theory precedes observation, indeed theory suggests hypotheses which constructs a position that suggests experiments to evaluate the hypotheses. The observations then support or reject the hypotheses which leads to gaining confidence in or to redefining (or fixing or rejecting) the theory. This will be the basic research methodology.

This view leads me to analyze all the experimental literature by identifying a theory, an hypothesis and a result. I then say if "fill in the theory" is true, I would expect "fill in the hypothesis" to be observed, in the experiment I observed "the result". As you know, in at least 95% of the experimental software engineering literature there is no stated theory. For these papers I identify the best theories that I can based on the discussion, experiment, results and conclusions, and then I fill in the blanks. Do that for a few months or a few years and you will be as discouraged as I about the software engineering literature. In most cases there does not appear to be any reasonable theory and related hypothesis that the experiment is to shed light upon. In many others the authors draw conclusions from the results that are unrelated to any possible theory that the experiment could support.

Must There be a Theory of Software Engineering?

Above, I decry a lack of foundation (or theory) for software engineering. Before I try to convince you that I think I know a good direction to go to build such a theory, you might ask me why I think that there exists such a foundation for software engineering. We are here to work on a curriculum for an academic study of software engineering: upon what should we base the act of faith that brought us here?

Since many software engineering papers, research proposals and symposia begin with a discussion of how much money is and will be spent on software and how important software is to our economy, defense and intellectual development, we might ask if the expenditure and the impact on society alone justifies the curriculum, academic departments, research institutes, and research and development expenditures devoted to software engineering. This argument is not convincing; there are many problems in our world that involve more money and more problems and more impact on people than software and yet do not have a specific academic field devoted to them. For example, alcohol and illegal drugs involve more money and jobs, and impact more people than software. The computer industry just passed the automobile industry in terms of dollars, but automobile engineering existed as a curriculum for only a few years in a few universities (similarly for railroad engineering that was an option of mechanical engineering in the early part of this century).

A second argument is that there must be a field called software engineering because there is a demand for software engineers in industry, and therefore, it must be possible to build a theory of software engineering to teach. I call this "I teach software engineering, therefore it exists." Counterexamples abound; there are education departments all over the country with scant evidence of a theory of education. The recent introduction of computers into elementary school classrooms illustrates this lack of theory. We know from controlled laboratory experiments that computer based rote learning is more effective than human instruction. The experiments using computers in the classrooms to teach rote learning have been declared a failure. Either teachers don't know what they are doing in the classroom or (what seems to me more likely) the computer scientists and education professors don't have an adequate enough model about what really goes on in a classroom to build a system that can help students learn [note 4]. Business schools, professors, research programs abound with even less evidence that anyone knows what a foundation might be for the subject.

Generally, academic disciplines can justify themselves in universities only if they have an important problem and a set of approaches and research methodologies that have been demonstrated to lead to significant results. For example, despite the fact that there is little money and few jobs in linguistics, there are more linguistic departments in the United States than software engineering departments. Linguistics has a set of theories and models and a scientific approach that has led to a better understanding of language.

The bottom line is that there are no imperative reasons of the type "there must be an intellectually sound field of study for software engineering because...." Any proof of existence must be by construction; we must show the foundation of the field and must demonstrate that its use produces results that are not otherwise available.

If the essay so far has been at all convincing, then I have gotten you in a good frame of mind for what follows. Either I will convince you that I have a way to save software engineering and with it the livelihood of the software engineering academics or we will all go home believing that software engineering will quickly follow railroad engineering, automobile engineering, urban studies, etc. and that all the academics should quickly find jobs in industry or other academic fields.

What Is the Software Process?

The first step is to clearly define what the foundations of software engineering is a theory of. The present approach to software engineering limits the object of study to a description of the current practice with an emphasis on work products. An approach that hopes to be a foundation for not only what is but also for what might be needs a broader perspective. I will call this the software process. The software process captures information that is then transformed and transmitted across space and through time. The process transforms (e.g., requirements to specification to design to HOL to machine code) and transmits across space (e.g., across a desk, a room, an organization or to a subcontractor) and through time (e.g., to a requirements group to designers to programmers to testers to maintenance people).

An important characteristic of this process for large projects is that the amount of information is too vast to be mastered or even known by a single individual. Also the representation of the information must stand independent of any and all particular individuals. This requirement that the totality of information which at any time resides largely within the minds of individuals must be preserved as individuals come and go is in my judgment the single most important distinction between systems that are developed and maintained by a single individual or an unchanging small group and those that software engineering is concerned with. I believe that this property is the single most important determinant of the difficulties we experience with large projects. Even if we could design large projects with small modules with few interactions and thereby decompose the information, the requirement to represent the information completely independent of particular individuals makes large projects fundamentally different (and harder).

Does an information view of software capture the dominant software
activities? Two studies surveyed how software personnel spend their
time:

Programmers at Bell Labs [29]

reading programs and manuals	16%
job communications	32%
writing programs	13%
personal	13%
miscellaneous	15%
training	6%
mail	5%

Maintenance personnel at IBM [34]

study requests	18%
study documentation	6%
study code	23%
update documentation	6%
implement	19%
test	28%

Maintenance is the most costly phase of the life-cycle; the first three
maintenance categories that could roughly be called "understanding"
account for roughly half of the personnel time. For projects where maintenance costs dominate, roughly half of the life-cycle costs are associated with reading and understanding code, documents, manuals
and other software products. Other data shows that the number of
words of documentation per line of code increases sharply with problem
size; this suggests that the production and subsequent reading and understanding of software products is not only the most dominant activity
in software production but is also a factor in the nonlinearity of effort with
scale.

The software process creates, transforms and transmits information.
Software engineering is the creation of the various notations needed to
capture and transmit this information over time and space and the
development of techniques to transform this information from one notation to another. With some notable exceptions (e.g., the translation of
HOL to machine code), the overwhelming bulk of the transformations of

information is done by humans with minimal help from machines. The dominant activity is input to humans ("understanding") with relatively little output (modify code, write documents). Most of the energy that is pumped into the system is consumed by the humans and most of this is lost as they leave the system [note 5].

What Is Cognitive Science?

Cognitive science is a recent coalescence of several approaches to the study of the mind. The original questions were first studied by the ancient Greeks. The modern viewpoint focused about 30 years ago; the term cognitive science has been used for the past decade. Cognitive science is not so much a single academic/research field as a group of researchers in several disciplines with a shared set of problems, assumptions and biases. The core disciplines are cognitive psychology, artificial intelligence, philosophy of the mind, and linguistics with some contributions from anthropology and neuroscience. By no means all or even most of the researchers in the component fields regard themselves as cognitive scientists; in fact, rival points of view are active in each of the core disciplines.

For a field so young, cognitive science is lucky to already have an excellent intellectual and personal history of the field in Gardner [45]. For a reader who is acquainted with the basic issues and problems in one of the component fields, Gardner's book is an outstanding description of the web of intellectual connections among the component disciplines. Unfortunately it is not as effective as an introduction for the reader with no prior knowledge in the field. A simple introduction is not possible because the problems are hard, the concepts are tricky, and there is a long history of false trails and tempting fallacies. My own introduction was via reading in cognitive psychology including [19], [72] and [89]. My seminar (CS4510 Cognitive Science and Computer Programming) includes cognitive psychology with some readings in AI and philosophy.

Gardner [45] lists five key features that characterizes cognitive science:

1. Cognitive science believes it is necessary to assume the existence of mental representations. They believe that a scientific field can successfully deal with abstract notions like mind, thinking, etc.

2. The computer has been a strong influence on cognitive science. The information processing model of the brain is modeled after a Von Neumann machine.

3. Cognitive science feels that in the short run it is necessary to factor out whenever possible emotion, culture, history and other individualistic traits.

4. Cognitive science has a strong belief in interdisciplinary studies.

5. The classical Greeks' philosophical problems are accepted by most cognitive scientists as part of their intellectual history.

Cognitive View

As described, the activities of software development and maintenance are virtually all cognitive. That is, they are involved with the process(es) of knowing or the act of knowing and could be described with terms like perception, imagery, retention, recall, problem solving and thinking [note 6]. Some of the activities are carried out by computers, so they might be called machine cognition. As described, contemporary software activities are done mainly by humans; so they involve human cognition. The contemporary study of cognition provides a unified view of both kinds [note 7].

A cognitive view of software engineering would assume that as human factor researchers are designing physical artifacts that are to be compatible with human senses, software engineers are designing artifacts to be compatible with human cognitive processes. The information is held mainly by people. When a critical maintenance programmer leaves a project, the project has less information until his replacement has fully mastered his job. The code and the documentation contain information that is used in part to regenerate the information that the departed worker had. To view the non-human artifacts as the exclusive objects of study with the humans treated as black boxes is to ignore the bulk of the information and energy flows and to lose sight of the motivations for the design of the system.

A cognitive view does not accept the code or the processes generated by the code as the principle objects of study. For one, the code is static. The coding object of interest is really the thousands and millions of meaningful variations of code. A given instance of the code contains little information about what variations are possible let alone meaningful. "To understand" the code means to be able to conceive and eventually produce any of the other possibilities. Secondly, although in principle we could automate the software production from specification through to code, in practice we do not seem to be able to build such a machine for large problems; and present attempts at small scale do not exhibit the "understanding" that would allow it to make minor changes without "replaying" the whole process.

Cognitive Science and Software Engineering

What are the present and possible future relationships between cognitive science and software engineering? Clearly software engineering is not and will not become a part of, or a major contributor to, cognitive science because the goals of software engineering do not include any attempt to resolve the long standing epistemological questions on the nature of cognition. On the other hand, software engineering will be the beneficiary of advances in cognitive science, but even more I think that computer programming and software engineering will become the basic experimental science upon which cognitive science will rest. That is, I believe that the study of programming by individuals and the development of systems by software engineers will become the basic model for, and example of, the study of cognition. Among the human tasks for possible intense study by cognitive science like reading, language understanding, stacking blocks, solving cryptarithmetic puzzles, why do I think that computer programming will become the central problem?

1. Programming is about the right level of difficulty; reading and language understanding are too tough and the work on cryptarithmetic puzzles shows it to be too simple.
2. Because it is based on transformations of formal symbols, it is easy to exclude the considerations of emotions, cul-

ture, history and other factors that virtually all cognitive scientists, for either practical or philosophical reasons, want to ignore for the short run.

3. Software development is partially computerized; the trends to automate more of the software task allows excellent opportunities to gather data. Programmers will become to cognitive scientists what rats were to generations of behavioral psychologists.

4. Compared to other engineering design tasks, software development can involve more levels of abstraction and is less limited by physical attributes.

5. There is a large and growing expenditure on software that makes money for experimentation available and suggests economic returns from increased understanding of the task.

6. The scale and modularity of large software development is just about right when compared to a single individual. The modularity allows small one person tasks to be studied. The scale of the whole project has complexity of the order of magnitude of a single individual.

Perhaps the most important reason that the study of software (especially large projects) will be so important for cognitive science is that it forces a sophisticated view of the differences between knowledge (facts) and information. The machine allows us to easily and quickly generate an absolutely staggering amount of data. We can get a list of all variables, modules, and interconnections; and we can build program graphs and do variable analysis. In addition to this static analysis, we can simulate the process and we can obtain output, traces, execution profiles and other dynamic measures. All this data can be economically gathered, and if stored properly, it can be economically retrieved. Yet, when that is all done, there remains a clear distinction between data and understanding. It is this mountain of facts together with experiences (human experiences) and intentions that yields the capacity for purposeful action that I call information. Facts plus X yields information, which is the capacity for purposeful action. I claim that X is clearly cognitive, and I am not convinced that X can be replaced by some formal symbol process like production (or expert) systems.

Note that this analysis lays clear the fundamental hypothesis of expert systems approaches to software (and other fields): namely that cognition is computation and that facts organized into rules yields information. Cognition is firing production rules and the apparent complexity of what we call cognition and understanding are largely illusions produced by the action of a very large number of rules (and that if AI researchers only had bigger and faster computers they could demonstrate behavior that we would call intelligent).

How might software engineering benefit from the study of computer programming and software development by cognitive science? First, I don't think that cognitive science will make any direct contribution to our methodologies. That is not their goal; they want to study cognitive processes by means of studying programmers. We should not expect otherwise; after all, after a half century of maze work by behavioral psychologists there is no definitive evidence that present day rats are any smarter than their turn of the century compatriots. Their work in cognitive science will help us in another more profound way. They will help form and sharpen our vocabulary to talk about and think about software engineering. They will suggest to us an evolving conceptual framework to clarify our thinking and allow us to develop a better research agenda. And — getting back to the purpose of this workshop — they will help us develop a vocabulary and organization that will allow us to teach the theories and techniques of our field more effectively.

Examples of How Cognitive Science Will Help Software Engineering

What evidence is there that cognitive science will help us develop a foundation for software engineering? My present list is short; each item is underdeveloped with more promise than substance. But even this tentative beginning has gotten me excited about software engineering research and has helped me think more clearly and to teach more effectively.

1. Knowledge domains - Brooks: [19] Brooks presents a theory of the organization of the knowledge acquired by a programmer who understands a program. The programmer's knowledge is described as a succession of "knowledge domains" that form a bridge between the problem and the final executing program. Each of these domains (for example, problem, algorithm, programming language, etc.) "consists of a closed set of primitive objects, properties of the objects, relations among objects, and operators which manipulate these properties and relations" [19]. This theory involves two kinds of information — the first is about things within a particular domain; the second involves translating information in one domain to information in nearby domains. The second type is clearly harder and more difficult to automate, and yet, it is done effectively by humans. This analysis gives a clear view of what is happening in the software process. The present software engineering view focuses on the work products (objects within a domain) and is largely blind to the processes (mostly human) that translate a work product in one notation to a work product in another notation.

Perhaps more importantly Brooks shows the utility of a theory; he uses the theory to make predictions about the effectiveness of documentation and then compares it to experimental data. This general procedure leads to an acceptance, rejection, or modification of the theory. The software engineering literature is long on experiments, but these experiments are not as useful as they might be because of the absence of theories.

2. Memory as reconstruction - Neisser: [72] The classical view of the human memory is that one retains memories as slightly faded copies of sensory experiences; they exist always and on occasion are aroused. Neisser's view is that we do not recall memories; rather we reconstruct them through an active (not passive) process and that this reconstruction is based on "traces" of the experience that we retain. More provocative (at least to me) is Neisser's proposal on the character of these traces: "The only plausible possibility is that it consists of traces of prior processes of construction" and "we store traces of earlier cognitive acts, not the products of those acts" [72], p. 285.

This leads me to consider software documentation from a new prospective. Typically documentation has not conferred significant benefits on the writer or the reader. Current documentation has the classical view as its basic premise: external memories (cognitive science jargon for memories like notes that exist outside the mind) are the things that we are trying to remember. Neisser says that we don't remember things from internal memory this way; so I ask if we should build external memories (documentation) in this way. We need to view documentation as being dynamic with an entirely new concept of dynamic. Documentation should be constructed to help humans in the reconstruction of the internal state called "understanding."

Documentation (unlike good literature) is boring to write and read because we have so little insight on how people construct facts to understand technical material. We should devise more "intuitive" notations for documentation. By intuitive I mean the nonverbal and partially verbal knowledge about how the software really works. This knowledge can then be used by the reader to construct or reconstruct an understanding of the software. With high resolution dynamic displays we have a new medium in which to rethink our approach to documentation. Together with a more sophisticated view of human memory processes we may be able to make some significant progress on documentation.

3. Schemata (context, environment) - Neisser: [72] Another aspect of Neisser's theory of memory is that the construction is not limited to the object being remembered. We remember in reference to "frames of reference" or "schemata." Neisser presents a detailed discussion of why this view is supported by common sense and by some experiments. We would like documentation that only tells the reader things that he/she does not already know. This is difficult to achieve because documentation is prepared for potentially many readers. This analysis suggests we should think about on-line documentation where the system has some knowledge about the state of the user's knowledge and understanding. This suggests documentation systems that can use some knowledge of the state of the user's knowledge to determine what and how much material to present. This is clearly an ambitious undertaking. A more modest approach would eliminate from view some comments but put their retrieval under the control of the reader. For example, the comments and elaboration could be hidden behind the code, the user would then display them if it was needed. This is not unlike a spreadsheet where the formulas are hidden or a outline program that shows lower levels of the document only if requested.

4. Programming as a learned skill - Sheil: [87] In an outstanding review of the software psychology literature, Sheil attributes the unimpressive results of the behavior research in programming to "the results of sloppy methodology, of a poor choice of hypothesis from computer science and of the considerable practical difficulty of investigating complex behavior." He goes on to say the "basic problem is a fundamental misunderstanding of the nature of the programming skill." He discusses two flawed views and concludes with, "More fundamentally, programming is a learned skill, and therefore, what is easy or difficult is much more a function of what skills an individual has learned than any inherent quality of the task." By this he means that the expert programmer's skill is not exclusively or even primarily determined by his/her innate ability nor is it based on some small body of expertise like the syntax of a programming language. Rather the "the programmer's expertise is made up of an enormous number of interrelated pieces of knowledge." Now this view will suggest the futility of setting up experiments with a group of programmers, some doing a new technique and the others not, and expecting significant differences. This also has implications for the training of programmers and their support on the job. Our training and support must recognize that we need to support a much larger set of facts for programmers, and the organization of these facts may be different for each programmer.

One is struck immediately that the approaches to improving software engineering suggested by this new perspective are harder than those we have today. This seems right because we have always known that the development of software was a task more sophisticated than the intellectual tools we had to think about it. The harder and bigger problems suggest multiperson, multiyear, well organized research efforts; but the potential reward for a more sophisticated approach is correspondingly greater.

Conclusion

In my view the integration of a cognitive science perspective into a framework for software engineering offers us the possibility of a coherent foundation for the field that will allow a clear and more ambitious research agenda. Some of this "new view" has already been developed by a few software engineering researchers with little or no explicit mention of cognitive science; the explicit use of this viewpoint will provide a vocabulary and organization to integrate this work. I think it is premature to try to name this new view until it is more fully developed. However, some aspects are coming into focus. We need a better description of the software process. I think that the information approach sketched here is a possible candidate. Any candidate must clearly emphasize the transformation of information not just the products and must not treat humans in the process as black boxes. As discussed, the new view should proceed top-down. This says that we must build relatively high level models of the process and that we are going to have to include models of human cognition. We are going to have to set aside our engineer's reluctance to deal with models of humans and with models that rest on ill-defined concepts like thinking, design, remembering and so on.

Another implication of the new approach is that we are going to have to think about new dynamics of the processes. We will have to think about documentation that grows and adapts to humans or other parts of the system that are also changing. Our views on training and the support of programmers will have to better recognize the nature of the programming skill.

A final word about our enterprise here: as described, I think that a new foundation of software engineering is needed and that a greatly improved version is within view. I don't think that a new organization will be completed within the next several years, and like many of you I have a software engineering class to teach next quarter. I think our time is well spent clarifying the goals of a software engineering education, and the effective approaches and techniques of our field. I am much less comfortable with any attempt to impose a rigid taxonomy on the field or to try to more carefully define our present vocabulary. Using a

Christmas tree analogy, I think we can agree on the shape size and purpose of the tree. We can work on the beautiful decorations that we have and are building, but we should avoid locking in on today's structure for the limbs. In short, in preparation for a better and more effective foundation for our field, we should do nothing that would tend to further legitimize in any way the present framework.

NOTES

1. This is a preliminary version of an essay on the foundations of software engineering.

2. One symptom of the inadequate research agenda is that most, if not all, software engineering researchers are personally involved in the development of software. I don't think this is solely or even primarily because we want hands-on experience. In a well founded field, researchers pursue an agreed upon agenda that is related to, but not identical with, what practitioners do. Another symptom is that the literature tree in virtually all software engineering subfields is shallow with many involving only one or two papers and only one or two authors. The lack of a coherent foundation makes it difficult to build on the work of others.

3. I believe most of the experimental software engineering papers should be characterized as bottom-up and atheoretical. It is not simply the absence of theories and models that provide a plausible mechanism or explanation for the results; in addition, most authors seem to really believe in black box experimentation and apparently believe that it is incorrect methodology to *a priori* posit a theory that would predict and explain the results. If they were psychologists, we would call such an approach behaviorism.

4. With less theory and experience than education professors, I wonder how we will be able to design a "software environment" or "software factory" that will generate positive benefits, let alone justify the cost of its development and maintenance. This is surely a instance where "nothing is more practical than a good theory."

5. From this perspective the development of large software systems does not look that much different from other large information intensive projects like developing a major federal tax change. Public sentiment is translated into

legislative intent, which is translated into tax code, then into regulations, algorithms for computation, manuals and preparation materials, interpretations and judicial rulings.

6. Cognitive scientists are no more able or willing to give a definitive definition of cognition than we are willing to unambiguously define module or user friendly.

7. A more controversial view held by a few is that there is only one type of cognition, sometimes performed by electro-mechanical devices and other times by organic devices.

Software Engineering Education:
An Idealized Scenario

Richard E. Fairley
Wang Institute of Graduate Studies

Abstract. The ideal scenario for software engineering education incorporates a broadly based undergraduate program in computer science, mathematics, science, social sciences, business, and management; followed by one to two years of programmer-level work experience; followed by a professionally oriented masters program in software engineering; followed by a one to two year period of professional-level apprenticeship; followed, for some, by training at the doctoral level. Completion of each stage of the idealized program qualifies the graduate for a corresponding level of duties and responsibilities as a software engineer. This paper describes an idealized, comprehensive program of software engineering education, and is extracted from the technical report, "The Role of Academe in Software Engineering Education," TR-85-19, Wang Institute, October, 1985.

Many professions follow an educational model of broadly based undergraduate programs (political science for law, biochemistry for medicine), professional graduate level training (law school, medical school), and apprenticeship (law clerk, intern) under the guidance of skilled practitioners. This model seems appropriate for software engineering. The ideal scenario for software engineering education thus involves a broadly based undergraduate program in computer science, math, science, social sciences, business, and management; one to two years of programmer-level work experience; professional training at the masters level; a professional-level apprenticeship; and, for some, training at the doctoral level. Some of the functions and skill areas required of professional software engineers are itemized in Table 1. In most cases, the level of maturity and sophistication indicated in Table 1 can only be achieved through a combination of undergraduate education, work experience as a programmer, professionally oriented graduate education, and a professional-level apprenticeship.

The most desirable preparation for a software engineer is an undergraduate computer science major (including courses in computer engineering, math, science, business and management) with a minor program of study in an application area; followed by one or two years of work experience; followed by a master's program in software engineering, and concluded with one or two years of apprenticeship to gain experience in most, and preferably all, of the areas listed in Table 1. Following this, some individuals may wish to pursue advanced practitioner training, or to pursue a career in research and teaching. Doctoral programs in software engineering would provide these opportunities.

This ideal scenario is depicted in Figure 1. Appropriate courses at the undergraduate level are listed in Table 2 and master's level topics are listed in Table 3. The structure of the master's program in software engineering at Wang Institute is presented in Figure 2 . A detailed description of the Wang Institute Master of Software Engineering degree program is presented in the accompanying paper, "Core Course Documentation: Master's Degree Program in Software Engineering," Wang Institute Technical Report TR-85-17, September, 1985.[1]

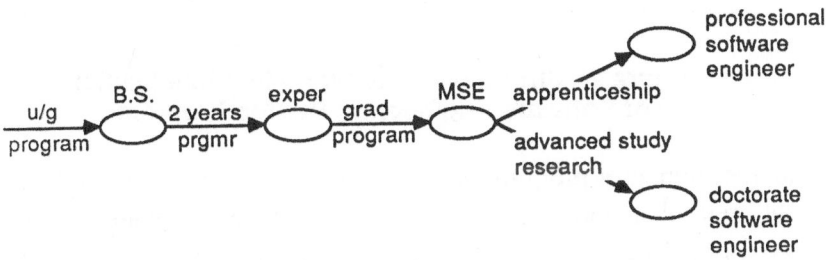

Figure 1. Ideal Scenario of Software Engineering Education

Table 4 presents the structure of a proposed PhD program in software engineering. Doctoral programs in software engineering will be distinguished from doctoral programs in computer science by the emphasis placed on methods, tools, and techniques oriented to the technology of software development and modification, and by research endeavors

---

[1]To obtain a copy please write to the author at the Wang Inst. of Grad. Studies, Tyng Road, Tyngboro, MA 01879

such as experimental studies, case studies, and development of exemplar software artifacts, in addition to endeavors that advance the theory and methodology of software technology.

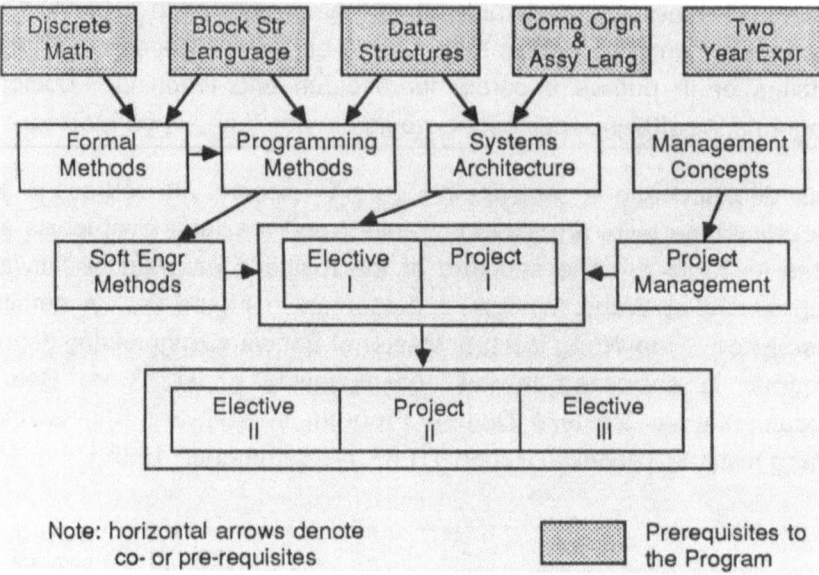

Note: horizontal arrows denote
co- or pre-requisites

Prerequisites to
the Program

**Figure 2. Structure of the Wang Institute Master
of Software Engineering Degree Program**

The importance of programmer-level work experience and professional-level apprenticeship in the education of software engineers cannot be overemphasized. Much of the material indicated in Table 1 will be unappreciated by undergraduates who have no basis of experience to understand the importance or relevance of the topics. The need for programmer-level work experience is analogous to the need for work experience in business education: business curricula are, for the most part, timely, appropriate, and important to modern society; yet, most students in undergraduate business programs view the programs as easy paths to bachelor's degrees. This is partly because of the "soft" (non-quantitative) nature of much of the material in business curricula, but it is primarily a result of the student's lack of maturity and real world experience. After a few years of work experience, the material presented in business schools is much more meaningful to students.

Apprenticeship at the post-masters level is also important in the development of professional software engineers. The need for an apprenticeship in software engineering is similar to the need for an apprenticeship in architecture, law, and medicine. Newly graduated architects do not design skyscrapers, law clerks do not argue cases before the Supreme Court, and interns do not perform open-heart surgery. Yet, new software engineers often find themselves in analogous situations.

Apprenticeship with a qualified mentor allows the apprentice to apply various methods, tools, and techniques of software engineering under a guiding hand, and tempers academic treatment of the topics listed in Table 1 with the realities of the profession. A somewhat formalized apprenticeship also provides an avenue for the apprentice to infuse new ideas and new technology into the sponsoring organization. The apprentice can experiment with, and demonstrate the feasibility of, new ideas in a sheltered environment.

Some software engineers will have the desire and the ability to pursue doctoral level training in software engineering. There are several paths at the doctoral level: contributions to the theory and methodology of software engineering, development of outstanding software artifacts, experimental studies involving human subjects, and significant case studies of technological and/or managerial issues.

Doctoral topics in software engineering must pass the litmus test of orientation to technological and/or managerial issues surrounding the development and modification of software products. In many cases, the nature of the emphasis placed on a topic will determine its suitability as doctoral work in software engineering or doctoral work in computer science. Currently, doctoral students who pursue software engineering topics in computer science departments often distort their true contributions and emphasize minor theoretical points in order to satisfy the appropriate criterion for computer science.

It is important to note that many research topics in software engineering are not acceptable computer science topics (for example, development of software artifacts, experimental studies, case studies); similarly, many

topics in computer science, such as theories of computational complexity or abstract families of formal languages, are not suitable software
engineering topics.

Computer science and software engineering are distinct, but strongly
related disciplines — just as physics and electrical engineering and
chemistry and chemical engineering are distinct but related. The differences in viewpoint and orientation to subject matter arise because
science and technology serve distinct intellectual, economic, and social
needs in modern society.

The career path for a doctorate in software engineering might be a
university career in research and teaching, or a career in industrial
research and development. The incentives and rewards in universities
and industry should encourage easy movement between the two
arenas. This would appear to be advantageous to all concerned parties.

Table 1. Functions and Skill Areas for Software Engineers

Requirements Analysis
Familiarity with the application area
Familiarity with analysis tools and techniques
Oral, written, and interpersonal communication skills

Functional Specification
Functionality, performance, design constraints, quality criteria, functional
interfaces
Ability to identify and specify appropriate abstractions, interfaces,
and constraints
Ability to establish quality and performance criteria
Familiarity with appropriate notations, tools, and techniques

Software Design
Thorough understanding of the hardware and operating system environment
Ability to decompose complex systems, specify interfaces, and document the
design using appropriate methods, tools, and techniques

Implementation
Familiarity with the necessary algorithms and data structures
Proficiency in the operating system(s) and programming languages(s)
used to implement the system
Proficient coding style to enhance understandability and
modifiability

Inspections, Walkthroughs and Reviews
Ability to effectively participate in inspections, walkthroughs, and reviews
Ability to function as a member of a team

Debugging and Unit Testing
Deductive and inductive problem solving skill
Familiarity with debugging and testing tools and techniques
Understanding of unit testing coverage criteria and ability to design test
cases to meet those criteria

Integration and Acceptance Testing
Familiarity with methods, tools, procedures, and techniques for integration
and acceptance testing

Configuration Management and Quality Assurance
Familiarity with tools and techniques
Ability to work with, and function as, configuration management and quality
assurance specialists

Preparation of Users' Manual and Maintenance Guide
Written communication skill
Ability to work with users and technical writers

Software Maintenance
Familiarity with tools, techniques, and procedures
of software maintenance
Ability to perform emergency fixes and scheduled enhancement, adaptation,
and repair.
Ability to work with customers and organizational procedures for change control

Project Leadership
Ability to work within an organizational framework
Ability to plan a project and lead a team of five to seven programmers

Table 2. Topics in an Undergraduate Software-Oriented Curriculum

Computer Science
- Introduction to Computers and Computation
- Algorithms, Data Structures, and Structured Programming
- Computer Organization and Assembly Programming
- Computational Complexity and Analysis of Algorithms
- Computer Architecture
- Computer Logic and VLSI Design
- Language Translation

- Programming Paradigms
- Operating Systems
- Systems Programming
- Database Systems
- Scientific Computation
- Expert Systems Technology
- Computer Communications
- Real-time Systems and Programming
- Performance Evaluation

Math

- Calculus
- Differential Equations
- Linear Algebra
- Appropriate Discrete Math
- Probability and Statistics
- Symbolic Logic

Business

- Introduction to Business
- Micro-Economics
- Financial Accounting

Management

- Theory and Structure of Organizations
- Human Relations and Organizational Behavior
- Oral and Interpersonal Communication Skills

Software Engineering

- Software Analysis and Design Methodologies
- Software Development Tools and Techniques
- Problem Solving in the Technological Disciplines
- Team Project in Software Engineering

Table 3. Topics in a Graduate Software Engineering Curriculum

Technical Issues

- Computing Systems Technology
- Tools and Techniques for User Requirements Analysis

- Practicum in Conducting User Requirements Analysis
- Preparing a User Requirements Document
- Applications of Formal Methods in Software Engineering
- Tools and Techniques of Formal Specification and Verification
- Practicum in Formal Specification and Verification
- Practicum in Rapid Prototyping of Software
- Survey of Design Methods, Tools, and Techniques
- In-depth Study of One or More Design Methods
- Practicum in Software Design
- Issues of Detailed Design and Coding Style
- Practicum in Detailed Design and Coding Style
- Practicum in Debugging and Unit Testing Techniques
- Practicum in Integration and Acceptance Test Planning
- Issues, Tools, and Techniques of Software Maintenance
- Conducting Reviews, Inspections, and Walkthroughs
- Development and Execution of a Test Plan
- Development and Execution of a Documentation Plan
- Format and Content of Software Project Documents
- Issues, Tools, and Techniques of Change Control, Configuration Management, Quality Assurance, and Validation and Verification
- Standards, Policies, and Procedures in Software Engineering

Managerial Issues

- Organizational Structures and Management Concepts for Software Engineers
- Customers, Contracts, and Business Plans
- Marketing and Distribution Considerations
- Lifecycle Models, Milestones, and Reviews
- Tools and Techniques for Planning a Software Project
- Practicum in Developing a Software Project Plan
- Software Economics: Cost Estimation Techniques, Risk Assessment, Cost-Benefit Analysis, and Trade-off Studies
- Tools and Techniques for Monitoring and Controlling Software Quality and Programmer Productivity
- Tools and Techniques for Monitoring and Controlling Schedules and Budgets
- Practicum in Technical Writing and Oral Presentations
- Motivational Issues for Programmers and Software Engineers
- Participating in A Software Engineering Team
- Leading A Software Project Team

- Practicum in Software Engineering Team Projects
- Management of Software Maintenance Activities
- Standards, Policies, and Procedures in Software Engineering

Table 4. Structure of a PhD Program in Software Engineering

Breadth
- 12 Graduate Level Courses
- 6 from Masters Core
- 4 areas:
  - Software Engineering Methods
  - Software Engineering Management
  - Quantitative Methods
  - Computing Technology

Depth
- Courses
- Seminars
- Directed Study

Dissertation Areas
- Case Studies
- Exemplar Artifacts
- Experimental Studies
- Theoretical Advances

Research Orientation
- Technology of Computing Software

Essential Elements of Software Engineering Education Revisited

Peter Freeman
University of California, Irvine

The Thesis

Ten years ago an intellectual basis for software engineering education (SEE) was proposed that identified a set of components that should underlie any curriculum in the field [38]. Those components included computer science, management science, communication, problem-solving, and design; they stressed the integration of management and technical issues in software engineering.

A review of that proposal convinces me they are still the right elements. However, events of the intervening ten years and the current requirements for SEE lead me to the conclusion that the design component is being seriously underemphasized.

Further, I believe that the lack of progress in building the structures to deliver SEE is highly problematic. This perception leads to some other observations about SEE and what we should be doing about it. This paper develops these two theses and suggests some directions we should be taking.

Essential Elements Reviewed

The 1976 paper noted that, "We believe that five content areas should form the basis of any software engineering curriculum." For each of the areas (computer science, management science, communication skills, problem solving, and design methodology), we addressed three topics: how the content is used by the software engineer, the range of knowledge needed, and the depth of understanding required.

The paper implicitly stressed the principle that software engineering is an applied activity that must carefully integrate managerial and technical concerns and techniques. It went on to address the issue of teaching software engineering (a topic expanded on in several later papers [41, 101, 54]) and ended with the following:

"Any such curricula must meet the following criteria:

1. Be based on the five content areas outlined here;
2. Be flexible so that they can change easily and be adapted to substantive developments in the field;
3. Be based on computer science and be viewed as "applied computer science." Other alternatives will lead to suboptimal educational programs.
4. Prepare students to push forward the boundaries of knowledge and techniques, not just apply what is already known.
5. Include a large amount of realism and practical work.
6. Provide for multiple implementations, dependent upon career objectives and backgrounds of students and upon the academic home of the program;
7. Build on existing curricula to the extent possible."

I would write the same paper today. While much has happened in the past ten years and while there are certainly some refinements I would make, I think this is still the foundation on which software engineering (and educational programs to support it) must be built for the foreseeable future.

Let me note some of the needed refinements here without going into detail. "Management science" should be broadened to "management"; many of the things the software engineer needs to know about management are not quantitative and never will be. "Design methodology" should be broadened to "design practice" or just "design"; (more on this below). Although implicit in the emphasis on computer science (in the broad sense) in our original definition, the long range importance of automated and/or mathematically based techniques in software engineering means that the software engineer must have a strong foundation in those parts of computer science that are relevant to effective use of these techniques; the loose nature of the definition of computer science argues that a tighter definition of what we intend for the software engineer to know is needed.

My revisitation to this proposal and the added perspective of ten years thus confirms (for me, at least) that it is indeed the proper foundation. But, that does not mean I am sanguine about our present situation.

On the contrary, I am disturbed by two things, one procedural, one substantive. Procedurally, I fear that the software field is like some of America's basic industries, which for years refused to acknowledge that changes were needed; the lack of progress in software engineering usage and education is extremely serious. As an educator, I must take a share of the responsibility.

Substantively, my experience of the past ten years argues even more forcefully that design must be the integrative knowledge and activity that is the core of software engineering. That part of the content of software engineering education must be emphasized and put into effective action.

Before expanding on these two topics, permit me to share my perceptions of some of the significant events (for software engineering) of the past ten years and the current demands on and for software engineering education.

What's Been Happening Since We Talked Last?

Although there have been numerous public sessions at meetings, undoubtedly many private gatherings, and some curriculum development efforts, I believe this is the first effort since 1976 [39] to address strategically the question of where software engineering is or should be headed. In reflecting on the past decade, I have tried to identify the events or trends that are most relevant to our present considerations:

1. The general expansion of computing in all its aspects;
2. The creation of a significant software package industry, as well as the great expansion of custom development services;
3. The microcomputer revolution and the consequent growth of software development for small machines;
4. The emergence of microcomputers as a tool for the software engineer;
5. The growth in number (and size) of very large software systems;
6. The growing perception that automation (especially AI) is important to the software engineer;

7. Greatly increased investment in tools and, to some extent, training for programmers;

8. The focus on the front-end activities of development;

9. Lack of attention to the design activity;

10. Creation of national research and technology-transfer programs in a number of countries;

11. Failure of most universities to get into SEE activity;

12. Failure of most industries to do anything significant about on-the-job training for software engineers;

13. Lack of integration of software engineering content into traditional computer science or information science curricula;

14. Lack of any significant breakthroughs or greatly deepened understandings of software engineering;

15. The small increase in the general level of usage of what we do know.

These are not listed in any particular order; further, I am sure you have your own opinions about relative importance — indeed, you may not even believe that some of these have actually occurred. They are, however, the things that stand out for me. My purpose here is not to discuss the ramifications of these events since that will show up in my later comments. Rather, I will limit my discussion of them to the two that help drive my major theses.

In a sense, when I review where we have been in the past ten years, I feel that we have simply jumped over the design activity. The early 70's were characterized by attention to programming methodology. Around 1976 many people started to become concerned about the "front-end" activities of requirements analysis and specification; that concern continues to the present. With some exceptions, there has not been an analogous focus on what happens between the time the requirements and specifications are "known" and the programming activity begins.

There is no question that front-end activities are critical and that some high payoff can be had by improving them. What we as a field seem to have skipped over, however, is the critical activity of taking the results of those front-end activities and turning them into coherent systems — that is, design, as distinct from programming.

When I consider how systems are built today by most organizations and consider how they were built ten years ago, I don't believe we have much of which to be proud. Likewise, when I ask what my students know today about software engineering compared to what students of ten years ago knew, I cannot see much difference. Over the past decade the knowledge base of software engineering has grown, and many improvements in the ways we can build systems have been developed. The apparent failure simply to disseminate and use that knowledge concerns me deeply.

Even though these perceptions alone are enough to drive quite a lot of activity in SEE and technology transfer more generally, it is important to ask what the world around us is asking for.

What are the Demands of 1986?

The demands of 1986 seem simple to me:

1. High quality software;
2. Flexible designs to permit easy modification and un-foreseen usage with other software;
3. Shorter development times;
4. Better prepared professionals;
5. More people.

That these demands (and others that may seem more pertinent to you) are not always attainable, and may even be contradictory given current techniques, is clear.

We can certainly generate a long list of specific demands for SEE — more training in use of formal techniques, better command of Ada, ability to

organize and manage projects, and so on. While that may be useful when trying to design a curriculum, it doesn't shed much light on strategic considerations until we abstract them.

The task for SEE in the light of these general demands is to identify the essential knowledge necessary to satisfy them and find effective ways of imparting that knowledge to the relevant professionals (and professionals-to-be). That, of course, is nothing new, but may be worth keeping in mind.

The core of my thesis is that while all the elements reviewed above are important, design is the absolutely essential element that must be transmitted to all software engineers in some form. Further, I think there are some ways of going about it that should have significantly more success than what we have been doing. That is the subject of the remainder of this paper.

The Central Role of Design
in Software Engineering

My long-standing interest in and study of design (see, for example, [36]) has led me to stress the importance of design in software development [37], [40], [39], [42], [44]. The more I learn about software development, both abstractly and pragmatically, the more I am convinced of its absolute centrality.

Rather than repeat what has appeared elsewhere, I want only to summarize those arguments here and move forward to consider what we should be doing in the area of design education.

What Is Design?

Professor Simon's definition, "devising artifacts to attain goals" [88], still captures the essence of what design is all about.

In software, the artifacts of ultimate interest are programs. Until recently (and, still, for many people) those programs were small, produced by one person, and were the only "tangible" result of the development process. This, among other things, has led to a focus on the programming process.

There is no question that creating a program is a design problem. Yet, the nature of the problem (devising a sequential set of instructions, in most cases, and data structures that will carry out a desired computation) conditions strongly what the program designer does.

When coupled with the small size of individual programs, this has meant that program design (or programming) is not much concerned with issues of structure in the larger sense of definition of the components of a system and their interrelationship.

Software developers repeatedly learn (usually the hard way) that when dealing with large systems of programs, it is precisely the issue of component definition and relationship that is critical. This level of design (typically called architectural or general or preliminary design) should thus be concerned with structuring the entire system (devising the artifact) in order to attain the specific goals at hand.

The process of system or architectural design is one that naturally occurs between the specification activity and the detailed design of programs. Because of its place in the process and because of the importance of the system structure that it establishes, system design is where the developer has the opportunity to bring together all the considerations, requirements, constraints, and possibilities of the design situation to achieve a superior product. It is this set of unique opportunities that make this form of design so essential; the more so as our demands become more stringent and our systems larger. Yet, we largely ignore it in our educational programs and only infrequently do a good job of it in practice. The connection is obvious.

The Breadth of Design

Design in the general sense of Simon is quite pervasive in software engineering. We design when we correct a system deficiency by devising a fix for it. We design when we create the specifications for a system. We design when we plan a set of tests to determine if our system has a desired set of properties.

One of the continuing confusions is between internal and external design. Most of the instances of design discussed above are concerned with the way in which functions are implemented — that is, with the internal design of the system. Most of the design knowledge and techniques of software engineering are concerned with this type of design.

But, we are also designing when we decide what functions a system should have, how they should behave, and what the relationship should be between them. This design of the external characteristics of a system, usually carried out initially during specification, but often perverted as development proceeds, is rarely treated as a form of design to which some of the same knowledge can be applied. Even more importantly, there is, or should be, an intimate connection between the internal and external designs of a system.

Software engineering is essentially a synthesis activity. Everyone involved in the systematic creation of software-intensive systems is involved with design. That does not mean, however, that everyone is or must be a master designer.

Some people need to know the most about external design. Others need to focus on design changes, while others will be detailed designers, perhaps in particular specialty areas. Managers need to understand the management of the various design activities as well as be able to apply some of the design problem-solving techniques to problems they face such as the design of an effective working group.

Design as a process and as a body of knowledge is the single thing that is common to just about everything in software engineering. Every software engineer must know something about design and the critical path of technical development must be driven by the designer.

The Curriculum Implications of Design

There are three curriculum aspects relative to design:

- Processes of design
- Design knowledge
- Training mechanisms

Because there is much to discuss on each of these, and many different viewpoints, I will only sketch enough here to indicate my meaning.

Design is a process. There are things to be done, decisions to be formulated, decisions to be made, results to be validated, information to be collected. One can (and often does) proceed intuitively through design.

However, we do know some things about how to structure the process in particular situations. Popular "design methods," such as structured design or Jackson design, are examples of highly organized design processes that have been packaged explicitly. Other knowledge about how to proceed and how not to proceed in the design of large systems can be codified and passed on to new designers. Techniques of managing a design activity can be formulated and applied to practice situations. The results on the process of using different types of design tools can be studied. The history of design projects, both successful and unsuccessful, can be reviewed. These are some things relating to the design process that should be a part of the curriculum.

Design knowledge is harder to delimit. In one sense, everything known about software or computers is knowledge that may someday be needed by a designer in order to make a decision; it is the overall task of SEE to winnow out the most relevant of this mass of information and make sure that the software engineer has access to it.

There are some specific kinds of design knowledge that can be imparted, however. One of the most important is the study of successful design structures. Another is the study of system architectures as related to specific functional architectures. Knowledge about trade-offs between different algorithms or data structures, while clearly a general subject, is relevant to the task of making design decisions. The contribution of different system elements to desired quality criteria such as reliability is a highly relevant piece of design knowledge. As we focus more on the process of design, additional topics will arise.

The third aspect of the design curriculum is the set of mechanisms for training designers. Fundamentally, design is a skill which must be practiced to be learned. A close integration of the preparation for doing design (learning the processes and the design-oriented knowledge) and the practice whereby it is really learned is essential; further, an often overlooked aspect is the continuing feedback to the designer on his performance and the need for refreshers. (More on this below as I look at the second issue: technology transfer.)

Software Engineering Education — The Process

Let me return now to a consideration of the broader picture of SEE, not just the design component. As noted in the introduction, I think that we have been unsuccessful in the past ten years in getting software engineering established in any broad sense as part of the educational scene.

That statement is in no way intended to diminish the accomplishments that have been made: The establishment and continuing growth of Wang Institute, the establishment of the Software Engineering Institute at Carnegie Mellon University, the creation and successful operation of IBM's Software Engineering Institute, the institution of several extensive corporate training programs, the publication and successful sales of several general textbooks are all important achievements. Yet, compared to what is needed (viewed either from the supply or the demand side), we have barely scratched the surface.

There are no masters-level degree programs (to my knowledge) specifically oriented to software engineering at a major university. Most schools do not even have a software engineering course in the context of a computer science curriculum. The one serious attempt at curriculum development [54] by a group that could represent a broad spectrum of the field was stillborn, apparently the victim of turf wars. Attempts to infuse some software engineering into other curricula have had little success.

My own situation is illustrative. My department started a professional master's program in 1975, aimed at top quality students who wanted to pursue serious careers as computer science professionals. The most popular option (with more than 50% of the students) within the program was a concentration on software engineering. Although successful, the department chose to phase out the program beginning in 1982 due to lack of resources (both monetary and faculty) and a need to focus our energies on research. The result has been good for the department, but detrimental to our ability to provide software engineering education.

Two things are relevant in this vignette to understand why the field has not made much progress in SEE. One is that we got little financial support from local industry for the program; moral support was plentiful, but it is hard to pay salaries with that. The other is that the pressures of a research university are generally for increased research accomplishment; in a new field like computer science, the pressure can be particularly strong. Further, in the face of severe shortage of faculty one must strongly prioritize the allocation of resources.

I don't believe there are any silver bullets in SEE. We face a situation that is fundamentally one of changing people's attitudes toward the importance of what SEE has to offer at a time when there are severe shortages of people capable of providing it and in the face of increasing competitive pressures that make the addition of what is seen as simply additional costs highly problematical. This state of affairs has existed the past ten years and is worsening, if anything.

Viewed in this context, perhaps we have done as well as we could have. The only constructive course of action, in any event, is to try to find ways of moving forward more effectively. To that end, I have several suggestions regarding the process of providing SEE; some of these are not terribly new, so consider them a reaffirmation!

Some Steps Needed to Move Software Engineering Education Forward

1. Establish more institutes like Wang. Although the number of graduates that Wang is able to produce is small, it has high value to the field as a showcase and model. I think the establishment of several (probably less than six) more institutes like Wang would be beneficial.

They should probably be geographically dispersed and might well follow fundamentally different patterns (although having two or three similar, semi-competitive institutes like Wang would probably be useful). Several could exist in the context of established educational institutions of different sorts (indeed, Carnegie Mellon University-Software Engineering Institute may turn out to be exactly this). One might be a non-profit service center for a consortium of industries in some region;

one might be profit-making (a fair amount of money is made delivering courses of marginal value; why couldn't someone make a go of delivering quality education?); one might be specialized to a particular industry or application (for example, building software for automated factories).

Although I believe the need is great enough to warrant support by the federal government, the current financial climate probably prevents that. The issue, in any event, is to provide more visible examples of how to provide SEE.

2.   Integrate software engineering concepts into undergraduate curricula. There are a number of techniques and concepts of SE that can be assimilated by undergraduates.   Given that most computer science majors go to work in industry, we could certainly raise the general level of competence significantly and provide a better base for further professional training if they were better prepared.   Although warming to the task slowly, most departments are at least receptive to the idea of incorporating material into their curricula that will better prepare students for their professional careers.

I believe this has not been done largely because of the lack of published curricula by the professional societies. The existence of Wang and an increasing selection of textbooks will help, but some formal curricula suggestions by recognized bodies that represent a broad sample of the community are urgently needed.

3.   Create some master's programs in major universities. Universities are just as competitive as anyone else. If two or three quality, professional master's programs are started at leading universities, the idea will catch on. How to do it is more problematical, but I suspect that the combination of renewed support for education in general and the competition among states for high-tech industry will produce some start ups soon.

4.   Encourage industrial retraining. Again, the changing tax laws and budget situation remove some of the incentives, but the value should still be clear. If industry needs N software engineers, we certainly don't need to turn out N people educated and trained from scratch. Many people already in industry have a good bit of the background necessary to be good software engineers. Further, they often have the advantage of maturity, leadership ability, and application knowledge. A good bit of work needs to be done, however, to find ways of identifying those that will most benefit from such retraining and ways of providing it in different situations.

The American industrial system has often been faulted, properly I would say, for throwing away its employees instead of retraining them. This is a situation in which this would be foolish to an extreme. There simply is no way that we are going to educate enough people from scratch to carry out the tasks at hand, and doing the tasks with poorly trained people is increasingly counterproductive. Further, one of the things that seems clear about software engineering is that the more professional maturity and application knowledge one has the better; many people currently working have acquired these traits without proper training in software engineering.

5. Establish a tradition of continuing education. Software engineers need to have continuing professional education, just as medical doctors do. As we establish the educational mechanisms for software professionals, we must educate students to expect this and at the same time start to provide for it.

6. Carry out some solid economic studies of the impact of software engineering. Certainly one of the primary inhibitors to the adoption of software engineering in practice has been the lack of much believable supportive economic data (at least data that is publicly available). Studies that strongly support the value of using software engineering should make it easier to obtain the funding necessary to provide the needed education.

There are other possibilities, of course. Similarly, there are a number of suggestions for improving the actual delivery of SEE. In closing, I will only mention the need in the area of design for educational structures that permit students to alternate between the classroom and the development shop (but under some carefully fashioned monitoring), allowing them to move through several cycles of obtaining formalized knowledge and learning how to apply it.

Conclusion

The basic elements of software engineering education seem to be constant, although there are strong arguments that design should be the essential ingredient that ties the other elements together. Our progress in establishing SEE has been slow and the prospects for the future are not much better; however, several strategies are suggested.

The survival of American economic capability depends in no small way on our success. Providing software engineering education and making sure that the knowledge so imparted is actually put to use is an essential enabling technology for the renewal of our industries.

Software Engineering and Computer Science: How Do They Differ?

Robert L. Glass
Seattle University

Abstract. "Thermodynamics owes much more to the steam engine than the steam engine owes to thermodynamics... if we look at the usual course of events in the historical record... there are very few examples where technology is applied science. Rather it is much more often the case that science is applied technology" (from "Sealing Wax and String: A Philosophy of the Experimenter's Craft and its Role in the Genesis of High Technology," Proceedings of the American Association for the Advancement of Science, annual meeting, 1983; D.D. Price).

I am a software practitioner of thirty years experience, and an academician of four years experience. My background traces back to the origins of computing as a profession. Out of that long background, I have formed some biases and discovered some truths. I would like to share some of those with you here.

First of all, a definition: software engineering, I would assert, is applied computer science. For those of you with an academic background, this may be a sufficient definition. Just as there are applied mathematics and pure mathematics, there can be applied and pure computer science. For those of you with a practitioner background, however, this definition may be begging the question. It defines one term with reference to another that isn't that well defined. Let me explain.

Back in the 1950s, when I first began my professional career as a programmer, there was no computer science, and there was nothing called software engineering. Computer science came along nearly a decade later, creating a science out of the existence of computers in the same way that, as Price described above, thermodynamics was born out of the existence of the steam engine. Then came software engineering, lagging computer science by another half decade.

Those of us in the practice were a little uncomfortable with computer science. It put a neat and tidy framework around some things that to us weren't that neat and tidy, no matter how much we wanted them to be.

But when software engineering came along, it was like a trip home after a long absence. Software engineering seemed to care about what the good programmers had been doing for a decade and a half; it was based on the reality of the practice.

Some examples might help here. Computer science, as the years have rolled by, has come to be things like research into automated programming and proof of correctness. Software engineering, as the years have rolled by, has come to be research into things like "empirical studies of programmers." Computer science research efforts currently lie under the cloud of condemnation contained in the Parnas papers on Star Wars. Software engineering research is still evolving, but the claims it makes for the future are at least buttressed by an understanding of the realities of the present.

But enough of the past. Given that software engineering has a kinship with software practice, and that computer science develops and formalizes computing theory, what can we say about the difference between software engineering and computer science as educational forces of the 1980s and beyond?

There are some things which good computer science and good software engineering should have in common:

- They should present a menu of solution methodologies, not a single blueprint. Single blueprints ignore the reality that different kinds of applications require different kinds of solution approaches.
- They should be taught by people who understand both the theories of computer science and the realities of software practice. For software engineering, the scale should be tipped toward experience; for computer science, it may be tipped toward theory.

There are some things which good software engineering should stress:

1. A knowledge of computer science theory is a necessary but not sufficient part of the software engineer's tool bag.

2. Computer science theory sometimes does not work in practice. The software engineer must know enough about the theory to know how to avoid these failures.

3. Software development experience really is worth something. The grizzled veteran of half a decade probably has achieved and surpassed several levels of evolving maturity in the course of reaching that experience level (assuming that five year's experience is not one year's experience five times). Those levels of maturity need to be passed on to junior people by experienced senior educators.

4. The world needs bridge builders between theory and practice. In the U.S., everyone wants to do the "R" of "R and D." Poor theories will never be discarded and good theories put into practice until someone is willing to play the "D" role, trying out theories in a realistic setting to see if they work. Software engineers should not only be able to move into the practice of software smoothly, but they should take with them the informed yet questioning mind that allows them to pursue and evaluate new proposals for professional improvement.

Seen in this light, the fields of computer science and software engineering are siblings that have all the similarities and uniquenesses that siblings in general have. It is important, in building an education program in either field, to use the similarities as a foundation and stress the uniquenesses as end goals. With that approach, we will be able to capture the best of both disciplines — the framing and formalizing of computer science, and the reality base of software engineering.

The Environment for the Software Engineer

A. Nico Habermann
Carnegie-Mellon University

Abstract. The task of education and educators is threefold:
- to teach basic principles that have a lasting value and can be applied in the analysis of events, phenomena and artifacts;
- to provide insight into the current state of the art and the historic development that led to this state;
- to teach a body of facts, procedures and mechanisms for the application of knowledge.

The fundamental aspects of education apply to every discipline, including software engineering, which has the objective of producing high quality software products and software tools. When software engineering emerged as a separate subdiscipline, most of the effort went into the development of concepts and methodologies. It has become clear in recent years that these concepts and methodologies will not be effective without the support of integrated tools and task-oriented programming environments. It is therefore necessary to pay sufficient attention in education to the engineering of these tools and environments.

Introduction

It is often hard to define a discipline accurately in terms of primitive notions that are familiar to everybody. For instance, an attempt to describe computer science might be: "Computer science is the discipline that involves the study of algorithms, including their properties and issues of representation, implementation and execution, and that involves the design and application of algorithms and supporting equipment for the creation of information systems that can be used for information retrieval and for the generation of new information." Although such a definition characterizes the field in general terms, it clearly fails to convey the nature of the problem domain in which computer scientists are interested. It would be hard to derive from this description, for instance, that programming languages constitute a major topic of interest in computer science. It is not uncommon that scientists avoid all problems of describing their discipline with a phenomenal characterization such as: "Computer science is what computer scientists do."

In the case of engineering, we can do a little better than: "Engineering is what engineers do." The *Dictionary of the American Language* says that engineering is the application of scientific knowledge or technical know-how to the creation of mechanisms that facilitate the achievement of a goal. This description applies well to various forms of engineering as we know them, including civil engineering, mechanical engineering, chemical engineering and electrical engineering. It also applies well to software engineering, where the mechanisms are software tools and programming environments, and the goal is the production of reliable and user-friendly software systems that perform well and that are constructed according to specs, on time and within budget.

It is interesting to note that software engineering has the peculiar characteristic that the mechanisms it creates are of the same nature as the goal it pursues: both mechanism and goal are software systems. Mechanical engineering is in some respect in a similar position since it may devise machines to produce machines. Civil engineering, on the other hand, is not likely to employ mechanisms of the same nature as its goal: the construction of an airport, for example, requires the use of heavy machinery and trucks. There is no particular need for another airport as one of the construction tools.

The point I wish to make in this short paper is that an important aspect of software engineering is its application to itself and that this observation is relevant to software engineering education. Since mechanism and target are both cast in software, one may expect that similar development support tools will work for the creation of both target and mechanism. After a brief discussion of the foundation of software engineering and the nature of education, the application of software engineering to software engineering education is further discussed in the last section.

The Foundation of Software Engineering

In order to do a good engineering job, one has to understand both the target product and the available means very well. This implies that the software engineer must understand the construction and application of software systems and also the techniques for analyzing and improving systems. This is obviously a tall order, because it requires the software engineer to know the core of computer science and to be more than familiar with application fields such as business management or natural sciences. It also requires him or her to know the typical techniques and mechanisms that have been developed to control and improve the software production process.

Since a thorough knowledge of the main body of computer science is a necessary prerequisite, software engineering should not become the major topic of study until a level has been reached equivalent to that of a senior college undergraduate in computer science. If an under-graduate program in computer science is to prepare for further study in software engineering, it should emphasize programming languages and systems and leave room for electives in other disciplines such as business administration or physics and chemistry. It is clear that, if one also takes into account the need for sufficient background in discrete mathematics, computer technology and computer literacy, the proper place for a software engineering program is at the master degree level as one of several possible specializations in computer science.

The Nature of Software Engineering Education

In the planning of the Software Engineering Institute, we made a clear distinction between training and education [6]. This distinction has been clearly stated in various documents and is also reflected in the structure of the SEI, notably in the creation of a Technology Transition & Training Division and a Research & Education Division.

The emphasis of training is on "how to do a job" rather than on analyzing the job and on considering alternative methods for carrying out the job. Education, on the other hand, is always analytic in nature: it not only presents new material to students, but it also teaches the students to discover common features as well as differences and to make relative value judgements. Another difference between training and education relates to an aspect that many science and engineering disciplines have in common: the experimental approach to testing a hypothesis or to providing evidence for an idea or a viewpoint. While training concerns primarily the acquisition of factual information and know-how, a major aspect of education is to teach students to apply the scientific method of analysis and experimentation.

The task of education and of educators is
- to teach basic principles that have lasting value and can be applied to the analysis of events, phenomena and artifacts;
- to provide insight into the current state of a discipline and the development that led to this state;
- to teach a body of facts, procedures and mechanisms for the application of knowledge.

In this paper, we will concentrate on the first issue, the basic principles. Software engineering builds on principles that can be categorized along three dimensions inherent to the construction of large software systems. These dimensions represent
- the quality of the target software product;
- the process controlling the development of a product;
- the interaction and communication between people creating a product.

The first category, which may appropriately be labeled "product control," consists of product properties such as reliability, user-friendliness, performance, fault-tolerance, etc. Software engineering involves tools and techniques that measure software products with regard to these various properties and help us improve products along this dimension.

The second category, for which "process control" is an appropriate label, comprises issues concerning what is generally known as the "software lifecycle," which describes the development of a software product as a sequence of steps that starts with requirement specifications and leads through design specifications, implementation, system construction and testing, and finally to software maintenance [Fa85]. Recent experience has shown that these steps should not be considered as successive development phases ordered in time. It has, for instance, generally been recognized that requirement specifications are initially bound to be incomplete and need refinement when design and implementation take place. It seems to happen frequently that specifications are still being modified when software has reached the maintenance stage [12]. One should therefore treat these steps as coexisting product views, each describing a different aspect of the software product in which we are interested. Requirement specifications describe the purpose of a system, design specifications the functionality, implementation how the system works, system construction how the pieces are put together, testing how well it works, and maintenance what kind of trouble was encountered, what changes were made and which extensions were implemented.

The third category is generally known as "project management." It deals with issues that arise when people have to work together in an organization that is charged with the creation of a product within a predetermined period of time and with limited resources [18]. The task of project management is twofold:
- to enforce rules of behavior, and
- to generate and provide access to project information.

Rules of behavior primarily concern policies on documentation, modification rights and deadline control. When code or documents are modified, programmers must be forced to leave a trace of their actions and should not be able to bring a project into an ill-defined intermediate state. It is also likely that one wants to enforce certain documentation and coding standards that make it possible for programmers to read and use each other's material. The purpose of project information is to enable programmers to inspect the overall state of the project and to assemble versions of program modules into system configurations.

The partitioning of the software production process into the three dimensions, "product control," "process control," and "project management," can serve as the basis for a coherent software engineering curriculum. It can be used to categorize the principles of software engineering and can also be used to survey the current state of the art. Once a good overview of the existing techniques is assembled along the three dimensions, one can analyze the status of each individual piece with respect to availability, accuracy, adaptability, formal foundation, etc.

The Educational Environment

Software engineering concepts were first developed in the early seventies when programming-in-the-large became an issue. Their development is quite different from that of other subdisciplines such as operating systems, programming languages and databases. These other subdisciplines gave rise to a large variety of products, all built around an increasing body of common knowledge and expertise. This has unfortunately not been the case in software engineering. Early on in the development, an irreparable rift emerged between two camps, one consisting of proponents of formal verification and the other consisting of those promoting the informal method of code testing. That rift has not been healed to this date. In addition, many measurement and development support tools have been developed in an ad hoc fashion and in relative isolation. The result is a large collection of tools adequate for specific purposes, but lacking coherence and common principles.

The lack of coherence in software development tools is apparent in the programming environments that most programmers work in today. It is common that people work with text editors that don't know anything about programming languages, with programming languages that don't know anything about the file system and with debuggers that understand object code, but not the source language in which programs are written.

The recent development in the design of integrated programming environments is an encouraging sign of improvement. There is a general tendency to create environments that provide coherent sets of tools in support of specific software development tasks. There is no doubt that a major task of software engineering in the near future is going to be the production of marketable programming environments that offer integrated sets of task-oriented tools.

The main point to be made here is that a good program in software engineering must integrate the traditional oral and written communication between teacher and student with experimental programming environments. These environments should contain software engineering tools that can be analyzed and applied by the students. The motivation for such an integrated organization of the curriculum is twofold:

- first, we argued that software development and measurement tools are objects of study and apply to the software engineering process itself;
- second, students should be provided with a rich underlying environment in order to carry out worthwhile software engineering experiments.

Software engineering and operating system courses have suffered for a long time from a lack of adequate programming environments. Experiments in these classes have usually failed, because students had to implement even minimal support environments for their work from scratch. The resulting environment was usually too poor to perform any realistic experiments and absorbed most of the time available for doing a class project.

Having a good environment available to support education has proven to be extremely valuable for programming-in-the-small as has been demonstrated by systems such as the Program Synthesizer and Gnome [93, 46]. Benefits will be even greater when environments support the complex tasks of programming-in-the-many and programming-in-the-large (software engineering).

The programming environment for a software engineering curriculum must provide common software engineering tools for the development and measurement of software products and the software production process. It is totally inadequate to rely on a traditional environment which provides a text editor, a compiler, a debugger and a file system and, at best, an additional text preparation facility.

Curriculum design should not proceed without a parallel design of one or more educational support environments. If this task is taken into account from the start, there is good hope that the curriculum will have an impact on the design of the support environments and vice versa. An additional benefit is acquired if the development and enhancement of the support environment(s) is considered as a continuous task that keeps up with further developments and revisions of the course material. The experiences with the Program Synthesizer and with the Gnome system are very encouraging in that respect. Both systems have progressed considerably since their inception and have included many facilities that provide specific support for the courses taught with them.

It seems pretty clear that software engineering will undergo further automation in the future. There exist right now some interesting software development systems and language systems exist that provide integrated tool sets for the task at hand (e.g., Interlisp [94], DSEE [62]). However, a serious drawback of these systems is their handcrafted nature. These systems are examples of designs that applied good principles, but provided little flexibility or evolution. It is to be expected that further automation of the system generation process will be one of the major challenges in the near future. Possible approaches to further automation have been explored by the Synthesizer Generator project, the Gandalf project [73] and others.

Conclusion

The main objective of software engineering is to facilitate the production of high quality software systems within budget and on time. Software engineering is peculiar in that its target product and the mechanisms to create a product are of the same nature: both are software systems. As a result, an important activity of software engineering is the construction of tools to construct tools. A software engineering curriculum must pay attention to this important aspect of software engineering. It must supplement oral and written communication with a rich software engineering environment that provides an integrated set of tools first for analysis and application, but also for the construction of new tools.

A proper framework for a curriculum in software engineering is provided by a partitioning of the field along three dimensions, respectively describing issues involving the software product, the development process, and the management of a project. This framework can be used for classifying the principles underlying software engineering and for overviewing the existing tools and mechanisms.

Educational support for software engineering must be developed in parallel with a curriculum design so that the one can have an impact on the other. It is totally unrealistic to rely on software support that students write during the course. Such an approach always leads to poor support and absorbs most of the available time in class and out. As a result, the experiments carried out are inevitably small in scale and narrow in scope. Creating a permanent educational support environment has the additional advantage that gradual improvements can be tuned to changes and revisions of the curriculum.

Considerations for Graduate Software Engineering Education: An Air Force Perspective

Walter D. Seward
Thomas C. Hartrum
Gary B. Lamont[1]
Duard S. Woffinden
Air Force Institute of Technology

Abstract. This paper presents a graduate curriculum for software engineering education, as proposed by the Air Force Institute of Technology (AFIT). In order to define such a curriculum, it is first necessary to define what is meant by the term "software engineer," and what capabilities are expected in a graduate of such a program. The process of "software engineering" is examined in the context of requirements for software system development and management within the Air Force. These requirements help define the fundamental concepts and techniques, as well as the support tools, which must be integrated into an effective curriculum for software engineering. The program presented incorporates both the theory and practice of software engineering. The proposed curriculum for a Master of Science degree with a major in software engineering is based on AFIT's experience with software engineering education and its ongoing contact with many Air Force agencies involved in software development. Many of AFIT's student thesis efforts have involved large-scale software developments which often extend from student to student over several years. This paper presents this program, along with supporting discussion of program objectives and course content.

Introduction

A basic requirement for developing any educational curriculum is the specification for the expected capabilities of the graduates. The capabilities required of the graduates must be defined in the context of the generally accepted definition of a given discipline, as well as the specifics of known users if possible. A curriculum for software engineering education therefore depends upon an accepted definition of software engineering. Since the creation of the term "software engineering" in 1967, there has been a great deal of interest in the subject and its definition. The impetus for the creation of the term was the perception that a "crisis" existed in terms of the development and management of

---

[1]On sabbatical, Department of Computer Science, Wright State University, Dayton, Ohio.

software systems. Since that time, significant effort has been expended in the pursuit of methods and tools which will lead to the design and production of reliable, efficient, and cost effective software products. In addition to this effort, there have been many attempts to define the discipline of software engineering and its relationship to other disciplines [12], [16], [29], [57], [80], [81], [90], [103].

Software Engineering and Software Engineers

A precise definition of software engineering cannot be made any more than can one for electrical or mechanical engineering. The field of software engineering covers many areas of interest, as does electrical engineering. The profession of engineering is continually evolving. As technological developments create new opportunities for the advancement of society, new fields of engineering develop in response to the needs of society. For example, computer engineering and aerospace engineering, which were originally facets of electrical and mechanical engineering, respectively, have developed in response to new technological capabilities. Furthermore, as technology advances, problem and solution approaches tend to converge in certain areas, for example, computer engineering and VLSI engineering. Likewise, software engineering is a discipline which has evolved because of a specific requirement of society.

An engineer is one who solves problems in a technical area. This includes both the ability to analyze existing systems to determine problem sources, and the ability to analyze requirements and then apply scientific principles to design a system to satisfy those requirements. It is the process of synthesis which distinguishes an engineer from a scientist. A software engineer is an engineer whose primary field of expertise is software systems. A software engineer applies scientific principles to the design of efficient, cost effective, and reliable software systems which meet a specific need of society.

In defining software engineering and the functions of a software engineer, it is equally important to examine those tasks which are *not* the normal functions of a software engineer. Just as electrical engineers in properly supported environments do not, in general, wire circuits, but have technicians available to do so, software engineers should be *able* to write and debug computer code, but should not do so as their primary task. Rather, they should be involved with the analysis, modeling, design, and development of software systems to solve practical problems. Note that the standards by which such systems are evaluated include both technological and management issues.

Software Engineers in the Air Force

Within the domain of software engineering, the Department of Defense and the Air Force find themselves in a somewhat unique situation. The dramatic increase in the numbers of computer-based systems in use in the Department of Defense is well documented. The most significant increases have been in the number of embedded computer systems. Furthermore, many of these systems are very large scale, such as systems for command, control, communications, and intelligence (C3I). This increase in computer-based systems throughout the military services has dictated an increase in the level of knowledge required by both the personnel who are involved in the design and implementation of these systems, and those who use and maintain them. However, the brunt of responsibility for ensuring that the fielded system is reliable, responsive, and maintainable falls on the software engineer. These systems are becoming increasingly dominated by software, and software provides the primary basis for user interaction with the system. Further complications arise because much of the actual development and implementation of these systems is done by contracting organizations, which depend upon the service's project office for requirements definition, guidance, and assistance throughout the system development. In order to meet the requirements for software engineering in this environment, a curriculum in software engineering must ensure that graduates possess a number of capabilities in both technical and management skills.

Requirements of a Graduate Software Engineer

A graduate software engineer should possess a number of capabilities which span both technical and managerial skills. The graduate must have a firm grasp of the fundamental elements of software system development. These include programming (in several languages, both assembly level and high level languages), data structures, operating systems, and an understanding of hardware architectures and their relationship to software systems in differing environments. The latter is especially critical in the area of embedded systems, which is one of the Air Force's primary requirements for software engineers. Furthermore, the engineer must be able to apply the concepts and methodologies of software engineering to practical problems. This includes the ability to determine the proper tools and methodologies most applicable to a specific problem, and the ability to apply them in the proper manner.

Management of a large software or embedded system project is also required of software engineers in the Air Force environment. Management of the development team throughout the definition and implementation phases, and configuration management of the system once deployed are both required. The necessary management skills include the ability to apply techniques of software cost estimation to specific applications, to understand the software acquisition process, and to be able to apply effective leadership to the planning, control and maintenance of the project.

Graduate Curriculum in Software Engineering

The objectives of the Air Force Institute of Technology's (AFIT) graduate program with a specialization in software engineering are to provide the student with an integrated curriculum of both analytical and hands-on courses oriented toward the identification and solution of practical problems in software engineering. These objectives are in addition to the overall goals of the Graduate Computer Engineering and Graduate Computer Systems programs. The goals of these programs are to educate graduates so that they are able to assimilate new technologies as they evolve and maintain their technical expertise throughout their professional careers. Students entering the program must have a bachelor's degree in computer engineering, computer science, mathematics with computer emphasis, or another scientific or engineering field with computer system experience. Students are expected to satisfy the basic mathematics requirements stated for the Accreditation Board for Engineering and Technology (ABET) and the Computing Sciences Accreditation Board (CSAB) degrees of computer engineering and computer science respectively. In addition, as a minimum, the students must have had experience with high order language programming with Ada (due to the DOD environment), basic computer architecture and assembly language programming, algorithm design, and digital logic design and application. Those students who do not have this background must make-up these deficiencies during the program.

A distinct advantage for AFIT is the stronger than usual maturity and experience, both technical and managerial, of most of the students. Although some students arrive directly from undergraduate school, most have had one or two Air Force assignments where they have managed or worked on computer based systems development. This experience and maturity provides them with an appreciation for the real world problems that a software engineer must face.

At AFIT, software engineering is considered as an area of specialization in computer engineering or computer systems. The graduate program in software engineering at AFIT has been evolving for the past four years and continues to evolve as the resources necessary to implement the desired curriculum become available. These resources include both the necessary manpower and computer hardware and software. Presented here is the curriculum structure planned for the coming year. Also presented are the plans for near term changes.

Assuming that the background requirements are met by the student, the curriculum consists of a core sequence, a specialization sequence, two graduate level math courses, formal courses in technical writing and research methods, an independent study (thesis), and sufficient technical electives to create a program that adequately covers a broad spectrum of topics, yet allows depth in one or two areas of computer or software engineering. In the eighteen month program at AFIT, the student will take seventy-two hours, with at least twelve hours per quarter. Since the degree requirements are for forty-eight credit hours of graduate courses including the thesis (12 credit hours), a student with a strong background can either graduate in less than eighteen months, or can expand his program by in-depth study in more areas of computer engineering.

The Sequence of Core Courses

The core sequence provides the coordinated sequence of courses that integrates the principles of computer hardware, software, and hardware/software interfacing to insure that the software engineer is able to apply software system development to both stand-alone and embedded computer systems. The problems associated with embedded system development are the more demanding of the two environments, and therefore receive the primary emphasis in these courses. The sequence includes the following courses:

Operating Systems

In this course the student learns to apply the principles of operating systems to the design and evaluation of specific operating systems. The students apply quantitative measures of performance to evaluate and compare systems of software and hardware. The course includes a project which involves the design and development of a simple operating system.

Computer Systems Architecture

The objective of this course is for the student to be able to apply the principles of computer system architecture in the areas of processor control, memory system, and I/O system design. The emphasis is on the relationship between digital system components, performance objectives, and specific applications.

Software Engineering

The objective of this course is for the students to be able to apply software engineering methodologies and tools related to the requirements definition, structured design, coding, test and maintenance phases of software development. A course project involves group development of the requirements and specification of a large-scale software system. This project is carried forward in the "Software Systems Laboratory" course.

Minicomputer/Microprocessor Laboratory

In this course the students learn to apply the concepts and techniques of digital logic design and assembly language programming to the design, implementation, and evaluation of the performance of hardware and software modules for computer system interfacing. This course emphasizes chip level and assembly level design and development.

Software Systems Laboratory

The objective of this laboratory is for the students to apply the principles and techniques of software engineering and operating systems concepts through a group development of a large scale software project. The project in this laboratory course is begun in the software engineering course, and completed here. The students develop the software systems to support a local computer network protocol. The project is completed using the programming language "C". Portions of the project require the students to integrate assembly level modules with the higher order language routines.

Software Systems Acquisition

The objectives of this course are for the students to apply the concepts and techniques of software engineering to software acquisition; and understand and be able to apply the techniques employed in planning, developing, procuring, and maintaining software systems in the Air Force. This course stresses the integration of concepts and techniques of the software life cycle with those of project management and procurement within the Department of Defense environment.

The intent of the graduate programs at AFIT is for the students to progress as much as possible in their education while at the Institute. In those cases where the student has had an exceptional undergraduate program or has completed some graduate work prior to coming to AFIT, there are more advanced courses available for each of the core sequence courses. These students are required to enroll in the more advanced courses and to take additional elective courses.

Specialization Sequence

In addition to the core sequence, students are required to take at least one sequence which develops in depth a specific area of computer engineering. The specialization sequence for software engineering includes required courses which delve into specific aspects of software system development and recommended elective courses which provide breadth of knowledge in specific application and support areas. The courses in the sequence are as follows:

Advanced Software Engineering

The objective of this course is for the students to apply the concepts and techniques of software reliability, software system security, and software test and evaluation to software system design and evaluation. Automated design tools are used where applicable.

Advanced Software Environments

This course explores current knowledge of software development environments. Students apply software engineering principles to the development and evaluation of development support tools. A large scale Ada-based group project is used to demonstrate course concepts.

The student is required to complete the sequence by taking at least one course from one of the other specialization sequences within computer engineering and computer science. These specialization sequences include the following:
- Artificial Intelligence
- Computer Graphics
- Computer Communications Networks
- Computer Performance Evaluation
- Compiler and Formal Language Theory
- Database Systems
- Computational Analysis

Each of these sequences include three or more courses that pursue in depth a specific topic area. Hands-on experience is a critical part of any engineering program. Each of the courses in the above sequences include projects to reinforce concepts presented in the classroom.

The Mathematics Requirement

A firm theoretical foundation is essential for examining such issues as algorithm complexity, design and analysis of complex simulation models, and hardware and software system performance. Hence, each graduate of the program is expected to have had at least an undergraduate mathematics course in each of the following subjects:

- Discrete Mathematics
- Finite Automata and Formal Language Theory
- Probability Theory
- Statistics.

If the student has not had courses in each of the above, then he is required to make up the deficiency as appropriate. In any case, at least two graduate mathematics courses must be selected either from those above, or from other approved courses. The appropriate courses are determined based on the student's background and planned course of study.

Elective Courses

The students complete their course requirements by selecting elective courses from a wide range of available support sequences. These courses cover a range of topics from computer engineering and computer science, and include, in addition to elective sequences listed above, VLSI system design, computer architecture, and numerical analysis.

Independent Study

Perhaps the most important element in the AFIT program is an independent study by the student on a problem of importance to the Air Force or other DoD agency. There are twelve quarter hours of credit allotted for the student to solve a software system design problem from the requirements analysis phase through the system integration and test phases. The results of this work are documented in a thesis. The thesis research provides the ultimate project, in which students apply the tools and techniques presented in the classroom to analyze and design a practical system.

Observations and Future Trends

As stated previously, the curriculum is evolving. It must evolve not only because of resource limitations which prevent full scale implementation at this time, but also because of ongoing developments in computing technology. To adequately present the discipline of software engineering, there must be available to the student computer-based tools to support the software system design process. Without these tools increased software productivity will be stymied by the "sweat shop" environment of yesteryear. Likewise, advancements in software engineering education depend upon readily available support tools in the educational institutions and integration of those tools into the curriculum. Software development environments must be available to the student to provide education in things desired and not with mundane tasks. Laboratory courses and large scale programming projects are essential to software engineering education. The projects must be large enough to be realistic, but must be assigned in increments to be achievable within a quarter or semester. Automated support tools are necessary to accomplish these requirements. Our experience at AFIT indicates that realistic projects require more time than is available in a quarter or semester. Although it is more difficult to coordinate than a single long-term project, two closely coupled project phases can accomplish the same objectives.

Artificial Intelligence and distributed computing are two rapidly evolving areas of computer technology. As software engineering methodologies evolve to support AI programming, or as knowledge-based software development methodologies are developed, the curriculum must be updated to incorporate these technologies. AFIT is already active in the AI area both in research and with a sequence of courses available in the area. Software development methodologies for distributed processing systems present a challenge. Few such methodologies exist. AFIT courses address the development and application of distributed systems, but include little discussion of software development in such environments. As distributed architecture systems become available, AFIT is incorporating distributed software system development concepts into the curriculum.

Conclusion

AFIT has included formal courses in software engineering in the curriculum since 1975. The number of courses and the course content has evolved based upon the requirements of the Air Force for software engineers, the availability of tools and techniques to support software development, and AFIT experience with differing approaches to presenting the concepts and techniques of software system development. The curriculum will continue to change as new technologies modify the environment and objectives of the software engineer, both in terms of support tools and changes in applications.

Why Is Software Engineering So Difficult?

William E. Richardson
United States Air Force Academy

Abstract. The development of computer software has taken on significant proportions in relation to other aspects of system development. As a result, overall system development efforts have become more difficult rather than easier in recent years. This weak link effect has done little to enhance the overall image of the field often called "software engineering."

The inability to accurately define software engineering undoubtedly presages some of the difficulties of the discipline (if I can go so far as to call it a discipline). Most attempts at definition involve a set of general properties at one of three levels: the software development level (the micro view), the software lifecycle level (the macro view), or the system development level (the system view).

If we assume one of these definitions then we should be able to isolate and categorize the problems with software engineering from this perspective. It appears to me that there are four major categories of difficulties to address if we are to truly make software engineering a discipline of its own. These categories are:

- the eclectic software engineer
- the lack of a physical product
- the complex problem set
- the lack of good tools

This paper discusses these areas in some detail, not with an eye toward defining the solution set, rather with an eye toward a more rational definition of the problem.

Introduction

The development of computer software has taken on significant proportions in relation to other aspects of system development. As a result, overall system development efforts have become more difficult rather than easier in recent years. We often hear the cries of "software crisis" whenever a system is late, over budget, or does not meet the user's requirements. This weak link effect has done little to enhance the overall image of the field often called "software engineering."

The purpose of this position paper is to present three different views of what constitutes software engineering and a brief discussion of why software engineering is so difficult to accomplish correctly. It is unlikely the problems of software engineering presented here will be new to any readers but I hope to present these problems in such a manner as to make them more comprehensible and coherent. To do this, I have categorized the problems into four abstract capsules: the eclectic nature of software engineering, the lack of a physical product, the complex problem set, and the lack of good tools. Each of these abstract issues must be conquered individually if software engineering is ever to become a mature discipline in its own right.

What Is Software Engineering?

The inability to accurately define software engineering undoubtedly presages some of the difficulties of the discipline (if I can go so far as to call it a discipline). Most attempts at definition involve a set of general properties at one of three levels: the software development level (the micro view), the software lifecycle level (the macro view), or the system development level (the system view).

The micro view was the earliest approach to a software development strategy and embodied the ideas of many pioneers in the field of programming. The basis of this strategy is that programming is a new and difficult art/science combination that requires new tools and philosophies in order to handle the logical complexity. Theories such as top down decomposition, modularity, and the definition of the three required unit control structures helped to bring some order to the new task of implementing software. The focus in these early theories was very definitely on the software implementation process, although the result of many of these approaches was also to affect the broader issues of software maintenance and modifiability. It is common to hear these theories lumped together and called "structured programming." This micro view is still a very important field of study today but the emphasis has changed from the theory and techniques of programming to the tools of program development, especially program development environments. There are still a few who cling to the view that software implementation (programming) is at the heart of software development and hence is the essence of software engineering.

With the recognition of the "software crisis," the idea that program development was but a small part of the overall software process became a common axiom. As a result, the macro view or software lifecycle approach to software engineering became popular. This approach states that the software engineer should be responsible for the software product throughout its life: from problem definition to software system phase out. The macro view recognizes that the problems introduced in the programming phase of the software development are minor in comparison to the problems introduced in problem definition and requirements specification. Indeed, it is a common theory that the post-implementation cost of software is outrageously high as a result of the pre-implementation ineffectiveness. That is, the macro definition of software places its emphasis on reducing the overall cost of software development and maintenance by reducing errors of problem definition and solution design as well as correct programming. Hence, the macro view of software engineering is a superset of the micro view. Success in defining the software lifecycle process has been very slow in coming. Indeed, like in the micro view, attention is being turned toward the development of tools and lifecycle environments. Unlike the micro approach, the theory and practice has not as yet formed a firm foundation upon which to build these tools.

The final view is the most general and most recent of the possible levels of definition of software engineering. From this point of view, software is considered to be only one aspect of a larger body of effort called a system. The system approach accepts the premises that support both the micro and macro points of view, but it goes the step further to require that total system lifecycle cost is what is really important. Hence, from a system perspective the software must have its own integrity and must also help build the integrity of the total system. This perspective has been greatly advanced by the U.S. Department of Defense as a result of its less than spectacular success with embedded weapon system software. In systems applications the cost of failure is usually even more significant than in the more classical software applications. The other interesting aspect driving many people toward this level of software engineering definition is the rapidly decreasing cost of computer hardware. With hardware costs steadily declining we see that it is becoming more cost effective to include some "intelligence" in new systems. Hence the demand for system application software is the most rapidly increasing segment of software development. To a large degree we have not even begun to develop the theories, much less the tools, with which to conquer the system level software requirements.

In this explication of the possible divergent levels of definition of software engineering, I have obviously over simplified in two significant areas. First, I have ignored the theories of software engineering that fall between the three given, and there are many theories of this sort. For example, there are theories of software engineering that gladly embrace the design, implementation, and testing phases of the lifecycle but consider the early lifecycle phases of problem definition and requirements specification to be too esoteric for real software engineering.

The second oversimplification is that I have carefully chosen not to specify what actual properties should be included at each level of definition. For example, should the macro level software engineering definition allow classical analysis techniques or does software engineering by its very nature exclude certain of the fuzzier approaches? The actual tenets of software engineering that comprise each level of possible definition is set aside for a different discussion.

This attempt to quantify, even partially, the discipline of software engineering is necessary to create the context for the body of our discussion about the difficulty inherent in software engineering. For this discussion, I will assume the broadest definition possible, that is the system view including all reasonable underlying tenets.

Why Is It So Difficult?

This question is undoubtedly so multifaceted that it will never be completely answered. However, there is certainly significant benefit in attempting to characterize the problems inherent in software engineering so at least an abstract answer to the question can be given. With this abstract answer in hand, perhaps it will then be easier to identify the areas of education and research needing to be refortified or rethought in order to produce better software engineers.

In attempting to determine such an abstract framework for the various problems of software engineering, I found the following four themes kept recurring. By no means are these themes mutually exclusive but they do provide a convenient foundation from which to discuss the software engineering dilemma.

The Eclectic Software Engineer

Consider for a moment the task of the software engineer using the system definition of software engineering. Without a doubt, this individual must be a master of many different disciplines. One of his /her primary tasks is to interface with the user to determine the exact requirements of the system. From this perspective the software engineer must be proficient with classical analysis techniques, able to abstract, and articulate. Additionally, he/she must become an expert in the area of application, understand the interfaces to the remainder of the system, and comprehend the organizational environment in which the system operates. He/she will be required to understand enough psychology to ferret out unstated requirements and develop insight into unmentioned problems and organizational idiosyncrasies. Finally, the software engineer has the very difficult task of conveying to the user and to management technical information and difficult concepts. To a very large degree, the entire effectiveness of the project depends upon his ability in these very "fuzzy" areas of interpersonal communication, psychology, and the ability to abstract and synthesize.

Another area where the software engineer must have expertise is in the area of design. Design requires a combination of two talents: creativity and the ability to reuse previous design parts, sometimes called cumulativity. Again, abstraction and synthesis play an important part in the design process. As in any design endeavor, the insight of the artisan can make or break the product. Unfortunately, the design process in software development is unlike many other forms of design in that two of the overriding criteria of the design must be the ability change the product based on the effect of ever changing requirements and the ability to maintain (read correct or evolve) the software product throughout its lifetime. This concept of design to a moving target seems self-defeating but is necessary when the user is a tyro in the area of automation and the software engineer is a novice in the area of system application.

Of course, the technical management of a software engineering project is a whole other area of expertise that is too often overlooked and understressed. Further discussion of this point will be put off until the next section, but it is important to note that classical as well as specialized management skills are required to control a software project. Additionally, the sheer size and complexity of software systems, the lack of experience on software projects, and the requirement for interfaces to other system components often increase the management difficulty by orders of magnitude over more conventional development efforts.

Finally, we come to another difficult area of expertise for a software engineer: the technical tools and technical ability. This is also the area of greatest divergence of opinion as to what is appropriate for the practitioner to know and use. Some methodologies require a significant mathematical training and understanding. Others see mathematics as a dead end which obscures the correct technical path. Until the technical discord is finally resolved the software engineer will have the same difficulties encountered in any discipline where technical standards are flimsy or nonexistent.

Where Is the Product?

The second significant problem area is the logical nature of the product of software engineering. This to my mind is the major difference between software "engineering" and "real" engineering. Because of this logical nature there are few physical laws which can be used to model, describe, or predict the behavior of software. Obviously, some mathematical and logical "laws" are relevant to software, but these have not yet been demonstrated to fill the role that physical laws do in other forms of development. It is because of the lack of physical laws that the software aspect of computer science is sometimes called an artificial science (like political science, or social science) rather than a natural science (like physics or chemistry). Another negative effect of software being a logical rather than a physical product is the lack of visibility of the product to the user and to management during the lifecycle, especially during design and development phases. It is exceedingly difficult to control and manage that which we cannot see. It is also difficult to quantify the status of such a project — we have all seen the 90 percent complete syndrome gives managers fits when trying to budget resources for a project. Perhaps even more distressing, based on our previous discussion about the effect of the user presenting a moving target for the requirements, is that the product is typically not visible to the user until late in the development process. This means that changes in the requirements are either determined very late or are never determined at all — either of which results in significant cost inflation. Of course, rapid prototyping and other techniques help to mollify this problem somewhat, but the fact that scaling is generally not possible on logical products means that it is difficult to keep the user in the development loop to the necessary degree early in the lifecycle.

Complexity of the Problem Set

One of the problems in software engineering where we continue to lose the battle is in the area of complexity. Over the last twenty years, the technology for developing hardware and the capability of the hardware being developed has increased at a very high annual rate. Meanwhile the cost/capability ratio of the hardware has shrunk significantly. Through this period the capability to produce and deliver software has risen only slightly. The net result is more applications are becoming economical for automation and even the more complex, science fiction like applications are being attempted. Consequently the hardware is driving the already stretched software industry further into a deficit position.

The more complex and larger scale projects also have another interesting side effect: the longer the lifecycle of the typical project the more it depletes the reservoir of software engineering experience and the more difficult it becomes to create and test theories and methodologies of software development. If systems are eight years in development, how long will it be before enough evidence is gathered to validate the techniques used to develop the system's software and, at the rate the software development theory is changing, how useful will the techniques be once they have finally been validated? Again, the problem cries out for the ability to simulate or scale the process. Certainly the drain on our experience is a significant problem because we are already in a personnel crisis of substantial proportion.

Absolutely the most crushing damage the increasing demand and increasing complexity inflicts on software development is because we have never found how to reuse much, if any, of what we develop. Each project takes on a uniqueness that causes us to reinvent the same wheels over and over again. In very few cases has reuse of significant pieces of software been successful and in very few cases has reuse of designs been attempted.

No Tools Is Not Good News

The final category of software engineering problems center around the fact that we have an absence of good tools or even methodologies in which to use good tools. As mentioned in the introduction of levels of software engineering, the tools for structured programming are now coming to maturity, but the tools for the other two levels are still years from maturity. The difficulty in developing methodologies and tools is the result of the three previous problems. For example, a methodology must attempt to be universal in both its coverage of the lifecycle and applications. It must include structuring, formal, and management components; it must require few or no transitions of tools, symbology, and techniques; and it must, thereby, ease the burden on the software engineer. It certainly must be coherent and provide visibility of the product. Finally the methodology must supply sufficient infrastructure and support to ease the complexity of the development process. Without a good methodology and compatible tools, the previous three categories of problems seem insurmountable.

The tool development has recently gone into high gear, but we must be careful that we do not outsmart ourselves by making very good tools which do not fit into any coherent methodology. The development of tools is probably the one problem in which there is some room for speeding up the maturation process; however, it will certainly be at a substantial cost. And if we proceed along too many tangents that are unproductive and hence only deplete our resources for developing useful tools, we will likely find that trying to rush out of our adolescence has only set us further back.

Conclusion

As promised, this paper did not introduce any particularly new ideas but simply attempted to organize a number of thoughts about our current state of software engineering. It appears when all is said, the overriding problem is the discipline is still very immature. As a result, we do not have the background or experience base from which to draw to help solve our problems. The immaturity also brings with it the inability to specialize, which may be the only natural solution to the complexity and eclectic software engineer problems. Therefore, we must continue to be flexible and to support partial solutions while we continue to search for the ultimate paradigm.

Technology Selection Education
for Software Engineers

Rocky Mountain Institute of Software Engineering

William E. Riddle
Software Design & Analysis, Inc.

Lloyd G. Williams
University of Colorado

Abstract. Creating and improving an adequate software engineering work force requires several different types of continuing education for software professionals. Task-oriented education is needed to make already well-educated managerial and technical personnel effective for specific jobs, projects and organizations. Improvement-oriented education is needed to upgrade experienced personnel with a working knowledge of new software engineering technology. Selection-oriented education is needed to provide an exposure to new techniques and concepts sufficient to impart an appreciation of the technology's cost/benefit and allow well-founded decisions about whether or not to adopt it. We discuss the need for selection-oriented education, the characteristics of a successful selection-oriented education program, the requirements it levies against other education programs, and the attempt being made at the Rocky Mountain Institute of Software Engineering to provide such a program.

Introduction

Creation and improvement of an adequate software engineering work force requires significant educational effort on several fronts. Pre-employment, academic education must provide for the continual infusion of the requisite numbers of new personnel. Post-employment, continuing education must provide for "modernization" of the work force and job-specific training. Both forms of education are extremely important but continuing education is critical because software engineering technology is changing so rapidly.

Continuing education may take the form of "refresher" courses, short courses on specific topics, or on-the-job training with new methods, tools or techniques. A specific continuing education activity will serve one or more of the following intents:

- *Task-oriented education* assists in developing specific skills. This type of education is needed to make already well-educated managerial and technical personnel effective for specific jobs, projects, and organizations. It moves these personnel closer to the state of practice.

- *Improvement-oriented education* assists in upgrading a professional's capabilities in general. This type of education provides experienced personnel with a working knowledge of software engineering technology that is new to them. It contributes to moving these personnel closer to the state of the art by improving their general capabilities.

- *Selection-oriented education* provides an exposure to new techniques and concepts at a level sufficient to impart an appreciation of the technology's applicability and cost-to-benefit ratio. This type of education is needed to enable management and technical personnel to make well-founded decisions about whether or not to adopt a particular technology. This also contributes to moving the personnel closer to the state of the art but addresses the preliminary step of deciding in which direction to move.

In this paper, we focus on the critical, but often neglected, category of selection-oriented education. We begin with a discussion of the need for continuing software engineering education in general and selection-oriented education in particular. Then we discuss the technology selection task itself, indicating what it involves, how it contributes to improving the state of practice, and why it is key to technology improvement in general. This is followed by discussions of some criteria for selection-oriented education programs and the relationship of selection-oriented education to other types of education. We then provide an example, describing the selection-oriented education activities at the Rocky Mountain Institute of Software Engineering **rMise**. We conclude with a brief summary, in which we also relate some problems encountered in establishing the **rMise** selection-oriented education activities.

The Need

Continuing education is an important aspect of training for software engineers and will continue to be for the foreseeable future. The need for continuing education is based on several factors, chief among them the lack of directly relevant experience in academic computer science programs and the rapid change in software engineering technology. This latter factor, in particular, leads to a need for selection-oriented education.

Academic Training for Software Engineers

Managers of software projects have complained for some time that graduates of computer science programs do not enter the working world with skills that are relevant to "real world" software projects. Entry level software engineers invariably must serve an apprenticeship while they acquire necessary skills that were not included in their education. Relevant skills include requirements analysis, design, team work, and software maintenance.

Some of these skills are beginning to be included in undergraduate computer science courses, and it is likely this trend will continue. Specialized graduate programs, which grant master's degrees in software engineering, have been developed [29], and many computer science departments are developing more than token strength in the area. As we gain more experience in treating software engineering as part of an academic program, we are increasingly able to include this subject matter in undergraduate courses [61]. As a result, students may, through required courses and judicious choice of electives, receive better training for typical work situations.

New Technologies

The mismatch between academic experience and on-the-job requirements is not unique to software engineering; many other disciplines (e.g., chemistry, journalism) have also noted the problem. What is unique to the software engineering arena is the rapid rate of change to both its conceptual base and fundamental technology, and hence to the discipline itself.

Research over the past five years has produced numerous advances in software tools, automated environments, and software methodologies. During this time our model of the software process itself has undergone major revision. The rapidly changing nature of the technology which supports software engineering has produced a significant gap between the state of the art and the state of practice. This gap is a consequence of the long delay apparently required between the conception of new software engineering technology and its introduction into practice [82].

The Need for Selection-oriented Education

We seem caught in a never ending spiral. There is a mismatch between what is learned in pre-employment education and the skills and knowledge needed for many work situations. And the technology is expanding and improving at a pace that makes it difficult to keep courses in tune with both the state of the art and the state of practice.

Part of the solution lies with the introduction of software engineering material. This material tends to be closer to real world situations, and these courses can include group exercises that more closely "simulate" real world projects and work situations. They also provide real world-related knowledge structures (e.g., life cycle models) that can be effectively used to relate the state of the art and the state of practice.

The cure does not, however, lie solely in revamping the computer science curriculum. While there is certainly room for the inclusion of more software engineering in the curriculum, a student's experience can never be completely realistic because of the confines of an academic environment and calendar. And, in fact, experience in general supports the time-honored view that the proper goal for academic education is the acquisition of general knowledge and skills as well as an understanding for and appreciation of the process of learning. The preparation for a "lifetime of learning" that comes from general education is especially important for software engineers who will need to cope with rapidly changing technology, and possibly many different application areas, during their careers.

Given the limitations of an academic environment and calendar, it is unrealistic to expect academic computer science programs to service **all** the educational needs of software engineers. Continuing education programs are needed to "correct" for the inevitable mismatch between the skills and knowledge developed through an academic education program and those needed for specific work situations. In fact, it is the specific aim of task-oriented education to provide this "correction."

The other forms of continuing education meet the need to decrease, or at least keep constant, the gap between the state of the art and the state of practice. Selection-oriented education helps to speed the movement of technology into practice by assisting the selection of new technology applicable and beneficial to particular work situations. Improvement-oriented education helps to close the gap by providing the follow-on education needed to make effective use of new technology. Continuing education, therefore, plays a significant role in transferring new technology into practice in a timely fashion. And selection-oriented education is the key in that it supports the critical first step of deciding what technology should become part of the state of practice within specific target communities.

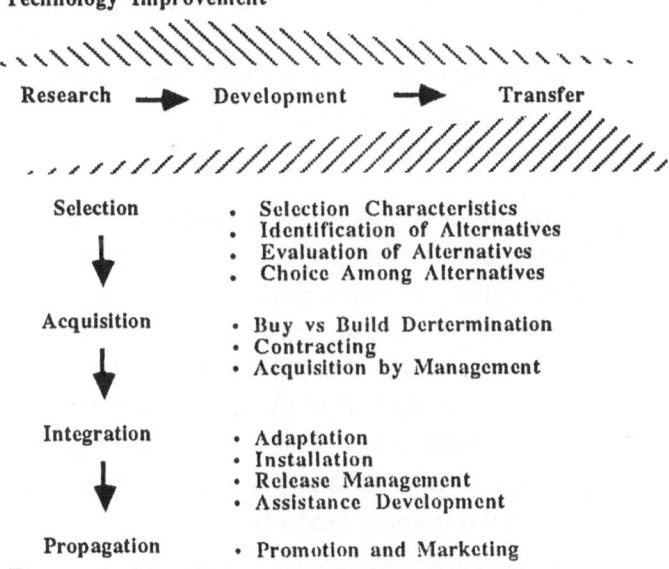

Figure 1. The Role of Technology Identification

Technology Selection

The process of narrowing the gap between the state of practice and the state of the art is pictured in Figure 1. Once new technology has been conceived through research and been sufficiently developed to become state of the art, it is the aim of *technology transfer* to make that technology part of the state of practice within some community. If the technology has limited applicability, the target community will be narrow and the transfer activity will be specific to the technology being transferred. When the technology is of general utility, however, the target community and transfer activity will be correspondingly broad and general.

Software technology comprises the technical and managerial methods, techniques and (automated and manual) tools for the *software process*, that is, the process of creating and evolving software systems. At present, the state of the art and state of practice in software technology are both immature relative to what has been achieved in other disciplines (for example, electrical and civil engineering). Lacking fundamental knowledge and insight about software "building blocks" and the processes for using them, the software process remains a craft in which most systems, even when they are variants of existing systems, are built from scratch using *ad hoc* procedures. New software technology, therefore, tends to be general rather than specific to particular situations. Because of this generality, new software technology tends to have potentially broad applicability.

As a result, there are a wide variety of software technology transfer situations. The target community can be a specific project, a division within some organization, an entire organization itself, or a entire sector of the community at large. On the one hand, the transfer can concern a particular method, technique or tool that fills a specific gap; on the other hand, it can concern a collection of methods, techniques, and/or tools that meet a more general need. The transfer can take place prior to using the technology, or transfer and use can be integrated, with actual use helping to guide the transfer process.

A general software technology transfer paradigm, which can be adapted to meet the needs of specific situations, is also pictured in Figure 1. The paradigm comprises four activities: *selection* of technology satisfying some criteria, *acquisition* of suitable versions of the technology, *integration* of the technology with existing technology, and *propagation* of the result throughout the target community. These activities will typically occur sequentially, but it would not be unusual for them to take place in parallel.

Technology selection is the process of determining which methods, techniques and tools satisfy criteria reflecting the target community's requirements. Selection requires several capabilitiés: the ability to *identify* a set of candidates to be considered; the ability to (comparatively or "absolutely") *evaluate* the candidates; and the ability to *choose* among the candidates, based on the evaluations and with respect to the driving criteria. More often than not, a single pass through these steps will not produce a final choice. One pass may, therefore, serve to support the identification step in a subsequent pass.

Selection characteristics that discriminate among alternative methods, techniques and tools, are critically necessary for technology selection. In support of identification, they must (at least) provide a rough categorization of alternatives. In support of evaluation, they must provide a set of dimensions along which evaluation may be performed. In support of choosing among alternatives, they must support interpreting the evaluation results in terms of the criteria driving the selection. In addition, they should generally support understanding the benefit to be derived from adopting the technology versus the cost, effort and "pain" of acquiring it and putting it into service.

Technology acquisition also requires several capabilities. The selected methods, techniques or tools may be commercially available, but it may be more cost effective to develop new versions rather than purchase existing ones. For example, the need to make extensive modifications to commercially available versions will usually swing the balance in favor of building a new version. Technology acquisition, therefore, requires the capability to make build-versus-buy decisions. Technology acquisition will also require a contracting capability. If the technology is purchased, this capability must support many activities, including the negotiation of royalty and service arrangements. When it is decided to develop a new version, the contracting capability may additionally have to support working out a development contract. Finally, technology acquisition requires an overall management capability to guide the process to successful completion with the eventual delivery of the selected technology.

Technology integration is the activity of consolidating new and existing technology. Several methods, techniques and/or tools may be jointly selected, and integration may also involve the consolidation of these pieces of new technology with each other. In part, integration involves tuning, customizing, extending, or otherwise adapting the pieces of technology so they can successfully be used in tandem and so they appear consistent to the users. It also involves installing, on the hardware used by the target community, any software embodying the technology. Adaptation and installation will typically be done in several steps over a period of time; therefore, some process for the management of successive releases will usually be required. Finally, materials that aid learning and usage will have to be developed, including: documentation and other assistance materials; on-line, automated "help" facilities; and instructors and consultants who can provide off-line assistance.

Technology propagation involves active promotion and "marketing" with the intent of achieving the technology's widespread use throughout the target community. This includes activities such as demonstrating applicability, demonstrating value, providing introductory tutorials, and responding to trouble reports and requests for modification. The propagation activity is, in essence, a miniature (recursive) version of the overall transfer process in which individuals in the target community decide to select the technology, acquire it, and integrate it into their daily routine.

Technology selection is constrained by the activities preceding and following it. Technology obviously cannot be selected until it is researched and developed. These prior activities will provide much of the knowledge and experience needed to identify, evaluate and choose technology before it has been extensively used. In addition, the characteristics used in selection must reflect the ease or difficulty of subsequently acquiring, integrating and propagating the technology.

Technology selection is, however, **the** key to technology improvement and transfer. The process of selection can be instrumental in improving the general state of affairs through the identification of gaps to be filled through research and development. It can also aid in identifying the need for new acquisition, integration and propagation techniques, and perhaps even suggest the general nature or operational details of these techniques. Thus, in addition to being a critical first step in improving the state of practice, technology selection is also critical to guiding improvement to the state of the art and the transfer process in general.

Criteria for Selection-oriented Education Programs

Technology selection requires a broad knowledge about software technology in general, an understanding of the general state of practice, and a familiarity with technology on the state of the art horizon. It also requires a number of basic skills, among them: design of experiments, instrumentation, data interpretation, and survey design. Finally, it requires insight, intuition and experience so that definitive decisions can be reached when interpreting what will undoubtedly be inconclusive, if not inconsistent, evaluation data.

Education alone cannot prepare personnel for the task of technology selection. It is unrealistic to assume that any person or team can be broadly enough educated to successfully handle even a small proportion of the situations that will arise. A major determiner of success will, therefore, be the ability to freely formulate teams having the requisite knowledge and skills for each specific situation. In addition, the levels of insight, intuition and experience required for even the simplest of situations cannot be imparted through education. Another major determiner of success will, therefore, be the extent to which the teams can be populated with personnel experienced in both the technology under consideration and the selection process itself.

However, education can obviously contribute. Formal education and improvement-oriented education can provide the requisite skills, and task-oriented education can impart the requisite understanding of the requirements and constraints of specific target communities. It is the specified intent of selection-oriented education to complement these other contributions. The role of selection-oriented education is discussed in this section in terms of both general and specific criteria that must be met by an selection-oriented education program. The role of the other forms of education and their relationship to selection-oriented education are discussed in the next section.

General Criteria

Selection-oriented education must provide the ability to identify, evaluate and choose among alternative methods, techniques and tools. In addition, it must impart an understanding of the other activities in technology transfer — acquisition, integration and propagation — so that the concerns imposed by these activities can be adequately accommodated.

Selection-oriented education is intended to augment and be augmented by other forms of education. It need not, therefore, be "complete." It can, instead, provide a partial understanding sufficient to help the student understand whether or not further, more in-depth, education is needed and in what areas. The major task is to provide sufficient insight into a piece of state of the art technology to allow it to be evaluated in comparison to other state of the art and state of practice technology. Other tasks include introducing general paradigms for technology selection; making the student aware of a variety of identification, evaluation and choice techniques; and relating the general community's experiences in performing technology selection.

Because it is a form of continuing education, selection-oriented education must meet several contextual constraints. The education must be packaged to fit the time constraints and flexibility requirements of the target student audience. It must be modularly packaged so that customized sequences can be used to meet individual needs. Finally, it must capitalize on the student's former education and (generally extensive) experience.

Specific Criteria

Within the confines of these general criteria, a selection-oriented education program must meet several specific criteria. These pertain to the content of the program, its general form, the pedagogical tools that are used, and the instructors.

Content

Exposure to State of the Art Technology. A primary intent is to impart an understanding of the state of the art sufficient to provide a starting point for technology selection. Students should understand what lies on the technology horizon. They should also understand any concepts fundamental to assessing this technology with respect to their work situations. And they should appreciate the prospects and timeframes for developing usable, transferable versions of the technology.

Technology Transfer Coverage. As indicated previously, successful technology selection requires consideration of the feasibility and ease of subsequent acquisition, integration and propagation. The education program should provide the opportunity to understand what techniques are available for these subsequent activities and how they interact with the task of technology selection.

Technology for Identification, Evaluation and Choice. The program must introduce students to a variety of techniques for identifying, evaluating and choosing among instances of software technology. It must help them understand the similarities and differences among alternative identification, evaluation and choice techniques. The students should understand these techniques in the context of general approaches to technology selection in particular and technology transfer in general.

Experience-based Content. The content of the program should reflect actual experience as much as possible. This should include experience with using various technology selection paradigms and specific identification, evaluation and choice techniques. It should also include experience with using technology that the students might actually be considering for adoption. The experience data should reflect a reasonable and extensive set of selection-support characteristics and be useful in demonstrating how identification, evaluation and choice may be conducted.

Decision-making Orientation. It can be expected that the majority of students will be decision makers within their organizations. They will be responsible for making technology transition decisions, developing a plan for making these decisions, and managing the technology transfer process in general. The program must meet their needs for general information about possibilities as opposed to the details of specific software technology instances or technology selection techniques. And it must help them plan a decision-making process, decide how to upgrade the skills of their support personnel, and guide the process to successful completion.

However, not all students will be in the position of making decisions for larger groups. Instead, they will be interested in making decisions regarding the technology they themselves use. The education must also service their decision-making needs, which, while similar to those of the majority of students, will generally be more specific to particular pieces of technology. In addition, the program should provide these students (and also the majority to some extent) with the information needed to convince their management to invest the required resources.

General Form of the Program

The program must be strongly experiential. We have already noted the need to include information on actual technology transfer, selection and usage experiences as much as possible. The program must, however, go beyond this and provide students with the opportunity to gain their own experiences. Because of the necessity to base selection decisions, in the foreseeable future at least, upon insight, intuition and experience, imparting this experiential knowledge must be a cornerstone of the educational program.

To this end, the program must include demonstrations and hands-on exercises. These can be simple, "canned" ones intended to highlight specific points. More extensive exercises — that run over several days, involve team work, and have rather general goals — should also be provided. There should be the opportunity for students to gain insight, intuition and experience through "open laboratories" separate and independent from the structured courses.

In providing extensive demonstration and exercise capabilities, we encounter two severe problems. One is the general inability to provide demonstrations and exercises that reasonably reflect "real world" situations. The other is the lack of support for scientific investigation of software engineering issues.

Certainly, there is a large disparity between the experience acquired in a typical educational exercise and that provided by "real world" software engineering projects. Real world projects involve large, complex systems developed by teams of programmers. These systems may take years to develop and have useful lifetimes of ten to fifteen years. During their lifetime, they may require a significant amount of maintenance.

Typical exercises, on the other hand, are chosen so they illustrate specific principles and can be completed within a short period of time. They are, therefore, small and of limited complexity, and the scalability of their results is suspect. They are usually designed to be completed by a single individual and generally do not have significant lifetimes. It is extremely rare for educational exercises to include the evolution that takes place during the maintenance phase of real world software projects. Some of the important differences between educational projects and major software development efforts are summarized in Figure 2.

	"Real-World" Projects	Educational Projects
Size	>10,000 lines	<500 lines
Lifetime	10-15 years	"until it works"
Complexity	many modules	single module
Development	teams	individual
Developer/User	developer ≠ user	developer = user
Maintenance	extensive	throw-away

Figure 2. Differences Between "Real-world" and Educational Projects

In many other disciplines, the means have been developed for making valid inferences concerning actual phenomena from small-scale experiments or exercises. We lack this capability in computer science in general, and it impacts our ability to "simulate" real world situations in educational exercises and demonstrations. We can certainly perform exercises and demonstrations. But the methods used rarely scale to meet the demands of large projects. The skills and conclusions obtained are hard to transfer to more complex situations.

Thus, in developing the experiential component of selection-oriented education programs, we must carefully develop the demonstrations and exercises, and prepare convincing, valid arguments of their implications for the real world. Until we have developed the capability to perform valid, scientific experiments, we must caution students to correctly interpret any exercises they may conduct on their own. In part, this involves monitoring the use of any self-help laboratory we make available and assisting the students in interpreting the results of experiments they perform. It will also require the inclusion of courses in experimental techniques.

Pedagogical Tools

Interactive Sessions. Students will rarely come to selection-oriented activities with well-formulated questions. And, in our experience, when they do, the questions are frequently the wrong ones, (e.g., which methodology is the best?). The educational program, therefore, must encourage the students to voice their concerns and interests during class time. These can then be refined interactively by the instructor and the other students. Interactions with other students is particularly important, if only to find out "the situation" is a little different at other locations.

Laboratory Components. As indicated before, all selection-oriented courses should have some laboratory component. Lack of facilities may reduce this to merely the inclusion, in the course materials, of transcripts of previous demonstrations, exercises and experiments. The norm will probably be to offer guided exercise time in conjunction with a course, during which the students can receive individual help from the instructor. In any event, the development and presentation of effective in-class demonstrations will place severe demands on the facilities available at even the best of organizations.

Instructors

Instructors obviously must be technically competent. They must also have an intimate knowledge of both the state of the art and the state of practice. The ideal instructor is a researcher, actively involved with advancing the state of the art, who is instrumental in moving the technology they have developed into practice within some representative community.

They must also have demonstrated an above average competence as a teacher. They must be familiar and comfortable with teaching for the short, intense periods common in continuing education situations. They must be able to synthesize and explain difficult concepts quickly and articulately. They must be able to provide insight without having to give detailed explanations.

The interactive nature of selection-oriented education imposes additional burdens. The instructors must be willing and able to seek out the needs of the individual students. They must be receptive to questions and other interruptions, and demonstrate superior interpersonal skills in handling them. They must be highly flexible and able to rapidly mold the material to the needs of the students.

Relationship to Other Types of Education

Selection-oriented education cannot take place in isolation. It must be developed and administered in conjunction with the other categories of continuing education described in the introduction. Selection-oriented education also relies on a particular set of fundamental skills (e.g., data reduction, data analysis). The teaching of these skills is most properly part of pre-professional education. Thus, selection-oriented education is also strongly dependent upon knowledge and abilities acquired during formal, academic education. As will be seen, selection-oriented education can also have a significant impact on academic education.

Task-Oriented Education

The goal of task-oriented education is to move well-educated personnel closer to the state of practice for specific jobs, projects, and organizations. For example, task-oriented education might be used to help a technical individual accomplish the transition to a managerial role within their company. Task-oriented education should typically precede selection-oriented education.

While task-oriented education usually has a very specific focus, it can be used to assist selection-oriented education. This is important because those individuals making use of task-oriented education are often charged with the responsibility of selecting new technologies to be used in their particular tasks. During task-oriented education, professionals can develop a recognition and appreciation of project and organization criteria that are important in selecting new technologies. These criteria could then be used to guide the identification, evaluation, and choice stages of technology selection. Support for selection-oriented education during task-oriented education requires little effort beyond sensitizing professionals to the criteria that are important from the point of view of the task in question.

Improvement Education

The goal of improvement education is to provide experienced practitioners with a working knowledge of current software engineering technology. Improvement education typically involves in-depth, hands-on experience with a particular tool or technique. This experience should involve classroom-style learning to provide an overview and introduction to the technology coupled with exercises that give students experience in using the technology on meaningful example problems. This category of education, in many instances, logically follows selection-oriented education. Once a particular technology has been selected for a project or organization, the target community needs to be trained in its use.

It is not necessary, however, to view improvement education as completely separate from selection-oriented education. They are, in fact, complementary and may be considered to be co-requisites in some circumstances. Those actually involved in technology selection may need to have in-depth, hands-on training with various technologies in order to make an informed evaluation. One way to accomplish this is to provide activities whereby evaluators can gain hands-on experience with new methods, tools and techniques in situations which lend themselves to comparison. These activities should include exercises or sets of exercises designed to reveal the relative strengths and weaknesses of the tools or techniques under consideration in a variety of contexts (e.g., both real time and data-processing applications). The exercises must exhibit many of the characteristics for exercises supporting selection-oriented education. The exercises will need to be sufficiently detailed and realistic to enable meaningful evaluation. They will also need to be simple enough to allow completion within a reasonable time. Thus, exercises developed for improvement-oriented education can be useful for selection-oriented education. Conversely, those exercises developed to support selection-oriented education can provide appropriate vehicles for improvement education.

Academe

Selection-oriented education has two important ties to traditional academic education. First, in order for selection-oriented education to be effective, or even possible, there are fundamental, prerequisite skills. These skills build on foundations that must be laid during formal education. Thus, selection-oriented education levies some requirements against academic programs. Second, selection-oriented education also impacts formal education by assisting in the selection of new material for inclusion in the curriculum.

Requirements from Formal Education

Technology selection has as prerequisite skills the ability to compare and evaluate competing technologies. These comparisons and evaluations need to occur along two dimensions. The initial selection of a new technology will involve identification, evaluation, and choice. These activities are aimed at determining which technologies are appropriate for a given project and/or organizational context and selecting those which best meet a particular set of needs. Once a new technology has been selected, its successful transfer into practice depends strongly on the benefits which the technology provides in relation to its costs. These costs may be measured directly in financial terms (as in the cost associated with construction or acquisition of a new software tool) or in more indirect terms (such as the "pain" associated with a steep learning curve for a tool or technique).

Measurement along both dimensions requires the ability to perform empirical investigation as well as the use of less formal comparison and evaluation. Specific aspects of comparison and evaluation skills will be context-dependent and thus the domain of post-employment continuing education. The foundations for these skills must, however, be established as part of pre-employment formal education.

Provision of basic skills for technology choice and evaluation will require some revisions in the computer science curriculum. Experimental skills are typically not included in a computer science education. Indeed, there is a need for considerable research in this area to determine what types of experiments and experimental skills are appropriate for computer science. Also missing from the computer science curriculum are fundamental empirical skills such as data reduction and data analysis. While computer science is likely to have special needs that differ from those of other disciplines, the basic concepts and techniques have been well established and can be adapted from other disciplines such as physics and psychology. The inclusion of these topics in the computer science curriculum is also likely to hasten the development of experimental methods in software engineering.

Impact on Formal Education

As noted in the introduction, software engineering principles and practices are beginning to have an impact on both the graduate and undergraduate curriculum. This trend is likely to continue and accelerate. As new software engineering tools and techniques are developed, many of them will find their way into the curriculum.

The selection of those technologies that are to be included in the curriculum is an extremely important activity for educators. The particular criteria used by educators will differ from those used by practitioners;

educators will be more interested in pedagogical issues such as illustration of basic principles and exposure to a broad spectrum of topics. While the criteria used by educators and practitioners may differ, however, the selection process will be fundamentally the same. Thus, the nature of technology-selection education for educators is not significantly different from that for practitioners.

The need for selection-oriented training for educators cannot be underestimated. Traditionally, the best way for educators to stay current has been to be active in research, be familiar with the current literature, and attend professional conferences. These avenues are still of fundamental importance, and support for research clearly needs to be expanded. Where selection of technology for inclusion in the graduate or undergraduate curriculum is concerned, however, the problem has dimensions that cannot be addressed via the traditional research route alone. Software engineering technology is changing rapidly on many fronts. Research activity typically provides in-depth experience in only a narrow area whereas educators typically teach in more broadly-based contexts (e.g., survey courses). Selection-oriented education is, therefore, necessary to provide appropriate exposure to topics outside an individual's research specialty.

There is also a widely recognized shortage of educators in computer science and software engineering. Many institutions, particularly the smaller ones, are forced to "borrow" faculty from related fields, such as mathematics, to teach computer science courses. These faculty often take advantage of improvement education by auditing courses and using sabbatical leaves to fill in their computer science backgrounds. However, since their primary allegiance is to another discipline, these faculty are usually not in a position to evaluate and select new material for inclusion in the curriculum. The problem is further aggravated by the fact that, at smaller institutions, research is often not a high priority. Selection-oriented education coupled with improvement education offers a viable approach to training for faculty in these cases.

rMise Selection-oriented Education Activities

The Rocky Mountain Institute of Software Engineering (**rMise**) is a non-profit organization supporting research and education in software engineering. Its intent is to serve all segments of the software engineering community, including researchers, developers, practitioners, managers, administrators and educators. Its primary focus is the transfer of modern software technology from the research arena to the broader professional community.

rMise sponsors many different types of activities, including demonstration "fairs," workshops, study groups, tutorials, and research projects. These activities are organized into several programs, each oriented towards a specific segment of the community. For example, the **rMise** Technology Improvement Program is oriented toward the research and development community and includes activities such as: evaluation-oriented demonstrations of emerging state of the art technology; technical workshops and study groups to address issues concerning the gap between the state of the art and the state of practice; tutorials addressing where the state of the art is, can be and should be; and research projects to advance the community's technology transfer capabilities.

A selection-oriented view of **rMise** activities and programs is shown in Figure 3. The Education Program is central in this arena. It provides a wide variety of selection-oriented education activities for practitioners, managers and administrators. It is supported by two more narrowly focused programs: the Technology Improvement Program helps the research and development community understand the state of the art/state of practice gap and develop selection-oriented technology to narrow it; the Education Support Program assists educators through the development of innovative selection-oriented education support capabilities and materials. As the figure indicates, a broad spectrum of selection-oriented activities are already underway. For those activities still in the planning stage, the figure gives an example of the types of activities envisaged.

PROGRAMS

	TECHNOLOGY IMPROVEMENT PROGRAM	EDUCATION PROGRAM	EDUCATION SUPPORT PROGRAM
RESEARCH PROJECTS	research and development of measures supporting technology selection	development of a prototype technology demonstration laboratory	investigation of electronic media supporting software engineering education
TUTORIALS	tutorials on the past, present and future of Ada™ environments	Summer Tutorial Programs <hr> Aspen, 1984 <hr> Colorado Springs and Aspen, 1985	tutorials on integrating selection-oriented education into "traditional" academic programs
STUDY GROUPS	Software Environments Improvement Workshop, Boulder, November 1985	Boulder, 1986 preparation of a white paper on "Selection-oriented Education in the Area of Software Testing"	preparation of a white paper on "Use of In-class Demonstrations for Software Environments Education"
WORKSHOPS	Third International Conference on the Software Process, Breckenridge, November 1986	Software Methodology Workshop, Colorado Springs, July 1985	workshop on the preparation of technology selection-oriented exercises
DEMONSTRATION "FAIRS"	evaluation-oriented demonstrations of alternative leading-edge technology	Software Methodology Exposition, Boulder, July 1986	education support material exposition

(Left axis label: ACTIVITIES)

☐ planned and already-conducted activities   ☐ examples of possible activities

Figure 3. A Selection-oriented View of rMise Activities and Programs

In the remainder of this section, we first describe several **rMise** activities from a technology selection point of view and then use these sample activities to discuss the **rMise** approach to selection-oriented activities.

Example of rMise Activities

Summer Tutorial Programs

Each Summer for the last two years, **rMise** has offered an extensive tutorial program. The programs have included about twenty tutorials each and have been attended by hundreds of participants, primarily from the United States but also from overseas, in both directions. A list of the tutorials in the 1985 Summer Tutorial Program appears in Figure 4.

Management Technology

- **Project Management of Software Engineers**
  R. Fairley, Wang Institute
- **Building a Software Project Team**
  R. Fairley, Wang Institute
- **Measurement for Management**
  D. Weiss, Naval Research Laboratory
- **Improving Software Productivity**
  A. Pyster, Digital Sound Corporation

Tools and Environment

- **Software Engineering Tools and Environments**
  L. Osterweil, University of Colorado
- **Source Text Analysis Tools**
  F. DeRemer, MetaWare™ Incorporated
- **Tools for Software Testing**
  L. Clarke, University of Massachusett L. Osterweil, University of Colorado
- **Pre-implementation Description and Analysis of Software**
  W. Riddle, Software Design & Analysis, Inc. J. Wiledon, University of Massachusetts
- **Software Maintenance**
  C. McClure, C.L. McClure & Associates, Inc.
- **Software Environment Design**
  L. Osterweil, University of Colorado W. Riddle, Software Design & Analysis, Inc. L. Williams, University of Colorado
- **Distributed Software Development Environments**
  L. Williams, University of Colorado
- **Ada™ Environment Issues**
  R. Taylor, University of California

Figure 4. rMise 1985 Summer Tutorial Program

Individual tutorials have treated state of the art and state of practice technology in a variety of areas, among them: software methodology, project management, software tools, software engineering environments, software analysis, and modern programming languages. The tutorials have been organized into sequences, with the earlier ones treating fundamental concepts and the latter ones treating advanced topics. This organization has allowed participants to choose a subset meeting their needs and experience levels. Many participants have taken advantage of this; the average length of attendance at the Institute's Summer Tutorial Programs has been three days.

The programs have also included tutorials that directly address technology transfer and technology selection. A *Technology Transition* tutorial was part of the program in 1984. The software methodology tutorial sequences have included tutorials specifically designed to compare alternative methodologies. Several of the tutorials on software engineering environments have covered general paradigms for moving technology into practice.

Software Environment Design Tutorial
Many of the tutorials in the Summer programs have provided the opportunity for first-hand experience through exercises and demonstrations. Some have had first-hand experience as their central focus. An example is the *Software Environment Design* tutorial, held both Summers.

In this tutorial, participants work in groups to complete an extended, multi-day design exercise. Initially, three scenarios are presented: a large independent software house with branch offices in several cities; a small, two-person company that produces application software for several brands of personal computers; and a major industrial firm that makes medical monitoring and control equipment that relies on embedded computer systems to perform most major tasks. Each group first prepares a requirements definition for a software environment servicing the needs of software personnel under one of the scenarios. Each group then presents their requirements definition to "management," with the other groups serving as management consultants. Depending on their needs and experiences, the groups then focus on either project management issues, and prepare a project plan, or technical issues, and prepare an architectural design. In either case, they must address how existing state of the art and state of practice technology can be used for their environments. These plans and architectures are also presented to management. Throughout the tutorial, the instructors play the dual roles of "senior management," visiting the groups as they work and inquiring about what is happening, and "consultants," helping the groups develop feasible plans and modern architectures that take reasonable cognizance of modern technology.

Executive Summary of Software Engineering Issues

The audience for **rMIse** activities was broadened, in the 1985 Summer Tutorial Program, with the inclusion of a multi-day tutorial, *Executive Summary of Software Engineering Issues*, designed specifically for top-level administrators. The intent was to provide senior managers with intense introductions to a broad spectrum of software engineering topics, in a way that would help them evaluate the potential for their organizations.

This tutorial covered a wide variety of topics: artificial intelligence, rights and data issues, human factors, large-scale systems, measurement technology, software methodology, tools and environments, and management support technology. For each topic, the emphasis was on basic concepts, potential benefit and (both good and bad) experiences. A large portion of the time was used for open discussion and interaction. The instructors were themselves top-level administrators, allowing them to interact with the participants on a peer basis.

Software Methodology Workshop

In conjunction with the 1985 Summer Tutorial Program, there was a Software Methodology Workshop, co-sponsored by the Department of Defense's STARS Program. It was attended by over 100 professionals, primarily from industry and government. In the workshop's initial segment, several technology developers, instrumental in founding specific methodologies, gave presentations on the philosophy underlying their approach to the software process. A open discussion among the developers and the workshop participants ended this initial segment. In the middle segment of the workshop, full-day tutorials on six different methodologies were provided and each participant attended three. In the final segment, each participant picked one of the three methodologies they had studied and used it, with the instructor's and other participants' help, to solve at least one of three specific problems. This final segment ended with a plenary session in which representative solutions in each methodology were presented and a group discussion addressed the differences and similarities among the methodologies.

Software Environments Workshop

The primary activity in the **rMlse** Technology Improvement Program has been a study group-style *Software Environments Workshop*, co-sponsored by the National Science Foundation [83]. The goal was to determine how to improve the state of the art in software environments over the next decade. It provided an indirect contribution to selection-oriented education by developing estimates of both the current and future state of the art in the software environments arena.

Participants formed groups to determine fundamental issues and required activities in several areas: tools, distributed systems, database systems, extensibility, artificial intelligence, integration, prototyping, measurement and evaluation, monolingual versus multilingual environments, human interfaces, and evolutionary versus revolutionary approaches to improvement.

They also addressed several global topics. First, to provide a context for the issues and activities, they developed a characterization of the software environment situation in the mid-1990's in comparison to the situation today. Second, they considered the general nature of organizations that could successfully undertake the required activities. Third, they reconsidered the results of a similarly-intentioned workshop, held five years ago [74], and updated this previous workshop's assessment to reflect the community's emerging concern for general systems issues and the software creation and evolution process.

The rMlse Approach to
Selection-oriented Education

State of the art Technology. Many factors have influenced the choice of topics covered by **rMlse** activities. Within the ever-present boundaries imposed by resource availability, attention has primarily been given to topics where the state of the art is well-developed and the gap between the state of the art and the state of practice is larger than average. Several studies (see, for example, [109]) have indicated that the state of practice is quite far behind the state of the art in software methodologies and software tools/environments. **rMise** has emphasized these topics. It has also treated subjects, such as project management, that directly relate to these topics and affect the extent to which this technology is used in practice.

The **rMise** approach to addressing the state of the art has, therefore, been to emphasize "high payoff" areas in which there is a significant amount of available state of the art technology that is not being used in practice.

Coverage of Technology Transfer. With the exception of the *Technology Transition* tutorial, few **rMise** activities have focused exclusively on the processes involved in technology transfer. Rather, the coverage has been indirect, with the inclusion of material in some of the Summer Tutorial Program activities. The *Software Environments Design* tutorial and several of the other Tools and Environments tutorials have, for example, treated general paradigms for the transfer of tool/environment technology. It is expected that this indirect approach will continue for the foreseeable future, until our understanding of and experiences with software technology transfer mature significantly beyond their present levels.

Identification, Evaluation and Choice Techniques. In **rMise** activities, these subjects are treated within the context of specific technology arenas. This approach emphasizes exposure to the state of the art, with specific selection-support techniques being discussed with respect to their use in specific technology domains. Selection-related material that has been included in the tutorials includes: cost estimation techniques, general paradigms for integrating technology, technology classification schemes, measurement technology, comparative evaluations of available technology, cost/benefit analyses, and techniques for effective participation in team efforts.

This indirect treatment of selection techniques has also included comparative evaluation exercises. Simple instances have occurred in the *Software Environments Workshop*, in which the participants differentiated between technology that should be emphasized in the near term and technology to be emphasized in the medium term, and the *Software Environment Design* tutorial, in which participants chose technology to include in their environments. More extensive comparison was done in the course of the *Software Methodology Workshop*. This workshop's format was generally judged to be successful at providing insight into a variety of modern technology options to a level of detail allowing (informal) comparative assessment. The format would seem to be of general utility for selection-oriented, experience-based studies of a wide spectrum of software technology.

As in the case of technology transfer in general, **rMise**, therefore, takes a primarily indirect approach to selection technology. For the foreseeable future, direct treatment will probably be limited to the Technology Improvement Program and include workshops and study groups on fundamental issues and concepts. The state of the art and state of practice in technology selection may eventually mature to the point that direct treatment in specific tutorials will be possible. But, because selection-support techniques will always be best understood in the context of their application to specific situations, it would seem that an emphasis on indirect treatment will always be most appropriate.

Experience-based Content. Reports on experiences in adopting and using software technology have been a part of the vast majority of the tutorials. The **rMise** approach has been to seek instructors who have had extensive experience. This approach was also used in choosing participants for the *Software Environments Workshop*: people actually involved in the design and construction of environments accounted for about half the participants.

Decision-making Orientation. The **rMise** approach has been to orient its activities specifically toward technology selection decision makers. The *Executive Summary of Software Engineering Issues* tutorial was specifically designed for top-level decision makers. Most of the offerings in the Summer Tutorial Programs have been oriented toward project managers and middle-level management, or people aspiring to these positions. In addition, decision-makers were specifically included in the *Software Environments Workshop* and this workshop's result was prepared for use by those responsible for deciding where to invest time and effort in the improvement of the state of the art for software environments.

Exercises. Exercises have been a key component of many **rMIse** activities. Tutorials offering extended exercises have been included in both the software methodology and tools/environments tutorial sequences (e.g., the *Software Environment Design* tutorial). A concentrated effort has been made to assure that these exercises do not suffer the problems noted in the **General Form of the Program**. In addition, several other tutorials have included simple, experience-providing exercises.

Unfortunately, it has not been possible to provide facilities for "live" demonstrations or provide a laboratory capability. This will be corrected, somewhat, in the upcoming *Software Methodology Exposition*. Manual and automated tools supporting a variety of methodologies will be demonstrated during the exposition, and participants will have the opportunity to gain hands-on experience with this technology. It is anticipated that this sort of activity will become an increasingly larger part of **rMise** programs, and plans are being made for eventually providing a full-capability laboratory supporting software technology demonstration and experimentation.

Interactive Sessions. The **rMise** approach to fostering interaction is to keep the number of participants small. Participation in the tutorials is restricted on a first-come-first-served basis to assure highly interactive learning opportunities. Study groups are held to a maximum of twenty-five participants to foster interaction. Even when the number of participants is small, the opportunity is sought to divide the group into working groups of three to five people (e.g., the *Software Environment Design* tutorial and the *Software Environments Workshop*). When the number of participants is large, as in the case of the *Software Methodol-*

ogy Workshop, the amount of time that the group spends together is held to a minimum and much of this is used for open discussion.

Instructors. rMIse has been fortunate to be able to attract instructors for its tutorials (and participants for its study groups) who are well-versed in their fields, quite familiar with both the state of the art and the state of practice, able to handle the rigors of short, intense sessions, and willing and able to participate fully in freewheeling discussions. The approach has been to find top-quality people who are heavily involved in defining and expanding the boundaries of their field of interest; no other approach would satisfy the instructor criteria specified previously.

Summary

Selection-oriented education provides an exposure to new techniques and concepts rather than an in-depth coverage of the techniques and concepts. The coverage is sufficient to impart an appreciation of the technology's applicability and cost-to-benefit ratio. The intent is to enable management and technical personnel to make well-founded decisions about whether or not to adopt a particular technology.

A selection-oriented education program must satisfy many criteria. It must provide an extensive introduction to the state of the art. It must cover all the activities supporting technology transfer and show how they interact with the specific activity of technology selection. It must cover a wide variety of techniques for performing technology selection and demonstrate their use. It must include information on actual experiences. It must service the needs of those responsible for selecting technology; often this is an individual who is trying to decide whether or not to upgrade his or her own capabilities. It must provide for a high degree of interaction among instructors and students so that needs of individual students are articulated and accommodated, the applicability of the material to personal situations is clear, and students are able to learn from each others' experiences. And it must be conducted by knowledgeable, experienced, articulate, flexible instructors who are well accustomed to short, intense, interactive sessions.

The Rocky Mountain Institute of Software Engineering (**rMise**) has sponsored a number of activities that contribute to selection-oriented education. The primary activity in this arena has been its Summer Tutorial Program. **rMise** also sponsored a workshop that emphasized the comparative assessment of alternative methodologies through large-group discussion of experiences gained in small-group exercises. The Institute organized and ran a study group to identify issues fundamental to improving the state of the art for software environments. Finally, a software methodology exposition is planned to provide more individualized learning through direct experience.

The **rMise** approach to selection-oriented education emphasizes exposure to the state of the art in software methodology and software tools/environments, two areas where the gap between art and practice is particularly wide. Techniques supporting technology selection are treated indirectly, in the context of their use rather than as subjects of direct focus. Experiential data is included as much as possible, primarily through the use of personnel who are actively involved in both developing the technology within their fields and transferring it into practice. The needs of decision-makers at the project management, middle management and top-executive levels are met by designing specific tutorials to meet these needs. Interactive sessions are assured by limiting participation so that groups are small, dividing participants into working groups of three to five people whenever possible, and devoting the majority of large-group time to open discussion. Quality instruction is assured by employing experienced instructors who are instrumental in defining and expanding the boundaries of their respective fields.

The **rMise** enterprise has provided a wealth of experience in setting up and running selection-oriented education programs. (And it promises to provide significantly more as its activities are expanded in the future.) The body of this paper has reported the positive experiences, and, in closing, we would like to offer a few experiential observations about what can go "wrong." First, we have found little interest in activities that directly address technology transfer and technology selection *per se*. There is interest in these topics within the context of specific situations — for example, which configuration management tools should be adopted and how should they be introduced — but there is essentially no interest in them as "stand-alone" subjects. Second, we have found little interest in revolutionarily new technology that, while it may be a "hot topic" in the research and development community, is sufficiently different from existing technology that its introduction would cause a large perturbation. The interest is in much more conservative advanced technology for which there is little question about applicability and ease of introduction. Third, the majority of students will be seeking **the answer** and feel that there must be something that will solve all, or most, of their problems if only they could find it. One of the major opportunities, and one of the hardest tasks, is to get students to realize that they have the wrong objective. Finally, some students (luckily a minority) will lack the flexibility and tolerance for ambiguity that is necessary when considering technology selection. They will be sophisticated enough to know that there is no single answer, but they will want structured courses that deliver logical assessments of what technology is good for a wide spectrum of specific situations.

Graduate-level Software Engineering Education: A Practitioner's Viewpoint

S. E. Smith
IBM Corporate Technical Institutes

Abstract. The definition of what software engineering is and what constitutes a software engineer are issues of continuing question and debate. In a sense, we find ourselves at the mercy of having created a title that has not yet been well reconciled with a body of scientific knowledge a la electrical or other fields of engineering. A consensus on its meaning is still ahead of us, the widespread acceptance of software engineering as an appropriate label reflects a pervasive sense of urgency that programming professionals must operate within certain bounds of discipline and control that become inherent in the profession. The breadth of acceptance of software engineering, as an urgent professional discipline need, embraces industry, government, and academia. Each of these segments of the community has made and continues to make significant contributions to the rapid evolution of the programming profession. As a result, we are in a position today to develop recommendations on the content of an academic program which can, in a concerted fashion, accelerate the cultivation of a software engineering profession. This paper will, based on my experiences, recommend a direction for a graduate-level program in software engineering. It does not attempt to define a specific set of courses and sequencing.

Introduction

The past two decades have been witness to significant progress in the field of software development. Much of that progress has been achieved empirically through the experiences of programming professionals with little of it having been captured in a form that can readily benefit newcomers to the profession. With that in mind there is a real need to identify and offer formal education programs which draw from the knowledge and experiences of government, industry and academia. The initiative of the Education Division, Software Engineering Institute, Carnegie-Mellon University to develop recommendations for a Master of Software Engineering curriculum is a timely and welcome effort, which I applaud.

Education Focus

A review and analysis of where and why software development projects experience difficulty is necessary to establish a frame of reference for identification of education needs for graduate software engineers. In software projects, success is measured in terms of the timely delivery of function that the target users need and will buy, in a cost effective way, and in a form that is non-disruptive to user's operations (i.e., reliable, installable, meets performance expectations, maintainable, usable) and facilitates extendability/enhancement. More often than not, most of these objectives are met; however, the increasing demand for software products, in increasingly complex applications and in an environment of scarce skills, requires that the technical and project management expertise of software professionals be as leading edge as possible. What does experience suggest is needed in a graduate-level software engineering curriculum?

MSE Curriculum Recommendations

Undergraduate computer science programs prepare students to be programmers. That is, the focus of training tends to limit graduate's skills to those that are operative on relatively small projects or in the latter stages of large programming projects where decomposition of development tasks has been done. Students are capable of quickly becoming effective in environments where their assignments are defined within bounds which facilitate intellectual control over their work. Large projects as well as small have a critical need for the talent and skill of these professionals.

In the case of large projects, in particular, there is an urgent need for additional skills which deal with the early or planning phases of development to assure that the identification, validation, and verification of requirements; estimation of work scope, specification, and design leads to a decomposition and description of the required product into entities which facilitate timely implementation by assigned programmers.

In addition to the product planning and structuring skills needed, it is critically important that an explicit process discipline be adhered to which provides for the control, management, and improvement of process productivity and predictability as well as product quality in terms of functional capability, reliability, installability, maintainability, performance, and usability.

The foregoing provides a frame of reference for identification of a core of base set or graduate level courses in software engineering, primarily for students who will be members/leaders of relatively large software development projects, and which have two fundamental objectives. First, develop an appreciation for, an understanding of, and a commitment to certain principles:

- Software is developed to satisfy customer needs and produce profit.
- Discontinuities in the course of product definition, specification, design, implementation, integration, use, and maintenance require communication through the creation and maintenance of effective product description materials.
- Early reconciliation of product capabilities and customer needs is essential; e.g., prototyping.
- Development process discipline is fundamental and must be rendered explicit; e.g., discrete steps with entry and exit criteria, measurements, data collection/retention and analysis.
- Management of defect content must reflect a philosophy of defect prevention versus defect detection; e.g., correctness of design, intellectual control, statistically based testing for verification purposes.

The second objective of the core material is to provide students with alternatives on "how" to deal with the "what" reflected in the first objective. Specific material to be covered would be comprised of surveys, case studies, and theory from texts, periodicals, and professional society proceedings. The intent is to give students knowledge and understanding of what is considered the "best of the breed" current practices and information on viable, yet unproven, alternatives. Lecture and study would be complemented heavily with workshops. In addition, a significant team project, which brings the key principles and their importance into play, would be required.

Beyond the core, students would have an opportunity to enroll in selected areas of specialization within the context of a general software development environment; e.g., requirements, testing, fault tolerance, asynchronous design. There should also be an opportunity to selectively enroll in courses dealing with product technology specialization; e.g., database, data communications, storage management, etc.

Graduates of the program would be well positioned to deal with the planning, control, and management of any large software project. Their specialization selections would position them for specific roles on a programming development team. Elective courses in product technology areas would develop students' expertise for development of specific classes of products. Figure 1 depicts a model which represents the concept of the curriculum being recommended. The core (which includes the masters project) comprises 2/3 of the total credit with electives (either development process or product technology specialization) making up the remainder.

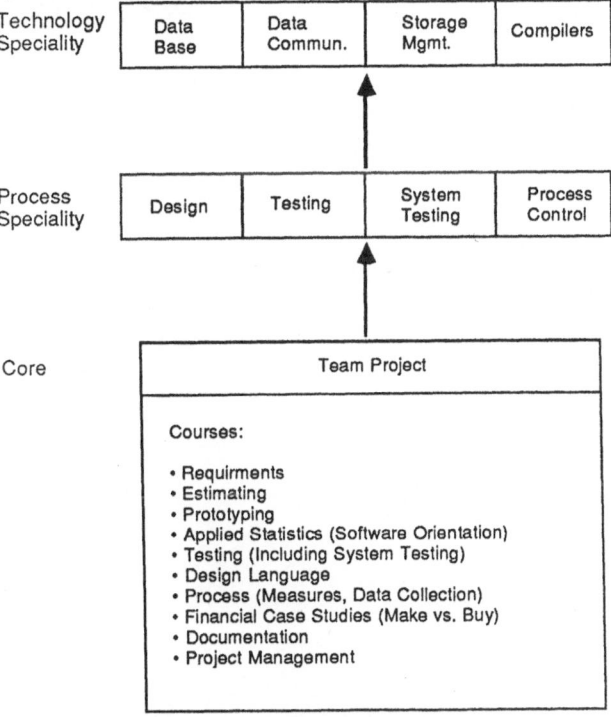

Figure 1. MSE Curriculum Model

Summary

There are several technical subjects relevant to the advancement of software engineering in areas such as design methodologies, testing, statistical quality control, etc. However, in my view, the highest priority for a MSE curriculum is best placed on the planning, management, and control aspects of software development.

Some Observations on the Nature of the Software Engineering "Problem" and Their Implications for Software Engineering Education

William A. Wulf
Tartan Laboratories

Abstract. The term "software engineering" is somewhat synonymous with "methodology." Yet, methodology should not play a major role in professional education, because a methodology is a tool, which will become obsolete: it should be taught, but it should be treated as a tool, not as the central topic of the discipline.

Introduction

I intensely dislike position papers that take a negative, "anti-" position. Yet, guess what — that's exactly the kind of paper I've written here. Specifically, I'm going to be anti-methodology. At least I am going to be anti- the notion that methodology ought to play a major role in a professional educational program.

In the context of this paper, I intend the term "methodology" to span a very broad spectrum of topics, including programming languages (notably the structuring features such as strong typing and data-abstraction/encapsulation), programming methodologies (such as "top down design," "modular decomposition"), formal lifecycle models, structured requirements analysis, program design languages, and so on.

I am concerned that the term "software engineering" has become almost synonymous with "methodology." To the extent that this is true, and hence there is a tendency to organize professional software engineering curricula with this bias, I think we are making a serious mistake.

The Rationale

I will discuss my reasons for my concern under several headings:
- Misplaced Emphasis
- The Character of the Problem Will Change
- Methodologies are NewSpeak
- Formalized Methodologies Aren't Self-Evidently Useful

I trust the reader will understand that I am not anti-methodology, per se. I have made research contributions to several of the topics listed above, and I remain a strong proponent of many of them. Rather, my concern is that software engineering is a broad and evolving topic, and that an educational program should not narrowly focus on the hot topic of the moment.

Misplaced Emphasis

Every educational program is a balance between material of immediate utility and long term stability. The electrical engineering student, for example, both learns Kirkoff's laws and experiments with contemporary components and equipment. Kirkoff's laws will not change, but, frankly, are not of as much immediate value as a working knowledge of the latest oscilloscope. Merely a knowledge of the latest oscilloscope, however, is of only temporary utility.

Methodology is, at best, like an oscilloscope. At worst, it is like a tube-tester, a device whose utility will be made obsolete by advancing technology.

Software engineering is, in many essential respects, no different from other kinds of engineering — and, in particular, like other engineering, good software engineering is based on solid science and mathematics. Methodologies are neither of these; they are, rather, management techniques based on a collection of observations about our human limitations in dealing with complexity and/or communicating with each other.

Computer science as a whole, and software engineering in particular, is a young field. We don't know exactly what mathematics, for example, is most germane. Some of us may even suspect that the "right" form of mathematical models for algorithmic process remain to be invented.

Faced with uncertainty about the "right" mathematics and science, there is a tendency to place a heavier emphasis on shorter-term, obviously utilitarian material — e.g., methodology. I believe this is misplaced. It would better serve both the student and the field to teach the "wrong" mathematics; doing so would at least increase the mathematical maturity of the students.

The Character of the Problem Will Change

The available data suggest that the amount of code required to support a single application doubles roughly every three years (i.e., it grows 25% per year). It is interesting to contrast this with the growth in primary memory size, which has doubled every 2.2 years. I believe that this indicates that the demand for functionality, as reflected by program size, is essentially unbounded and that only the availability of memory and our ability to produce software limits its growth.

Programming productivity has increased only 4-6% per year over the last 20 years. As practiced, programming is a craft, not engineering. It is labor intensive, and all dimensions of the quality of the programming product are determined by the craftsmanship of the programmers that created it.

The demand for functionality over that period has been satisfied by increasing the number of programmers, not by increased productivity. That technique will not work indefinitely; indeed, we are rapidly approaching the point at which productivity is the limiting factor in satisfying the demand for new functionality.

Faced with these observations, there are only three alternatives:

- demand is not really unbounded, and happily, we are just about to satisfy it, or
- we will not be able to satisfy the demand, or
- software must be produced some different way.

I don't believe the first, and I won't accept the second without having explored the third. Methodological approaches have not, and will not produce a compounded 25% per year increase in productivity. Therefore, software **will** be produced differently. We may not yet know what that different method will be, but of necessity it will not contain the problems that spawned the current methodologies.

Methodologies are NewSpeak

All software methodologies are management techniques — either management of people, in the obvious sense, or management of complexity, in the sense of the various structured design and/or coding techniques.

They are, further, restrictive techniques. Like Orwell's NewSpeak, by prestructuring what can be said, they try to prevent the designer/programmer from uttering bad programs. NewSpeak is the antithesis of good education, which strives to broaden the student's perspective, foster understanding, and prepare them to think independently and constructively.

Strong typing is a good example. The usual argument for strong typing is that it prevents certain kinds of programming errors, or at least catches them during compilation rather than forcing much more expensive debugging. This is quite true. Alas, what is also true is that the present state of the art in typing mechanisms also prevents writing perfectly correct, and frequently more understandable and maintainable programs.

Formalized Methodologies Aren't Self-Evidently Useful

I don't believe people are stupid, at least not all of them are stupid all of the time. Thus if most people behave in some particular way, perhaps there's a good reason for it.

Demonstratably, most of the popular topics in software engineering, whether the use of ever higher-level programming languages or one of the structured design techniques, have little appeal for the programmer. They can be enforced by management fiat but, they are not techniques of choice.

How many of the people attending this workshop regularly use a complete formal methodology, from formal requirements analysis through configuration control in their personal programming? I don't.

Why? Objectively, methodologies are more burden than help for programming in the small — which is what the average programmer does most of the time. Moreover, if the industry is to achieve significant and sustained increases in productivity, an objective ought to be to make **all** programming problems into programming-in-the-small problems.

Conclusion

Should methodology be taught in a professional software engineering program? Of course! But it should be treated like an oscilloscope, like a tool that will become obsolete, not as the central topic of the discipline.

Perhaps, in fact, the most useful role for methodology in such a program would be to discuss their limitations. Like Knuth's well-known paper on programming with GOTOs, discussing the limitations that all methodologies have, even to the point of interference with constructing good programs, would be extremely enlightening.

Section II
Part 2
Current Software Engineering Curricula

Since the late 1970s, several programs leading to a master's degree in software engineering have been started. The papers in this part describe the content of four of these programs, and the experiences of the implementors.

The two American programs have existed long enough that changes have been made in response to different perceptions of the discipline and need. James Comer and David Rodjak chronicle the evolution of their curriculum at Texas Christian University, and Everald Mills evaluates the state of his program at Seattle University. Both universities are in urban settings with considerable high technology industry in the area. They share an orientation toward educating experienced practitioners.

In contrast, the pair of United Kingdom programs are aimed at "undergraduates" in the sense that the students in them do not normally have work experience in software engineering. Imperial College in London, as described in M. M. Lehman's paper, has a four year course leading to a master's degree. David Budgen and his colleagues at the University of Stirling in Scotland have a curriculum that includes a significant internship period in industry.

Adapting to Changing Needs: A New Perspective on Software Engineering Education at Texas Christian University

James R. Comer and David J. Rodjak
Texas Christian University

Abstract. In response to the need for skilled software engineers, Texas Christian University, in the Fall of 1978, established a Master's Degree in Software Engineering, the first such degree program of its kind in the country. After three years of experience with this program, the curriculum was revised in 1981 to reflect the changing needs of the software engineering profession. This revised curriculum, currently in place at Texas Christian University, is described and evaluated. Avenues of future curriculum expansion are explored.

Introduction

It has become evident in recent years that there are significant problems facing the computer industry with regard to the support and development of reliable computer software systems. Extraordinary advances in the development of hardware systems architecture has resulted in a much publicized software predicament. That is, as the costs associated with computer hardware fall, larger, more complex software systems become economically feasible. As such, the demand for computer software has accelerated to the point that the means of supply are being greatly exceeded. Consequently, the major technological concern for the 1990's is a rapidly expanding gap between the demand for software and the ability of academic, industrial, and governmental organizations to supply it.

The need for reliable, well engineered software has reached almost epidemic proportions. A current worldwide market of $18 billion, two-thirds of which is held within the United States, is expected to increase to approximately $55 billion by 1987 [70]. With increases of this magnitude, it is of paramount importance that industry be provided skilled individuals who are able to apply sound engineering and management principles to the analysis and design of computer systems software.

This is obviously not the situation that currently exists. To further underscore the problem, one is referred to various onerous predictions being made by knowledgeable software scientists. In November, 1983, it was estimated that the demand for software at the national level was increasing by approximately twelve percent per year while the supply of skilled software developers was increasing at the rate of four percent per year. Coupling these percentages with an estimation that the productivity of these same software developers was increasing at a rate of about four percent per year results in a cumulative four percent gap. At this rate, it is projected that industry will be left with a shortfall of between 800,000 and 1,000,000 software personnel by the year 1990 [13].

In recognition of the need for advanced study in the field of software development, Texas Christian University (TCU), in the fall of 1978, instituted a graduate degree in software engineering. Due to external pressure, prompted by the absence of an engineering college at TCU, the program was renamed Master's of Software Design and Development (MSDD) in 1980. The original intent of the program was to examine prevalent programming practices and methodologies that might be useful for furthering the development, management, and maintenance of reliable systems software. These goals continue to serve as the primary thrust of the program.

However, since the program's inception, the field of software development has changed considerably. Many important new techniques and methodologies have evolved and have come to the forefront. In an effort to respond to this maturation, the degree program at TCU was recently examined and updated. The purpose of this paper is to assess the current status of software engineering education at TCU and to discuss the current curriculum and the motivations for its evolution.

The Early Days

Historical Perspective

During the mid-1970's, a dramatic increase in the use of computer software was experienced by many of the nation's high technology companies. In particular, companies involved with aerospace and semiconductor manufacturing, geophysical exploration, and communications systems development found themselves face to face with a growing need for more sophisticated software. In some cases, this need was created because the software was embedded in the product being manufactured. In other cases, the software was needed to support other aspects of the product line such as engineering research and development, material management, product manufacturing and testing, and worldwide logistics. All too frequently, attempts to develop specific software in support of these areas were less than successful. Common problems often included missed schedules, budgetary overruns, and software that simply did not meet necessary technical requirements. Consequently, upper management soon realized that software was a problem looking for a solution. They just as quickly recognized that they did not know how to achieve a solution.

The emerging problem confronting high technology companies of this period was twofold. On the one hand, software was generally perceived to be a "...black box created by programmers who practiced their art..."; as such, many companies did not possess the skills to manage or measure the progress of the software development process. At the same time there was a rapidly growing shortage of individuals having the skills to develop this critically needed software. The traditional approaches for solving such personnel shortages were not viable. Not only were software engineers not being produced by academia but there was a shortage of experienced personnel to be lured away from other companies (methods frequently used to staff more classical engineering disciplines). In response to these shortages, an occasional company turned to a different staffing approach, that of establishing programs, internally, for the purpose of cross training employees in the disciplines of software engineering [68, 9]. It is generally difficult for an outsider to judge the success of such a program. However, such cross training efforts frequently produce individuals who are able to code, but who often lack the depth and breadth of understanding of the entire software life cycle. Clearly these are processes that characterize the software engineer. Overall, the best approach to satisfying the shortage of skilled software designers seems to lie with the establishment of curricula by academic institutions.

The Original Curriculum

TCU responded to this early need by instituting a Master's Degree in Software Engineering in the Fall of 1978. The formulation of the initial curriculum began with a careful analysis of:

- existing surveys of software engineering needs and objectives [100],
- discussions with local industrial managers and experts,
- ACM's preliminary work on a master's curriculum [28, 56], and
- observations of what courses were being offered by various other universities [51].

It was determined, as a result of this analysis, that TCU's curriculum should be based upon the life cycle approach to software engineering with heavy emphasis on the management of software development. To be included in the program requirements were courses in verbal and written communication techniques, software design and development methodologies, and group participation methods.

As a result of early evidence, it was determined that the program should be oriented towards part-time students who could be accommodated, at the outset, through evening college classes. This was largely due to the decision that admission to the program would be limited to professionals already having practical experience in the software development environment. It was also felt that since TCU was within easy commuting distance of a large number of high technology companies, there would be an adequate number of students attracted to the program. These early decisions proved to be successful as the program has now grown to approximately 50 students — all of whom are full time employees within the software development community in and around Ft. Worth.

A list of the courses offered as a part of the original software engineering curriculum is shown in Figure 1. Of these courses, all were required, with the exception of SDD 6104, which was provided as a "leveling course" for students having insufficient background in the computer sciences. In addition, the program required that each student take at least six hours of electives. These were most generally taken in the school of business or the Computer Science Department. A detailed discussion of the original degree program can be found in Appendix I.

TCU MSDD COURSE TITLES

SDD 5143 - Introduction to Software Design and Development.
SDD 5193 - Communication Techniques in the Software Design
             and Development Environment.
SDD 6104 - Overview of Computer Science.
SDD 6113 - Methodologies of Software Development.
SDD 6123 - Requirements and Specifications for Software.
SDD 6133 - Software Design.
SDD 6142 - Software Design Laboratory.
SDD 6153 - Management of Software Development.
SDD 6163 - Economics of Software Development.
SDD 6193 - Effective Participation in Small Task Oriented Groups.
SDD 7113 - Software Implementation.

Figure 1. MSDD Courses — Before Revision.

As evidenced by Figure 1, the original software engineering curriculum was oriented towards teaching the management of software development as professed by Boehm [11] in 1976. From its initial inception the program was conceived and administered as a professional program to be offered only to software managers and developers already having significant industrial experience. As such, students entering the program came from a broad cross-section of industry. Experience ranged from business and management environments to more technical engineering environments, and while each student was interviewed prior to admission into the program, the level of technical and management expertise varied greatly. Consequently, as with all new programs, difficulties were frequently encountered. Course content often had to be adjusted to meet the needs of both classes of students, that is, both technical and nontechnical. An even greater problem concerned the lack of quality textbooks. Indeed, in some cases textbooks simply did not exist at all — good or bad! Thus, many of the early courses were taught using seminar notes, personal knowledge or experiences, or whatever other resources an instructor might have available. Clearly, not an altogether desirable situation from the student's standpoint.

The Current State

Changing Needs

In 1981 the content of TCU's curriculum for the Master's Degree in Software Design and Development was re-examined and subsequently revised. The basic changes were intended to accomplish a balance between the technical and management components of the program. By now, it was understood that training in the management of software engineering projects was important but was not, in and of itself, sufficient to solve the many problems confronting the software development community. It was clear that there was a new, even greater need for sound technical training in the methodologies and techniques of software engineering.

Many early software managers were not able to assess the risks and benefits of new technologies that could be directly applied to their various projects. Quite frequently this failure was due to a lack of understanding of the new technologies that were available. Clearly, in an industrial environment, new concepts must be accepted and appreciated at the management level before changes can be implemented. In an effort to address these needs, TCU's curriculum was modified to include courses that would provide a sound foundation in the technical aspects of software engineering. Many of the existing management oriented courses were combined in an effort to reduce the overlap existing from one course to another. They were, however, not altogether removed from the curriculum.

Attempts to revise the program were aided by the increased availability of published materials in the various areas of the emerging software engineering discipline. In the three years from its inception to its revision, significant new material had been published and was now available for incorporation into the curriculum. Indeed, in some instances, the revision was directly guided by the proliferation of new textbooks and published papers attesting to the growing universe of software engineering knowledge.

The New Curriculum

As a result of the revision, several new course subjects were considered and integrated into the curriculum in an effort to introduce new software engineering topics. Courses were designed in such areas as software metrics, data bases, Ada, computer architecture, and security and privacy. Also included was the study of the various automated tools related to the software development life cycle. Figure 2 contains a list of the courses comprising the revised MSDD program. The reader is referred to Appendix II for a full discussion of the new program.

Figure 3 shows a typical degree plan sequence that most students are counseled to follow. As indicated, it is possible to satisfy the degree requirements in seven semesters by enrolling and successfully completing at least two courses per semester. Since the majority of students enrolled in the MSDD program are employed as professional software developers, most are unable to attend classes more frequently than twice a week. Consequently, in order to accommodate part-time students, all classes are scheduled in the evening college and meet once a week for three hours.

TCU MSDD Course Titles

SDD 5143 - Introduction to Software Design and Development
SDD 6013 - Ada Design and Development
SDD 6023 - Advanced Topics in Systems Software
SDD 6033 - Computer Facilities Management
SDD 6043 - Software Quality Assurance and Metrics
SDD 6053 - Security and Privacy
SDD 6104 - Programming Structures
SDD 6113 - Modern Software Requirements and Design
          Techniques
SDD 6123 - Applied Design, Programming, and Testing
SDD 6153 - Management of Software Development
SDD 6163 - Economics of Software Development
SDD 6173 - Computer Systems Architecture
SDD 6183 - Database and Information Management Systems
SDD 6193 - Effective Communication in Small Groups
SDD 7113 - Software Implementation Project I
SDD 7123 - Software Implementation Project II

Figure 2. MSDD Courses — After Revision.

Year	Semester	
	Fall	Spring
1	• SDD 5143 (Intro. to SFW Design & Develop.) • SDD 6104 (Programming Structures) or elective	• SDD 6173 (Computer Systems Arch.) • SDD 6113 , (Modern SFW Requirements)
2	• SDD 6123 (Applied Design, Prog., & Testing) • SDD 6153 (Mgmt. of SFW Development)	• SDD 6183 (Database & Info. Mgmt. Sys.) • SDD 6163 (Economics of SFW Develop.)
3	• SDD 7113 (SFW Implementation I) • elective	• SDD 7123 (SFW Implementation II) • elective
4	• elective Δ Comprehensive Orals	

Figure 3. Typical Degree Plan Sequence.

A concerted effort was made to capitalize on new, readily available textbooks and to eliminate duplication within the courses being offered. Included in Appendix II are textbook titles that have been used most recently in each of the courses now being taught. Further, to reduce inconsistency, several adjunct professors from industry were identified and now regularly teach in the program. Additional software development tools were identified, and where feasible, were procured along with a VAX 11/780 computer system for use in the program. Since the installation of the new curriculum, dramatic results have been observed. The MSDD program is now well established and is beginning to experience a steady growth rate.

The prerequisite graph for courses taught in the MSDD program is shown below in Figure 4. All students are required to complete a core curriculum consisting of nine courses. In addition a variety of MSDD elective courses are regularly scheduled and students are allowed to take these or to choose electives from outside the Computer Science Department. Currently, due to the present size and makeup of the student body, all courses are offered but once during the academic year.

As such, students are encouraged to closely follow the degree plan sequence shown in Figure 3. As mentioned earlier, the "leveling" course, SDD 6104, is required of those students having insufficient formal background in computer science. This course may be taken concurrently with SDD 5143 during the student's first semester at TCU.

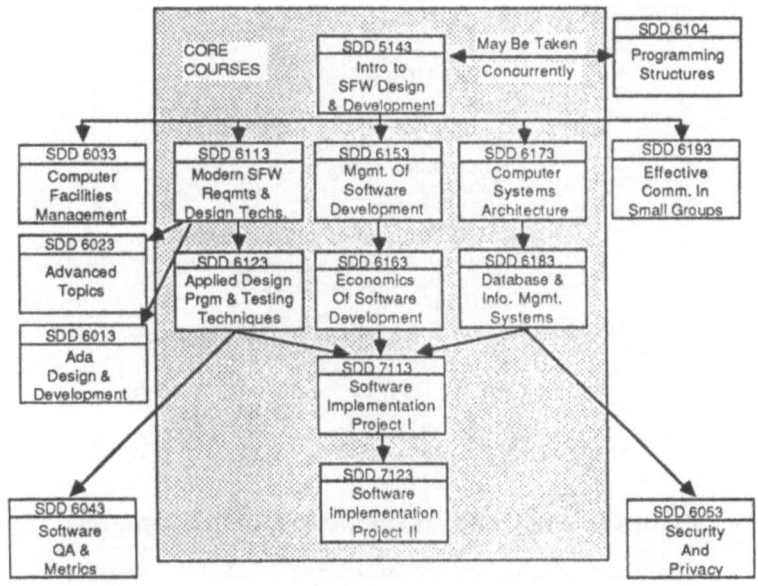

Figure 4. Prerequisite Graph for MSDD Program.

The Curriculum Environment

Within the past two years, significant new computer resources have been acquired and made available to students enrolled in the MSDD program. Many of the hardware and software tools that are available are shown in Figure 5 below. The two mainframe computers, the IBM 4341 and the VAX 11/780, are used in the majority of the courses being taught. However, several specialized hardware tools are available in the form of personal computers, micro-processor development systems, and artificial intelligence systems. In addition, several varieties of software packages are available. Included among these is a relatively complete set of programming languages, editors, and debuggers as well as a limited number of software development tools. Most of these tools are used in the classroom environment and in support of students pursuing independent research.

MSDD Facilities

- IBM 4341
  - 12 Megabytes Main Memory
  - 3.7 Gigabytes On-Line Disk
- DEC VAX 11/780 (VMS/UNIX)
  - 4 Megabytes Main Memory
  - 1.5 Gigabytes On-Line Disk
- Texas Instruments Explorer Systems
- Personal Computers
  - Tandy Radio Shack
  - Macintosh
  - Apple II Plus
- Graphics Equipment
  - VT 240 Tektronics Compatible Display
  - VS 11/Vax Graphics System
  - AED 767
- Software Tools Available or Planned

- UNIX	- HOS USE.IT	- SDDL
- SYSREM	- RXVP80	- STRUCTURES
- PL/1	- Modula-2	- Smalltalk
- PROLOG	- COBOL 74	- FORTRAN 77
- LISP	- Pascal	- Ada

Figure 5. Facilities Available to MSDD Students.

The Near Future

During the Fall semester, 1985, the authors conducted a brief survey of selected students associated with the MSDD program. For completeness, and in an effort to gauge the success of the revised curriculum, several students were polled who had graduated under the old curriculum and several who were currently enrolled under the new curriculum. The objective of the survey was to ascertain whether the approach and content of the MSDD curriculum were meeting the needs of those students working in industrial software development environments. Conclusions drawn from the data supplied by these students are discussed in the following section. A copy of the questionnaire used in the survey can be found in Appendix III.

Student Survey

Of the students surveyed, approximately seventy percent completed and returned their questionnaires. Of these, it was learned that approximately seventy-five percent of the respondents were actively employed in the development of business-oriented software systems. Various application areas included financial systems, cost accounting, personnel record systems, inventory control, and fleet expense and maintenance systems. The remaining twenty-five percent were involved in various engineering software development efforts such as aircraft/pilot trainers, automatic test equipment, and real-time radar simulations. With regard to the respondent's degree of responsibility within these project areas, it was learned that the data was heavily skewed toward higher level job classifications. In particular, one-quarter of the respondents specified their job classification as managers of software development. One-third indicated a job title of project leader, and the remaining indicated job classifications such as chief programmer, systems analyst, or software designer.

The following comments briefly summarize the more significant results of the curriculum survey:

1. The traditional software life cycle "waterfall model" (that is, serial, overlapping phases of planning, requirements, design, coding, testing, and maintenance) is very definitely applicable to the vast majority of both business and engineering software development efforts.

2. The course material currently required for successful completion of the MSDD degree is unquestionably relevant to the industrial work environment.

3. Students are generally able to apply the methods and techniques which they have been taught. However, in many cases, established management directives have acted to place limitations on the introduction of new methodologies. For example, while a chief programmer might easily be able to apply design methodologies, coding standards and guidelines, he or she might find difficulty in influencing the adoption of a new software cost estimating approach if there exists little management support for such a tool.

4. There is not a large number or variety of software tools currently in use. Text editors and language translators were the most frequently mentioned tools that are generally available in almost every development environment. It is perhaps not surprising that the use and

availability of software tools was most frequently mentioned by students involved with the development of business software applications. Problems frequently cited in connection with engineering software tools included that they were simply "too specialized" or that they "required too much labor to use them."

5. There were several recommendations made for additional technical courses and new areas of instruction. The most frequently requested new courses included:

- Artificial Intelligence
- Rapid Prototyping
- Communications and Networking
- Technical Personnel Management and Motivation

In addition, several new areas of instruction were requested. Included were topics such as: personal computer applications, programming environments, and hands on experience with software tools.

Finally, the majority of the students responding indicated a great deal of satisfaction with the revised curriculum. It was felt that it was especially beneficial to have instructors who had significant industrial software development experience. In general, the students indicated that the MSDD curriculum provided substantial preparation for their particular work environment.

Departmental Response

With the changes instituted in 1981, the MSDD program was substantially improved. Much of the overlap that existed between courses was eliminated, increased rigor was introduced into the program, and several new, more substantive courses were added to the curriculum. However, in an evolving and maturing discipline such as software engineering, change is inevitable. If the program is to remain current and applicable, new alternatives must be considered and new courses must be continually introduced into the curriculum.

In response to recent student requests, a course in artificial intelligence will be offered in the Spring, 1986, semester. Additional courses, as suggested by students, will be offered when appropriate faculty can be identified to teach such courses. Obviously, the introduction of new courses into any curriculum is largely a function of the availability of teaching expertise. However, additional software and/or hardware resources to use in support of these new courses must also be available. Consequently, the decision to teach or not to teach a new course, is almost always driven by economics. Certainly, the situation at TCU is no different from that found in many of the nation's universities.

The department is currently preparing the necessary paperwork required to become an affiliate with the Software Engineering Institute (SEI). Such an affiliation would pay great dividends, in that new ideas and teaching strategies may be directly derived from the Institute itself. With state of the art input being obtained from SEI, TCU's program, or any other, should find itself in an enhanced position to remain relevant.

Summary

The Master's of Software Design and Development curriculum at Texas Christian University provides students with the managerial, technical, and communicative skills that are required for successful software development and maintenance in all software environments. This curriculum, which has been in existence since 1978, has evolved over time and has been structured to be flexible to the changing needs of the software engineering profession. A recent student survey has confirmed that the program's approach, which is based upon the waterfall model of the software life cycle phases, and course content are unquestionably applicable to the industrial software development setting. As faculty, hardware, and software resources become available, new courses will be added to the curriculum in order to ensure that it remains relevant. The objective of the MSDD curriculum at Texas Christian University is now, and always has been, to provide a program of instruction that is adaptable to the changing needs of the professional software developer. Clearly, this program is helping to fill the critical need for skilled software engineers.

Acknowledgment

The authors wish to thank Dr. Robert R. Wier and Dr. David F. Addis for reading this paper and offering helpful comments concerning its contents.

APPENDIX I: The Original Curriculum

Requirements for Admission: Enrollment is limited. Admission to the program will be by application to AddRan College and approval by a Software Design and Development Admissions Committee. Both academic background and professional experience will be considered. It is expected that individuals with the following minimum qualifications will fill available spaces: 1) Admission to graduate study in AddRan College and either 2) B.S. in Computer Science and some software development experience, or 3) substantial job related experience in software development.

Degree Requirements: A 40-semester hour program with either 1) 34 hours of Software Design and Development (SDD 5143, 5193, 6104, 6113, 6123, 6133, 6142, 6153, 6163, 6193, 7113), plus 6 hours of approved electives or 2) 30 hours of Software Design and Development (without SDD 6104) plus 10 hours of electives. Both programs include an oral examination.

SDD 5143 - Introduction to Software Design and Development. Prerequisites: Admission to the Software Design and Development Program. May be taken by seniors majoring in computer science on a space available basis. Techniques of software design and development. The software life cycle. Methods for requirements definition, system specification, and design. Design concepts and methods. Improved programming methodologies. Methods for testing, validation, and quality control. Documentation. Software economics. Management of programming projects. Case histories. Organization of presentation materials. Preparation of graphics for presentation. Maximizing the use of multimedia. Writing style for software documents. Development documents — requirements, specifications, design, and implementation. Technical documentation. User documentation, automated aids. Reports. Proposals.

SDD 5193 - Communication Techniques in the Software Design and Development Environment. Prerequisites: SDD 6113. Organization of presentation materials. Preparation of graphics for presentation. Maximizing the use of multimedia. Writing style for software documents. Development documents — requirements, specifications, design, and implementation. Technical documentation. User documentation, automated aids. Reports. Proposals.

SDD 6104 - Overview of Computer Science. Prerequisites: SDD 5143. Technical overview of the software design and development environment. Computer systems architecture. Software structures such as compilers, operating systems, assemblers, file systems, and data management systems. Hardware/software tradeoffs. Storage management. System support packages.

SDD 6113 - Methodologies of Software Development. Prerequisites: SDD 6104 or permission. Structured programming. Modularization. Top-down development. Levels of abstraction. Stepwise refinement. Hardware, software, and user tradeoffs.

SDD 6123 - Requirements and Specifications for Software. Prerequisites: SDD 6113. Requirements analysis. Techniques for representing requirements. Specification development techniques. Specification languages. Automated aids. Laboratory will consist of case studies.

SDD 6133 - Software Design. Prerequisites: SDD 6123. Design process. Major design methods — composite/structured design, data structure driven design, structural analysis, and others. Evaluation of alternate designs. Automated design aids. Design documentation.

SDD 6142 - Software Design Laboratory. Prerequisites: Should be taken in parallel with SDD 6133. Case study designs using design methods contained in SDD 6133.

SDD 6153 - Management of Software Development. Prerequisites: SDD 5143. Organization context of software development. Analysis of life cycle costs. Scheduling and budgeting techniques. Specification and control of standards for products, processes, and equipment. Personnel development and utilization. Team techniques.

SDD 6163 - Economics of Software Development. Prerequisites: SDD 6153. Fundamentals of economics. Distribution of costs through software life cycle. Relative hardware/software costs. Economic analysis for decision making. Economic feasibility studies.

SDD 6193 - Effective Participation in Small Task Oriented Groups. Prerequisites: SDD 5143. Recognizing and supplying actions necessary for task oriented groups to achieve their objectives. Group maintenance roles. Group orienting roles. Task directed roles. Evaluative roles. Closure and action items. Systematic approaches to problem solving. Problem definition. Developing the solution domain. Means-end analysis. Provisions for feedback. Delineation of subproblems. Assignment of priorities. Time lines.

SDD 7113 - Software Implementation. Prerequisites: SDD 6133 and SDD 6142. Transfer of design to code. Testing techniques. Validation. Verification. Certification. Security. Case studies.

APPENDIX II: The Revised Curriculum

The Master of Software Design and Development program offers a professional graduate curriculum in the software development discipline. Software Design and Development requires that professional expertise, technical skill, and managerial ability be focused on the design, implementation, and maintenance of reliable and cost-effective software systems.

Requirements for Admission

1. Admission to graduate study in AddRan College, and
2. Appropriate level of technical competence demonstrated by an appropriate transcript or resume, and
3. Two or more years of experience in software systems development, and
4. Knowledge of assembler language programming (e.g. CoSc 1603), and
5. Programming skill in using a block structured programming language such as Pascal, PL/I, Ada or Algol, and
6. An undergraduate course in data structures or its equivalent.

A student may resolve requirements (5) and (6) by successfully completing SDD 6104, if items (1) through (4) are otherwise satisfactory for admission.

Degree Requirements: A 36-semester hour program (40 hours if SDD 6104 is necessary) with at least 27 hours of SDD courses and 9 hours of electives (which must be approved by the Computer Science Department in advance of enrolling). SDD 6104 is required of students entering the SDD program without qualifications (5) and (6) listed above.

The following courses are required of all students to complete the degree: SDD 5143, SDD 6113, SDD 6123, SDD 6153, SDD 6163, SDD 6173, SDD 6183, SDD 7113, and SDD 7123. Prior to scheduling the final oral, each student must have submitted a paper, based on current coursework or related areas, to an appropriate journal for publication. Each student must pass a final comprehensive oral during the last semester of coursework.

SDD 5143 - Introduction to Software Design and Development. Prerequisites: Admission to the SDD program. May be taken with SDD 6104. An introduction to software design and development, oriented towards the software development life cycle phases. The need for discipline in software development is established, using software cost relationships and case studies. An overview of techniques for systems analysis, configuration management, software quality assurance, and maintenance activities provides insight to all activities required for successful software development. An overview of communication skills, economics of software, and project management is also included. (Text used: R. S. Pressman, *Software Engineering: A Practitioner's Approach*, McGraw-Hill, 1982).

SDD 6013 - Ada Design and Development. Prerequisites: SDD 6113. The impact of the new DOD standard language on the design and development of software systems will be studied. Particular attention will be given to the development of software systems in Ada. The evolution of Ada, and its standardization and current status will be studied. Ada language data types, program structuring, the Ada support environment (APSE), and systems programming in Ada will be emphasized, including program development. (Text used: G. Booch, *Software Engineering with Ada*, Benjamin/Cummings, 1983).

SDD 6023 - Advanced Topics in Systems Software. Prerequisites: Permission of instructor and SDD 6113, SDD 6153, and SDD 6173. Advanced topics of current interest in systems software, such as: Networking and Distributed Systems, Performance Evaluation, Object Oriented Architecture (e.g., iAPX432), etc. Students will study current literature. (May be repeated for credit when topic changes.)

SDD 6033 - Computer Facilities Management. Prerequisites: SDD 5143. A comprehensive study of problems associated with management of data processing and computer facilities. Particular emphasis is placed on problems of cost effectiveness, machine configuration, personnel and human factors, security, systems planning, facilities requirements, and office automation.

SDD 6043 - Software Quality Assurance and Metrics. Prerequisite: SDD 6123. The impact of software quality assurance upon the software life cycle development phases will be studied. Particular software testing philosophies such as top-down, bottom-up, and sandwich will be compared. Software metrics for reliability, flexibility, maintainability, performance, resources, and structure will be discussed, as well as methodologies for the collection of software metric data. Finally, software metrics will be linked to the requirements of software quality assurance and reliability. A summary of industry-wide software metric data will be presented. (Texts used: T. Gilb, *Software Metrics*, Winthrop, 1977; B. Beizer, *Software System Testing and Quality Assurance*, Reinholt, 1984).

SDD 6053 - Security and Privacy. Prerequisites: SDD 6183. This course covers the technical, legal and ethical aspects of security and privacy of information. Technical issues covered include encryption techniques, database security, and implementation of protection schemes in operating systems and programming languages.

SDD 6104 - Programming Structures. Prerequisites: Admission to the MSDD program. Introduction to block structure languages including scope rules, recursion, pointer variables, and control constructs. Study of data structures including arrays, stacks, linked lists, trees, graphs, and files. Examples are selected from operating systems, compilers, and systems programming. A number of programming assignments in Pascal, C, or Ada will be made. (Text used: G.M. Schneider and S.C. Bruell, *Advanced Programming and Problem Solving with Pascal*, John Wiley & Sons, 1981.)

SDD 6113 - Modern Software Requirements and Design Techniques. Prerequisites: SDD 5143. A comprehensive study in state-of-the-art techniques for design and development of software systems. Automated tools for requirements, design, and documentation are used in a comparative study of functional decomposition, structured analysis, PSL/PSA, Higher Order Software, SAMM, SREM and rapid prototyping techniques. Emphasis is on contrasting the application of different methods for a selected methodology. Appropriate methodologies will be applied to sample problems. Structured design, Petri-nets and Warnier Orr methods will be compared to distinguish applications of each methodology. (Texts used: K.T. Orr, *Structured Requirements Definitions*, Orr & Associates, 1981; L.J. Peters, *Software Design Methods & Techniques*, YOURDON Press, 1981.)

SDD 6123 - Applied Design, Programming, and Testing Techniques. Prerequisites: SDD 6113. Emphasis on object oriented design, Jackson methodology, levels of abstraction, top-down, bottom-up, sandwich, Nassi-Schneiderman, Hamilton-Zeldin and SDDL methods of design. Software quality assurance and testing methods to measure cohesiveness and robustness are studied along with static and dynamic testing concepts. Automated testing methods and software maintenance considerations with respect to reduction of life cycle cost are also studied. (Texts used: G.J. Myers, *The Art of Software Testing*, John Wiley & Sons, 1979; G. Parikh and N. Zvegintzov, *Tutorial on Software Maintenance*, IEEE, 1983.)

SDD 6153 - Management of Software Development. Prerequisites: SDD 5143. A complete methodology for managing the planning, design, construction, evaluation, documentation distribution, and maintenance of software products with emphasis on top-down design, management by objective, configuration management and motivation. Human factors related to quality, productivity metrics, chief programmer teams, egoless programming, democratic teams, structured walkthroughs and formal inspections are investigated. Automated project management tools are used to enhance and simulate a real-world environment for project management. (Texts used: T. DeMarco, *Controlling Software Projects*, YOURDON Press, 1982; R.C Gunther, *Management Methodology for Software Product Engineering*, Wiley Interscience, 1978.)

SDD 6163 - Economics of Software Development. Prerequisites: SDD 6153. An in-depth study of software life cycle cost distribution with major emphasis of Boehm's Software Economics model COCOMO; the parametric models PRICE S, JENSEN, and SLIM are also covered. The work of Aron, Brooks, Baker, Wolverton, Parr and Putnam will also be analyzed to cover the full spectrum of software economics. Individual projects will include application of PRICE S/SLIM automated parametric models to industry problems. (Text used: B.W. Boehm, *Software Engineering Economics*, Prentice-Hall, 1981.)

SDD 6173 - Computer Systems Architecture. Prerequisites: SDD 5143 and SDD 6104. The logical organization, conceptual structure, and functional behavior of computers are studied from the user viewpoint. First, the CPU, I/O devices, and memory components of a fundamental uniprocessor are presented. Secondly, a multiprocessor configuration is established using the fundamental uniprocessor as a building block. Distributed processing and commercially implemented networks such as DECnet, Ethernet , USnet, SNA, and the Open Systems

Interconnection Model established by ISO will be compared. Telecommunications will be addressed. Finally, the criteria for evaluation, selection, and performance measurement of a computer system that is part of a larger product will be studied. The topics include the advantages and disadvantages of uniprocessor and multiprocessor configurations, reliability, maintainability, software support, throughput analysis, and rapid prototype modeling. (Text used: D.L. Kuck, *Structure of Computers and Computations*, Wiley & Sons, 1978.)

SDD 6183 - Database and Information Management Systems. Prerequisites: SDD 6173. The requirements analysis and design criteria of database and information management systems will be studied. The impacts of the operational environment, quality control, security, human/system interface requirements, system specification and design will be investigated. Hierarchical and relational databases will be studied, along with commercially available databases and information management systems. Design techniques for optimization, application to large databases, and restructuring existing databases will be discussed. The design review methodologies of MCAUTO and IBM will be considered. (Texts used: D.M. Kroenke, *DATABASE PROCESSING: Fundamentals, Design, Implementation*, SRA, 1983; W.H. Inmon, *Effective Data Base Design*, Prentice-Hall, 1981.)

SDD 6193 - Effective Communication in Small Groups. Prerequisites: SDD 5143. Technical communication requires the exchange of information in an accurate, concise, unambiguous, and timely manner. In software development, technical communication takes a variety of forms: interaction with existing and prospective customers, oral and written progress reports to management, memos and presentations to colleagues, proposals, requirements documents, specifications, design documentation, code documentation, formal and informal project reviews, test plans, test results, user's manuals, training sessions; and maintenance reports must all be prepared and delivered in the course of a software life cycle. (Text used: R.W. Griffin, *Task Design: An Integrative Approach*, Scott-Foresman, 1982.)

SDD 7113 - Software Implementation Project I. Prerequisites: SDD 6123, SDD 6153, and SDD 6183. This course is the first of a contiguous two-semester sequence which applies the techniques of modern software development to actual problem solutions. Group projects will be assigned, based in part on the student's professional background. The projects will require the development of operational software, emphasizing group development processes to accomplish feasibility analysis, costing, planning, requirements specifications and preliminary design of the assigned project.

SDD 7123 - Software Implementation Project II. Prerequisites: SDD 7113. Preliminary design of the project assigned in SDD 7113 is reviewed and the detailed design is executed. A critical design review is performed and the implementation, testing and documentation is completed as a group process. Acceptance testing is accomplished to ensure that the software satisfies the user specification requirements.

APPENDIX III: The Student Questionnaire

Part A: You and Your Work
1. Your name:_____
2. Your mailing address:_____
3. Day telephone number:_____
4. Night telephone number:_____
5. Your current employer:_____
6. Approximately how many software professionals are at your employer's site?_____
7. Your job title:_____
8. Briefly describe your software application.
9. What is your particular involvement with this software application?

Part B: THE TCU MSDD CURRICULUM
1. Is the traditional software life cycle "waterfall model" applicable to your work? In what respect?
2. Has the course material you have learned been relevant to your work?
3. Are you able to apply the techniques and methods of software engineering that you have learned to your work?

4. What automated software tools do you regularly use? What is your evaluation of these tools?

5. What specific changes would you recommend in the content of the MSDD courses?

6. What new technologies do you think should be included in the MSDD course of study?

7. Please describe your overall opinion of the MSDD curriculum with respect to the "real-world" of software development.

The Software Engineering First Degree at Imperial College, London

M.M. Lehman
Imperial College of Science and Technology

Abstract. This brief paper, with its appendix, provides a broad view of the four year Master of Engineering course at Imperial College. A more complete description, including fuller syllabi will, it is expected, be available at the workshop.

British University Course Structure

Undergraduate courses in British universities differ from those in the United States in a number of ways. Two such differences in particular must be brought to the attention of participants at the Software Engineering Education Workshop.

First, in the great majority of British universities, degree courses are largely predefined. Students will have, at most, to select only a small number of options; choices that permit a degree of specialization within the selected subject area — computing science or software engineering in the case of this department. Thus while a student must pass examinations in the courses that he or she attends, the concepts of major and minor subjects with independent course "credits" that are summed, does not apply.

The second major difference arises from the fact that British first degree courses, awarding a Bachelor degree, are generally of three year duration. Some years ago, however, the engineering community realized that the length of such courses did not allow time to provide both the breadth and depth of knowledge and understanding required by an engineering executive in the world of today. Four year courses, termed "Dainton" courses, were, therefore, introduced to permit the exposure of the potentially, most capable students to management and related topics as well as to a period of industrial experience.

Four Year Advanced Engineering Course

More recently, following publication of the Finniston report, [33] four year courses have been set up in engineering departments at selected British universities. These courses include a significant amount of advanced technical and management material. The treatment of topics, particularly in the final year, is similarly advanced.

As a reflection of the standard achieved (and also to make them competitive with an alternative educational route comprising a three year bachelor's degree course followed by a one year specialist master's course), the four year courses now generally award a master's degree (M. Eng) as a first degree. Detailed regulations differ somewhat between universities. Some will permit the switching of qualified students from the three to the four year course (or vice versa) at the end of the first or second year. Optional completion of a four year course at the end of three years with the award of a bachelor's degree is, however, in general not permitted.

Four year courses are, generally, more demanding than the three year courses; entry conditions are, therefore, more stringent and are clearly intended to attract the best students. At the output end of the higher education process, graduates may be expected to advance rapidly once they enter industry, and ultimately reach senior management or executive positions, by virtue of both greater ability and of knowledge, understanding and experience gained.

The Imperial College Software Engineering Course

Imperial College has been running an undergraduate course awarding a BSc (Eng) degree in computing science for some twelve years. The annual intake is about 100 students. Some years ago it was decided that developments in software engineering and the importance of this topic in the world of tomorrow suggested a need for a specialist course awarding a software engineering degree. Moreover, the wealth of material, much of it advanced, needing to be included, suggested that such a course should take the form of one of the new four year courses.

Such a course is now running — the first intake of 10 students in their second year and the second intake of 16 students in their first year. The first students will be graduating in 1988.

The first two years of this four year course, which will award a master's degree in software engineering, are identical to the first two years of the computing science course, making a switch at the end of that time possible though not, in general, encouraged. That is, all the Department of Computing's undergraduates go through the first two years together. The divergence starts in the third year, although some individual courses are still shared, being offered to three year Computing Science students as options.

The Course Structure

The appendix provides outlines of the course structure and content. Detailed syllabi of the individual lecture series are available from the author.

From the description in the appendix it will also be seen that students spend a total of six months gaining practical experience in industry which, while considered too little, appears to provide the best compromise, under existing time and other constraints, between provision of material considered essential, additional material which is, at the very least, desirable, and practical experience of the industrial software development environment and of the application of what has been studied.

The descriptions included in the appendix do no more than provide a top level indication of the topics included in the course. A lecture series, as identified by title, may range from, say 11 to 44 hours and will be supported by half that number of tutorial hours. Additional time is set aside for laboratories and projects. More precise syllabi, down to three levels of detail, are available, although in the final analysis the actual content of a course will be decided by the lecturer. Detailed syllabi, even if not precise in their descriptions of ultimate course content, do permit better judgement about the amount of time to be allocated to each lecture and assist the process and control of lecture coordination and the avoidance of overlap.

The amount of material one would like to include in the course greatly exceeds the time available, in terms of both potential breadth and depth. It is believed that the material presented here represents an acceptable starting point for a new academic discipline. It is certain that the course will change and evolve as a consequence both of experience and of evolution of the discipline.

Imperial Software Technology Ltd.

In connection with the provision of industrial exposure and experience, it is appropriate to mention Imperial Software Technology Ltd, (IST), a company set up in 1982 by the College in partnership with the National Westminster Bank PLC, the Plessey Company PLC and PA International. IST is already achieving a leadership position in the programming environment and software tools industry. Its conception arose, at least in part, from the perceived need by the software engineering course designers to provide a realistic and advanced industrial software technology working environment providing a base for realistic student industrial exposure and experience.

To fulfill this role effectively, such an organization must be an independent, technically and commercially successful organization with clients, products and services in the software technology field. Only then can it provide facilities, support and the technical and managerial environment to permit student experience and exposure that reflects the real world of software development. Only in this way can it convincingly demonstrate to the observing students (and to others) the industrial and commercially successful application of the methods, techniques and tools studied in their courses.

The role of the company in software engineering education was perceived to be somewhat analogous, though in detail quite different, from the role of teaching hospitals in the education of medical students. Whether this will be achieved in practice and how it will all work must await actual experience. This will commence with the entry of the first students to industry, IST and elsewhere, in the spring of 1987.

The sad fact is that software engineering today is still largely pragmatic. Its relevance appears only in projects of such dimension that they cannot be adequately reproduced in an academic environment. To produce graduates of real immediate value to industry and who can transfer advanced software technology to industry requires universities to provide knowledge, understanding and insight into the technology, its mathematical foundations, theory, processes, methods and tools in the context of an industrial, profit seeking, resource constrained, client demanding, environment. Academic courses in software engineering must be complemented by open-eyed experience. It is believed that involvement that provides this can be achieved and, at the same time, while profitable to the student, the employer and the employer's clients. Though IST has a wider mission and charter it will also serve an an instrument to prove this.

Summary

This brief paper, with its appendix, serves as an introduction to the four year master's degree course in Software Engineering at Imperial College. A more complete description, including fuller syllabi is available. To obtain a copy please write to the author at the address supplied in the list of participants.

Appendix

Four Year Course in Software Engineering

Course Structure

Year 1, 2:   Common with Years 1, 2 of BSc (Eng) Course
summary follows

Year 3   <u>Terms 1,2:</u>   Courses as listed, associated Lab Work
and Group Project

Students take Compulsory Courses[1]
totaling x modules

and (9 - x) Optional Courses[2]
each of 1 module[3]

<u>Term 3:</u>   Industrial Placement (April-September)
(approximately 6 months)

Assessment by course work and tests only.

Year 4:   <u>Terms 1, 2:</u>   Courses as listed

Students take Compulsory Courses[2]
totaling y modules[3]

and (9 - y) Optional Courses[2]
each of 1 module[3]

<u>Terms 2, 3:</u>   Individual Project - may be industry based
Assessment by course work, laboratory work and examinations at the
beginning of the summer term.

A Module comprises 22 hours of lectures, together with associated
tutorials.[3]

Courses are listed on the attached sheets. Over two years, the selection of Optional Courses must include at least <u>one</u> course from each of the four subject areas (Technologies, Systems, Applications, Environment).

---

[1]Classification as Compulsory or Optional not yet finalized but $3 \leq x,y \leq 6$

Three and Four Year Courses

Part I Courses

110: Computing Systems I

120: Programming

140: Theory of Computing I

141: Logic

145: Mathematical Methods

161: Integrated Laboratory

Part II Courses

210: Computing Systems II

220: Advanced Program Design

221: Language Processors

230: Computing Applications

240: Theory of Computing II

245: Statistics

261: Integrated Laboratory

Software Engineering Degree: Part III Courses

<u>Compulsory Courses:</u> Provisionally 66 hours lectures

SE311 Software Engineering Process

SE312 Calculus of Software Development

SE313 Database Technology

SE314 Introduction to Macro Economics and Financial Management

SE315 Introduction to Management

Provisionally Optional Courses:[2] Each one, 22 hours lectures

Technologies

SE321 Functional Programming Technology I

SE322 Artificial Intelligence Technology

SE323 Compiler Technology

Systems

SE331 Computer Networks

SE332 Object Oriented Architecture

SE333 Interface and Microprocessor Technology

SE334 Performance Analysis of Computer Systems

Applications

SE341 Graphics

SE342 Silicon Compilation

SE343 Applied Mathematics

Environment

SE351 Industrial Sociology

SE352 Government Law and Industry

SE353 Humanities

---

[2]Up to three of the courses classified here as Optional may become Compulsory

Software Engineering Degree: Part IV Courses

Title

Compulsory Courses: Provisionally 66 hours lectures

SE412 Methodology of Software Development

SE413 Language Definition and Design

SE414 Programming Support Environments

SE415 Standards, Ethical and Legal Considerations

Provisionally Optional Courses:[3] Each one, 22 hours lectures

Technologies

SE421 Advanced Logic

SE422 Theorem Proving

SE423 Concurrent Computation

SE424 Human-Computer Interaction

SE425 Expert Systems Technology

SE426 Functional Programming Technology II

Systems

SE431 Advanced Operating Systems

SE432 Parallel Architecture

SE433 Distributed Systems

SE434 VLSI

---

[3]Up to three of the courses classified here as Optional may become Compulsory

Applications

SE441 Robotics

SE442 Computing in Engineering

SE443 Natural Language Processing

Environment

SE451 Micro-Economic Concepts

SE452 Industrial Relations

SE453 Innovation and Technical Change

SE454 Humanities

The Master of Software Engineering Program at Seattle University after Six Years

Everald E. Mills
Seattle University

Abstract. In 1977-78 Seattle University initiated a series of discussions with representatives from local business and industry. In those discussions, software engineering emerged as a critical area of need for specialized educational programs. As a result of this cooperative effort, Seattle University established the Master of Software Engineering [MSE] program. This program is now in its seventh year of operation and has produced four graduating classes. Rather than preparing students to enter the software engineering profession, the MSE program is a way for those already engaged in software engineering to improve their educational background and technical skills. The program is intended to cover both the technical and management aspects of software engineering. This paper discusses the philosophy, objectives, and implementation of the program.

Introduction

It has now been nearly twenty years since the first use of the term software engineering [71]. These first two decades have seen much activity and even some progress in this exciting new discipline. During this time, a generally acceptable list of activities and responsibilities involved in software engineering seems to have emerged. Still, a single, precise and universally acceptable definition of software engineering has not.

This is clear from even a brief perusal of current classified advertisements, which indicate that many jobs in the software development world are being labeled as software engineering positions or activities, and that employers are eager to recruit software engineers. However, the detailed specifications for these various positions point up the sometimes significant differences in interpretation of the term software engineer.

The inability to establish a precise, universally acceptable definition of software engineering has especially hampered the development of educational programs in this area [63]. Thus, even though software engineering has now long been identified as a complex activity for which some sort of specialized educational program is necessary, few such programs have been developed. One notable exception is the graduate program in software engineering at Seattle University, Seattle, Washington.

Seattle University is an independent urban university committed to the concept of providing rigorous professional educational programs, but within a sound liberal arts background. In 1977-78, the University initiated a series of discussions with representatives from local business and industry. In those discussions, software engineering emerged as a critical area of need for specialized educational programs. Leading software professionals were invited to assist in the development of such a program at Seattle University. Larry Peters and Leon Stucki, both employees of the Boeing Company at that time, were heavily involved in this effort.

The result of this cooperative effort was the establishment of the Master of Software Engineering[MSE] program at Seattle University. As originally established, the curriculum was similar to that described by Peters and Stucki in their 1978 ACM Conference paper [2,3]. The curriculum has subsequently been modified slightly, and is described in more detail below. This program is now in its seventh year of operation and has produced four graduating classes, starting in 1982. In the following, the philosophy, objectives, and implementation of the program are discussed.

Philosophy and Objectives of the MSE Program

The Seattle University MSE program is described as one specific response to the need for educational programs in software engineering. It is not necessarily presented as a model curriculum but rather as a response to the particular needs of the computing community in which it resides.

First of all, the Seattle University program addresses itself to professionals working in software development activities. This choice of audience for the program has two important immediate consequences, as follows.

1. Such students are typically currently employed, and wish to continue working while pursuing a graduate degree.
2. Classes for such students must be held in the evenings to avoid conflicts with work schedules.

Obviously, other audiences, such as more conventional undergraduate students [BSE degree], or recent graduates with no required work experience, could have been targeted. At the time the MSE program was established, however, the need for additional educational training for those already involved in software engineering was identified as an extremely pressing one, and it was selected as the main thrust of the Seattle University program.

Secondly, having established the professional software experience requirement, it is probably best to regard the MSE program not as a preparation to enter the software engineering profession, but rather as a way for those already engaged in software engineering activities to improve their educational background and technical skills. The prior experience required of all MSE students must include extensive programming experience, involving at least some use of contemporary languages such as Pascal as well as involvement in other phases of the software development life cycle.

It has often been noted that software engineering involves an extremely broad range of activities and responsibilities. These activities and responsibilities involve both technical and management issues as well as complex combinations of both. The goal of the MSE program is to prepare its graduates to cope more effectively with this broad range of activities and responsibilities. Specifically, the graduates should be able to:

1. Engage effectively and productively in the various phases of the software development life cycle, including requirements specification, analysis, design, implementation, testing and maintenance.

2. Understand, select among, and use state-of-the-art methodologies and techniques.

3. Manage effectively a project of non-trivial size (at least 4- 6 people over 1-2 years)

4. Communicate effectively, both orally and in writing, with various parties involved in the typical software project: users, analysts, programmers, managers, etc.

5. Recognize, learn, and evaluate new concepts, techniques, and methodologies for possible use in future projects.

As indicated previously, the MSE program is intended to cover both the technical and management aspects of software engineering. Although some students will prefer the management aspects over the technical, or vice versa, a minimum level of expertise in both areas is essential for all students. Beyond this level, students may take elective courses which emphasize either the technical or management aspects.

The MSE Curriculum

Basis and Required Background

Working software professionals have been identified as the target group for the MSE program. Beyond that, the program is intended for the members of this group most capable of benefiting from such a graduate program and of making continued contributions to the field after completion of the degree. Thus, the requirements for application to the MSE program can be summarized as follows:

1. A minimum of two years professional software experience. Extensive use of and/or experience with software does not satisfy this requirement. The work experience must have had the production of software as its primary goal.

2. A baccalaureate degree in a quantitative discipline. In this requirement, computer science is recognized as the essential scientific basis for software engineering and is the preferred degree background. However, many practicing professionals do not have computer science degrees for various reasons. Degrees in other disciplines, such as the various areas of engineering, the sciences and mathematics are acceptable. In any case, a required minimum of expertise in computer science is insured via the foundation courses described below.

3. Graduate Record Exam (GRE) or Graduate Management Admissions Test (GMAT) Scores. Students must demonstrate reasonable probability of success in the graduate program via satisfactory scores in one of these standard exams.

MSE Courses

In the following, the MSE curriculum is described as it currently exists. Of course, individual courses have undergone the usual evolutionary process, and the curriculum as a whole has been recently revised. Nevertheless, the basic format is similar to that proposed by Peters and Stucki [92], as well as by others such as Freeman and Wasserman [41].

The MSE coursework can be classified into the following areas, each of which is discussed in more detail below:

Foundation Courses

ESW 500.   Information Structures and Algorithms

ESW 501.   Computer Systems Principles

Core Courses (24 credits)

ESW 508.   Technical Communication

ESW 510.   Software Systems Analysis

ESW 512.   System Design Methodology

ESW 514.   Programming Methodology

ESW 516.   Software Quality Assurance

ESW 518.   Software Metrics

ESW 531.   Software Project Management

ESW 543.   Formal Methods

Elective Courses (12 credits)

ESW 533.	System Procurement Contract Acquisition and Administration
ESW 541.	Database Systems
ESW 551.	Distributed Computing
ESW 553.	Artificial Intelligence
ESW 560.	Human Factors in Computing
ESW 562.	Data Security and Privacy
ESW 564.	Computer Graphics
ESW 566.	Real Time Systems
BUS 507.	Organization Behavior
BUS 580.	Organization Structure and Theory
BUS 582.	Decision Theory

... and other appropriate courses from the MBA program.

Software Engineering Project (9 credits)

| ESW 585, 586 and 587. | Software Engineering Project 1, 2, 3. |

A. Foundation Courses

Computer science is recognized as the basic underlying science for software engineering. Thus, students must demonstrate a minimum competency at least equivalent to the courses ESW 500 and ESW 501. If students are admitted without this background, they must complete these courses. ESW 500 is essentially a junior-senior level data structures and analysis of algorithms course. ESW 501 is not directly comparable to any single undergraduate course in most curricula. It includes a wide range of topics such as computer architecture, programming languages, operating systems, and hardware/software relationships. These two courses are not counted in the 45 credits required for the MSE degree.

B. Core Courses

These courses are intended to address all of the major areas of activity of software engineering. The importance of communication skills is addressed by making it the first course in the required curriculum (ESW 508) as well as by requiring various forms of communication throughout the MSE program. These include written expositions, as well as oral presentations, with appropriate visual supporting materials, for example. Some core courses, such as ESW 510, 512, 514 cover the more technical areas, while courses such as ESW 531 are more directed toward the management aspects. However, there is no attempt to artificially separate the technical from the management concepts. Management and/or technical issues may be discussed as required in any given class, depending upon the orientation and background of the students and instructor. ESW 518 is an interesting case in point. Although the course could be taught from a strictly technical viewpoint, the current approach is to teach about metrics and their use in the management of software projects. The students are required to have previously completed the ESW 531 Software Project Management course.

C. Elective Courses

Students are required to complete 12 credits in elective courses. Here they may extend their technical background, by taking courses such as artificial intelligence or database design, or they may opt to take additional management oriented courses, either in software engineering or in the regular MBA program.

D. Software Engineering Project

All MSE students must complete this three quarter sequence (9 credits) involving a software project. These projects are group projects, typically involving 4 to 6 students. The objective is to carry out a software development project from start to finish, beginning with a brief statement of the project requirements and (hopefully) ending with a finished, marketable software product. This is very much a student project, managed and carried out by the students themselves, with overall direction by a faculty advisor. During the course of the project, students are required to participate in the management of the project as well as the technical tasks and communications/presentations required. Formal reviews are required, usually coinciding with the major phases of the software development cycle. These reviews also involve the faculty advisor and/or user/customer for the software. The software project may originate from within the university or from outside. If from within, it may result from a request within the department, or from some other academic or administrative unit in the university. Projects originating outside the university may arise from student suggestions, or from requests from business or industrial firms. Selection of appropriate projects is extremely important, because of their central role in the completion of students' degree requirements.

Although the software projects may involve almost any type of software system, it is essential that certain requirements be met. Among the most important of these are the following :

Project Size. Project teams consist of 4 to 6 students. Each student is expected to work on the project an average of 10 to 12 hours per week, over the life of the project, which is three quarters or approximately nine months. Also, during the approximately three months preceding the project, students are required to do some preliminary familiarization and preparation for initiation of the project in earnest, beginning in the fall quarter. This is usually done at a fairly relaxed pace but is essential for the success of most projects. Thus, projects selected must be of appropriate size to be possible to complete by the student team in the time allowed.

Project Complexity. The effort required to complete any project depends on both the size and the complexity of the system to be implemented. Thus, the complexity of the system must also be considered in the selection process.

Required Schedule. The projects are constrained to the academic year time frame, with initial identification of the projects done in the spring quarter, and the actual project work done in the following three quarters (September through June). Thus, it must be possible to complete the project within this time frame, and the user/customer must be amenable to it as well.

Project Support. The project must, of course, also be within the scope of the total resources of the department, including hardware and software available to it. Projects originating outside the university often require facilities not possessed by the university. Such projects are still possible, if the requesting agency is willing to provide this additional support to the project, and this has been done quite successfully in some projects. In addition to computing resources, the projects also require significant commitments of time and effort from the user/customer agency. This commitment will primarily be in the form of extensive communications with the project team and in participating in the required project reviews. Since these are student projects, which can conceivably fail, the customer must make this commitment knowing that they do not have an absolute guarantee of a finished product.

The software project is seen as the capstone of the MSE degree program. It provides an opportunity to focus and use all of the principles and techniques covered in the coursework. For these projects, "real-life" tasks have usually been chosen, rather than mere academic exercises. Previous projects include accounts payable, computer-aided instruction, computer graphics and library circulation systems [64]. Projects currently underway include an artificial intelligence expertise transfer system, robot programming language and hardware simulation software. In general, the results of these projects have been quite good, even though not all projects have produced acceptable software systems. The results clearly demonstrate that such projects can be carried out in a real world atmosphere and still be controlled to provide a useful final learning experience.

As indicated previously, the typical student in the MSE program is fully employed in the software business. Under these circumstances, the MSE program should require three years to complete. The recommended schedule for completion is as follows:

YEAR	FALL	WINTER	SPRING
1	508, 510	512, 531	514, 516
2	518, elective	543, elective	elective, elective
3	585	586	587
	(Software Project.....................)		

Table 1. Recommended Completion Schedule

Implementation Considerations

The MSE curriculum at Seattle University was first implemented in the fall of 1979. As originally implemented, the curriculum included a first course, ESW 505 Introduction to Software Engineering. As experience was gained with the program, and the qualifications of entering students increased over the first five years of the program, this course was no longer felt to be necessary or desirable. It was dropped from the program in 1984. Thus, the curriculum in use is that described in the preceding section.

A number of difficult issues complicate the implementation of a program such as the MSE degree. Among these are :

1. Initial placement of the academic unit in the university
2. Faculty/staffing considerations
3. Academic/industry balance
4. Computing resources
5. Curricular/text materials
6. Rapid rate of technological change

In the following, each of these issues will be discussed with regard to the Seattle University program.

1. Initial placement of the software engineering program in the university. Although this author was not personally involved with the program at its beginning, it is my understanding that this was not a significant problem at Seattle University. The program was initiated by Fr. Francis Wood, S.J., then Chair of the Electrical Engineering Department. The university includes a School of Science and Engineering, in which electrical engineering is housed, and the new program was also established in that school but as a separate graduate program. The fact that the founder was an engineer, and the new program was a graduate program rather than an undergraduate program, probably eased the problem of where to place the unit. In other environments, the placement of software engineering within the university, or even the recognition of software engineering as an academic program, may arouse considerable controversy.

2. Faculty/Staffing. The acquisition and retention of qualified faculty is one of the most severe problems to be faced in implementing a software engineering program. Even among computer oriented disciplines, those suitable for software engineering positions are among the most attracted to and sought after by industry. Industry can offer more attractive salaries and more sophisticated and exciting computing environments. Even with regard to the selection of faculty, questions abound. What qualifications should prospective faculty members have? What disciplinary background is required? What about industrial experience? Management experience? All of these questions are difficult and are further complicated by a dearth of qualified applicants of any type. At Seattle University, the first priority has been placed upon recruiting PhD's in computer science, with extensive professional experience in software — a nearly impossible task.

At the present time, the regular MSE faculty at Seattle University is part of a faculty group that supports both computer science and software engineering. This group includes a total of eight full-time regular faculty, three of whom are committed almost entirely to software engineering. In addition, some of the other regular faculty members occasionally teach software engineering courses. At best, however, this regular support totals about four full time equivalent (FTE) faculty positions. This is clearly not an adequate number to staff all of the courses required for the MSE program. In addition, it is practically impossible for three or four people to cover all of the areas of expertise required. Thus, it has always been part of the implementation philosophy of the program to use adjunct faculty persons from local business and industry to supplement the regular faculty — both in number and in areas of expertise.

Thus, approximately six courses per year are covered by adjunct faculty from local industry who have expertise in particular areas such as computer graphics or real time systems. This allows the coverage of a broad range of elective courses in an effective manner with a relatively small faculty group.

3. Academic/Industry Balance. An appropriate balance must be struck between the underlying theoretical and conceptual bases of software engineering and the practical everyday demands of the industry workplace. This is a major issue for almost every course in the MSE curriculum. The overall approach has been to attempt to present basic concepts and fundamental principles, and then to relate these to the practical conditions of the business and industrial environment. A good example of this is the analysis and design courses. Attempts are made to cover the basic concepts as embodied in a number of major methodologies. In addition, students are required to use at least one methodology extensively in the program. The emphasis is upon trying to teach concepts of lasting value, plus the ability to learn and adapt to new concepts and methodologies which may be encountered in the future. Although the university remains the best place to teach underlying formal concepts in a reasonably short time, there are other skills and techniques that can better be learned in an on-the-job setting. Furthermore, in the computing industry especially, there are conditions and situations in the real world that are impossible to duplicate in the university setting. This is true for a number of reasons, including costs and the fact that no standardized industrial software environment exists. The key then to some degree of success in this area is to recognize these different areas and concentrate our efforts on those most suited to the formal setting.

4. Computing Resources. A successful program in software engineering must, of course, have access to computing resources at least comparable to that which students are likely to confront on the job. Computing resources at Seattle University have been fairly limited to systems such as an HP 3000/48, VAX 11/750 and IBM PC or PC/XT systems. However, it has been possible to augment these facilities significantly, especially in the software project courses, via the use of equipment provided by the project sponsors (outside business or industrial firms). However, as more sophisticated software development environments come into general use, it will continue to be difficult to provide the computing environment necessary for a viable program.

5. Curricular/Text Materials. There still exist very few programs offering software engineering degrees. Thus, there are few software engineering curricula, and many courses in our curriculum for which it is difficult to find good texts or other curricular materials. This results in a number of effects, including placing a tremendous burden upon faculty members to develop their own course materials. The resulting strain often results in lowered course quality and/or the loss of qualified faculty members due to burnout. Although this situation is improving, it will continue to be an important consideration. This also exacerbates the general problem of attracting and retaining qualified faculty members. The teaching job is simply that much more difficult, and a good faculty member is correspondingly more difficult to replace, when good text/course materials are not available.

6. Rapid Rate of Technological Change. The rapid rate of change in the basic technological environment for software engineering will continue to present tremendous problems for the implementation of academic programs. It intensifies most of the problems already listed. It makes it even more difficult to find good faculty members — and difficult for good faculty members to remain so. It makes it more difficult to provide adequate computing environments — and difficult to maintain those, once available. It is probably the single most important factor which both makes software engineering challenging and exciting — and at the same time overwhelming and discouraging. Faced with limited resources, there is no obvious way to resolve this problem. Possibly the most important part of dealing with it is to try to recognize those aspects of change which are so essential that they must be dealt with — and ignore, if we must, those which are not so essential.

Results of the MSE Program

The Seattle University MSE program began in the fall of 1979. The first expected graduation date was then June 1982, and four classes have graduated to date. Approximately 33 students have been admitted each fall since 1979. The number of students graduated each year since 1982 has averaged 22. Thus, approximately two-thirds of the students admitted have completed the degree program. However, the performance of classes to date has varied considerably.

As in many other graduate programs, MSE students are required to complete the degree requirements within six years after the coursework is begun. Thus, it is reasonable to expect that almost all students who intend to finish the program will have done so within six years of their admission. Only the two classes admitted in 1979 and 1980 will have encountered this six-year limitation by the end of this year. Thus, probably all or most of those students who will finish the program will do so by June 1986. The time required by students in the various entering classes to complete the degree program is shown in the following table.

Number Completing Degree After n Years:
(Percentage of number originally admitted)

Year Admitted	Number Admitted	n = 3	4	5	6
1979	41	18 (44)	24 (59)	31 (76)	33 (80)
1980	34	8 (27)	16 (45)	19 (54)	20 (59)*
1981	36	13 (36)	22 (61)	23 (64)*	
1982	31	14 (45)	15 (48)*		
1983	28	10 (37)*			

* -- Projected numbers for June 1986 graduation.

Table 2. Admissions and Graduates

Seattle University Software Engineering Program

Table 2 above indicates that although the program should be completed in three years, almost half of those who graduated from the first entering class took more than three years to do so. The delays (and probable eventual failure to graduate) were even greater for the class entering in 1980. In that case, 8 (27%) of the 34 entering students graduated after 3 years, and 11 more, for a total of 19 (54%) after 5 years. Since the typical student is fully employed and often married, the pressures of job and family life often dictate the rate of progress through the program.

This is true not only on a year-to-year basis but also on a quarter to quarter basis. Table 3 shows the number of students enrolled each quarter since the program began.

Number of Students Enrolled in Quarter:

Academic Year	Fall	Winter	Spring
1979-80	49	44	37
1980-81	76	65	63
1981-82	94	84	79
1982-83	92	84	80
1983-84	95	90	80
1984-85	87	80	76
1985-86	94	87*	80*

*Projected for remainder of current year.

Table 3. Number of Students Enrolled Each Quarter

Seattle University Software Engineering Program

As indicated by Table 3, approximately 80 to 90 students are enrolled in the MSE program in any given quarter. Previous studies indicate that students' academic backgrounds vary widely, with about 30% in mathematics, 20% in computer science, 40% in engineering and physical sciences, 20% in business administration and management, and 20% in other disciplines [64]. The total of the indicated percentages exceeds 100 because many students hold second degrees or dual undergraduate majors. In addition, almost 15% of the students held advanced degrees in other disciplines prior to admittance to the MSE program.

In terms of expertise, the previous study indicated a distribution of about 40% in scientific/engineering, 35% in business/administrative applications, 20% in real-time applications, 15% systems programming, and 15% "other." This corresponded roughly to the figures for computer professionals employed in the Seattle area. The level of software experience ranged to over 15 years, with a median of 4.5 years at the time of entry to the MSE program.

It is difficult to measure the real success of the MSE program. How should it be measured? In terms of salary of the graduates? By apparent job status or rank? The program cannot easily be measured on the basis of job placement upon graduation since nearly all of the students are employed as they progress through the program and do not necessarily seek new employment upon completion of the program.

One measure of the success of the Seattle University MSE program is the high regard in which it is held by local software professionals. This is probably most visibly evidenced by the large number of applications for admission received each year. During each of the past three years, approximately 115 applications have been received, while only about 35 new students have been admitted each fall.

On a strictly qualitative basis, many favorable comments return to the program from local industry. Local industry and business organizations support the program well both by sending students to it and by providing financial support for those students. Informal contacts with both current students and alumni of the program yield many reports that they are indeed using the concepts learned in the MSE program and that it has enabled them to get the job done more quickly and effectively. In the final analysis, this may be the highest rating the program might receive.

Seattle University will, no doubt, continue to struggle with all of the implementational problems outlined above. Nevertheless, the favorable feedback received from our students and their employers clearly indicates that the MSE program has very effectively addressed an important educational need in the local computing environment.

Appendix

MSE Course Descriptions

ESW 500. Information Structures and Algorithms

Theory and applications of linear, tree and graph structures; memory management, sort-merge, algorithm design and analysis.

ESW 501. Computer Systems Principles

Survey of computer systems architecture, programming languages, and operating systems. Relationships among hardware and software.

ESW 508. Technical Communication

The role of communication skills in software engineering. Organizing ideas, writing, speaking, structure and content of proposals, reports, manuals and other software project documentation.

ESW 510. Software Systems Analysis

System requirements analysis and functional specification methodology, tools and techniques. Prerequisite or corequisite ESW 508.

ESW 512. System Design Methodology

Software system design methodology, tools and techniques. Prerequisite ESW 510.

ESW 514. Programming Methodology

Software system implementation methodology, tools and techniques. Programming language capabilities. Programming style. Principles of unit testing. Prerequisite ESW 512.

ESW 516. Software Quality Assurance

Managerial and technical aspects of verification, validation and quality assurance. Theory of testing. Prerequisite ESW 531.

ESW 518. Software Metrics

Quantitative approach to software engineering and management. Metrics and tools to evaluate, control and estimate the software life cycle. Reliability, size, quality and complexity measures. Prerequisite ESW 531.

ESW 531. Software Project Management

Organizational context of software development. Analysis of life cycle phases. Scheduling and budgeting techniques. Management, planning and control techniques. Personnel development and utilization. Prerequisite ESW 508.

ESW 533. System Procurement and Contract Acquisition

An introduction to the software procurement environment, contract law and the fundamentals of negotiation. Specification and control of products and process. Prerequisite ESW 516.

ESW 541. Database Systems

Review of database management techniques. Survey of database management systems; their use, architecture, design, implementation and cost/benefit/performance tradeoffs. Prerequisite ESW 514.

ESW 543. Formal Methods

Theory of program function and structure. Proof of correctness techniques. Automatic programming. Prerequisite ESW 514.

ESW 551. Artificial Intelligence

Survey of the field of artificial intelligence. Expert systems, robotics, language and pattern recognition. Prerequisite ESW 514.

ESW 560. Human Factors in Computing

Automation of user processes, design of user interfaces, data presentation techniques and the human-factor aspects of operations and maintenance procedures. Psychology of computer programming. Prerequisite ESW 508.

ESW 562. Data Security and Privacy

Encryption, database security and implementation of protection schemes in operating systems and programming languages. The legal and ethical aspects of security and privacy. Prerequisite ESW 514.

ESW 564. Computer Graphics

Analysis and generation of pictures by computer graphics hardware and software. Prerequisite ESW 514.

ESW 566. Real Time Systems

Design, implementation and maintenance of real time systems. Data acquisition systems, process control systems, interface techniques. Prerequisite ESW 514.

ESW 585. Software Engineering Project 1
ESW 586. Software Engineering Project 2
ESW 587. Software Engineering Project 3

A three quarter sequence in which students are grouped into teams that undertake a software project using tools and techniques presented in previous courses. Sequence generally begins in the fall and ends in spring quarter. Prerequisite ESW 516, 518, and satisfactory service as project reviewer on an assigned prior project. ESW 518 may be taken concurrently with ESW 585.

Academic/Industrial Collaboration in a Postgraduate Master of Science Degree in Software Engineering

David Budgen, Peter Henderson, Chic Rattray
University of Stirling

Abstract. This paper outlines the organisation of a new Master of Science (MSc) in Software Engineering that has been set up as a specialist conversion course[1] for graduates who have had some experience of computer programming. The most distinctive feature of the programme is that this degree involves the participation of an industrial partner in providing some of the teaching and a period of industrial placement. Some observations upon the first year of this degree have been included.

Introduction

The Stirling Structure: To clarify some of the points that will arise later, it is useful to provide a brief outline of the academic structures that exist at the University of Stirling. Historically, the Scottish education system has followed a broader and less specialised path than that of England and Wales, and traditionally, a university education begins a year earlier in Scotland.

However, while a General Degree programme lasts for three years, an Honours Degree programme has a four year span, and so an Honours graduate from a Scottish university will normally have been educated to the same level as their English counterparts.

Stirling is the newest of the eight Scottish universities, having been granted its charter in 1967. It currently has about 3100 undergraduates and postgraduate students. Unlike any other university in the U.K., Stirling operates a scheme of two semesters in preference to the usual

---

[1]For American readers, the British often use the term 'course' for both 'course units' and also to mean a degree programme. (DB)

three terms. Each semester lasts approximately fifteen weeks, including a teaching period of twelve weeks. All course units are modular in form, and normally consist of three hours per week of lectures, together with one hour of tutorial (or two to three of laboratory). A grade for each course unit is issued at the end of semester. This grade is normally made up from assignment grades plus the examination grade.

An undergraduate will normally take three course units in each semester. In the Scottish tradition, undergraduates do not specialise during the first four semesters, but those selected for an Honours programme at the end of this period will then undertake eleven honours units over the next two years. For computing science students, the final year project will usually occupy two of these units.

The MSc in Software Engineering: To help meet the demand for software engineers, the SERC (Science and Engineering Research Council) has supported a number of specialist postgraduate conversion courses at selected universities.[2] The Stirling degree is one of the most recent of these to gain approval, and is distinguished by having an extensive component of industrial collaboration and experience within its structure. The programme occupies eighteen months, rather than the conventional twelve months, and involves a six-month placement in an industrial setting. This part is currently provided and funded by International Computers Ltd./Standard Telecommunications Ltd. (ICL/STL) the U.K.'s major computer manufacturer, and takes place at their main software research centre. In the future, it will also be possible to accommodate some students who are sponsored by other industrial partners and who will undertake their placement with their sponsor.

This joint project arose from the strong research links that already existed between ICL/STL and Stirling, represented by research projects funded from ICL/STL, Alvey and Esprit. Within the U.K. this represents an uncommon degree of collaboration between industry and academia at this level of postgraduate education.

---

[2]A postgraduate conversion course is one that takes graduates from other disciplines and 'converts' them to the chosen discipline.

As the final authorisation for the course was only provided in the late Spring of 1985, the course is still in its first year, and not all aspects are in their 'final' form. However, sufficient progress has been made with the first intake for us to be able to provide some initial observations on this form of MSc programme.

Course Objectives

The MSc in Software Engineering is intended to form a 'specialist conversion course,' producing software engineers who will be of practical use to industry. Candidates are expected to have had some exposure to computing in their first degree; of the first intake, two have joint degrees in computing science, although others have only had fairly limited programming experience.

In teaching the course, we sought to create a programme that would provide a sound foundation of applied computing science, followed by a period of industrial placement, and finally ending up with a project and dissertation as the final assessment item. Within this framework we had to construct our programme with only limited additional resources being available for teaching new courses, and so we sought wherever possible to integrate existing courses. Since our industrial partner was willing to provide some lecturing effort and seminars, we also needed to include these. So the programme for the MSc contains new courses, courses drawn from the undergraduate honours programme, and in one case, a course taken from an existing postgraduate diploma programme for Information Technology.

Course Structure

course occupies eighteen months, beginning at the start of the Autumn Semester (mid-September). The student calendar for the course is:

i)	Sept-Dec	Semester 1 (Stirling)
ii)	Jan	Two-week industrial acquaint visit (ICL/STL)
iii)	Feb-June	Semester 2 (Stirling)
iv)	July-Dec	Industrial placement and project (ICL/STL)
v)	Jan-Mar	Final project and dissertation (Stirling)

We look at these in more detail below.

Academic sessions (I & III): Postgraduate Master's degrees at Stirling usually require students to complete four course units per semester (undergraduates normally complete three units per semester), and the MSc has followed this form. The first semester is concerned with bringing all students up to a base level of technical competence. It has a theme of *fundamentals*, and the four course units are:

1. Pascal programming/practical specification
   (P. Henderson's 'me_too')
2. Data structures, files and basic computer forms
3. Programming language syntax and semantics
4. Software Engineering principles

Unit (1) was devised especially for this MSc; (2) is taken from the syllabus of another postgraduate taught unit; (3) is the third year Honours core unit, which must be completed by all Honours students, and (4) is an elective unit from the fourth year syllabus. This last unit is primarily concerned with specification and design, although some lectures are devoted to such issues as testing, documentation, project control, etc.

In the second semester the theme is *software systems*, and the students proceed to study more specialised topics, pursuing a programme which is made up from the following course units:
1. Methods of formal specification
2. Concurrency and operating system concepts
3. Computer networking
4. Compiler design or expert systems

A major deficiency of this programme is that there is no material covering database issues, primarily due to resource limitations. In future years we intend to find ways to remedy this and to include some database aspects in the second semester.

Industrial Components: There are two major components to the industrial side of the course. The initial acquaintance visit (January) is intended to provide the students with some idea of the organisation of ICL/STL, and with the form and range of research projects that are being undertaken there. At the end of this visit, each student (with the aid of ICL/STL staff) should have determined which project they will be joining in the summer, and have established contact with their future supervisor.

During the spring semester, a member of the Stirling staff will be appointed to liaise with a student, and with the student's project supervisor, so that we have a triangle which is formed by the student, the industrial supervisor and the academic supervisor.

The main project period occupies six months, and during that time, each student will work as a member of the chosen ICL/STL project team, funded by ICL/STL. (This keeps the SERC contribution to the normal twelve month grant.) The students will also take part in the normal graduate induction programme at ICL/STL and will operate as a single group for such purposes. At the end of this period, each student will produce a short written report detailing their experiences during the six months. A copy of this report will form an annex to the final dissertation that is submitted for the degree.

Project and Dissertation: For the final three months, the students will return to Stirling and undertake a 'traditional' MSc project - the topic for this having been agreed upon with the academic supervisor during the previous spring semester. This topic need not necessarily be directly related to the project that was followed during the industrial placement.

In addition to the industrial placement, ICL/STL supplies a number of 'guest lecturers' and seminar speakers during the teaching period. As an example of this, Dr. Barbara Kitchenham has lectured on the 1985 autumn course unit on software engineering, and there are similar lectures arranged for two of the units that will be held during the spring semester. For 1986 a number of guest lectures on database issues have been arranged for the MSc students in order to partly meet the shortcomings of the course units. Since some of these units are also attended by undergraduates, the benefit of the industrial collaboration is spread more widely than just the immediate MSc course.

Observations

The first intake of twelve students was in September 1985, and we are now organising the recruitment for September 1986. Two students opted out from the MSc within the first few weeks; the remaining ten have successfully completed the first semester and the industrial acquaint visit.

Comments on progress have been divided into three main sub-headings: *social* dealing with how the postgraduate students have integrated, *technical* concerned with the facilities provided for them and how these have been used, and *academic* describing the academic aspects of the course as completed so far.

Social: As only one student was a Stirling graduate, the ten students formed a small group, which had no direct links with the rest of the students on campus. Most of the group resided on campus. A problem that was identified in the first semester was that for each of their course units, they mixed with a different group; one course was for them alone, the others were joint with the Information Technology Diploma postgraduates, final year honours students, and third year students. This led to some problems of identification - accentuated by the knowledge that they were the first students on this particular course.

With that in mind, ICL/STL have taken care to keep them as a group for the initial acquaint visit, and have made clear to them that it is the intention to continue this for the induction sessions during the six-month placement. In the second semester they will mainly share course units with honours students, and with that in mind, our early attempts at social events with the postgraduate students from the information technology course may have been the wrong approach.

This aspect should not be given undue emphasis, but in a small campus university a sense of identity is important, and has significant effects in terms of how quickly the students settle and are able to concentrate effectively.

So far there is no indication that the distance between the ICL/STL and Stirling sites (at least 250 miles) forms any problem for the students.

Technical: For the course units of the first semester, the main computer tools have been UNIX^{TM3} Operating System (System V on an AT&T 3B5) and the Pascal programming language. Some care was taken to limit the use of other tools during this early stage, although towards the end of semester the students did use Wang PCs.

The third and fourth year students also use the department's own UNIX engines and terminal rooms, and we had hoped that the shared use of these facilities would result in the postgraduate students being assisted by the undergraduates in getting up to speed with UNIX and Pascal. Partly for the reasons given in the previous section, this did not happen as much as we had hoped. For 1986 it may be useful to try some more 'bribery' in the form of joint social events with the final year undergraduate students in order to assist the progress of integration for the postgraduates, which was only beginning to take effect by the end of the autumn semester.

At present, we do not have an Ada environment that is adequate for use in teaching, but one possible development for the future might be to begin this course by teaching a subset of Ada instead of Pascal. This might help with the spring semester courses where we will currently need to introduce Modula-2 as well as Prolog and/or Hope.

Academic: In the first semester, we feel that the choice and the balance of the units was quite successful, and this seemed to be confirmed by the quality of the grades produced.

For most course units, the postgraduate students were assigned to their own separate tutorial groups. Sometimes these met for a few extra sessions at their request. The only exception was the software engineering unit, where we traditionally run small seminar groups in which each student is asked to make a short presentation on a (short) paper selected from the current literature. A list of these papers is given in Appendix A. While this presentation is not directly assessed towards the final grade on the course, it is made clear to the students that we regard

---

[3]UNIX is a trademark of AT&T Bell Laboratories.

the ability to present an idea, or set of ideas, as an important skill that needs to be acquired. On this course unit the postgraduate students were deliberately mixed in with the final year students in making up the seminar groups, so that the discussions and presentations could spread the experience more fully. Overall, these tutorial arrangements worked well, and a similar pattern is planned for the course units of the spring semester, with special tutorial groups on most course units, but using 'seminars' on the expert systems unit.

Most of the course units that are taught within the Department of Computing Science result in a final grade that is based 40% on coursework and 60% on examination. This leads to a fairly high loading of assigned course work, and during the first semester it proved necessary to adjust this for some course units. While postgraduate degrees normally involve completing four course units per semester, these course units are not usually taught to third or final year students at the same time, with the appropriate expectations as to experience. We found that the volume of assigned work on some of the courses proved to be rather demanding for the postgraduates who also had less experience of handling this form of assigned work. At Stirling we also require extensive, formal documentation of assigned work, and simply learning these practices can be time-consuming to a student who has not had previous practice at providing the required information in these forms. Some further problems of clashing deadlines also added to the demanding course load. In the end, some adjustments proved necessary both to the volume of assigned work as well as to deadlines. For the current semester some adjustments to the number of assignments have already been made, and it is likely that we will extend the policy of giving to the postgraduates assignments that are slightly different to those that are given to the undergraduates on the same course unit.

Overall, the results from the first semester were encouraging, and we plan to make relatively few changes to this part of the programme for next year. The lack of database material in the second semester still causes concern, and we will need to investigate some means of including this. One possibility might be to replace the concurrency/operating systems unit that is also taught to undergraduates with a new unit for the postgraduates, which will be made up from half a unit on concurrency and half a unit on databases.

So far, we have only had limited industrial involvement in the teaching of the course material, though there will be more of this in the present semester. Most students appear to have made good use of the opportunities presented during the two-week industrial acquaint course at ICL/STL.

Future Developments

Obviously we have yet to experience the effects of the most distinctive feature of the course - namely the industrial placement. This course is intended to provide trained software engineers who are ready to begin to practise in industry rather than academics, and so this is an important aspect. Liaison between ICL/STL and the staff at Stirling is still developing (we had a group visit to ICL/STL in October) and is likely to become a major item in the success of the course. For that reason, we will be giving this a lot of attention over the next twelve months, and encouraging visits between the staff of the two organisations.

Student response has been encouraging, and there is an added useful side benefit in that the final year students are also gaining some exposure to industrial experience and practices through the guest lectures and seminars. We are currently building up a **Centre for Software Engineering Technology** within the department that will act as a focus for local industry, and we also expect this to play an increasingly important role in supporting the MSc in software engineering, by providing students with further exposure to the particular needs of industry for problem-solving skills.

Appendix
Software Engineering Seminars
University of Stirling
Department of Computing Science

The seminars form an important part of the course, and you should try to read as many of the recommended papers as possible. They should give you some additional background feeling for the problems of the subject. The papers chosen are reasonably short and fairly self-contained, and so should not require you to read all the references too!

Everyone in the class will be expected to lead the discussion on one of the selected papers. We will normally discuss two papers per session. In addition, there will be at least one seminar with a guest speaker, and a class discussion session at the end.

All the papers listed are available in the library. We will provide you with a photocopy of the paper that you are presenting. Please do not take any of the relevant journals out of the library, as this prevents others in the class from accessing them. The presentation should make some use of the overhead projector (we will provide transparencies and pens) — and if necessary we can make copies of *short* summaries for the other members of the group.

Seminar Themes:

Week 1: Life Cycle and Its Limitations: i) "Stop the Life-Cycle, I want to get off", G R Gladden, ACM SigSoft, Software Eng Notes **7**, 35-39, 1982.

i) "Life Cycle Concept Considered Harmful", D D McCracken and M A Jackson, ACM SigSoft Software Eng Notes **7**, 29-32, 1982.

"ii) "An Assessment of the Prototyping Approach to Information Systems Development", M Alavi, Comms ACM, **27**, 556-563, 1984.

Week 2: The User Interface: i) "Ease of Use: A system design challenge", L M Branscomb & J C Thomas, IBM Sys Journal, **23**, 224-235, 1984.

ii) "Thoughts on Specification, Design and Verification", J Goguen, ACM SigSoft, SE Notes, **5**, 29-33, 1980.

Week 3: Design Methods: i) "A Design medium for Software", J F Leathrum, Software Practice and Experience, **12**, 497-503, 1982.

ii) "Pragmatic Problems with Step-Wise Refinement Program Development", J L Diaz-Herrara, ACM SigSoft SE Notes, **9**, 80-88, 1984.

Week 4: Management of Software Projects: i) "Software Quality Assurance", F J Buckley & R Poston, IEEE Trans on Software Eng, **SE-10**, 36-41, 1984.

ii) "Managing and Predicting the Costs of Real-Time Software", R D Warburton, IEEE Trans on SE, **SE-9**, 562-569, 1983.

Week 5: Programmer Productivity: i) "The parable of two programmers", N W Rickert, ACM SigSoft SE Notes, **10**, 16-18, 1985.

"The parable of two programmers, Continued", W D Maurer, ACM Sig-Soft SE Notes, 19-21, 1985.

"The parable of two programmers - Still More" T E Barrios, ACM SigSoft SE Notes, 21-22, 1985.

ii) "Reviews, Walkthroughs and Inspections", G M Weinberg & D P Freedman, IEEE Trans on SE, **SE-10**, 68-72, 1984.

Week 6: Maintenance of Software: i) "Issues in Software Maintenance" B P Lientz, Computing Surveys, **15**, 271-278, 1983.

Week 7 and 8 will be used for guest seminars and class discussions. **Week 9** will be used as a revision class.

Section II
Part 3
Experiences With Existing Courses

Papers in this part are centered on evaluating the experience of teaching software engineering and its associated project courses. Susan Gerhart reflects on her tenure at the Wang Institute, and William McKeeman presents the project course he teaches there. Other project courses are described by Richard Thayer and Leo Endres of California State University at Sacramento and David Wortman of the University of Toronto. Jon Bentley and John Dallen discuss their experiences using smaller exercises.

Skills versus Knowledge in Software Engineering Education: A Retrospective on the Wang Institute MSE Program

Susan L. Gerhart
MCC Software Technology Program

Abstract. The author was a faculty member for three years (1982-1985) in the Master of Software Engineering (MSE) program (hereafter abbreviated as WIMSE) at the Wang Institute of Graduate Studies. This paper distills that experience, organized in the form of questions on the following topics:

- What is a software engineer?
- What is software engineering?
- What has been learned about software engineering education?

A framework for analyzing the WIMSE experience will be constructed and followed throughout the questions, with interspersed recommendations appropriate for the SEI Education Workshop. The purpose of this paper is to provide some informal and subjective (and probably idealized) observations on the WIMSE curriculum to complement the more formal and objective information that is available in [2]. The state of software engineering is also seen from the view of software engineering education.

What is a Software Engineer?

A few years ago the classified ads in Sunday newspapers asked for programmers of various specialities. Today they request "software engineers," which may show an expansion of the role of people who do something to produce software; programming is only one of those roles. This trend emphasizes a broader range of products related to software and the more professional sounding "engineering" title. To start off our discussion of software engineering education, we need to know more about what a software engineer does and is.

Is There Only One Kind of Software Engineer?

A software engineer may be found doing any of the following tasks:

- writing micro-code
- designing user interfaces

- running potential products on test data
- building simulators for hardware designers
- acquiring requirements
- participating in design teams
- preparing detailed designs
- identifying reusable parts of code as it is developed
- building tools for other software engineers
- experimenting with prototypes
- supervising programmers
- writing documentation
- managing projects
- identifying new product lines

Some of these roles are full time multiyear jobs, even spanning careers. Some are performed periodically or within the scope of single projects. Some software engineers are generalists, while others see themselves as specialists in the above areas. There is no such concept as the "monolithic" software engineer. The software engineering field includes many specialities and requires most of its members to be able to perform a variety of functions. We need this distinction among specialities to adequately discuss details of software engineering education.

> Recommendation: A software engineering curriculum should be designed to support a number of (specified) roles for software engineers. One test of a curriculum, then, is its coverage of the basic skills and knowledge for specified specialities.

> Recommendation: Identify and describe the specialities of software engineering to clarify the needs of a software engineering curricula.

How Do You Know a Software Engineer When You See One?

Here comes our framework for the rest of the paper. In this definition, we are not trying to distinguish a software engineer from a programmer, rather to characterize a kind of technical professional. A software engineer:

1. *Understands his or her current role within an organization, a project, and the individual's career.* Software engineers are able to work in several ways with several kinds of other specialists.

2. *Knows several ways of doing particular tasks.* A software engineer has a choice, at least conceptually, of doing jobs in different ways, either through previous experience or from education. These methods can be articulated and adapted. The software engineer knows how to evaluate the results of using a method, can make a legitimate choice among methods, and understands the basis for each. Likewise with tools, a software engineer knows of several tools possibly appropriate to the tasks at hand and how to use them effectively.

3. *Has an educational familiarity with a variety of relevant technical material.* A software engineer knows of books and journals which might serve as sources of information on methods, tools, or algorithms. A software engineer also is aware of professional organizations, both local and national, and the services they provide.

4. *Plans his or her work.* By virtue of having choices of methods and awareness of resources, a software engineer makes choices on how to work. Furthermore, a software engineer has the experience to gauge how long tasks will take and is able to trade off tasks and quality.

Though these might seem like obvious characteristics, we'll see that some of the easily omitted characteristics (1 and 4) are the prominent ones in the experience of the WIMSE program.

Notice that this definition excludes characteristics of responsibility that are associated with professional engineers (licensing, ethics, etc.); true professionalism ought to be addressed also, but separately. And the definition also purposely excludes a large number of people in the field who can only do what they are told to do and how to do it. Also, the definition is watered down by requiring not specific knowledge or skills, just a well informed choice and ability to grow. We do this to emphasize the theme of this paper — that skills are as important as knowledge in software engineering education. Moreover, we argue later that the state of the field makes this rather minimal looking definition the maximum one currently possible.

> Recommendation: Adopt a definition of a model software engineer to be produced by a Master's of Software Engineering program.

We'll use this framework — roles, techniques, culture, habits — throughout the paper.

How Does an MSE Program Affect the Students' Career Paths as Software Engineers?

Students come to the WIMSE program to learn better ways of doing their jobs, and the skills and knowledge to move them on to new jobs. Typically they have several years of experience in a narrow slice of software engineering and often they feel stuck. Often, they have been trained in a field other than computer science or software engineering, perhaps a non-engineering field, and are now making a commitment to the software engineering field. Many of the students entering a "professional" degree program today are those lured away from graduate school in the past by the opportunities of the field. They are excellent students who like to do interesting technical work at good pay. Their return to school is often motivated by intellectual needs as much as vocational ones. They just know they aren't well enough educated to work the way they want. They want choices and control in their work-life. They already have role experience, good work habits, minimum formal knowledge, little formal training in technique, some exposure to tools, and a vague feeling for the literature of software engineering. They want to feel, and be, more professional in their job performance.

Many students end up in jobs that they never would have found interesting or qualified for without the MSE degree. For example, the intersection of artificial intelligence and software engineering creates unique jobs, e.g., in quality assurance of AI products and the application of AI to software engineering functions. The MSE emphasis on software development processes leads other students into quality assurance where they can have the widest influence. Some students find ways of avoiding management responsibility by increasing their technical skills while others find technical areas that enhance their management roles and some develop management skills. Within the WIMSE, a strong career influence may be the multiple roles played within projects and assignments. These roles are not always taken seriously, but some students have the chance to experience for the first time planning of projects and responsibility for design decisions. Tools, or possibilities for tools, may be seen for the first time and suggest new fields of specialization, e.g., tool-smithing. Some students find certain technical areas that they might have moved into quite repugnant or attractive, e.g., detailed product testing and quality assurance. In each case, they learn at least a little of the basics required for that speciality and a feel for where it fits into the total software production organization. By studying with other students experienced in various specialities, they gain more insight into new roles.

The fourth of our characteristics of a software engineering is also a strong determinant of career change. The WIMSE is intense, in different ways for part-time and full-time students, but always requires concentration, steady work, and interaction with other students.

Of course, there is specific knowledge gained along the way, but the experience is much broader than just that knowledge.

> Recommendation: An MSE program should be as explicit as possible about its effect on participants' career goals.

> Recommendation: An MSE program should recognize the factors that are brought to the program by a mixture of experienced students. Mixtures of full-time and part-time student bodies may both enrich and complicate software engineering education, and should be carefully thought out.

While concern for MSE students' careers was always high at the WIMSE, this recognition of roles and their influence was never explicit. The reason for stressing the career aspects of a professional school is the need for making a program attractive and realistic in the education it delivers to its students.

What Has been Learned about Software Engineering Education?

The SEI workshop has provided the opportunity for comparing MSE program content. Experience with WIMSE will now be described.

Some Questions Regarding the Necessary Skills and Knowledge of a Software Engineer

- What should a software engineer know, before and after a MSE degree program?
- What skills are lacking in entering students?
- What skills and knowledge are gained from the MSE program?
- What skills are still lacking upon graduation?

Following our framework, we'll address these questions for each factor.

Roles

Experience preceding an MSE program with some role within an organization brings both maturity and knowledge. The sad difficulty of getting anything done, well or poorly, is a lesson easily acquired through almost any job and helps to provide the motivation for studying management topics. It also adds realism to the idealism attached to many methods and tools. As mentioned above, an MSE program graduate should know more and different roles and how they interact. A management career path will show wider familiarity with what specialists do and what their particular problems are. A technical career path will be more productive through awareness of the demands and interactions of various specialities.

> Recommendation: The variety of skills of software engineers provides a possible theme for organizing a MSE program. However, there should not be too much specific training for roles.

Techniques

It is often surprising how few techniques known within software engineering literature are actually practiced. One reason is that few are taught within computer science programs, e.g., systematic testing or technical reviews, and many persons performing software engineering have no formal training. Another reason is simply that few of the techniques work well at all. And, many programmers just don't want to try or use them. It seems reasonable to expect that an entering MSE student would have some control over coding practices, since these are most widely known, but little else. That has been true in the WIMSE, though even rudimentary coding skills may be lacking if a software engineer has been pursuing specialities with minimal programming.

It would be nice to say that, upon leaving an MSE program, a software engineer would know various methods (and tools), how to use them, and what to expect from them. Unfortunately, the state of knowledge within the software engineering field can't support this. Certainly an MSE should know the existence of methods and tools but broad or deep experience is hard to come by. Almost all methods require substantial projects to prove their usefulness, or their deficiencies, and these projects cannot be performed within the scope of a degree program. It is easier within a single company or a group of similar companies (e.g., government contractors or Ada-based developers) to teach methods that are enforced or conventional; these, too, often lack an established scientific basis but are "more valuable" because they are required.

Indeed, the measures of experience might be better gauged in terms of frustration: level 0, when nothing is seen to solve a known problem; level 1, when a promising method is seen, but not used; level 2, when a method is used but the project is too large to really assess it; and level 3, when a method is used on the right size project and still fails to solve most of the problems. Only in the sales literature of methodology peddlers are methods given uniformly high praise. Of course, some of this frustration may trace to inadequate teaching or faculty inexperience, but it is a wide-spread opinion that the methods themselves are at fault.

MSEs will usually gravitate toward one or two viewpoints that match their own or which intrigue them, and then pursue the methods that fit that viewpoint. For example, Parnas' document-driven approach to software attracts many students. Viewpoints seem more valid and enduring than specific methods given the current state of knowledge within software engineering.

Recommendation: Present different viewpoints; don't sanctify methods or masters.

Educational Familiarity

Few entering students to an MSE program seem to have read widely in the literature. A survey at WIMSE showed that about 1/3 were members of ACM, 1/3 members of IEEE Computer Society, and (after overlap) about 1/2 were members of neither of the major professional organizations. It's fair to expect then that the primary journals and conference proceedings will be known to only a few students. With so many students coming from other disciplines, it's not surprising they lack a systematic introduction to the field. Of course, this characteristic of knowing technical resources should be present after graduation. But it's not as easy as it might seem, since, at least in the WIMSE, there's a tendency to hand out all readings and not require students to forage through the library for their own material.

> Recommendation: An MSE program should contain some assignments that require the use of software engineering literature.

> Recommendation: Pointers to the most accessible journals should be explicitly given.

Also, there is a body of literature that doesn't fall into traditional academic frameworks, e.g., the software products reviews and guidebooks. This is particularly relevant in topics like reusability models of software production.

Many students are not familiar with the path of papers from technical reports through refereeing, what degrees of refereeing are applied, or how the whole publication process works.

> Recommendation: Explain the publication process to interested students and encourage them to participate as reviewers and contributors.

One chronic problem of journals and conferences is getting "practical" input from authors and reviewers directly from industry; the MSE program is a place for addressing that need.

Although the picture of methods mastered is pessimistic, there are many general concepts that an MSE should know; for example, the strengths and weaknesses of testing versus proving, the various ways of representing design information, the process of transferring technology, principles of good documentation, and some of the past and present trends in viewing software. Even more important is having a structure for organizing software engineering knowledge, e.g., knowing how to relate theory and methodology to a tool.

> Recommendation: Organize an MSE curriculum through structure
> and relationships of knowledge, not through specific knowledge.

For example, a good idea may be traced through theory, methodology, technology, and management and evaluated on its contribution. We argue later that little specific knowledge, e.g., Method X, is worth-while.

Habits

As mentioned, one major effect of the WIMSE is the production of work habits that allow a student to survive the program. People who can't concentrate or don't have the drive are weeded out in an oral examination that measures, at least, intensity and drive.

Any rigorous professional program should produce such a strong effect, although it might be over-looked as a factor in success. The WIMSE requires the ability to plan one's work when there isn't possibly enough time to do everything, get down to business in an hour's meeting time, switch contexts of topics and people, always write up every important idea and scrap of work, work with incompatible people, and trade off better work on one piece with tolerably inferior work on another. In several ways, a professional program may be much more demanding than a PhD degree program.

Methods, Tools, and Techniques

- What methods, tools, and techniques are being taught and used?
- Which ones bomb? Which are successful? Why?

It is important to emphasize again the variety of specialities within software engineering and the different needs and backgrounds of students in an MSE program. Any course which covers many different kinds of topics will automatically end up with a diversity of responses (and course evaluations) from students; some topics will really strike a strong chord, while others will completely bomb with different types of students taking the course.

> Recommendation: Don't expect uniform acceptance of topics
> taught; recognize individual differences in students.

Here are some topics and recollections of them from the perspective of teaching the software methods courses (Programming Methodology and Software Engineering):

<u>Program</u> <u>Testing</u> is a subject about which almost none of the students have systematic knowledge, though most have been bloodied, and they can learn a great deal in a short time. Unfortunately, the methods (black box and white box) are unpleasant to use and easily foiled. The big lesson is how hard testing is to do at all thoroughly and how fallible it can be. In WIMSE, theory of testing was covered in Formal Methods with testing practicalities and exercises covered in Programming Methodology. Tools for testing make a modest impression, e.g., coverage analyzers and profilers. Systematic testing is a nice way of introducing the principles of using methods.

<u>Program</u> <u>Proving</u> is always controversial and difficult. The concepts of programming language semantics, problem domain knowledge, invariant methods, and logic all come in one large mind-boggling package. Taught in Formal Methods, this is difficult to reinforce in Programming Methodology since the students generally lack the logic and notation skills to perform any exercises and have seen only a few, narrow methods. The concepts that are retained are the distinction between program and specification, the existence of methods like loop invariants, and the proof difficulties presented by certain program organizations. The possibility of specification proving and correctness-preserving transformations can be introduced and used to motivate alternative software production models. However, some students find a strong attraction to the material and are capable of using it well.

<u>Abstract</u> <u>Data</u> <u>Types</u> is probably the best link between formal methods and programming methods with the emphasis on program structuring and the support offered by programming languages such as CLU and Ada. There should be many good exercises using abstract data types.

<u>Software</u> <u>Design</u> <u>Methods</u> are a problem area since there are so many, each addressing different kinds of problems. The IEEE tutorials are the best source of articles but few of the articles are instructive enough. Standard design exercises don't exist in the literature and are hard to find for a course context. The design methods all appear rather weak and narrow, except for Jackson's methods which are more fully explicated. The existence of commercial design tools can be demonstrated

and these tools are excellent candidates for substantive and user interface evaluations.

Technical Reviews are controversial and difficult to teach in a methods course, but invaluable later during project courses. The procedures are laid out in Weinberg's work, for example, but require a lot of experience on the part of the instructor to avoid hurt feelings and to produce the right critical review information. This is one of the most successful industrial practices and often catches on well with WIMSE students.

Software production models, i.e., lifecycle, prototyping, iterative enhancement, reusability, etc., make for some good reading and discussion but need project courses for experimentation with alternative approaches. The software engineering literature shows a tension between the large-scale government needs and the processes used in small, product-oriented companies. This is an area of topics where there are more opinions than results, and where it's often hard to get down to the crux of the approach.

Requirements Analyses are taught within WIMSE as course "definition study" projects using an obscure method from the data processing world. Real-life problems are solicited from within the Wang Institute and from outside in local companies, with identified clients for each. Teams of students follow the method on selected problems by gathering data on the problem, existing procedures, and the organization, then analyzing the data, and formulating and evaluating alternative approaches. These projects almost always produce valuable analyses and give insights on the complexity of the environment into which software systems must fit. The problem always looks different at the end, often the data gathered teachs a lot in itself, plus the formulation of alternative approaches is a good exercise. While time-consuming, these projects also offer the chance to apply project management methods and, sometimes, requirements tools. Follow-on projects often occur. The method used over 20 times has been found successful, although it required adaptation to work.

<u>Specification</u> <u>methods</u> <u>and</u> <u>languages</u> are only given cursory attention.

<u>Standards</u> may be discussed through the IEEE and NBS reports, but these are often dry and hard to motivate.

In general, there are no textbooks that fit the WIMSE courses and articles from the general literature must be sought and used. This is a continuing problem, since there is so much poor literature to sort through and so little that fits the needs of the curriculum.

> <u>Recommendation:</u> Establish a network or clearing-house for exchanging good literature, exercises, and educational material.

> <u>Recommendation:</u> Develop a good set of exercises along with a curriculum.

The quality of an MSE program is highly dependent on the projects and exercises performed along the way. Developing good exercises is one of the great challenges for MSE curriculum instructors and developers.

There are many ways of delivering the software engineering material. Panels of experts, e.g., practitioners in quality assurance, are good vehicles for covering material and invited lecturers can often supplement a faculty member's experience. Occasionally, videotapes are available on selected topics and can be accumulated over time, e.g., of past panel discussions. Often class discussions are more effective than lecturers, but are equally challenging to the instructor to direct.

Technological Needs

- What technology base is needed for offering software engineering programs?
- How is it to be developed and used?

The WIMSE used a fairly standard UNIX environment supplemented by PCs. Specific software tools were supported by a project [67] that identified and imported worthwhile tools, helped train faculty and students in their use, prepared supplementary tutorial material, and generally provided the base for easing selected tools into the curriculum. This effort was invaluable to faculty for demonstrating tools such as AIDES (Hughes), PSL/PSA, and PC-based design tools, as well as more mundane environment support such as revision control systems.

The commitment to using software technology should be a major issue facing those developing a MSE program. The technology exists and can be obtained with modest resources (many vendors can be talked into educational discounts), but the expense lies in the personnel to procure the technology and make it usable. A minimum of six months lead time is usually required to bring in a tool. At least a week of a faculty member's time is required for learning each tool adequately to teach it and to set the context for using the tool. Even making full use of some of the UNIX utilities is a big task. Add that to the need to integrate students into simple fundamental utilities, such as news and mail and document preparation systems, and the technology base for supporting a MSE program is substantial. The operating system base can be handled by many people, but the specialized software tools require specialized training. Note that the training need for curriculum demonstration is different from that for production use of a tool, because the curriculum goal is most likely a demonstration of the essential capabilities of the tool and minimal exercises for getting a feel for it.

> Recommendation: Recognize the need for substantial support for software technology in developing an MSE program.

A minimum technology base for an MSE program might include such tools as: program profiler, program test coverage analyzer, revision control system, data-based design tool with graphics, specification processor and analyzer.

> Recommendation: The Software Engineering Institute could develop a model minimum environment suitable for demonstration purposes in a MSE program. Training courses for faculty and tutorial material in using the software tools should be provided.

Faculty Training

- Where does a faculty member acquire the knowledge and skills to teach in an MSE program?
- What are the challenges?

Certainly, an MSE faculty member should have the same characteristics as a software engineer, plus the experience to choose what should be taught and to teach it. That would mean about five years, say, of practical software engineering experience and the same of graduate education training. It would be desirable that experience be within the past five years, since the field has changed and memory fades. The person should also have broad exposure to the software engineering literature as well as that of their field of speciality within, probably, computer science. They should have experience with a variety of software production methods, both formal and informal, and know many of the tools available to software engineers today not just UNIX. They should hold some strong viewpoints on how software should be produced, but be open to alternatives outside their experience. And they should be able to work on projects with groups of people as well as individually be able to direct their own research.

Such people don't exist. Real industrial experience may be acquired before or after graduate school. If before, it's likely to have been blotted out by the graduate school experience; if after, it's probably not typical of the MSE student's experience. People who have good careers going in industry don't usually want to go into the cold, cruel world of academia. Unless the faculty member went to one of the few graduate schools that expose their students to software engineering concepts, e.g., The University of Maryland, they are probably limited in recent knowledge to their speciality within computer science. And without explicit effort during prior industrial experience, the faculty member is unlikely to know any of the software engineering methods (how many thesis students use the Jackson Design Method and technical reviews in their dissertation projects?). Finally, the work modes of traditional graduate schools emphasize individualism and exploration, both of which differ from the MSE group project and discipline approach. The traditional academic looks forward and dreams, while the professional school academic must deal with the problems of the present. Unfortunately, the career path for a faculty member in a professional school environment is unclear: What industrial or academic paths would be followed after leaving the professional program? And research often must play some role for the professional school academic, but what research models apply? And where do consulting and other forms of academic/industrial interaction fit into the professional development of faculty?

Does teaching in an MSE program require a PhD? Of course not, but academic institutions usually do.

Recommendation: Consider the career paths of MSE faculty members and their relationship to teaching in an MSE program. Don't bar well educated practitioners who only lack a PhD

It's a hard job, but somebody has to do it.

This is probably the greatest challenge to starting MSE programs — the ideal faculty member should have come through an MSE program! On-the-job training teaching management courses, or even methods courses, is rough on the faculty and on the students. Yet there isn't any way around it, short of really putting each class of MSE instructors though an MSE program to teach them management, methods, tools, and theory at the right level. Certainly, a faculty member can learn the material one course at a time but is unlikely to learn a greatly different area from their own past experience and this still doesn't make up for lack of experience. And even one course at a time is rough, since most courses have several topics.

Recommendation: In preparing a description of an MSE program, also provide the background for faculty — how to get started in an area, where to find the best literature, who to consult for exercises, what's important and why. Provide practical information that will allow faking experience.

Is Software Engineering Well Enough Developed as a Discipline and as a Body of Knowledge to Support a MSE Program?

Intellectually, no; pragmatically, yes.

Intellectually, the software engineering field is a hodge-podge of invalidated ideas; some are rooted in theory; others are market-driven. Practically, however, there are enough good ideas to warrant an effort to package some and teach them. There is a structure to knowledge and a variety of viewpoints that can be transmitted. Furthermore, there are role experience and work habits characteristics that may be gained while studying different topics with experienced students in an environment where it's possible to try new tools and techniques. However, *it would be wrong to believe that a professional degree program can add much intellectual power to a person when the field lacks the necessary scientific basis and experience to make advocated methods and tools work well.*

Software engineering education is at the state where computer science education was 15 years ago before the first textbooks started to come out. However, software engineering faces a bleaker future, since it is multidisciplinary and since the demand across the field for people to build software leaves few to study the building of software.

> Recommendation: Software engineering education is not a matter of taking recognized techniques and packaging them; the field is still in need of scrutiny and further development.

What Approaches Might be Used to Generate MSE Curricula?

There are several approaches to developing a software engineering curriculum:

1. Base the curriculum in one existing field and spread branches to others, e.g., from a management base into computer science, from business information systems into computer science, from computer science into management, etc.

2. Assume that the software engineering field is represented by its literature and structure a curriculum that will present the best portions of that material.

3. Identify the great (or, at least, the best) ideas of software engineering and base a curriculum around them.

4. Select a theme, such as software engineering specialities, and develop sub-curricula for each, unifying into a whole.

5. Survey practicing experts in the field and determine how they do what they do well and what they need further, then package that into a curriculum.

6. Decompose the knowledge of software engineering into theory, methods, and tools and then structure courses to cover each.

7. Select faculty who seem to have the right kind of knowledge and allow them to teach what they know.

> Recommendation: Adopt one such strategy to generate an MSE curriculum.

Across any of these, we feel that the best work has to be the basis, not the breadth of the available material.

> Recommendation: Identify the few great ideas that have gained acceptance or show the greatest promise and test any curriculum to see that it adequately covers these.

What is the State of the Quality and Quantity of Software Engineering Literature?

Even the best ideas are unlikely to have found wide applicability, and so to have been encountered in practice. Unfortunately, the best ideas are often buried in the mass of software engineering journals and conference proceedings. Almost any article can be published in one of the journals or conferences. The objective of the professional organizations is often to create conferences that attract the most people and make the most money. The result is a glut of conferences, some with virtually no quality control.

The MSE faculty member has a responsibility to continually scan the software engineering literature for new ideas, good tutorial papers, pointers to tools, trends, and potential colleagues to recruit. This is impossible to do today. The volume of literature is simply too great and the density of worthwhile (in the context of software engineering education) material too small. If there were a few top-notch, sure-fire sources the problem would be less, but the good material is widely spread. *IEEE Software* and *Computer* provide frequent sources of good software engineering education material, but often one, and only one, good paper will appear in an off-beat or otherwise worthless conference.

> Recommendation: Establish prizes, or other forms of recognition, for the best papers, the best workshops, and the best research within software engineering, perhaps in different categories of theory, methods, and tools.

The problem with books is much less severe, since few appear and publishers are usually good with samples. IEEE tutorials are the best book source since somebody has screened the paper collections, but even these may be unreliable. Several survey textbooks exist for context, but lack the necessary depth on most topics.

> Recommendation: A network should be established of educators who filter through the literature for the best new, and old, papers appropriate for an MSE curriculum.

> Recommendation: The WIMSE reading lists provide a good first start as filters of the software engineering literature.

Indeed, many of the best papers are the older ones that appeared in the early 1970's as the field was forming. The identification of really good material could go a long way toward helping MSE faculty assemble material, not to mention possibly improving the quality of work throughout the field.

What are the Strengths and Weakness of the Wang Institute MSE Program?

Consider again our framework for being a software engineer.

The WIMSE provides an opportunity for exploration of many roles and specialities within software engineering. However, this isn't an explicit goal of the program, but rather an occasional way of organizing projects. This feature of the curriculum has been seen to influence the career paths of several students.   Not enough foundation material or experience is provided, however, for students who may want to pursue several specialities, e.g., related to management.

Many methods have emerged from five years of courses in WIMSE that are teachable and appear valuable in the students' eyes.   Some of these are more like viewpoints, e.g., Parnas' document-driven approach; others are off the path but have been made useful, e.g., the SDM requirements analysis method; and some are extremely useful, if fallible, e.g., systematic testing techniques. However, there are still too many methods considered and too few given the opportunity for deep use within projects. The problem here is one that pervades the software engineering field and is aggravated by faculty inexperience with many methods. This becomes a vicious circle for both faculty and students, trying to learn enough methods to select or synthesize the right ones, and never having the opportunity to explore any fully. There is always more frustration than satisfaction with any of the methods tried.

Similarly, many tools have been successfully integrated into the curriculum, others used occasionally in projects. However, this technology experience is fragile and limited. The main point is that it has been done to some extent and has proved valuable to many students.

The WIMSE provides broad exposure to software engineering concepts. Usually it is viewpoints that prevail over specific methods, especially since the methods themselves usually flop. Students sample a lot, experiment some, and pick up skills along the way. They form a structure for their growing knowledge and assimilate various viewpoints. However, the students are often spoon-fed the material and it is not always certain they will continue to grow after graduation.

As discussed amply, the WIMSE develops many skills and habits that lead to productive work. However, no explicit diagnosis of problems is provided, as, for example, occurs in some computer science courses on problem solving. Also, some basic skills in e.g., writing progress reports, may be ignored.

Conclusions

This paper has tried to emphasize that the WIMSE is more successful at providing skills and structuring knowledge than at providing specific knowledge. Certainly, knowledge is imparted and the WIMSE has gone a long way toward finding the right kinds of knowledge to teach and sometimes has been immensely successful in teaching it well. However, we have claimed that the specific knowledge is less secure, perhaps less valuable, than it looks because the software engineering field as a whole has little "well tested" theory, methods, and technology. A professional degree program can be no better than the state of knowledge in its field. Little of certainty has been learned about software engineering in general through the WIMSE.

Even though more is known, it is the knowledge residing in the faculty that determines what is taught and how well. WIMSE faculty have had to learn on-the-job most of what they teach and had little time to explore deeply what they did not know. We have recommeded serious consideration for extended faculty training for MSE teaching.

The skills acquired by the students are related to the ways the courses are run, the existence of project courses, and the intensity of the environment. Perhaps, this paper has attracted some attention toward the skills aspect of an MSE program.

In summary, we recommend a balance between skills and knowledge in considering MSE programs.

A Note on MCC and
Software Engineering Education

MCC's Software Technology Program is directed toward long-term research on the design of large, complex systems. The generic environment (tools, methodology, integration) to be produced is called Leonardo[1]. One feature of the Software Technology Program's approach is the study of teamwork among design specialists and the support for their individual and coordinated needs. The research will complement that of computer science by dealing with requirements and system-level design, rather than development after the system has been specified. A well-educated population of software engineers will fill some of the roles of Leonardo system specialists, although the system level knowledge goes well beyond what an MSE covers.

The Software Technology Program research in progress should soon be providing input to the software engineering field on various topics. Studies of designers working in groups may provide new models of the software design process. Additional input to those design process models is coming from study of design methods in general and from design experience in other fields. Exploration of possibilities for and multiple views of the product will be studied and ultimately supported. This broad approach to design process models may shed new light on the design methods now entrenched in the software engineering field. Visualization methods and tools are also being explored to better support designers' views of their evolving systems. Information bases of designs and problem domain information are being explored, heading toward reusability. Technology transfer is a specific function within the Program, involving coordination of liaisons from participant companies and planning and execution of events supporting technology transfer. In all, it is hoped that the broad approach of the Software Technology Program and its focus on "up-stream" problems will add both vitality and insight to the software engineering field. A better understanding of system design may help the software engineering field on a central topic which is difficult to teach.

---

[1]Leonardo is a trademark of MCC

Acknowledgement

Glenn Bruns, a 1985 graduate of the WIMSE and now a member of the technical staff at MCC, applied a test of reality to this paper. He's taught me more than I taught him.

Experience with a Software Engineering Project Course

W.M. McKeeman
Wang Institute of Graduate Studies

Abstract. This paper presents an approach to meeting the academic objectives of advanced software engineering project courses. The objectives are increased competence and confidence of the students in carrying out software development projects. The academic context includes a simulated industrial context. Part of the industrial context consists of industrial roles played for the student team by the instructor and others. The project itself is divided into tasks related to deliverables and collateral responsibilities. The software production model is a combination of the waterfall, iterative enhancement and document-driven techniques. A software development environment is mentioned although the details are presented elsewhere. A list of project courses offered at Wang Institute (1982-85) is appended. Further detail is given for four project courses conducted by the author.

Introduction

This paper is intended primarily for teachers of software engineering and secondarily for practicing software engineers. It presents a method for organizing and teaching an advanced project course.

Software Engineering Project is a required course in the Wang Institute Master of Software Engineering degree program. It has been taught 26 times at Wang Institute in the years 1982-1985. Six core courses in software engineering are pre- or co-requisite.

The project course organization reported here has been used four times (out of the total of 26). It simulates industrial practice in organization, methods and deliverables. The objective of the course is experience with the software engineering process. The objective of the simulation is a software product.

The experience reported here is dependent on the context provided by the Wang Institute MSE program. To the extent this context is duplicated elsewhere, this proposal should be successful elsewhere. Where some of the needed qualities in student background and facilities are lacking, the course should be modified to provide the students additional time and instruction during the project.

The Wang Institute MSE

Software engineering is the technological discipline concerned with systematic production and maintenance of software products that are developed and modified on time and within cost estimates. A software engineer must know what to do, when to do it, and how to do it efficiently.

The Master of Software Engineering (MSE) degree program consists of eleven one semester courses. Each course is designed to occupy thirteen hours of student time per week. Six courses constitute the core of the MSE — three in engineering methods, two in management and one in system architecture. Three courses are electives, usually covering technical material in computer systems. The remaining two courses are projects, taken near the end of the program.

The Project Course

The project course is designed to integrate the knowledge the student has gained from the prerequisite courses. Putting all the components of software engineering into practice in a project course requires the students to make hard decisions on what to leave out, where to put emphasis on what is tried, how to track product development quality and quantity and project time, and how to deal with other team members in a world of external demands and internal interactions.

The project course depends on the prerequisite courses; there is no time during the project course for lectures on software engineering methods. Project students often have to gain depth in the project application area during the course.

The central pedagogical challenge is to ensure that the academic exercise, sized to a team of three to seven students, and a time span of ten to thirteen weeks, scales usefully to industrial practice.

The Students

The attitude of the students is a critical factor in the success of any particular project course. The students all have industrial software development experience before starting the MSE program. That fact, together with prerequisite courses, ensures that all students are prepared to contribute. Grades are typically split into a common grade awarded to all members of the team and an individual grade awarded to each member. The team grade is weighted heavily (for example, 70%) in computing the final grade for each student. The planned result is to reinforce the team concept by demanding that success of the team is essential to the success of the individuals in it. This is in contrast to the Software Hut approach where motivation is supplied by a profit and loss game [53].

Each student must deal with the quality vs. quantity tradeoff. Student teams have been consistently overambitious, setting goals that are unattainable within the constraints of time, skill, and staffing. It is important to keep the scope of the exercise within bounds without sacrificing quality, the achievement of which is the central reason the students have entered the Wang Institute MSE program.

The C-Kit Projects

The author of this paper has recently supervised a sequence of project courses under the general title of C-Kit. Each student team has built some component of a compiler (record handler, lexer, screener, parser, decorator, abstractor...). All have been built under UNIX[1] on a Digital Vax 780.

Each C-Kit project has been designed to keep the deliverable software to a minimum, sufficient only to exercise the software engineering process. Typically, this leads to two hundred pages of process-related documents and a few hundred lines of delivered code. (In passing I add a defensive note in response to questions from my earlier reviewers. This is surely not the way to get a few hundred lines of code written;

---

[1]UNIX is a trademark of AT&T Bell Laboratories.

rather it is a way for my students to learn how to deliver larger systems, without letting the C-Kit coding exercise get in the way.) The emphasis on *the quality of the software engineering process* leads to products that are reasonable input to later project courses where extensions or integration tasks may be assigned. It is possible that C-Kit deliverables will be reworked to become Wang Institute supported packages.

Software Engineering Process Guidelines

Some project pre-structuring is available to the student team. This pre-structuring resides in style manuals, directory structures, document templates, and anything from any previous project courses. This collection is referred to here as the Software Engineering Process Guidelines. A collated document with this title will be available for Wang Institute students in the near future.

Models

Many different models have been tried for project courses at Wang Institute. It is easier to understand the model currently being used in C-Kit as one of a larger set of possibilities. The variables are product, production, and pedagogy.

Product Models

Before one can choose an engineering approach, one must have some idea of the task to be performed. This is called the product model.

Where the project lies between research (R) and development (D) is the most important parameter. Projects at the R end of the R-D scale require the team to discover much of what they need to know during the project itself. Typically a project ends up R oriented when some new technical application is to be attempted. Less often the team chooses to experiment with the engineering process itself. R projects start slow and have less time for process-related efforts. The effect is to risk the worst of industrial practice. Students under pressure can slip due dates and launch heroic hacking sessions at school as well as at work. On the other hand both the instructor and students are often motivated to new heights by an exciting challenge [14].

Projects at the D end of the R-D scale are low risk; someone on the team knows knows how to solve all the technical problems that are going to arise. D projects are much more predictable and are more likely to leave behind a usable legacy.

A second parameter is the degree of completeness of the project with respect to the product life cycle. A project that starts with requirements and ends up with delivered code is complete. One that does only part of the process (say a specification, or a design) is partial.

A third parameter is the independence of the project from earlier work on it. A new project is independent. An enhancement project is ongoing.

For C-Kit projects, the typical characterization has been:

```
R-D        Research    |--------------------x--| Development
C-P        Complete    |-x---------------------| Partial
I-O     Independent    |-x---------------------| Ongoing
```

One C-Kit project was much closer to the Research end of the R-D line. A planned C-Kit front-end integration project will be near the Ongoing end of the I-O line.

Production Models

There are several software production models in use, but none has gained universal acceptance in industry. This is reasonable because different kinds of problems require different kinds of approaches. It is also unreasonable because models known to be ineffective continue to be used.

Production models, when introduced to the profession, are presented whole. That is to say, an author of a production model typically presents a working system, usually encompassing the entire product life cycle. Within such a whole model there are two distinct concepts: the activities to be performed, and the ordering of those activities. The activities are closely related to the deliverables. Often an activity described within one model can be employed in a second model, replacing the analogous activity in the second model. The models relevant to this course organization are:

- Boehm is the spokesman for the "waterfall model" [12]. The activities are producing requirements, functional specifications, designs, code; unit testing, integration, and system testing; validation and verification, acceptance and delivery. The ordering is sequential, with successive activities partially overlapped. Because the waterfall model requires the early steps to be especially free of mistakes while it is well known that early in the project is just when ignorance makes mistakes most likely, some authors have objected to its use [23].

- Parnas advocates a document driven model [77]. Good configuration management and information hiding are major features of this model. Team members are required to rework the defining documents before fixing inadequacies discovered during implementation. In the most elaborate form of the method, change permission is controlled by an external bureaucracy. This would be typical of a large government-funded application.

- Basili and Turner propose Iterative Enhancement [7]. Iterative enhancement is a sequential model. In stage 1, a subset of the final functionality is built. Based on what was learned in stage N, stage N+1 is planned and carried out with increased functionality. In the simplest form of iterative enhancement, stage 1 is a prototype, and stage 2 is the final product.

A combination of the waterfall, document-driven and iterative-enchancement production models is used for C-Kit projects. This new model may be visualized as a sequential pair of highly overlapped, nearly vertical waterfalls — reminiscent of Yosemite Falls.

There are two complete stages. At the beginning of each stage, each of the waterfall activities is started almost immediately. Parnas' format for document definition is the starting point for deliverable documents [50]. The team must be alert to moving material from one deliverable to another when such movement increases a separation of concerns. As drafts of the conceptually earlier waterfall documents become available, some rework of the later, dependent material is expected. The first release of the completed deliverables is during week 6 or 7 (the end of stage 1).

The work in stage 2 proceeds with increased certainty as a result of the stage 1 experience. Stage 2 is planned to take the remainder of the available time, and is characterized by increased functionality, rework of process deliverables from stage 1, and the preparation of a public presentation of the results.

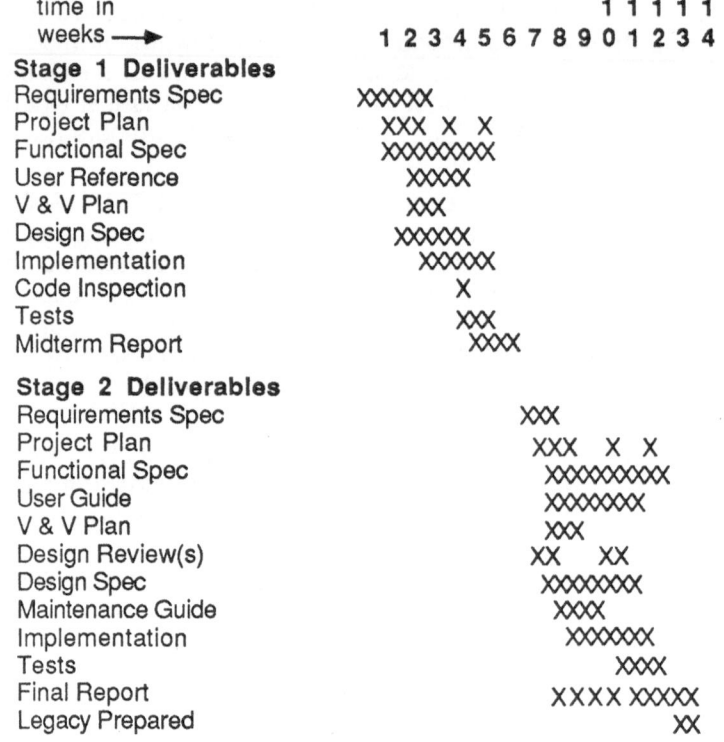

```
            time in                              1 1 1 1 1
            weeks ──►            1 2 3 4 5 6 7 8 9 0 1 2 3 4
Stage 1 Deliverables
Requirements Spec          XXXXX
Project Plan               XXX X X
Functional Spec            XXXXXXXXX
User Reference             XXXXX
V & V Plan                 XXX
Design Spec                XXXXXX
Implementation             XXXXXX
Code Inspection            X
Tests                        XXX
Midterm Report                XXXX

Stage 2 Deliverables
Requirements Spec                    XXX
Project Plan                         XXX   X  X
Functional Spec                      XXXXXXXXX
User Guide                           XXXXXXX
V & V Plan                           XXX
Design Review(s)                     XX   XX
Design Spec                          XXXXXXXX
Maintenance Guide                    XXXX
Implementation                       XXXXXXX
Tests                                    XXXX
Final Report                         XXXX XXXXX
Legacy Prepared                              XX
```

Figure 1. Double Waterfall Model

Typical C-Kit Project

Pedagogical Models

The driving pedagogical principle is to optimize the gain in student competence and confidence in conducting software development projects. It is acceptable for the team to fail to meet simulated industrial goals if the experience supports the academic goals.

A product-process tradeoff is made at the beginning of the project — the team may emphasize the delivery of the software product or emphasize the process. A product-intensive project tends to produce more code, and also tends to get into "industrial" kinds of trouble such as deadline slips, needing to reduce functionality at the last moment, and giving short shrift to documentation and testing. It is better to eliminate some tasks (that is, reduce the complexity of the production model) at the outset of a product-intensive project course rather than risk doing them poorly. Deliverables from a process-intensive project are usually professional in appearance. The content, however, may suffer. The phrase "full of sound and fury and signifying nothing" gives the flavor, although exaggerated. The instructor needs to guide the team into a safe middle ground.

Process in a project course may not lead to deliverables. A student-delivered lecture on revision control, or programming standards, may affect other deliverables but be associated with none. The instructor needs to ensure that the students carrying out "invisible" contributions are recognized and rewarded.

External Participants

To enhance the industrial simulation, various supporting roles are played for the project team. Often another member of the Wang Institute community, or someone from industry, is willing to play a supporting role. When the instructor plays such a role, he wears hats. The purpose of the hats is to ensure the team members react to the role, rather than to the real person. On occasion the students also wear hats to emphasize their roles when they are outside the expected pattern of team interaction (trainer, reviewer, etc.).

The external participants must have knowledge in the subjects required by the roles detailed below. In addition they must have the time to devote to student interaction, a perspective, a sense of humor, and a sense of the dramatic sufficient to make their roles "live."

Instructor

The instructor is outside the project, taking responsibility for the pedagogical experience. Except that a successful industrial experience is good for the self-confidence of the team, it is irrelevant to the course. For example, if the instructor believes that the team will gain an important insight thereby, risk-taking that would be unacceptable in an industrial project may be permitted. Similarly, a shouting match during a technical review may not be immediately quashed by the instructor if letting it play itself out will lead to a rich educational experience for some of the participants. The instructor wears no hat.

VP for Software

The VP is the authority figure on the project. The VP wears an intimidating dark blue hat, isn't knowledgeable about software, and is prone to Draconian measures. The team needs the signature of the VP for all deliverables and is careful to approach the VP only when the document to be signed is something the team is willing to stand behind. The instructor normally plays the VP role.

Customer

The customer represents the organization wanting the product. The customer has been played by the instructor, another member of the Institute, or by a "real" outsider from industry. The customer interacts with the team through periodic progress reports to ensure the correspondence between requirements and product. The earlier a divergence is detected, the less trouble it will cause.

Technical Consultant

Each project requires some technical knowledge beyond what the students bring to the course. A role of "technical consultant" is provided to fill the need. The consultant is ever willing to give advice but has no decision-making power. When played by the instructor, the consultant wears a gaily checkered hat with CONSULTANT written on the hatband. This is intended to emphasize to the students that they can safely ignore the technical advice (and not be worried that the consultant is really the instructor and in charge of grades). Occasionally the ground rules include the possibility that the VP for Software can also call on the technical consultant for advice.

Technical Editor

Some projects have access to a professional technical writer who red-lines draft documents according to the standards of technical writing. Like the technical consultant, the technical editor is willing to give advice but has no decision-making power.

Reviewer

Reviews of project deliverables often require a knowledgeable outsider, either as reviewer or review leader. The instructor is usually unable to play this role effectively, because a hat does not really hide authority and reviews are prone to emotional pathologies. Other students or members of the technical staff or outsiders can be invited to participate in reviews [35].

Project Leader (optional)

Rather than assigning the watered-down project coordinator role to a student team member, one can bring in an experienced project leader from outside the team. Experience to date indicates such a project leader must:

- Be more skilled than the rest of the team in software engineering methods.
- Have no personal stake in the product (e.g., not be the "customer" in disguise).
- Have a basis for authority of position (e.g., a say in the final grades).
- Have time to attend *all* project meetings.

Project Librarian

The librarian is responsible for documenting meetings, keeping the hardcopy files straight, and collecting materials for presentations. The project librarian position is not popular with the team members. Often we are able to get a less experienced graduate assistant to play this role for a specific project. This alternative has the side effect of preparing the project librarian for later participation as a student in project courses. The librarian of the Chief Programmer Team has, of course, other duties, some of which are allocated to team members in the course organization given here [3].

Secretary

The volume of the materials produced, and the need for multiple copies, makes a secretary desirable. The alternative is for the students to do secretarial work in place of other more instructive project work. At Wang Institute, the faculty secretarial staff often fulfills this role. The task is continuous from the start of the project but most intensive just before project presentation.

Project Course Deliverables

There are two stages to each C-Kit project. For stage 1, the requirements are minimal. The team nevertheless carries an entire life cycle to completion during the first half of the time allotted to the project course. One team member is responsible for each deliverable. For each responsible team member, a second team member is assigned as backup and assistant. The responsible team member is not expected to do all the work for the deliverable; several team members may be assigned to work on it. Not every member of the team is expected to work on every deliverable.

The assignments of tasks may change after stage 1 is complete. Each team member is encouraged to work both in an area where they feel special expertise and another area where they may feel the need to strengthen skills.

At the beginning of stage 2, the team and customer negotiate an increased functionality for the product. All deliverables are then reworked. Often most of the stage 1 deliverables carry over directly to stage 2.

The categories of deliverables are specifications, verification and validation, implementation, and documentation. The details follow.

Specifications

There are three specification documents: requirements, functions, and design. Writing specifications is often difficult for the students. One specific problem often encountered in preparing the specifications is that material is needlessly repeated in several separate documents. The details below supply the guidelines intended to minimize the duplication of material in specification documents.

Requirements Specification

The requirements document is usually provided by the instructor in draft form on day 1 of the project. The team is responsible for producing the final form and getting the signature of the customer. The purpose of the requirements document is to define the product to be developed in a way that is understandable and satisfactory to both the customer and the developer. A requirements document exhibits the following properties:

1. Each requirement is able to be validated ("met" or "not met").
2. It is in the language of the customer (no jargon, informal).
3. It contains no adverbs ("very", "fast", ...).
4. It is complete (no implicit requirements).
5. It includes requirements other than function (e.g. maintainability, performance).
6. It is explicit about constraints ("must use the VAX").
7. It is brief and readable.
8. It is signed by both customer and developer.

"Complete" in (4) above does not mean final. A requirements specification can be changed during the project by renegotiation but not by unilateral action by the development team. Periodic progress reviews keyed to the requirements document are the normal management control to insure that the team understands and accepts the task as defined. As a practical matter, the instructor monitors the team meetings and correspondence.

Functional Specification

A functional specification defines the functions to be supplied to the user, but not any invisible internal functions. The functions supplied must fulfill the requirements. The functional specification does not address how the functions are going to be achieved, although the specification writer generally has one (feasibility) model in mind when proposing the functions. Performance requirements for, and interfaces to, the user-visible functions are appropriate for this document. This document can be formal; often algebraic specifications are attempted.

Design Specification

A design specification describes how the product is to be built. It includes module definitions, inter-module interfaces, data structures, invariants, pre/post conditions, exception response, and algorithms[2]. The interface descriptions are most often procedural. It is appropriate to use implementation language notation to describe data structures, procedure headers, and the content of module banners. It is not appropriate to use implementation language notation to describe algorithms.

The design is a primary input to the work breakdown structure needed for the project plan, although timing constraints often force the planner to lump all implementation activity into an undifferentiated blob for the first few issues of the plan.

In industry, a design will often have a good deal more structure (architectural design, detailed design, pseudo code) than used in C-Kit projects. That level of detail has proven to be excessive for the project course.

Verification & Validation (V&V)

The V&V effort in a C-Kit project course has three components: technical reviews, the test plan and the test execution. (No team has attempted a proof of correctness to date.) Some related activities are carried out as collateral duties and do not result in deliverables.

Technical Reviews

Every project course should include at least one formal technical review [35]. It is most often a design review, but on occasion it has been more

---

[2]A hidden assumption here is the expected use of an imperative language such as Ada or C.

appropriate to have a code review or a review of some other deliverable. Inspections, focused on specific guidelines, have proven to be the easiest to conduct within the experience limitations of the students and the time constraints of the course. Walkthroughs are more difficult for inexperienced teams; it is too easy to get deflected onto side issues. Wide-ranging technical reviews are rarely successful in a project course context, partly because the accelerated schedule of the project makes the reviewed material obsolete before the review team can assimilate it and prepare for the review itself.

Test Plan

The testing group must validate the software with respect to requirements specifications, and verify the software with respect to functional specifications [8]. The test plan is directed at the final integrated product. The test plan does not include any unit testing unless unit testing is an essential component of the method for testing the integrated product. The testing activity is often expressed by command scripts and data files so that regression testing and test-set enhancement are automated. In C-Kit projects, we insist that correct results are never seen twice by human eyes. Once seen and approved, they are moved to an "approved" file and checked by file differencing thereafter.

The required tests are:

1. Smoke test (one path through the product).
2. Functions test (reasonable use of each function tested).
3. Limits test (every known or suspected limit n is tested at n-1, n and n+1).
4. Problem guesses (tests where trouble can be expected: function interference, boundary cases, machine/application mismatch).
5. Error response (reasonable response to violation of preconditions and other undesired events).

Test Execution

Each release of the product is tested; test failures are documented and the project coordinator (or leader) is notified. Conflicts over test interpretation are placed on the agenda for the next project meeting.

Implementation

A code deliverable consists of source modules that have been unit tested and integrated. The size of the code is deliberately kept small (a few hundred lines is optimal) by vigorous subsetting of any ambitious requirements. The assumption is that each deliverable is complete, correct, and meets all quality criteria — small but beautiful. All code is written with the two-stage delivery already in mind. Where possible, stage 1 delivered modules incorporate stage 2 hooks to simplify the planned extensions.

Documentation

Documentation specifically designed for the users and maintainers of the product include the manuals and the project report discussed in the following paragraphs.

User Tutorial

The user tutorial is designed to be read from front to back before, and during, a user's first experience with the software. It need not be comprehensive but it must leave the reader able to use a subset of the capabilities of the product and ready to continue using the software depending only on the User Reference.

User Reference

The user reference is designed for ease of look up. It is structured either by function or alphabetically. Tables are preferred to prose. It has an index and a glossary.

Maintenance Manual

The maintenance manual is intended to ease the task of systems programmers maintaining the delivered software for the customer, and for guidance in rework and enhancement by developers who may work on the software later. This manual gives an overview of the software, keying on the design document, installation, and software-change directives. Expected changes and the hooks provided are listed. An unanticipated change, requiring an extensive understanding of the software and substantial rewrite, is probably best carried out as a new life cycle; in effect, a stage N+1 of the iterative enhancement model. In the Parnas production model, for example, the maintenance documentation is identical with the design documentation [50].

Project Report

The project report includes the deliverables as well as retrospective statements by project participants: in particular, it includes the annotated and edited mail messages and memos, project statistics, customer evaluation, and presentation aids.

Collateral Assignments

In addition to the deliverable-related tasks of the project, students must do other tasks necessary to carry a project to a successful conclusion. These tasks, called collateral assignments, can be characterized as overhead, administrative, or housekeeping. In a lean-and-mean industrial world, these tasks are often unmentioned and often done badly. Our view is that they must be done well, and it is better to plan for them and carry them out efficiently.

Depending on the size of the team, each project member typically has more than one collateral assignment.

Project Coordinator

The project coordinator, a student role, is a watered-down version of project leader. The coordinator is responsible for:

- Publishing the Software Engineering Process Guidelines for the project.
- Seeing that meetings are scheduled, attended, and documented.
- Periodically checking on, and publishing the status of, each deliverable.
- Scheduling customer/team meetings for progress reviews.
- Ensuring that problems arising between team members are promptly dealt with (by personal action or by invoking higher authority).

There are several reasons why the above duties are limited. Most important is that singling out one student as "leader" is divisive. When the position is down-graded to administrative chores (as above), it becomes about as attractive as the other collateral duties. Also, among a group of students, there is rarely one that is sufficiently knowledgeable and mature to exert the necessary technical leadership; thus, the leadership role is transferred to the supervising faculty member or some other non-student outsider.

Planner

Early in the project a description of deliverables, a work breakdown structure, milestones, and project constraints are established. The planner takes the lead in ensuring that decisions are made. Then the planner collects the information and presents it in a project plan. The project coordinator uses the project plan to check team progress and the planner periodically reissues the plan with progress-to-date marked. Changes in the plan by team agreement or by imposition by higher authority are reflected back into the plan and it is reissued. Work breakdown structure tools and PERT tools are sometimes used.

Trainer

Often, despite the common background of the student team members, they are not all at the same skill level in some process necessary to the project. A team member is chosen to organize a tutorial on the required topic. The organizer is allowed to draw on external participants, in particular, on the technical consultant, for the actual presentation.

Directory Manager

The directory manager is responsible for the integrity of the common file spaces of the team.

Under UNIX, it is convenient to establish a project directory and sub-directories corresponding to the various team activities. The team members are directed to constrain their use of the common space by rules intended to enhance team efficiency and preserve information. They are also constrained to do all project work within the common directory. Each team member has a personal subdirectory for workspace.

The rules are published in a Software Engineering Process Guidelines established early in the project (usually a modification of a previous standard). Specifically, rules are given for the naming of files and directories (case conventions, name length, etc.), the content of README files, and the association of team member activity and the directory containing the results. The directory manager is not responsible for the contents of any files representing deliverables.

The directory manager periodically examines all the directories. Deviations from the published guidelines are brought to the attention of the owner of the file.

Document Manager

The document manager is responsible for the form and style of deliverable documents. In addition, the document manager is alert to information needlessly appearing in more than one document.

Team members produce hardcopy deliverables at intermediate stages of completion, usually as part of a formal or informal review. The document manager checks all presented hardcopy against the relevant Software Engineering Process Guidelines and brings any deviations to the attention of the author.

Where the deviation involves document contents — that is, where material has appeared in one document but apparently belongs in another — the document manager arranges for a discussion between the authors of the conflicting documents to resolve the conflict. The document manager does not inspect documents looking for missing technical material, because missing material is usually just a reflection of work-in-progress.

The document manager is also responsible for ensuring that all submitted documents contain information necessary for configuration control. This is discussed in more detail by Gill [47]; each document must be visibly identified by status, file location, version number, and date.

Code Manager

The code manager is responsible for the form and style of deliverable code.

The code manager is responsible for inventing specific program identifiers used by more than one team member (for example, for external procedure names and interface variables). The objective is consistency across the project.

Team members are encouraged to submit draft code for the code manager to inspect by submitting hardcopy, sending electronic mail, or specifying file location. The code manager checks the submittal against the coding rules (naming conventions, banner contents, paragraphing style, etc.), which are published in the Software Engineering Process Guidelines. The coder is notified of any problems, providing the coder with the opportunity to correct them before an official release is required.

Code cannot be released until the code manager certifies that it meets the guidelines.

Statistician

The project statistician is responsible for collecting and presenting the project activity record.

The data collected by the statistician includes the amount of time spent by each team member and on each activity. It may also include information on page, line, and word counts, bug tracking, or other product completion measures. Time cards, or an automated version giving the same information, must be designed and put into action almost immediately at project initiation. The information normally appears during the retrospective portion of the final presentation.

Mail Manager

Where electronic mail or memos are used for communication within the project, a historical record is preserved by the mail manager.

At a minimum the mail manager sorts communications into the appropriate categories and cross references where necessary. The mail manager may institute guidelines for mail headers so that the sender is required to state under what category the item is to be archived.

Legacy Manager

The legacy manager preserves the machine readable form of the final version of the deliverables for posterity.

The task includes the preparation of a subdirectory within the project directory, moving products into it as they are completed, and deleting all other files and directories shortly after the completion of the project.

Presentation Manager

The presentation manager is responsible for organizing presentations of the project and product.

A midsemester project presentation is given to the instructor alone. During this presentation, the instructor gives guidance to the team as they prepare for a public presentation at the end of stage 2.

The tasks of the presentation manager are:

- Organization of the presentation.
- Assigning presenters.
- Checking the presentation materials for accuracy and consistency.
- Scheduling the presentation time and space.
- Inviting the audience, always including the "customer," other students and faculty, and sometimes outside observers from local industry.

In addition, the hardcopy form of the presentation, usually several hundred pages of organized project materials, must be collected, collated, copied, bound, and distributed. At Wang Institute, the team members, the instructor, other requesting faculty, the department archives and the library all get copies. Extensive secretarial support is provided.

Software Development Environment

All C-Kit software has been developed under UNIX. It became clear during the first C-Kit project that the students were consuming valuable time establishing their workspaces and procedures. The difficulty was reduced semester by semester, by the increasing availability of legacy directories left over from completed project courses. The advantages supplied by the legacies, however, had the ill effect of inviting slavish copying of mature documents without the new author understanding the significance of some of the contents. The results were not always gratifying and required an inordinate amount of instructor time to correct.

The Institute supplies a project environment building facility to solve this problem. The builder provides a project directory structure and populates it with tools, document templates, and guideline documents. All work done by the team on the project is done within this directory structure. The builder, in its dormant form, resides as a shar file [79].[3] The details of a version of this environment, of considerable relevance to this paper, are documented by Gill [47].

The most important aspect of the project tools is that all project deliverable documents, using existing templates, automatically annotated with author(s), date and version, are kept with their revision history under rcs [96]. The rcs check in and check out actions use project-defined commands that ensure the integrity of this information. A typical use pattern includes a locked check out into a workspace directory, modification, check in, and draft printing.

The team must be skilled in the use of general tools as well as the use of project specific tools available in the environment. To some extent, the course prerequisites provides the initial familiarity; more detailed information is available in the tools seminars that are periodically given by the Institute professional staff outside the courses. Sometimes additional instructional time is necessary during the project. When this is

---

[3]Shar collects files and directories into a text file suitable for electronic transmission. The shar file is unpacked by running it as a Bourne shell script.

so, team members are assigned "trainer" collateral duties and time is allocated in the project plan.

The first environments grew naturally during projects (January 1982 to present). Professor Nancy Martin made available to the Institute community "A Short Discussion of Project Courses," a comprehensive collection of project course materials (January 1984). Various C-Kit projects drew on this material. An elaborate environment was set up by Tim Gill for the Wang Institute Static Analysis Project (October 1984). A common environment was set up for the faculty staff (early 1985). A project course entitled meta-project (September-December 1985) combined these experiences to build the first exportable project builder. The expectation is that several versions, each specialized to a particular style of conducting the project course, will be available to student teams at Wang Institute, and possibly available to outsiders as Institute-supported products.

Summary and Evaluation

This paper has presented a comprehensive description of one way of organizing and presenting a project course. The components are well trained, advanced students, a minimal product, an elaborate engineering process, good tools, and task assignments for external participants, deliverables and collateral duties.

It works. No one component is essential. It is usual to plan to experiment with some changes each time the course is run. The main determinant of success, in addition to the details laid out above, is the attention paid to the project and team by the faculty supervisor. Enthusiasm is contagious. A secondary determinant is the expectation that the product may someday be used, and that it will be looked to for exemplary practice by teams to follow. A third determinant is an element of risk; the mountain must be worthy of climbing. A measure of the success is the cohesiveness and mutual regard of the team at project end and beyond.

Serious problems can arise when equipment fails at a critical moment or when a team member fails to produce, or when the problem turns out to be beyond the time and energy of the team. There is little time to recover — at best the team falls back to a prepared reduction in functionality.

A project environment builder, containing much of the accumulated lore of the C-Kit projects, has been constructed. Here lies the hidden leverage of this kind of project course. Each year the students have ever improved examples and tools upon which to build. Information on the availability of the project environment for external distribution can be obtained by writing to the Wang Institute Faculty Technical Staff.

Acknowledgments

Several people contributed to this work. Some of it is traceable to Dr. Wang's original vision of the Institute and its articulation by the Institute National Academic Advisory Committee. The faculty and students who have struggled together to give meaning to the project courses will recognize the presence of good ideas that evolved in their courses, and the absence of bad ideas that they paid the price to explore. Dr. Nancy Martin contributed a depth of software engineering knowledge, the courage to try a variety of models, and finally a useful collation of materials which marked the beginning of the C-Kit efforts. The Summer 84 C-Kit team contributed the first consistent set of reusable materials. A member of that team, Tim Gill, took a research position at the Institute after graduation and further developed the project environment. Another alumnus, Dan Ligett, from his staff position in the Wang Institute Software Environment activity, and software specialist Sid Shapiro contributed much of the expertise needed by the Summer 84 team. Gill and Jim Kirby undertook the guidance of a student project to provide the first project environment builder. Several colleagues, most notably Susan Cardwell, Richard Fairley, Tom Fitzgerald, Jim Horning, Nancy Martin and David Weiss, made many helpful suggestions on the draft of this report. To all I am grateful.

Appendix I

Historical Log of Project Courses at Wang Institute

COURSE   INSTRUCTOR

Winter 1982
WICOMO   Bouhana
(implementation of Boehm's COCOMO model)

Summer 1982
Graphics Package Specification   McKeeman

Fall 1982
WISK Registration I   Martin
(a registrar's package for the Wang VS computer)

Winter 1983
Software Design Language   Fairley
WISK Registration II   Martin
WICOMO Enhancement   Bouhana

Summer 1983
Expert Systems   Martin
Software Design Language
& Processor   Fairley

Fall 1983
A Bibliography Manager   Gerhart

Winter 1984
Prototype Transformation System   Ardis
UNIX Instrumentation Tools   Bouhana
C-Kit Lexer   McKeeman

Summer 1984
C-Kit Screener   McKeeman
WICAL in Prolog   Gerhart
(an institute-wide calendar database)

Fall 1984
YACP   Martin
(a table generator for a C lexer)

Winter 1985
C-Kit Parser   McKeeman
Referee Management System   Bouhana

Summer 1985
TEDGEN   Ardis
(a syntax-sensitive editor in Emacs)
Prototype & Feasibility   Velasco
On-Line Survey Systems I   Bouhana
On-Line Survey Systems II   Perlman
C-Kit Decorator   McKeeman

Fall 1985
Meta Project   McKeeman
(a project course environment
builder)   Fitzgerald
Tool for JSD   Velasco
PM-KIT   Fairley
(a project management tool)

Appendix II

Recent C-Kit Project Experiences

The four projects below were run within the structure described in this paper. An outline of the deliverables and retrospective comments are given for each.

C-Kit Lexer

Semester: Winter 84 (13 weeks)

Team: Robert Marion, Susan Stefanec, Ephraim Vishniac

Reports: project report, includes draft requirements (1 p) requirements (4 p), project presentation materials (25 pp)

TOTAL 30 pp.

Reports - Stage 1:
project plan (9 pp), functional specification (11 pp),
test plan (13 pp), design specification (9 pp),
design specification (screener stub) (5 pp), design
specification (record handler stub) (5 pp),
Stage 1 status report (6 pp).

TOTAL 58 pp.

Reports - Stage 2:
project plan (8 pp), requirements (User Manual) (4 pp),
decision analysis for added functions (4 pp),
functional specifications (13 pp), test plan (9 pp),
design specification (5 pp), change specification (3 pp),
user manual (29 pp), project notebook (9 pp), memos (6 pp).

TOTAL 90 pp. (largely derived from Stage 1)

project code (deliverable, tests, stubs and drivers) (39 pp),
output (19 pp).

TOTAL 58 pp.

GRAND TOTAL 236 pp.

Retrospective:

The students delivered a lexer for the C programming language. The input was C program text; the output was a sequence of lexemes, containing the isolated text and associated information (what kind of lexeme, where found in input file, ...). The performance of the lexer set a standard for later project courses. The details of lexeme passing required a new concept — partially completed lexeme — which had to be added to the interface design in stage 2.

C-Kit Screener

Semester: Summer 84 (10 weeks)

Team: Susan Cardwell, Edmund Fung, Timothy Gill, Jim Haungs, Daniel Keller, Penny Parkinson, Ray Tackett

Reports - Stage 1:

document standards (5 pp), project plan (12 pp),
weekly Gannt charts (5 pp), requirements (5 pp),
functional specification (8 pp), design (12 pp),
QA plan (6 pp), user manual (6 pp), code (24 pp),
presentation materials (22 pp), document template (2 pp)

TOTAL 107 pp.

Reports - Stage 2:

document standards (5 pp), project plan (12 pp),
weekly Gannt charts (6 pp), requirements (5 pp),
functional specifications (15 pp), design (8 pp),
QA plan (7 pp), user manual (9 pp), code (50 pp),
test data and results (17 pp),
presentation materials (34 pp), document template (4 pp),
draft requirements (5 pp), administrative materials (74 pp),
directory structure (4 pp), retrospective (10 pp).

TOTAL 264 pp.

GRAND TOTAL 371 pp.

Retrospective:

The students delivered a screener for the C programming language. They completed an algebraic specification for the screener and did an elaborate job of testing. The performance requirement was that the lexer-screener pair had to be at worst twice as slow as the (existing) lexer. The emphasis on document standards was an interesting development — strongly affecting later projects.

C-Kit Parser

Semester: Winter 85 (13 weeks)

Team: Courtney Claussen, Ira Diamant, George Pfeiffer, Susan Trager, Allen Yen

Reports - Final Report Stage 2:

project plan (18 pp), requirements (5 pp),
functional specification (23 pp), design (7 pp),
V&V specification (30 pp), user manual (8 pp),
memos (25 pp), UNIX based test environment (14 pp),
meeting notes (18 pp), presentation materials (44 pp),
retrospective (4 pp)

TOTAL 196 pp.

Source Code TOTAL 150 pp.

GRAND TOTAL 246 pp.

Retrospective:

Stage 1 delivered a working parse tree builder for a small subset of C. Stage 2 delivered the same for most of C. This resulted in about 5000 lines of C code (far too much). The quality of the result was insufficient for later use, partly because of the excessive size of the task, and partly because of an error in the requirements (lay the fault to the consultant). Testing was a major consumer of team effort and was severely cut back for stage 2.

C-Kit Decorator

Semester: Summer 85 (10 weeks)
Team: Kyle Geiger, David Lui, Steve Shaw

Reports - Stage 1:
project plan (8 pp), requirements (4 pp),
functional specification (9 pp), design (7 pp),
QA plan (6 pp), project review summary (6 pp),
presentation materials (33 pp), meeting notes (13 pp)

TOTAL 86 pp.

Reports - Stage 2:
project plan (8 pp), requirements (5 pp),
functional specification (10 pp), design (7 pp),
QA plan (5 pp), presentation materials (33 pp),
meeting notes (8 pp)

TOTAL 71 pp (rewritten stage 1 materials were more concise in stage 2)

Source Code 60 pp.

GRAND TOTAL 227 pp.

Retrospective:

The students produced a program that, given a parse tree for a C program, would remove all declaration nodes and decorate all identifiers (terminal nodes) with the corresponding declaration. This is one way to do symbol table processing. The project took several weeks to get off the ground because neither the team nor the consultant knew exactly what was wanted. The project was well towards the R end of the R-D scale. Delivery was achieved by vigorous subsetting of the C language. (A fundamental design error in the C-Kit parser was detected causing the parser to be sent back for rework.)

Software Engineering Project Laboratory: The Bridge Between University and Industry

Richard H. Thayer
California State University

Leo A. Endres
Atkinson System Technologies Company

Abstract. The study of computer science, which concentrates programming languages, compiler construction, and operating system courses, does not adequately prepare an individual to build large software systems. This paper describes a two semester software engineering laboratory course to develop a student's understanding of software engineering and its relationship with computer science. This laboratory course also is intended to help computer science students make the transition from the school environment to the professional environment. It provides an opportunity to practice software engineering in an industrial/business situation under an engineering or product acquisition type contract. In addition the students assume project responsibilities broader in scope than they would normally have the opportunity to assume in their first years of employment. Problems and issues in instructing and managing a software engineering course of this type are discussed.

The Teaching of Computer Science Courses

University courses in computer science typically center around the areas of programming languages, software systems, data bases, and the applications of programming (e.g., graphics, business applications, engineering, etc.). The typical out-of-class assignment given to students is to write a computer program that will: (1) illustrate or show his understanding of a computer science concept, e.g., a database implementation, a different programming language, an assembler implementation, or (2) implement a computer application in a particular programming language, e.g., data processing problem, graph, computer aided design. The student is given one to several sheets of paper describing how the program is to be written. He is rarely told what problem is being solved. This is known as a homework assignment. The student demonstrates his knowledge of the subject by producing a computer program in source code and output data in accordance with specific instructions on the assignment sheet. Seldom is the student

required to establish a set of requirements from only some vague understanding of the problem; to design the system using one or more of the
acceptable design technologies; to develop a comprehensive test plan
and test specifications to test the system; and finally to make a written
or verbal report to the originator of the requirement. This is not to say
that no school does this; however, it appears to be the normal method of
doing a homework assignment in a computer science course.

The homework assignments are not large problems. Despite the many
hours students labor over terminals "hacking" at the program, they seldom develop a computer program with more than several hundred lines
of code. This creates a number of problems for the students after they
graduate.

Issues In Computer Science Education

The following paragraphs outline some of the issues in computer
science education.

Lack of Large System Development Knowledge

The graduating computer science student does not have a clear understanding of how to develop a very large computer program. It is difficult
for them to comprehend that even a relatively small program of 2 to 5
thousand lines of code cannot be tackled by hacking away at the computer program, and that this approach will not solve a problem that requires a team of more than one person.

False Sense of High Productivity

The student gets a distorted viewpoint of productivity. Those individuals
who have learned only to program, typically without a complete education in computer science, believe that producing several hundred lines of
code a day is usual, because they were able to program a short computer program homework assignment in that length of time. They do not
realize that code is only a small part of developing a software system.

Lack of Engineering Skills

Coding is reported to take only 15-30% of the available software
development time with the balance of the effort going to the engineering

efforts of system and software analysis, software design, system and software testing, documentation and a myriad of other things. For examples, see Boehm [12]. Despite this fact, the majority of university computer science courses are devoted only to programming and the applications of programming. This handicaps the typical graduate in that he has not been trained to do 70-85% of the professional tasks assigned to him.

Lack of Communication Skills

Graduates are hired as computer science professionals, are paid a professional salary, and work in a professional environment. Boehm [12] references studies that show that programmer professionals spend a large part of their time doing nonprogramming work, e.g., communicating with managers, customers, and peers. In addition, as mentioned, much of what a computer professional does involves writing technical documents and reports. Although an English course is required of most college graduates, this course alone does not adequately prepare them to spend a majority of their day talking and writing.

Software Engineering Crisis

Among the major issues involving large software systems are the following: They are often late, cost much more than originally budgeted, and frequently do not satisfy the "user," even though they may have met their required specifications. In addition, software systems are unreliable. They often fail to operate under what looks like normal conditions, are difficult to modify and change when necessary, and are not reusable later when the requirements slightly change. These failures in our ability to deliver a software system constitute what has been called, for the last twenty years, the "software crisis." Software engineering was introduced in the 1970s in an effort to bring an engineering discipline to software development and to solve and reduce the "software crisis." As far as industry is concerned universities produce coders, not engineers, and these people are not trained to tackle large software developments.

Software Engineering Courses

Software engineering courses will reduce the shortfall in computer science knowledge just as software engineering will reduce or eliminate the software development issues. This paper proposes a solution to this problem — teach software engineering courses at the undergraduate level and require software engineering courses in a computer science curriculum. Table 1 from Barry Boehm [15] does an excellent job of illustrating the differences between small and large computer systems. It dramatically points out that learning to program small systems cannot prepare individuals to properly build large software systems. This paper emphasizes an approach to teaching software engineering through software engineering laboratory courses.

Characteristic	Small Software Project	Large Software Project
User	Developer	Not the Developer
User Documentation	Memory Aids-Minimal	Tutorial-Extensive
Error Protection	Optional Minimal	Necessary-Extensive
Validation	Optional Minimal	Necessary-Extensive
Interaction to Consider	Few	Many
Cost To Modify	Low	High
Specifications	Optional-Minimal	Necessary-Extensive
Status	In one Person's Head	In Many Places
Version Control	Informal	Necessary-Thorough
Common Errors	Programming Errors	Programming Errors Plus: Interface Inconsistencies Inconsistent Assumptions Faulty Specifications

Table 1. Differences Between Small and Large Software Projects

What is Software Engineering: Why is it Different from Computer Science?

Software engineering can be defined as the practical application of computer science and other disciplines to the analysis, design, construction and maintenance of software and its associated documentation. All software engineering projects produce two things: the computer program, known as code, and the documentation necessary to operate, maintain, and use it. This, of course, has a perfect analogy in the hardware world, where we produce a hardware system along with its engineering drawings and operators' manuals. Software engineering has also been defined as an engineering science that applies the concepts of analysis, design, coding, testing documentation, and management to a successful completion of a large, custom-built computer program.

What Is a Large System?

The definition of a large system changes constantly. In the early 1960's IBM defined a large system as one with 35,000 lines of code. Today a large system is defined as having some 128,000 lines of code [12]. Some very large systems have one to two million lines of code. For the purpose of this paper, a "large system" is one that is too large to be done by more than one or two people.

Conclusion: The study of small personal software development strategies does not adequately prepare people to develop large software products.

Hardware Engineering Applied to Software

In the late 1970s, it was proposed that software be developed and managed in an engineering environment like hardware. Some of the hardware development ideas that were carried over to software were:

- Project management
- Lifecycle development methods
- Work breakdown structure (WBS)
- Formal and written requirements
- Design before you build concept
- Use of written specifications, e.g., requirements specification, design specifications, interface specifications, etc.
- Milestones and reviews

Today software engineering is comprised of a number of different activities, technologies, and tools. Figure 1 [95] presents a top-level structure of software engineering. This figure reflects that software engineering includes software development, project management, software quality metrics, and software maintenance.

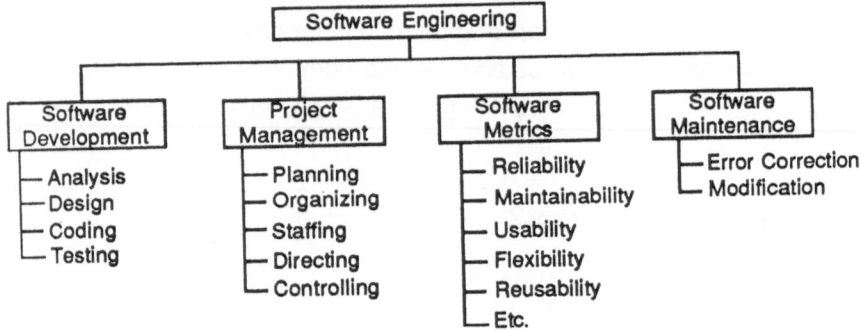

Figure 1. Top-level Structure of Software Engineering

Software Engineering Characteristics

Software engineering is comprised of tools, techniques, and methodologies that are used in software analysis, design, implementation, and testing. Software engineering has the following characteristics:

- Is applicable to large, multi-person projects
- Emphasizes communications
- Reduces system and development complexity
- Uses methodologies developed through "trial and error"
- Emphasizes the process
- Highlights visibility of progress
- Uses a systemic approach
- Is based on interdisciplinary foundation

Software Engineering Education

Software engineering is well defined and can be taught at the undergraduate or graduate level just like any other reasonably well defined discipline. Software engineering is typically taught using the lifecycle development model — requirements, design, coding and testing. In many cases, all these phases are crammed into one three-hour course.

In other situations the phases are paired, e.g., analysis and design, and taught together. In yet other courses, analysis, design, testing, management, quality assurance, etc. are taught as independent classes. Software engineering is also being integrated into the ordinary computer science curriculum. For example:

- One instructor does not provide the homework test data until 24 hours before the assignment is due.
- There is insufficient time to write the program after the data is released.
- This requires students to develop their own test procedures and test cases to validate their homework programs.
- Another instructor will not help debug the student's homework assignment in source form but only from the design.
- Only if the error cannot be found in the design will the source be looked at.
- Design is taught in lower-division classes along with coding.

Software Engineering Laboratory

A major issue that has come up in teaching software engineering is the attempt to make software engineering courses rigorous enough to compete with the coding courses. Coding is finite. When a program runs on a computer, producing the required output, the student knows that he is through. However, the requirements specification process is not finite. Occasionally neither the student nor the instructor can determine when the requirements are correct. Since it is not clear when requirement specifications are complete, students will typically short change this effort. The only positive way to solve this problem is to build (code and test) the system and see if it satisfies the requirements. This is complex and time consuming and can only be effectively accomplished in a software engineering laboratory.

Software Engineering Laboratory Courses

The purpose of having a university level software engineering laboratory course is to give the students an opportunity to practice what they have learned. It also provides an environment in which the student can see how the various components of a software project fit together. Depending on the type of software engineering laboratory course taught, facilities can vary from a very elaborate computer center facility to a room with a desk, chair and filing cabinet.

The following are examples of software engineering laboratory courses that have been culled from literature and from the authors' own experience. Many of these have been tried at California State University, Sacramento (CSUS). Some university software engineering laboratory courses will use a combination of laboratory types, such as the team approach with real world projects.

Everything In One Course Type

This type of laboratory course [107]completely covers software engineering from requirements to tested code. It is usually taught in one semester/quarter and contains both lectures on software engineering theory as well as a laboratory project. Many schools initiate a software engineering course using this method. Its advantage is that it is inexpensive and quick to implement; its disadvantages are that software engineering students get a shallow treatment of either the theory, the project or both.

No Project Type

This type of laboratory course uses the method of a "dry lab" to teach software engineering. The instructor will walk through a project on the black board. Its advantage is that it is inexpensive; its disadvantage is that the students do not get "hands-on" experience in software engineering.

One Class, One Project Type

This type of laboratory course [58] selects or assigns one group project to be completed by the class during the course term. Each student or team of students takes a different role in the project. Some students act as project managers, others write requirement specifications, while others conduct tests for software quality assurance and verification and validation on the engineering products. The advantage of this type of laboratory course is that it enhances interaction between project members and enables the class to take on a much larger project. Its disadvantage is that since projects are somewhat serial in nature, the design and the verification and validation team may be idle while the requirements team is extremely busy.

One Person, One Project Type

In this type of software engineering laboratory course [91] each student does one project individually. The advantage of this type of project is that it goes smoother as far as the student is concerned and is far easier for the laboratory instructor to grade. Its major disadvantage is that few projects are accomplished this way in industry. The students need to learn how to work with other computer professionals in building a software system that is too big for one person alone.

Project Team Type

In this type of laboratory course, [105, 21, 91] the students are grouped into small project teams. These are usually teams of 4-5; sometimes, however, team sizes range from 10-15 students. This increases personnel interaction problems, which increases the students' learning. The disadvantage is that lazy or incompetent students can "hide behind" their teammates and do little or no work for their grade.

Canned Project Type

In this project the instructor (and usually the student) knows the "answer" to the software engineering project. The design strategies and solutions for the project are limited. The student knows whether or not he has done the software engineering project correctly at each stage of the lifecycle. This laboratory is easier for the instructor to grade and less demanding on the student. However, this type of laboratory course does a poor job of representing a "real world" software engineering project such as the students will see after graduation.

"Real world" Project Type

In this type of laboratory course, [64], [21] the student finds or is assigned a small project, usually from a local business. There is no preconceived solution; in fact, there might not be a reasonable solution at all. This type of course maximizes the student's exposure to what he might expect to see after graduation. It is also the most frustrating for the student and the most difficult for the instructor to grade. Also, since the work is looked on as being "free" by the customers, they will accept less than originally asked for; i.e., they will let the students "off-the-hook."

Scenario Type 2

This is a variation [17] on the canned type of laboratory course. In this course various people, usually faculty, play different roles in a simulated real world environment. The student determines the requirements by interviewing the various actors/faculty. This type of project, like the canned project, does not present the students with the surprises they will encounter after graduation.

"Captive Slave" Type

In this type of laboratory course the objective is to build a software system to increase the software capabilities of their university or of a faculty member. Master and PhD students frequently fall into this category. This has many of the features of the "real world" project in that the project is for a "real" customer. The major problem with this type of project is that faculty are often inexperienced customers and may do a poor job of representing a real business; many of their projects are experimental in nature, with poorly documented requirements. They have more in common with research and development projects than software engineering development projects.

Multi-Semester, Large Project Type

This type of laboratory course has a very large project that requires a large amount of student help and many semesters to complete. The advantage here is that a much larger project can be attempted, therefore offering a better simulation of the large software engineering project to be encountered in real life. However, this type of laboratory course is very difficult to manage. A bad requirements specification or a bad design may have been done by a student who has already graduated (and received an "A" for his share of the course). As in a non-laboratory course, it is impossible to know if the requirements specifications are done correctly until the system has been coded and tested. The last students at the end of the lifecycle wind up doing more than their share of the work and learn all the lessons.

Teaching Assistant Type

A unique variation on the project team type [58] uses graduate students for team leaders or project managers. A graduate student with experience (either in industry or from doing this job previously) is assigned to a team of approximately five students. This has the obvious advantage of having an "experienced" software engineer "lead" the project. Learning is much faster, the students make fewer non-learning mistakes, and the projects have a higher completion ratio (which is motivating to the students). The disadvantages are that the students will frequently sit back and depend on the teaching assistant to make all the decisions, and the students do not have an opportunity to practice management.

Senior Projects: California State University, Sacramento

California State University, Sacramento (CSUS), Department of Computer Science, has implemented a software engineering laboratory course (called Senior Projects), which encompasses as a minimum set the analysis, design, coding, testing and management of a real software project. This laboratory course allows the students to produce a "large scale" software product. The students combine and practice what they have learned about software engineering lifecycle procedures and methodologies taught in earlier software engineering courses. This course is but one of several software engineering courses in the curriculum. Moreover, this course is required of all computer science majors. The course objectives for senior projects can be found in Appendix A.

Course Descriptions

Senior Projects is a two semester, two hour per semester course, which encompasses a project for the development and delivery of a computer product. It is a laboratory course designed to apply the knowledge gained by three or four years of college study to the development of a "real world" computer system. The course is only open to computer science seniors. The product to be worked on is selected by the student from industry or government. Group projects are required. The course emphasizes the software development lifecycle: proposal writing, project management planning, system requirements analysis, design, testing, documenting, and reviewing of a computer product.

The course is accomplished in two parts. Part One, done in the first semester, establishes the project, plans the effort, and analyzes and documents the requirements. Part Two, done in the second semester, contains the designing, coding, testing, and delivering of the product. The second semester should end with the acceptance of the product by the sponsoring organization. Course emphasis is on using the software system lifecycle development model. Each project, no matter how small, is expected to follow the software engineering lifecycle, i.e., requirements must be established before the product is designed, which must be done before the design is coded, to be followed by testing, etc. Even so, the limited size of the project (roughly 120 hours per semester per student) necessitates a few constraints, the primary one being more emphasis on "front-end" (requirements and design) of the project than would normally be expected with a small project. In addition, the *process* is emphasized as much or more than the *product*.

Although the course has both a lecture (one hour per week) and a laboratory (three hours per week), it is primarily a laboratory course. The lecture portion of the course provides instruction on what is to be done, not how to do it. For many of the students this is their first "real" project. The course takes them step by step through a typical software project and allows them to try out many of the computer science and software engineering principles and technology that they have learned. The following skills are needed for the course:

- Preparing written technical documents
- Preparing and presenting short oral technical reports
- Planning and scheduling an activity
- Analyzing a system and specifying its requirements
- Designing a system from requirements
- Coding a system in an acceptable language from a design
- Designing test procedures and test data
- Testing a completed system

As in private industry, the students are treated like professionals. They are allowed to establish their own schedule and set their own goals. As in industrym, the students are expected to meet their goals and achieve a standard of quality in their product.

Course and Project Requirements

Each student is required to participate on a software development team of from two to four students and participate in all phases and activities of a software development project. The student team will select their own project from a set provided by the previous senior project classes or seek their own from the local industry or government. Each project is expected to require between 200 and 250 hours per student over the two semester period. To gain credit for the first semester, the student team must complete the project through requirements specification and user's manual phases. Students with a grade of "D," "F" or "I" in the first semester are not allowed to enroll in the second semester. By the end of the second semester, the student team must have completed the project in order to receive a passing grade. The following steps or phases of a project are required:

First Semester

1. Identify sponsor/customer and product
2. Prepare project proposal
3. Plan project
4. Analyze requirements of product
5. Prepare user's manual
6. Prepare software requirements, review, and management status (verbal)

Second Semester

1. Prepare test document
2. Design product software
3. Code software
4. Test software
5. Prepare maintenance manual
6. Prepare final report (verbal and written)

Documentation

Each of the above phases and activities will terminate in an appropriate document. Each document should be self-contained and written for anyone with a general computer science background. It should not assume a detailed understanding of the specific project. The student is encouraged to consult the *IEEE Standards Style Manual* as a guide to good technical documentation. *IEEE Software Engineering Standards and Guides* are used as documentation models and outlines whenever possible.

Milestone Reviews

The students must prepare and present milestone reviews relative to their projects. The students do two oral presentations during their senior project. The first presentation (at the end of the first semester) is called a software requirements review and contains information on the current technical and managerial status of the project. The second presentation is the final review and contains information on what was accomplished and what lessons were learned. The oral presentation provides:

- Experience in making a formal presentation on a technical subject,
- Practice designing and fabricating visual aids,
- A chance to get feedback on style and communication skills,
- A well thought out presentation to be given to the project customer and the laboratory instructor on the present status of the project.

The listeners are given a rating sheet to provide feedback to the speaker as to style, presentation context, visual aids, manner of speaking, etc. This rating sheet is not used by the laboratory instructor in grading the student.

Senior Project Folder

The final class deliverable for the senior project is a bound 9"x11-3/4" folder containing all documentation and information about the project. The purpose of this folder is to (1) represent the final product of the course and (2) serve as an example for future classes.

Selecting a Project

The projects are selected by the students not the laboratory instructors. The laboratory instructor can veto a project that seems inappropriate. Since it is difficult to select a job that takes about 200 hours of work, many senior projects overrun the students' initial time estimate. Projects that do not live up to the original estimate are often adjusted in scope as needed during the first semester. However, projects must be on schedule to be reduced without penalty.

The students are expected to select a project in their application specialty, e.g., data processing, graphics/CAD/CAM, numerical computation, scientific computing, or system software. Students with non-application specialties, such as software engineering and database, can work on any application that uses their skills. Team diversification of talents is often especially effective.

Identifying an Acceptable Project

The following are some rules of thumb gained through experience that the laboratory instructor uses to identify an acceptable project:

- The product cannot be simply a game.
- "Home brew" projects are not allowed.
- The project must be big enough for 2-3 persons.
- The project must exhibit all phases of the lifecycle.
- The product must be coded in at most a third-level language (i.e., no GPSS, no simple databases).
- The product must be complex. (It should have 3 to 4 major dependent functions.)
- Each person should code at least 1 and, at most, 2 or 3 major modules.
- The product must contain 25-50% custom code (i.e., the project must not be all "packages").
- The product must be big enough that the project can fail.

Identifying an Acceptable Customer or Sponsor

The following are some rules of thumb gained through experience that the laboratory instructor uses to identify an acceptable customer. Experience has also shown that better results can be obtained by picking a good customer than by picking a good project:

- The customer must not be related to students.
- The students must not work for the customer.
- The customer must be legitimately in business.
- The customer should not be too "computer" naive.

Project Organization

Each project must have assigned a project manager, a project administrator, and as many programmers/analysts as necessary. The laboratory instructor acts as the "division manager for software projects." The project administrator (PA) is a student chosen by the instructor. Normally, each PA is responsible for 2 to 4 project teams. In general, the PA does man-hour accounting, task accounting, software quality assurance, class administration, record keeping, etc. Students filling this position are expected to have some previous non-classroom experience with software projects.

Senior Management

The laboratory instructor wears two hats: instructor and division manager. As instructor he is responsible for the student's education. As division manager for software projects he is responsible for the successful delivery of the product. In his role as a manager, he insists that the student comply with "company" procedures and policies. For example, all documents will be first turned in to the project administrator for review and acceptance. The project administrator will in turn forward the document to the division manager. The division manager does not accept documents directly from a project. However, if students are having trouble with the technical requirements of a document, the instructor must not act like a division manager but as an instructor.

Project Manager

The project team is headed by one student identified as project manager or project leader. The project manager is responsible for providing technical and supervisory guidance to the team members and for reporting personnel problems to the laboratory instructor or PA.

Project Administrators (PA)

The original purpose of the role of project administrator was to simplify the laboratory instructor's job. The ideal PA is a student who has already done a project and who has seen the lifecycle and its documentation from a practical point of view. Initially, the PA performed only the clerical duties involved in managing 6 to 10 projects: keeping track of time-sheets, scheduling meetings, collecting correspondence.

As the course evolved, the PA was also given the duty of performing the first level of documentation quality control. Since the PA is also enrolled in the course, often he can do no more than determine if the project team is following the outline correctly and doing some first level proofreading and editing. However, by the second semester, the PA is capable of a more thorough review of the documents.

Another important quality in a PA is that of subtle leadership. The PA is in a staff role to the laboratory instructor and without careful attention, the PA could become manager of the project team by default. It is an important part of the learning experience that the project team struggle with the problems of group management.

Management Analysts (MA)

One of the continuing problems in Senior Projects is that of obtaining new projects for each class of seniors. Since the emphasis is on real projects with real customers who change their minds and forget to mention essential requirements, the concept of using 'canned' projects was rejected. At the same time, it seemed too much to expect all students to find projects on their own; therefore, the solution was to have two or more students called management analysts (MA) appointed to go out into the community and recruit projects for the next class of seniors. This involves advertising in the local paper and contacting various business throughout the Sacramento area. The MAs also do some screening of the projects before the laboratory instructors review them. Originally, these management analysts were selected from the class; however, this was unsatisfactory — the students were not receiving sufficient education in developing large systems. The next attempt was to recruit management analysts from outside the Senior Projects class; unfortunately, these students did not know what kind of projects were appropriate. Our latest attempt is to have the PA to also perform the job of MA. This involves obtaining new projects from previous good customers if they have additional projects. Using these techniques, a fairly steady flow of 20-30 projects each semester is realized.

Team Members (Partners)

Selecting partners for a computer science project can be critical to the success or failure of a project. Students are encouraged to pick their partners with care. Consideration should be given to things like:

- Is there a balance of technical skills?
- Are the work habits of the team members compatible?
- Are the personalities compatible?
- Are the team members able to get together frequently?

Managing the Project

Each project automatically begins with the preliminary project plan from Table 2.

Week Due Activity	Deliverable	Pct of Total Time Spent
2 Identify Project		5
4 Prepare Proposal	Project Proposal	7
8 Plan Project	Project Management Plan	11
12 Analyze Requirements	Requirements Specification	16
14 Prepare Manual	Users' Manual	9
15 Software Requirements Review	Review	2
17 Prepare Test Plan & Procedures	Test Documentation	6
20 Design Software	Design Specifications	15
24 Code	Source Listing	15
27 Test Software	Test Results and Evaluation	8
28 Prepare Maintenance Manual	Maintenance Manual	2
29 Final Review	Review	2
30 Customer Acceptance	Final Report	2

Table 2: Preliminary Project and Cost

Project Management Plan and Requirements Specifications

The project proposal, project management plan, and project requirements specifications are the three major contracts signed by the student, the customer, and the laboratory instructor. Since the project has never been done before, it is highly likely that unforeseen problems will arise. Therefore, the project team, customer and instructor all must understand that the original contract is subject to renegotiation. If the original work has been planned well and the status kept up-to-date, then problems can be identified and the project can be easily replanned.

Project Schedule and Status

Each project team submits a schedule (in the proposal and again in the project management plan) to the Project Administrator, outlining the entire year. Each project team is responsible for reporting total number of hours worked at least once every two weeks during a laboratory period. The PA reports significant changes in the project status to the laboratory instructor and keeps a document/milestone log for the project.

Inch-Pebbles

Many laboratory instructors require intermediate "prototype" documents prior to the final deliverable document. These intermediate milestones are called "inch-pebbles." This approach allows both the students and instructors to get a first-cut look at the progress a team is making. Occasionally, a team's viewpoint is wrong and this can be seen and corrected from the inch-pebble. The danger with this approach has been the team assumption that if the inch-pebble is right, then the delivered document will be right, which is not always the case. Examples of inch-pebbles are: work breakdown charts prior to the project management plan, data flow diagrams prior to the software requirements specifications, and a preliminary architectural design prior to detail design.

Unit Development Folder

There has been some success with the Unit Development Folder (UDF) concept. The laboratory instructors have found it very helpful to have each project team maintain a three-ring, loose-leaf notebook containing a signed copy of all project documents. Every time a new document is submitted, the complete folder is turned in to the laboratory instructor for review and approval.

The Class

The course consists of one lecture and one laboratory period each week.

The Lecture

The lecture is one hour (50 minutes) long and covers topics pertinent to the completion of the project. In general, the lifecycle is reviewed and the activities of each phase are reviewed as the project advances into each phase during its development. Specifically, the lecture concentrates on the documentation required during the phases. Standard format, outline, and document content are presented and discussed.

The Laboratory

The laboratory is three hours (150 minutes) long and consists of status reports and dialogue among the students, instructor and project administrators. Often laboratory instructors set aside time for more private meetings with individual project teams. It is also expected that the project teams hold group meetings during this time. Typically, the teams meet with their project manager to:

- Discuss work accomplished the previous period
- Discuss and document problems
- Turn in the man-hour accounting sheet
- Estimate what will be accomplished during the next period
- Negotiate changes in project scope or schedule.

Document Review

Project administrators and instructors must make a concerted effort to have a quick turnaround on all completed documents. In order for the course to work, the documents must be reviewed and returned in less than one week. Toward the end of the semester, as the project administrators and laboratory instructors become more busy, the turnaround time may exceed one week.

Grade

In the "real world" the project (both process and product) is subject to review by management, which can affect one's salary or continued employment. Since the students are not paid for senior project work, their "salary" will be in the form of a grade. The grades are based on the quality and timeliness of each phase of the development lifecycle, plus credit for man-hour reporting and oral reviews. The quality of the work done is judged by the document delivered at the end of the phase, e.g., requirement specification, design document, etc.. Each semester is graded separately. All requests for due date extensions must be received in writing and at a suitable time prior to the scheduled date. Repeated slippages caused by procrastination are not permitted. Students who persistently fall further and further behind, until there appears to be doubt that they will receive a passing grade, are dropped from the course after a suitable warning. The laboratory instructor is solely responsible for grading the student. Project Administrators are primarily graded on their managerial ability.

Cheating

Cheating in this course is defined as (1) submitting somebody else's specific work as one's own and (2) forging somebody's signature. Copying documents from other sources that support a project is permissible and encouraged, provided the source document is properly referenced and/or credited.

Disclaimer

It was considered prudent to add a clause to the project proposal and to the project management plan that disclaims responsibility for the product.

Ownership

Since the students neither work for the school nor for the project sponsor/user, it is the students who are assumed to have nominal "ownership" of the final product and documentation. Students, instructors, users, sponsors or other interested parties who wish to have a clear legal title to the senior project product are told to get a separate agreement with all parties concerned signing the agreement.

Problems Encountered and Solved

The following section presents and discusses several problems that were encountered and solved in the last two years of teaching senior projects.

Completion of the Course

Several years ago it was customary for the senior project student to apply for and receive an incomplete grade (I) in the course. This allowed the student one extra year to finish the course. This resulted in numerous students never graduating. Today an incomplete grade (I) grade is rarely given or limited to an additional 2-4 weeks.

Completion of the First Semester

Before the application of milestone management and the insistence on project completion through requirement specifications and test documents in the first semester, it was not unusual for students to wait until the last 2-4 weeks of the year before beginning the project. This resulted in unreasonable pressure on both the student and laboratory instructor.

Grading

Once it was decided to treat grades like salaries, grading became somewhat easier. Typically, documents are rejected by the laboratory instructor and must be revised one or more times before they are satisfactory or acceptable. Since the project is graded on timeliness as well as quality, lower grades usually reflect that a document was accepted late, not that it was of poor quality.

Documentation

What has been found to be most beneficial (and what the students do not seem to be able to get enough of) are examples of good and bad documents. We have several years' worth of examples of previous projects in the library's reserve book room. Keeping them current and well-annotated is a major undertaking.

Data from Senior Projects

The Projects

The data for Figure 2.1 through 2.4 was obtained from one laboratory of the most recent senior project course (Sep-Dec 1985). Six projects were chosen, each with three students. All but one of these projects was implemented on a personal computer. All projects meet Boehm's [12] criterio for a "small" organic project.

The Deliverables

Figure 2.1 shows the project name, the language used and a brief description. It also shows the total pages of documentation and the number of lines of code delivered by the project. No attempt was made to define a "page" of documentation. Thus the table of contents and partial or blank pages may be included in the total depending on the project. Similarly, there were no standard margins, page sizes, etc. These numbers are provided to allow an idea of the "size" of the effort. The number of lines of code include comments.

Project	Language	Project Description	Pages of Document	Lines of Code
sms	basic	school records database	289	1800
pms	pascal+base	phone operator schedule	368	2750
raids	fortran	ram jet engines minulation	185	510
docpro	pascal	legal document processor	170	1563
lrs	basic	library reference system	381	1200
pms-mafb	dbase II	proj. scheduler-Mather AFB	386	3300
			297	*1854
			90	932

Figure 2.1. Hours Spent on Seven Phases of Projects

Time Spent per Phase

Figure 2.2 shows the hours spent for seven phases of these projects. Each of these phases resulted in a deliverable document (Proposal, PMP, SRS, UM, Design Spec., Test Spec/Report, and source code).

Project	Proposal	Planning	Analysis	User Manual	Design	Test Spec & Testing	Coding
sms	114	75	221	169	86	96	128
pms	119	70	69	76	269	78	185
raids	56	59	120	38	100	172	87
docpro	109	87	99	54	60	110	90
lrs	89	106	68	49	77	142	87
pms-mafb	126	82	124	34	150	65	120
Average	102.2	79.8	116.8	70.0	123.7	110.5	116.2
Std. Dev	23.6	14.7	51.5	46.3	70.7	36.8	34.8

Figure 2.2. Percentage Effort Spent per Phase

Figure 2.3 shows the same data as percentages of the total time spent on the project. The data was collected every two weeks and probably has as much error in it as data collected from industry.

Project	Proposal	Planning	Analysis	User Manual	Design	Test Spec & Testing	Coding
sms	13%	8%	25%	19%	10%	11%	14%
pms	14%	8%	8%	9%	31%	9%	21%
raids	9%	9%	19%	6%	16%	27%	14%
docpro	18%	14%	16%	9%	10%	18%	15%
lrs	14%	17%	11%	8%	12%	23%	14%
pms-mafb	18%	12%	18%	5%	21%	9%	17%
Average	14%	11%	16%	9%	17%	16%	16%
Std. Dev.	3%	3%	5%	5%	8%	7%	3%

Figure 2.3. Percentages of Total Time Spent on Project

Summary of Results

Figure 2.4 shows a summary of the effort (in terms of total hours expended) and then presents the results of that effort in terms of "deliverables": documentation and source code.

Project	Total Hours	Pages of Document per Hour	Lines of Code per Hour
sms	889	0.325	2.0
pms	866	0.425	3.2
raids	632	0.293	0.8
docpro	609	0.279	2.6
lrs	618	0.617	1.9
pms-mafb	701	0.551	4.7
AVERAGE	719.2	0.415	2.5
STD. DEV	116.0	0.129	1.2

Figure 2.4. Summary of the Effort

Conclusions

Minor Problems Yet to be Solved at CSUS

Design Reviews

It is apparent that this course suffers from the same malady that industry has "we can't seem to find the time and the people to do a 'good' design review." Although this is an essential part of the lifecycle, the students are already burdened by the amount of work that the course entails.

Code Walk-throughs

The same problem applies to code or design walk-throughs. Occasionally, code walk-throughs have been scheduled for extra credit. Unfortunately, most often the team that needs extra credit is the furthest behind.

Grading

One unsolved problem (which also appears in industry) is: How does the manager detect and grade a student who is not pulling his fair share of the load? Often the team is willing to cover up for a "slacker." In several instances it has been necessary to "fire" a student when this situation has gotten out of hand.(i.e., flunk or remove them from a project and assign them to another project to do by themselves).

Major Problems Yet to be Solved

Size

The major unsolved problem is that of really "simulating" a large project atmosphere. In general, most of the projects done by the teams are rather small and best done by one or two people. There should be a way to allow students to work on a project which <u>needs</u> a-team of 10 to 50 people for completion. Unfortunately, there are many obstacles to overcome:

- Getting enough students with similar backgrounds
- Finding (or building) a large enough project
- Doing the project in a one year time frame
- Finding the management for such a group of students
- Getting all students to participate in all project phases

The closest approach to such a project was one large, system-type project which lasted two years and was worked on by two three-man teams.

Maintenance Phase

The course does not allow students to experience any aspects of the maintenance phase. There do not appear to be courses in this field anywhere. Yet we realize that a majority of students will be hired in that capacity in their first job. An approach might be to have a separate course in which a student will have to maintain a previously delivered senior project. This would be an excellent experience in observing first hand the problems of delivering a correct software system.

The Major Successes of
Our Software Engineering Laboratory

This course has five major benefits for the student. It provides:

- A capstone course that provides an opportunity for the student to gather together all the information he has learned in three years of computer science education and practice how this information interacts to solve a non-academic problem.

- An opportunity for the student to experience <u>all</u> phases of a lifecycle and to participate in task and jobs (such as project management) that might not otherwise be available for several years.
- A chance for the student to demonstrate his capabilities in the "real world," thereby instilling pride and a sense of accomplishment.
- An opportunity to get "work experience" for the student's resume. Senior projects appear as work experience rather than as a classroom course on a resume.
- An exhibit that the student can be proud of, which provides physical evidence to a prospective employer or interviewer that the graduate is a software engineer or computer scientist.

Appendix

Course Objectives

Upon completion of this course, the student will have:

- Worked semi-independently from the academic environment while developing and implementing a software system.
- Taken responsibility for initiating, managing and delivering a software system from initiation to final delivery of the product.
- Demonstrated an understanding of lifecycle development phases.
- Worked in multi-person software development teams.
- Demonstrated the ability to accomplish all aspects of a software engineering project.
- Demonstrated an understanding of one software engineering development technique and methodology.
- Given a verbal technical report.
- Produced a software system through working with a potential software user and determining the software needs of that user.
- Written office memos or proposals to obtain resources necessary to initiate a project.
- Done a feasibility study, economical analysis, and top-level requirement analysis.
- Written a software engineering project proposal.
- Obtained user's concurrence with the proposal.
- Planned a software engineering project.
- Determined the cost and schedule for a software engineering project.
- Written a software engineering project management plan.
- Analyzed a software engineering requirement, i.e., converted users needs to testable requirements.
- Applied state-of-the-art software requirements representation techniques to a software requirement.
- Written a software engineering requirement specification (SRS): complete, consistent, correct, modifiable, unambiguous, testable, traceable, and process-free.

- Written a user's manual.
- Analyzed testing needs to assure that a delivered software system will satisfy the software requirement specifications.
- Written test plan, specifications, procedures, test cases, and test reports.
- Prepared and presented a software requirement review.(SRR)
- Designed a software system from a requirement specification; represented the software system with a state-of-the-art design and documentation system.
- Written a software design specification(SDS).
- Programmed a system from a software design specification.
- Tested the completed system in accordance with the developed test plan, test specification, test procedures and test cases.
- Written a test report.
- Written a maintenance manual.
- Obtained user's acceptance of the software system.
- Prepared and presented a final report.

Software Projects in an Academic Environment

David B. Wortman
University of Toronto

Abstract. This paper describes our experience in using a programming project as an adjunct to a graduate-level course in software engineering. It discusses the strengths and weaknesses of the project as a teaching tool.

Introduction and Background

For many years we have taught a graduate-level survey course called "Computer Program Engineering." The course is designed to familiarize graduate students with the a variety of topics in software engineering. It is similar to the course described in [58].

The Software Hut Project

In the course we use a software project called "Software Hut" [53]. The project was originally devised by J.J. Horning to introduce "real world" experience into a graduate software engineering course. The project involves a three-phase development of a software system by competing teams of students. In its usual form, the software is composed of an information producer (module A) and an information consumer (module B). In the first phase of the project, each team designs and constructs either module A or module B. In the second phase, each team obtains modules A and B that they have not written and integrates them into a complete working system. In the third phase, each team takes a complete system composed of modules A and B that they have not produced and makes some modification to the system. This modification is not revealed to the students until after they have selected a system for phase three so that their choice must be made in the presence of some uncertainty.

In the original software hut project, software modules were exchanged in a free market. Each team of students set a "selling price" for their software. They also made a decision to "purchase" software from some other team for use in phases two and three of the project. At least part of the student's grade for the project was determined by their net profit (proceeds from sales less cost of purchases).

The project was designed to simulate "real world" software development problems. It forced the students to think about issues like software structure, readability, maintainability, modifiability and software quality in ways that they had not considered before.

Course Project Goals

Before discussing the project, we examine its role in a software engineering course. We assume that the purpose of a graduate-level course in software engineering is to make the students aware of the problems and issues involved in the design, implementation, and maintenance of large software systems. This assumption biases our view of the purpose of the software project. If we were teaching a course that was more management oriented, e.g., a course for software managers or software entrepreneurs then the relative importance of the software marketing aspects of the project would be much higher. We believe that the software project makes several contributions to the education of the students.

1. *Experience with different program development styles.* Our course is taught to first-year graduate students who come into the course from a variety of backgrounds. We feel that the students benefit from exposure to the variety of program development styles that they encounter during the project.

2. *Designing and coding to a strict specification.* Although most of the students will have participated in programming projects as a part of their undergraduate education, we believe that they have usually never had to develop software that strictly followed a formal specification. The project format and the need to exchange software with other teams forces close adherence to the project specification.

3. Interfacing with foreign code. The students have to write programs that conform to an interface that they did not design. This teaches them the value of well specified, precise interfaces.

4. Designing and coding for unspecified future change. The need to make an as-yet-unknown modification to the software system in the third phase of the project introduces a concern for designing the software so that such modification is easy. This has an influence on the design of the software and is often a major criteria that the students use to select the software they will use in phases two and three.

5. Use of version control and configuration management tools. We encourage students to use available software development tools in their work on the project. This gives them a chance to learn about programming environments and about the issues of version control and configuration management. Most of the projects have used the sccs [84] or the rcs [97] version control system, and the make [31] configuration management tool.

6. Working to a strict schedule. The due dates for the phases of the project are set at the start of the project and are rigidly followed. The students realize that failure to complete their software by the end of a project phase will have a disastrous effect on their evaluation.

7. Assessing software quality. In making decisions on what software to acquire for the second and third phases of the project, the students have to examine various alternatives and make their own evaluation of the quality of each. Usually the programs and their accompanying documentation were placed on file in some place where they could be inspected by all teams.

It is important that the project should be more than just another programming project. The design of the project should focus the student's attention on software engineering issues that are typically ignored in other projects. This focus can be achieved through careful project design and through specification of an appropriate set of project goals.

Pedagogical Issues

There are a number of pedagogical issues that arise when a project is used as a part of an software engineering course.

Student Time and Effort Implications

The typical full-time student taking the software engineering course is typically taking 2 to 4 other courses simultaneously. It is unfair to the students to mount a course that requires an unreasonable amount of their time. Students can (and do) complain loudly if they think their workload is excessive.

The software project has to be planned with this constraint in mind. The instructor should monitor the student's workload throughout the project by watching his/her computer resource consumption and by talking with the student. The project description should allow the instructor some latitude for changing the project dynamically if he/she feels that the workload is becoming excessive.

Instructor Time and Effort

Consideration also has to be given to the amount of instructor and tutor time required to mount and administer the project. The project should be designed so that the amount of effort that they have to expend on the project is reasonable under the circumstances. The major pitfall for the instructor is to design a project that requires too much effort to evaluate and test between the project phases.

Suitable Test Bed — New vs. Used

In designing the project, a choice can be made between developing new software and working with an existing software system. There are advantages to both choices. Working with existing software reduces the project start up overhead and allows a much larger software project to be undertaken. A project starting with existing software might involve the analysis, design and implementation of some modification or enhancement to the software. The project can be self perpetuating because the result of one year's project can be the starting point for the following year. There are also drawbacks to this alternative. It requires the students to become expert in the working of some particular software. This may be a time consuming activity (e.g., the existing system might be a compiler or a database system). Students who had prior knowledge in the area of the selected system would have an advantage over those who do not. It is difficult to find a large, interesting system that avoids this bias. There is also a question of whether the students should be exposed to a system that is typical or exemplary. A typical system will teach them a lot about real software, but it will also mire them in the mistakes of others. We have observed a distinct shortage of large software systems of exemplary quality.

In many ways it would be desirable to turn the students loose on a really large (i.e., more than 1M source lines) software system and let them learn first hand the difficulties in working with software on this scale. We have never done so, because we felt that too much of the students time would be consumed in simply getting up to speed on that much software.

The other alternative is to have the project develop new software. This choice orients the course more toward the design and development aspects of software engineering. It has a high start-up overhead due to the need to design and implement a lot of code. It also limits the amount of software that can be developed in a one semester course. The student programming effort can easily become excessive unless the instructor monitors the situation carefully.

Timing of Project Relative to Lectures

There is a fundamental timing problem with the software project. To do well in the project, the students need to know the material presented in the accompanying course. This raises a conflict between the pedagogically desirable order of exposition and the order which best serves the needs of the project. It is simply impossible to present enough of the material before the start of the project or even to present enough of it early in the course so as to keep ahead of the students. The students should learn about specification techniques and methods of software design before they start the project. They should also be aware of various alternatives for organizing software development teams. Before software development begins, the students should learn about version control, configuration management, and programming environments.

We once tried doing the project as a separate (summer) project course in the semester following the lecture course. This experiment was unsuccessful and was not repeated. The failure may have been due to the way project courses are organized at our institution because one major failing was inadequate communication between the students and between the students and the instructor.

Choice of an Implementation Language

The choice of a programming language in which to write the software can be a critical factor in the project's success. Our students do not usually share a common programming language, so a compromise selection must be made and some of the students have the extra burden of learning a new language. This situation has become better in recent years since the students are now more likely to know Pascal or C.

In the early years of the software hut project, the students selected the programming language by majority vote. This sometimes led to disasters when the programming language turned out to be unsuitable for the project at hand. More recently the instructor has imposed a language on the students based on her/his foreknowledge of what the project will entail.

The instructor must also choose between a fairly unstructured language such as Fortran or C and a language that encourages structured programming such as Pascal, Modula-2 or Ada. An unstructured language probably gives the students a more realistic introduction to "real world" programming but it also burdens them with the overhead of fighting the programming language. The other choice makes it easier for them to develop modular, well-structured software. We believe that most of our students would opt for the second choice if the decision were theirs.

It is also important that there be a stable and reasonably efficient compiler for whatever language is chosen. Fighting compiler problems is not a productive or educational task for the students however realistic it might be.

Evaluation Algorithms and Creditability

The algorithm used to evaluate the quality of the software should encourage the students to learn "good" techniques. It should be repeatable and should be viewed by the students as being fair and rewarding excellence. We have tried different algorithms over the years, usually basing them on such factors as readability, efficiency, documentation, and programming style. We have found it difficult to devise an algorithm that does not ultimately involve the instructor's subjective judgements. Any evaluation algorithm with a subjective component is open to questions about its creditability. We do not believe that any of the presently available software metrics are suitable for evaluation of course projects.

Problems

In this section we discuss a variety of problems that have arisen in our use of a software project.

Small Scale Effects

The software project as described in Section 1 simply does not work if there are not enough students to form at least 5 or 6 teams. A similar result was observed by Woodward and Mander [106]. When faced with a small enrollment, we switch to an alternative project design in which the students work cooperatively to design and implement modifications to an existing piece of software. This gives them some of the same learning experiences as the larger project but avoids its complexities.

Presentation of Project Goals

It is important that at the beginning of the project, the goals for the software system be clearly explained. The students need to know what factors will be important in the evaluation of the software. If difficult to quantify criteria like "well-structured", "good style", "well documented" are used as goals for the project then it may be hard to describe these goals to the students in any simple way. One source of student complaints has been the lack of well defined goals for the project.

Evaluation of Software Quality

The greatest difficulty that we have had in administering the project has been the evaluation of software quality. The project format forces this evaluation to be done in a short time period, typically one week or less. During this time, the instructor or a tutor has to read the programs and make an assessment of the quality of each. The size of the software makes this a task of considerable magnitude. The assessment is subject to the problems of subjectivity discussed above.

Costing for Resource Consumption

A realistic evaluation of each team's performance would include assigning to each team a cost for the human and computer resources that it used in completing the project. Asking the students to accurately account for their own time is not feasible. In most universities, the students have access to a variety of computer systems using different accounts. In such an environment it is usually not possible to require the students to use a specific computer and account for the course project and thus it is not possible to determine computer resource usage for each team.

With the present project the best strategy for the students may be to use computer resources lavishly, especially in place of the scarcer human resource. The project is not intended to encourage this style of project development.

A Fair Evaluation Algorithm

Some algorithm will be used to evaluate the student's performance in the project and to calculate the project-related component of the their course mark. It is important that this algorithm be fair to all students. The evaluation of a student should be based on the merit of the student's work (or on the work of a team) and not on random events beyond the student's control. The algorithm should be fully disclosed at the start of the project and should not be altered without the consent of the students involved.

Over the years we have used algorithms that included factors for:

- the instructor's evaluation of the quality of the software. This evaluation was usually based on reading of the program and its documentation.
- results of program testing. The instructor or a tutor would devise a set of test cases and apply them to each program. A penalty would then be assessed for each error that was found in the program.
- the student's profit from buying and selling software. Software would be bought and sold between phases of the project. The student would be credited with the value of software that was sold and debited with the cost of software that their team purchased.

Student complaints about the fairness of the evaluation algorithm have been a continuing (and well justified) problem. Each of the evaluation components described above has its problems.

Evaluating the quality of a large piece of software by an (often hurried) reading is difficult. It is difficult to communicate the evaluation standards to the students in a way that allows them to try to achieve quality

In the early years of the project, the error penalty was exponential, a raw evaluation of the software was multiplied by a factor of $0.5^{**}N$ where N was the number of errors detected. This had the undesirable effect of creating a wide gap between programs that had no errors and programs that had even a small number of errors. More than 3 or 4 errors in a program could destroy a team's chance of obtaining a good mark.

Because we felt that the exponential penalty was too severe, in more recent versions of the project, the penalty multiplier has been of the form $X^{**}N$ with X in the range 0.8 to 0.95.

Our discouraging (but not unexpected) observation is that if we looked for errors in the student programs it was easy to find them. In general, the programs submitted for evaluation had not been adequately tested, even though the students knew about the high penalty for program errors.

Student Gaming and Collusion

Graduate students are usually good optimizers. Given an evaluation algorithm, they are quite clever about finding ways to maximize their marks relative to that algorithm. We have observed several student efforts to "game plan" the project in an attempt to obtain a good mark. Some examples:

- collusion in trading software. Different teams of students would agree to exchange their software at prices that either maximized their respective profits or guaranteed that all teams would have approximately the same profit.
- freezing out a successful team. If one team did exceptionally well in the first phase of the project, no other team would deal with them regardless of price/quality considerations in the second and third phases of the project.
- buying cheap software. Some teams would buy the cheapest software available regardless of perceived quality on the assumption that this would maximize their net profit. They assumed that they could overcome any problems that might arise with the software.

This game playing was not intended to be the major emphasis of the course. The original purpose of the free market exchange of software (i.e. to make the students think about price/quality) was being perverted. Many students objected to a course project in which they could only obtain a good mark at the expense of their peers.

Sufficient Penalty for Poor Software

In the ideal project, there should be a strong bias toward correct, efficient, well designed and well constructed software. We would like the students to develop a feeling for these characteristics and to favor such software. Unfortunately, in the scale of projects that we have been able to run, the penalty for acquiring poor quality software could not be made high enough to serve as a real deterrent. Some students choose to acquire the worst software available because it was also the cheapest and thus maximized their "profit." This is not what we had intended. With the relatively small scale of our projects the students were usually able to overcome any software difficulties without undue hardship.

Buying and Selling of Software

The original software hut project assumed a completely free market exchange of software among the teams. Each team set the selling price of its software and the terms under which it was sold. Some of the more imaginative teams made "sales presentations" and offered inducements such as a free software warranty. This approach was not entirely successful. If a team with good software priced it too high it would not be purchased in spite of its superiority. There was usually a very large difference between the "profit" of the best team and the worst team. This difference made it very difficult for a team that did poorly between phases 1 and 2 to ever recover. Although it might be argued that this approach is closest to the "real world", it also introduced an unnecessarily divisive factor, pitting student against student.

Several attempts were made to make the buying and selling of software more equitable and fairer to all students involved. First, teams we required to set their prices without knowledge of the other team's prices. This prevented the last team from setting its price to undercut all the others. The mechanism used was to have all teams communicate their price to the instructor who would then announce all prices simultaneously. The principle was established that the price of a piece of software was the same for all buyers. Buying software was done semi-secretly to discourage collusion. Each team would communicate its purchase decision to the instructor who would announce all purchase decisions simultaneously. The intent of these changes was to focus more attention on evaluation of the cost/quality of a piece of software and to discourage economic warfare between the teams.

More recently the price of the software was based on the instructor's evaluation of its quality and on the number of bugs it contained. This meant that the teams could concentrate more on the choice of which software to buy.

Lack of Testing

The present project organization does not encourage extensive testing and quality assurance of the software that is produced. Testing complex software can be very time consuming. Although we have been tempted several times to do so, adding a testing phase to the project would almost certainly increase the student's workload unacceptably.

Conclusions

The discussion in the previous section makes it clear that there are many pitfalls in the design of a software project. We now feel that the emphasis on buying and selling software in the original software hut project gave the whole project the wrong orientation. The course we teach is about the design and implementation of software, not about software marketing. The buying and selling aspects of the project consumed too much student time and energy and were divisive and disruptive. We now advocate a project in which the students are evaluated on the merit of the work that they do in each phase of the project, not on a haphazard software market. Two methods of distributing software can be used between project phases. Either the students can choose among the available modules or the instructor can randomly assign modules to each team.

A considerable amount of care and firm control is required to prevent the project from consuming inordinate amounts of student and/or instructor time. An effort should be made to organize the project so that the student's attention is focused on software engineering issues. The instructor should direct the project to prevent it from becoming just a large coding project.

We believe that a properly controlled and oriented project can serve as a useful adjunct to a software engineering course. It is desirable that the students gain experience with problems that only occur with large software systems. The interactions that occur in this project simulate (albeit on a small scale) many of these problems.

Appendix

Example Projects

This appendix describes several course projects that have been used at the University of Toronto. After each description, we comment on the relative success of the project

1. Assembler and Interpreter

This project involved the design and implementation of a primitive assembler and interpreter for a hypothetical mini-computer (similar to a PDP-8).

For several reasons, this was not a very successful project. The students chose to program in PL/I which turned out to be an inappropriate language for expressing the bit manipulation required for assembly and interpretation. They ended up spending far too much time fighting PL/I.

2. Distributed Calendar Tool

This project involved the design of a set of tools for scheduling individuals in an organization. An appointment secretary module would maintain a database of appointments for an individual. The individual could add and delete appointments as well as displaying a calendar of appointments for a specified interval. The students had to design the human interface to the program. A group scheduler module would intersect the calendars of a list of individuals and attempt to find an acceptable time for a meeting. Various constraints about acceptable meeting times could also be given.

This was a reasonably successful project. It contained the right amount of complexity and posed several interesting design challenges. The human interfaces designed by the students were fairly poor. Interface design is not a topic covered in any great detail in the software engineering course (it is covered elsewhere) so the students were unprepared for the task. This project had to be prematurely terminated at the end of the second phase due to excessive student workload.

3. Communications Package

This project involved writing two modules that communicated over a simulated channel using a standard communications protocol (DDCMP). In the first phase, each team wrote either a reader or a writer module and tested them using a perfect channel provided by the instructor. In the second phase, the teams integrated reader and writer modules to provide a complete communication system. In this phase the instructor provided a "dirty" channel that would randomly destroy information it was carrying. The dirty channel required the students to think carefully about error handling and recovery. In the third phase changes were made in the communication protocol and in the interface to the system.

This was one of the most successful projects. It had the right characteristics: relatively small code size, intricate algorithms, and a requirement to handle errors that made it interesting. The students came up with several novel algorithms for computing the checksum that was a part of the protocol.

4. Software Tool Design

The first phase involves the developing a complete specification for a software tool (module interconnectivity mapping tool) from a prose list of requirements. In the second phase, the students develop a detailed design based on a specification produced by some other team. There could be a third phase involving the implementation of a detailed design produced by some other team but this is typically omitted.

This project was developed as a response to student complaints about the excessive programming workload in previous projects.

Exercises in Software Engineering

Jon Louis Bentley[1]
AT&T Bell Laboratories

John A. Dallen
United States Military Academy

Abstract. Typical software engineering courses teach principles in lectures and readings, then apply them in the development of a single program (requiring several months). We recently taught a software engineering class that incorporated many smaller exercises (requiring several hours). The class was successful. Students were able to experiment with a broad set of ideas, and make interesting mistakes without jeopardizing the grades of their development team. This paper describes some tools and techniques we taught, and suggests how they might be incorporated into typical software engineering classes.

Introduction

In Fall 1985, we co-taught a senior-level software engineering course to fifteen computer science majors at the United States Military Academy. This paper describes a novel aspect of our course that might be profitably incorporated into many software engineering courses — small exercises in software engineering.

Section 2 describes one exercise in detail, and Section 3 surveys several other exercises. Criteria we used in designing and evaluating the course are sketched in Section 4, and our conclusions are offered in Section 5.

A Detailed Example

In this section we will give the flavor of the exercises by describing a two-class-hour exercise in some detail. The exercise was built around Parnas's [75] classic paper on modular decomposition of systems, which uses the example of a "key word in context" ("KWIC") program.

---

[1]During the Fall Semester 1985, this author was Visiting Professor of Computer Science at the United States Military Academy, supported by AT&T Bell Laboratories.

KWIC programs are often used in documentation systems. The input to such a program, for instance, might be a text file in which each line describes a program. A sort program could be described by the input line

```
sort  —  order input files
```

The output of the KWIC program is the ordered sequence of all key words in the file, each shown in the context of its line. Because the above input line has four words, it will appear in these four output lines:

```
sort — order input    files
       sort — order    input files
           sort —      order input files
                  sort — order    input files
```

Parnas's paper sketches two modularizations for this problem. The first was the style popular in the early 1970's; the five modules corresponded to phases of the program that might be overlayed in core memory (input, processing 1, processing 2, output, and control). The second modularization is driven by the principle of "information hiding". Parnas sketches the two solutions and then compares them; the second is superior in dimensions such as modifiability, independent development of modules, and comprehensibility.

In the final few minutes of a Monday class hour we described the KWIC problem and assigned the students the task of implementing a KWIC program by Wednesday; we also passed out copies of Parnas's paper to be read by Friday. Wednesday's class was a discussion of the KWIC programs, and Friday's was a more general discussion of information hiding, based on Parnas's paper and the programming experience.

Parnas's paper acknowledges that a KWIC program "is a small system"; it could be "produced by a good programmer in a week or two" and was "used successfully in a class project" in a software engineering course. The students in our course found it even simpler: a four-hour programming task using a UNIX[TM2] pipeline:

```
rotate infile | sort | print >outfile
```

---

[2]UNIX is a trademark of AT&T Bell Laboratories.

(This pipeline is presented on pages 134-139 of Kernighan and Plauger
[59] and corresponds roughly to the modularization Parnas found inferior; the students had no difficulty deriving it independently.) The
rotate program processes the lines of its input file in order; if a given line
contains *M* words, it produces *M* output lines. Each output line is of the
form

```
second part of line<tab>first part
```

where the second part of the line begins at each of the *M* words. For
instance, the input line

```
sort — order input files
```

generates these four output lines:

```
sort — order input files<tab>
order input files<tab> sort —
input files<tab> sort — order
files<tab> sort — order input
```

(Note that the sequence "—" is handled as a special case; more on that
shortly.) The standard UNIX `sort` program then sorts the lines in order
of their second parts (because it appears first in each line), and `print`
writes the lines in the desired format.

A major theme of our course was using software tools in the style
described by Kernighan and Plauger [59]. We emphasized the use of
existing programs; when the students had to write programs from
scratch, they used the AWK language described by Aho, Kernighan and
Weinberger [1]. (The appendix explains this decision.) The `rotate`
program can be written in AWK as

```
{x = " " $0
 for (i = 1; i <= length(x); i++)
    if (substr(x,i,1) == " "
       && substr(x,i+1,2) != " — ")
          print substr(x,i+1) "\t" substr(x,1,i-1)}
```

The code within braces is implicitly repeated for each input line. The
string `x` is the input line preceded by an initial space (so each word on
the input line is preceded by a space character). The `for` loop checks
each character in the string `x` , and if it defines a new word (i.e., a space
not followed by "—"), it is printed in the desired format (second part, tab
character, first part).

The `print` program is written in AWK as

```
BEGIN { FS = "\t" }
      { printf "%25s    %s\n", substr($2,1,25),
      substr($1,1,25) }
```

The BEGIN line is executed at the start of the program's execution; it sets AWK's field separator to the tab character. The substring operator substr is then used to print each input line in the desired format.

The first part of Wednesday's class surveyed the students' programs. The KWIC program described above is built from a 5-line AWK program, a 2-line AWK program, and a command line. The students turned in somewhat longer programs, but still fewer than 20 lines. The program we have described in this section incorporates several clever ideas contributed by the cadets.

Our students were familiar with the classic "waterfall" model of system development (the sequence of requirements analysis, specification, design, implementation, testing, maintenance) from classes on project management; we emphasized the importance of prototyping and iterative designs. The class discussion therefore turned to the next version of a KWIC program, dictated by the students' experience in applying their programs to an input file describing 28 UNIX programs with which they were familiar. The following issues are typical:

Function

Key words like "a", "and", "of" and "the" give no information; those lines should be deleted. The KWIC specification should include a facility for a "stop list" of undesired words (that facility can then be used to process "—" as an undesired word). The facility can be implemented using a member of the UNIX `grep` family to remove undesired lines after `rotate` and before `sort`.

Robustness

If an input line contains unexpected blanks, the `rotate` program generates superfluous rotations; unexpected tabs confuse `print`. A prototype program need handle only well-behaved input; a production version must be more robust.

Performance

The KWIC program handles only a few input lines per second; we could have assigned the students the task of making it more efficient. Instead, we made the more important point that efficiency is not an issue in many systems: a simple back-of-the-envelope calculation showed that the CPU time spent optimizing the program would far outweigh savings over many runs (and programmer time is infinitely more expensive anyway).

We discussed several other extensions suggested by the UNIX permuted index program `ptx,` such as parameterizing the spacing and preparing output suitable for input into document production systems. The class hour ended with a general discussion of issues such as problem definition, modularity, maintainability, performance, and building and using software tools.

Several weeks after the discussion, we examined a closely related problem. One of us described the suite of AWK programs he had built the previous evening to prepare the index of a book (Bentley [10]). Although the input and output were fundamentally different, the program suite was similar in spirit, and the above `rotate` program was quite similar to the indexer's `rotate` program that transformed "arbitrary term" into "term, arbitrary".

This exercise consumed two hours in class and four or five out of class hours. It isn't a typical exercise in standard software engineering courses; it involved no project planning, requirements analysis, formal specification, extensive coding, or documentation. Rather, the students built and used a small program to solve a task they found interesting. This exercise also exposed the students to the following.

Real Programs

The cadets studied both the production-quality UNIX permuted index program `ptx` and a single-shot program for a related task (index of a book).

Implementation Issues

The exercise gave concrete experience in exploring the design space of KWIC programs; the implementation gave immediate context for a general discussion of issues of modularity and maintainability. We preached rather little in our course about topics such as "building and using software tools" and "rapid prototyping"; we instead gave the students useful tools and required them to build interesting programs in a hurry.

A User's View

Students in typical software engineering classes are lucky to be able to run their system once on the last day of the semester; our students spent a large fraction of their time using the program they built. Parnas's paper provided an initial specification of their program; their experience in using that version was the most important input for the specification of the next version. We did not lecture them to "grow software rather than build it;" we made them do it.

The Professional Literature

This exercise started and ended with Parnas's [75] excellent paper on modularity; we kept a potentially hand-waving discussion of programming methodology concrete by relating it to a small, but subtle, program. (Our discussion followed Zave [108] in comparing Parnas's approach with Kernighan and Plauger's.)

Overview of Exercises

In this section we will briefly sketch several other exercises from the course, in decreasing precision. We chose our examples to represent the breadth of the course, rather than by a random sample (the KWIC program is the most typical of the exercises).

Sorting

A two-week unit was devoted to sorting (six one-hour lectures, from Monday of one week to Friday of the next week). Because the cadets had previously studied that topic in a course on data structures, Lecture 1 reviewed sorting algorithms. The assignment following that lecture was to modify a twenty-line C implementation of Hoare's quicksort algorithm. (This was the only exercise that involved programming in a language other than AWK. Our approach to sorting was unique among the exercises in its emphasis on performance; C is much faster than AWK—about two orders of magnitude for this problem — and has more predictable performance. We restricted the students to an "AWK subset" of C, with only minor problems.)

In Lecture 2 (Wednesday), we reviewed the exercise and assigned the next task, which was due Monday: a "sorting contest". (The winning team was promised a grade of "A+" and a surf-and-turf dinner at the Officers' Club.) Each team of two students[3] was to turn in two files: a C program to sort 5000 integers, and an input data set of 5000 integers. Each program was assigned the "score" of the sum of its run time on all input files; low score wins. Thus students were motivated to produce both efficient programs and inputs that would exploit weaknesses in their colleagues' routines. (Similar contests might teach Quality Assurance — given a specification, each team submits a program and an input to stress it — or specifications — each team submits a specification and a "wrong" program that might satisfy a poorly written specification.)

Lecture 3 was canceled to compensate for programming time, and the programs were due on Lecture 4 (Monday). That lecture was a discussion of the techniques used by each team, and a prediction of results. We graded the programs that evening and reviewed them in the next class. The winning programs — two tied — applied a few simple optimizations to clean initial programs; programs that were more baroque for the sake of "efficiency" were fast on the input supplied by their team but slower on other inputs.

Linderman [65] describes his experience in speeding up the UNIX system's disk sort by a factor of two; it was assigned as reading for

---

[3]The teams were not intended to simulate software development teams. Rather, having a partner allowed some work to be partitioned, and encouraged discussing ideas before coding them.

Lecture 6 (Friday). That class period was devoted to a brief presentation by Linderman (on aspects of his experience not described in the paper) followed by a question period.

The five lecture hours discussed the theory of sorting (1 hour), design alternatives (1 hour), implementations (2 hours), and a production sort program (1 hour). Outside of class, the cadets learned the C language (2 hours), designed and coded an interesting and useful subroutine (8 hours), and read a case history of a production program (2 hours).

Little Languages

Several weeks at the end of the semester were devoted to the study of small, special-purpose languages and their processors. Throughout the semester several students had complained about the succinct (some even said cryptic) arguments used by the UNIX system's sort command. We therefore assigned the task of designing a more appropriate language to describe sorting. (Our class emphasized the importance of using and building tools.) A sort program might be specified as

```
input infile1
input infile2
output outfile
field 2
        ignore case
        ignore nonascii
field 4
        compare numeric
```

They wrote AWK programs (a few dozen lines long) to translate from their languages into the language of the existing sort program; the output for the above program is

```
sort +1fi -2 +3n -4 -o outfile infile1 infile2
```

That was easily accomplished in two hours of in-class time and a few hours of programming. (Previous exercises concentrated on designing the internals of sort packages; this exercise turned to the user interface.)

The next set of linguistic exercises dealt with a language for drawing simple pictures. We provided a set of routines for drawing pictures in arrays of characters; the students designed and built a user interface.

The final "little languages" we studied were the interpreter and assembler for a simple single-accumulator, one-address machine. This
program reads a file of input numbers (terminated by zero) and writes
the sum on the output file.

```
# print sum of input numbers (terminated by zero)
input  get              # Read n,
       jz     done      #  done if zero
       add    sum       # Add old value of sum
       st     sum       #  then store the new value
       j      input     # Loop
done   ld     sum       # Load sum
       put              #  then print it
       halt
sum    const  0
```

Assemblers of this complexity used to be standard fare in "systems
programming" courses; they taught several important lessons, including
lexical analysis, symbol tables and multiple-pass algorithms. They also
taught how to organize a large program (as a college junior, one of us
wrote an assembler and interpreter for a similar machine in about 1000
lines of ALGOLW).

A Monday lecture described the assembler and the target machine; the
assignment due Wednesday was to implement them both in the
simplest possible code (we encouraged the cadets to concentrate on
correct inputs and ignore issues of error handling). Our implementation
of the assembler and the interpreter required 30 lines of AWK; the
cadets took under 50 lines.   (The emphasis on small size was a
response to ornate solutions to previous problems.) In Wednesday's
class we discussed the students' solutions, reviewed our program, and
presented a larger program (80 lines) with thorough error checking. On
a Friday field trip to Bell Labs, Brian Kernighan described to the cadets
how he used similar techniques to build a microcode assembler in AWK
for a special-purpose simulation machine.

Writing Aids

Steve Johnson originally implemented the UNIX system's spell
program as a one-line shell script; Doug McIlroy later rewrote it in C to
be particularly efficient. The cadets studied the history of that program

as sketched in Column 13 of Bentley [10] and as described in detail by McIlroy [69]. We assigned the problem of implementing a prototype spelling checker as a shell script and as an AWK program.

After a cadet pointed out several horribly misutilized words in a paper (including such gross offenders as "prioritize" and "utilize"), we assigned them to read Strunk and White's list of commonly misused words in *The Elements of Style*. They then implemented a simple `style` program to identify such words and suggest alternative phrasings (such as "Try 'used' instead of 'utilized'."). The cadets' first programs were effective but very slow; their second versions were efficient enough to find some glaring errors in long faculty manuscripts stored online. The students implemented several other small programs to deal with text.

Evaluation

Was our course successful? The fact that we are writing this paper shows that it gave us a warm fuzzy feeling; that sentiment was also expressed in the course evaluations by the students. Fortunately (or perhaps not), the West Point administration provides us with a more stringent test of success: can we convince the nation's oldest engineering school that software engineering should be granted the status of an engineering discipline?

The Military Academy requires all cadets, regardless of major, to complete a two-semester design sequence, chosen from any of the traditional engineering disciplines (such as civil, electrical or mechanical). The courses concentrate on principles of design and experience in applying those principles to interesting problems. The two-semester computer science design sequence (entitled Computer Systems Engineering) is a fairly typical software engineering course covering conventional software engineering principles and practices; it has not been accepted by the Academy's academic board as an acceptable design course.

Traditional engineering programs integrate three levels of study. The foundations are the science underlying a particular discipline, such as the study of strength of materials or device physics. The second level consists of design courses, where the various concepts are integrated and applied to design projects (within the Academy, this is the domain of the engineering design sequences). Collateral courses address management issues, such as CPM and PERT techniques, site layout and engineering economics.

Within this context, software engineering courses suffer from two shortcomings; the lack of a clear underlying foundation of principles and theory and, consequently, an emphasis on the management of the design process rather than the design. The concepts and principles associated with most software engineering courses are actually distillations of practical experiences and lessons learned, rather than firm science. While this does not reduce the importance of software engineering to a computer science education, the gap between foundations (data structures, database design, language concepts, etc.) and design management remains substantial by the standards of a mechanical or electrical engineer. Course projects in the foundation courses, while often complex, are designed to illustrate certain concepts and rarely integrate a wider spectrum of principles. Software engineering course projects, in order to achieve the goals of applying life-cycle concepts, typically have uninteresting design considerations to permit completion in two semesters. If the project emphasizes "real-world" tasks (as in the Academy's typical sequences), program design other than interfacing is most often trivial. Much is learned, but not about design.

Similarly, prototyping and the use of available tools are both mainstays of engineering design but are not well exercised in conventional software engineering courses. A civil engineer does not redesign an I-beam when building a trestle bridge, yet many software engineering students reconstruct each line of code from scratch.

We hope that the exercises that we have emphasized in this paper will be an important part of a future design course for computer scientists that is acceptable to the Academy. The next section shows how the exercises address several of the problems mentioned in this section.

Conclusions

We have a great deal of respect for typical software engineering courses; they currently play a central role at both the undergraduate and master's level. We would be hard pressed to suggest discarding any component of the current classes. We do feel, though, that the kind of exercises we have described in this paper could play an important role in future classes; they offer important content that is not stressed enough in typical classes.

Software Experience

The best way to get software experience is by working on the development of a real software project. Schools can provide several good substitutes, including the ever-popular team project, case studies, and exercises. We are confident that the exercises allowed the students in our class to make at least ten times as many mistakes as students in typical software engineering classes; the nature of the exercises allowed them to learn from this experience without their grades suffering.

Case Studies

Architects study the design histories of real buildings and aeronautical engineers study the design histories of real airplanes. Yet many software engineering courses have relatively little in the way of case histories of interesting software. The "Case Studies" section of *"Communications of the ACM"* describes large systems in general terms. Like the civil engineer who reads the history of a large bridge and then captures its interesting points in a balsa wood model, we used small exercises to reinforce lessons taught in large case studies.

Design Experience

Our students studied project organization and management in other classes; we concentrated on the design of software artifacts. In our class they studied many clever computing mechanisms, and made many design choices. Their experience taught them that thinking hard about a complex problem often yields a simple and elegant solution.

Application of Science to Engineering

The programming exercises provided an opportunity for the seniors to integrate material from several previous courses in interesting design problems (sorting, for instance, involved both algorithms and user interfaces). Such integration is an important component of typical engineering undergraduate programs, and is absent from typical software engineering classes.

Common-Sense Engineering

The exercises allowed us to make many important points without resorting to platitudes. Instead of repeatedly exhorting students to "Design with components," the exercises showed how components could turn a week-long task into an hour's work. Instead of exhorting to "Keep it simple," the exercises made them do so.

Fun

Software engineering has been defined as "the process by which all the fun is removed from computing"; our course did not suffer that sad fate. Fun is important for any field, both to attract the best students and to establish professional habits that can last a rewarding technical lifetime. The driving force in our class was the sheer joy of creativity; we also felt free to resort to devices such as contests, games, and wonderful literature.

We feel that similar exercises could be merged with the material in current software engineering courses to form a one-year design sequence in software engineering. The Fall Semester would cover the software tools to be used later in the course and part of the lecture material in current courses; exercises would be used to reinforce the abstract discussion. The Spring Semester (and perhaps the last part of the Fall) would be devoted to a large programming project, preferably one that builds upon (and uses) the small exercises studied earlier.

Acknowledgments

We would like to thank Al Aho, Stu Feldman, Brian Kernighan, John Linderman, and Norm Schryer for their various contributions to the course. We are indebted to Al Aho, Brian Kernighan, Doug McIlroy, Chris Van Wyk, Vic Vyssotsky and Pamela Zave for helpful comments on this paper. And to the fifteen cadets who suffered through the prototype offering of EF 485, thanks for your enthusiasm and effort.

Appendix
Discussion of the Tools

The UNIX system and the AWK language were essential to the success of the course; the exercises could not have been implemented in C or Pascal. A similar flavor might be available from other common tools, such as an integrated Lisp environment or a database system.

The UNIX system is well-known for its support of building and using tools. The library of existing filters and the use of pipelines allows the quick-and-dirty construction of useful programs, without exacting the substantial overhead normally expected in interfacing and modifying existing tools. Because the UNIX system is not currently the normal teaching environment at West Point, the cadets spent the first few weeks of the course learning the system. Although we felt that the time was well invested, it would be substantially reduced at schools where the UNIX system is standard.

Before we taught the course we decided that the students should learn exactly one new programming language; Pascal (which they knew) was simply not appropriate for the exercises we had in mind, and we couldn't afford the time to learn two languages. We seriously considered C, and finally chose the June 1985 release of AWK. We are delighted with that decision. Although AWK is significantly slower than C for many tasks, it provided the following important advantages.

An Implementation Language for Simple Filters
The `rotate` and `print` filters in the KWIC program were implemented in a few lines of AWK; Kernighan and Plauger implement `rotate` in 44 lines of Pascal and `print` in 34 lines. We believe that this is typical: AWK programs are an order of magnitude shorter than their counterparts in Pascal, C, or Ada.

An Implementation Tool for Little Languages
We introduced the students to a stylized use of AWK's features that allowed them to implement little languages with little effort (field definitions drive lexical analysis, pattern-action rules provide simple syntax, and associative arrays implement symbol tables).

An Introduction to Non-Algol Language Constructs

AWK introduced the students to many constructs outside the Algol heritage, including associative arrays and powerful string operations (including many operations on regular expressions). AWK encourages a coding style far outside the students' previous experience in Pascal, Ada and assembly.

An Introduction to C

Two months into the course, we introduced the C language as an AWK subset with minor syntactic changes and explicit type declarations. The cadets were able to implement a substantial sorting program in C with little difficulty.

Encouragement of Simplicity

Because AWK is well integrated into the UNIX environment, its presence encouraged the students to build a small filter that they could combine with existing tools. Because many of their filters required only a few lines of code, we encouraged them to reduce their programs to the bare essentials; that is much easier with a 10-line AWK program than with the corresponding 100-line Ada program.

Section II
Part 4
Future of Software Engineering Education

The next ten years will see radical changes in software engineering practice. In this part, Mary Shaw and George Rowland take non-traditional views of software engineering and think about the shape of the discipline in the 1990s. W. Richards Adrion and Bruce Barnes review previous and current National Science Foundation research funding in software engineering and the prospects for continued support.

Trends in National Science Foundation Funded Research and Their Impact on Software Engineering Education

W. Richards Adrion and Bruce H. Barnes
National Science Foundation

Abstract. Trends in software engineering education are discussed from the point of view of the changing environment for both education and research in computer science and engineering. Programs of the National Science Foundation and other federal agencies along with substantial contributions from private industries and foundations have dramatically changed the research infrastructure. These changes have generated important consequences for both graduate and undergraduate education.

Introduction

The National Science Foundation has as a mission insuring the health of U.S. science and engineering through support of science and engineering research and education. The Division of Computer Research is concerned with basic research in computer science and engineering, and provides support for this field through grants to academic institutions for the support of individual or small groups of investigators. Through the Coordinated Experimental Research and the Computer Research Equipment Programs, support for equipment, support staff and other infrastructure categories important to research and the educational environment is provided. An important part of all of this grant support is in the form of graduate and undergraduate student stipends.

Our years at the NSF have given us a unique perspective on the changing environment for graduate education in computer science and engineering, and in software engineering in particular. One of us (Barnes) has directed the Software Engineering Program at NSF since its inception. The other (Adrion) has directed the Coordinated Experimental Research Program, the CSNET project, and the NSFNET project. Both of us have served in a number of other NSF programs as well. The need to coordinate the NSF programs with those of other agencies and with industrial firms and private foundations has given us a unique perspective. These experiences enable us to observe the growth of computer research, the rapid changes in the structure and makeup of the field, and the trends in research investigations.

We hope that our observations will provide some insight into the environment which exists for software engineering research and education. Some of the trends we see affecting software engineering research and education are: a considerable increase in the use of networks and parallel computers; more emphasis on the total software lifecycle in evaluating the value of a project; an increase in the sophistication of the mathematical analysis used in research; and increased use of the computer as a research tool in computer science research.

In our view the goals of any Masters Degree program in Software Engineering should be similar to those espoused in other reports on software engineering programs. These reports point out the need to add to the student's prior skills and knowledge sufficient new material and experiences to qualify the graduate to assume a position of technical leadership on a software development team. We also expect that he or she will be well enough educated to be able to continue to learn and adjust to this rapidly changing field.

Changes in the Computer Science Research and Educational Environment

There are a number of programs in the federal and private sectors which have influenced and changed the academic infrastructure for computer research. Among these are the Computer Research Equipment and Coordinated Experimental Research programs of the NSF Division of Computer Research; the equipment programs administered through the NSF Division of Design, Manufacturing, and Computer Engineering; the NSF Engineering Research Centers Program; the NSF Office of Advanced Scientific Computing; the Department of Defense Advanced Projects Research Agency's Information Processing Techniques Office (DARPA/IPTO) and Strategic Computing Initiative; the DoD Software Technology and Research (STARS) Program; the DoD Strategic Defense Initiative; the DoD Office of Naval Research's Special Opportunities Program; IBM's Academic Computer Information Systems (ACIS) programs; Digital Equipment Corporation's External Research

Programs; the System Development Foundation; many state and local government programs; and workstation manufacturers too numerous to list. We can't describe all these activities or even a few in much detail, but we would like to try to give you a flavor.

The NSF Coordinated Experimental Research (CER) Program was created in response to the "crisis" in academic computer research. The research community reported to NSF through the Computer Science Advisory Committee and through reports such as the Feldman Report and the Snowbird reports that serious problems were arising in the field. Chief among these were the lack of or rapid deterioration of research facilities and the flight of faculty and graduate students to industrial laboratories. It was recognized that only three institutions (Carnegie-Mellon, MIT, and Stanford) were adequately capitalized to perform experimental research, and these had adequate support only as part of a few major DARPA/IPTO projects on the campuses. Remote access to these facilities for experimentation was usually not feasible because of the nature of experimental computer research and because access to the research results and accompanying discussions was available to only a few institutions over the DoD managed ARPANET. These problems caused computer scientists in academia to turn to primarily theoretical research resulting in even fewer trained scientists being graduated.

The NSF response was to create the CER program with three main thrusts. First the CER facilities program was developed to provide long-term (five year) support for facilities including equipment, maintenance, supplies, and supporting technical staff and long term support for major multi-investigator projects in experimental computer science. A second activity, to assist the research community in developing networking services in support of computer science research, resulted in the development of CSNET. The third activity, directed towards the problem of attracting experimentalists into a university environment, was a budget casualty later replaced with the much broader Presidential Young Investigators Program.

Through 1985, NSF has committed $75 million to 22 institutions for the support of experimental computer research. In addition, DARPA has major contracts with MIT, Stanford, Carnegie-Mellon, and California-Berkeley. These contracts include support for extensive experimental computer research facilities. While DARPA also has substantial contracts at Columbia, California Institute of Technology, UCLA, and others, these contracts provide only specialized or minimal facilities. When NSF began the CER activity, it expected to provide support at approximately fifteen institutions. With more than seventy PhD granting departments of computer science and engineering, it was estimated that 25-30 would require research facilities of the magnitude provided by the CER Program. In 1982, the DoD planned to expand their support, through ONR and DARPA, to include 10-15 institutions. This DoD program never materialized, but DARPA has upgraded facilities of their major contractors and provided an expanded number of smaller ($250-300K) equipment contracts. ONR has been able to provide a few "Special Research Opportunities" contracts in computer research which also include some facilities support. Without the planned DoD programs, the CER Program grew in an attempt to fill the need.

The DARPA Strategic Computing Initiative has a strong infrastructure component. The MOSIS fabrication facility developed by IPTO has been expanded and upgraded. The ARPANET continues to provide a communications testbed as well as serving as a medium for the exchange of information and software. DARPA/SCI is developing with university-industry consortia a number of radical new processor architectures, many of which it plans to make available to the general community in a next phase.

The NSF/CER, DARPA/IPTO, ONR, and various DoD and NSF equipment programs have benefited immensely from the rapid change in cost/performance of computing equipment and the willingness of the manufacturers to develop relationships with the academic community through joint research, equipment discounts and equipment donations. Most major research institutions are now reasonably well equipped with cd minicomputers and workstations. Special purpose processors such as the BBN Butterfly, the Intel IPSC, and the NCUBE hypercube and special purpose systems such as robot manipulators, image processors, graphics systems, and database machines are being placed in a number of universities.

The last few years have seen major changes in the academic computing research environment. Institutions have moved computer science up to a high level of priority, resulting in new facilities, laboratory space, and professional support staff growth. Coupled with the programs in the federal and private sector, these actions have resulted in a completely new environment for teaching and research in software engineering.

Trends in the Software Engineering Research and Education Environment

We see a number of trends in research and education as a result of the changing academic computer science infrastructure.   First, the widespread availability of powerful workstations has made possible the study, use, and development of software tools, methods, techniques, and processes in a contained and controlled environment. In much the same way that computer center machines are not suitable for computer research because of the service requirements, departmental minicomputers, now carrying the communications, management, document preparation, and general computing load, cannot be used for sophisticated software tools research or for reasonable educational software tools experiences. Research and education in this area are also helped considerably by the availability of powerful user interfaces and interface development tools. Bit-mapped graphics and pointing devices alone have greatly reduced the learning curve for new tools as well as provided the researcher with better insights into his/her problem space.

Beyond workstations, it is clear that software engineering has been a leading field in the general use of computing as a research and educational tool. To properly train new software engineers and to maintain adequate laboratories for research, it will be necessary to continue investment in computing hardware, software and systems. For example, software tool and method research and development involve the use of computer software which takes as data other software, for both the analysis and synthesis of software. Tool use, once the province of academia, has spread to industry. This trend requires that state of the art tools become an integral part of any software engineering curriculum. As tools, "toolboxes" and "environments" grow more plentiful and powerful, the need for academic research laboratories to develop, procure, and maintain these tools becomes even more imperative.

One of the most significant trends that we have observed in watching the research funding patterns is the shift from uniprocessor-based research to work with network, distributed, and parallel computation. This is very evident in recent NSF Computer Research Equipment program actions. Figure 1 illustrates the type of equipment supported by the grants from this program. Note the shift from mainframe computer facilities to network organization of computer resources. The CER Program has experienced an even greater emphasis on parallel and distributed computing with more than 75% of the CER facilities supporting this kind of research.

	80	81	82	83	84	85
Mainframe	13	4	6	4	6	5
Network	2	1	5	5	10	8
Parallel	0	1	0	0	0	1
Special Purpose	2	3	1	5	4	3
Total	17	9	12	14	20	17

Figure 1: NSF/CRE Actions by Year and by Equipment Type

Many other projects supported by NSF and certainly by other agencies, foundations, and industrial firms involve specialized or unique computational structures. Almost all experimental projects involve distributed computing in some way, many times in a heterogeneous environment. The implications of this trend for software engineering education are significant. The student will need a better understanding of computer architecture and structures, better understanding of how algorithm and programming language structure relate to distributed and concurrent processing, and an appreciation for the difficulties of expressing problems in a manner suitable for parallel solutions.

Dealing with computer software that is running in a parallel environment requires a deeper level of abstraction than one usually encounters in software engineering. Many of the projects supported by the NSF Division of Computer Research involve considerably more sophisticated mathematics than was the case a few years ago. Deep logical analyses and abstract mathematics are employed in program verification, programming language semantics, concurrent operating systems and data base modeling. Both computing theory and artificial intelligence research are requiring the use of richer mathematical tools in dealing with the models and processes employed in computer science. More mathematical ability, training and experience will be required of the student. Mathematical talent matures slowly. Thus the student must have a strong background when beginning the program and this background must be enhanced by courses and projects.

A clear trend in the proposals being considered by the NSF Software Engineering Program is the emphasis on the total software lifecycle. This can be illustrated by the current research in software testing and evaluation, where the goal of most projects is to find test data and testing policies that can be used throughout the total software lifecycle, rather than solely at the traditional testing stage following coding. In software performance evaluation, researchers are designing performance models for the early stages of software design which carry through to implementation and maintenance. While the software lifecycle has always been emphasized in software engineering, there is a trend towards formalizing the software process by identifying the information requirements and by requiring procedural consistency throughout the lifecycle. This emphasis on the software process and the lifecycle as a whole needs to be reflected in the courses and the curriculum. At a minimum, coordination and cooperation among the faculty will be required, and perhaps a major reorganization of the curriculum.

Two other trends are having significant impact on the software engineering student and researcher. The availability of tools like the MOSIS fabrication facility makes it possible for the student and researcher to implement algorithms directly in silicon. The line between hardware, firmware, and software is rapidly blurring. For education this means handling considerably more complexity to properly prepare the student. For the researcher this brings exciting possibilities for tradeoffs between fast "hard" implementations and flexible, but slower "soft" implementations in the software development process.

Finally, these new facilities have opened the door for major projects involving new systems, architectures, and ideas, projects involving many people, undergraduate and graduate students and researchers, faculty, and full-time researchers. These projects afford the software engineers at last a real opportunity to participate, observe, and measure "real" major projects right in the academic environment.

Conclusions

From these trends we see that the graduate of a software engineering program must not only be an expert in the design and construction of software, but must also be strong analytically, be exposed to major projects, learn the technology trade-offs, and be familiar with state-of-the-art workstations, systems, and software tools. Of course, the graduate must also communicate and manage other workers effectively. All of this puts considerable strain on the curriculum, the faculty, and the students. In order to accomplish all this, the student must be capable, motivated, and have a good mixture of academic and industrial experience. The faculty must develop a curriculum that is well-structured and coordinated.

These are exciting times in academia for computer science. Many new opportunities are opening up for experimental research. With these comes the promise of developing and refining software engineering as an academic subdiscipline through the educational and research processes. The trends we have observed at the National Science Foundation have been noticed by others as well. We feel strongly that these trends are pointing the way for the future of software engineering.

Software Engineering: Anomalies in Today's Education and a Prospectus for the Future

George F. Rowland, Jr.
United States Naval Academy

Abstract. "The only things that are new today are in the history that we have forgotten." The purpose of this effort is to set up a beacon in front of a few of the pitfalls that exist and lie ahead in the advance of software engineering as the focus of computing for the late 80's, 90's and into the 21st century.

The United States Government, the Department of Defense, and the Navy specifically have and are spending literally billions of dollars on software development, maintenance, and training. Yet these billions are delivering orders of magnitude less returns in field equipment efficiency, goal attainment, and mission-critical systems being delivered on time. The software crisis or gap in software management tools to handle tomorrow's problems today can be met and bridged. This paper will introduce a few of the tools that exist today, and describe how using current technology, these tools might enable our scholars, future scholars, and professional programmers to conceive, build, and manage the programming systems needed.

Introduction

Software Engineering Education: A Point of View

Software engineering is not something just thought of; since the early 60's formally, and much earlier in an abstract manner, designers and engineers have seen the need to apply sound engineering principles to the development of large software projects. The early techniques of providing formal and semi-formal languages for specification of requirements, software design representations, top-down development and software cost estimation — to mention only a few — are available, but the task yet seems to be too difficult. It is the rule rather than the exception for systems to be delivered late, over budget, and not within the standards of specification, reliability, or maintainability. The bottom line may be that the people implementing the techniques are not intellectually able to understand their use and implications in a design. [90, 82]

There is a shortfall somewhere. It must be defined, located, and eradicated.

Part of the definition may lie in common sense topics such as management science, problem solving, communication skills, and the psychology of the education process. Certainly it is a given that a firm theoretical understanding and expertise must exist in the process; but alone, that foundation cannot translate immediately to the real world.

Two major ideas are: (1) engineering sciences are based on hard premises that are rooted in real, representable, quantifiable, and provable entities; and (2) the environment of the software system may not always fit the engineering model. [60]

What is the synergism of a top down design versus that of an object-oriented design? Can the designer better fathom the synergism of one over the other? [90]

Software Engineering Anomalies:
Opinions on Requirements in Advanced Education
for Computer Curriculums

All the power of expressive languages and object-oriented languages and methodologies can lead directly to a new spaghetti code. If programming tool sets are not properly constrained and not properly managed (enforcement of standards in the production of tools and an overall tool management methodology), anarchy and chaos of disorder of purpose will cloud the overall design of problem solutions. Sound engineering premises and mathematical logic must be used in building tool structures. Will the structures crumble or decompose due to inadequate support? Can the mentality of top down design coexist with an object-oriented graph structure methodology? When does the disconnect occur between the ability to comprehend the whole of a problem and the need to functionally understand a problem and its end result? What is the application of interpreter-driven, interactive run time traces of computer science concepts? How do we use quasi-tools such as Turbo Pascal[TM1], execution Pascal, etc., in expressing the interrelations in computer engineering design?

---

[1]Turbo Pascal is a trademark of Borland International, Inc.

Views on the Subject of Controversy

Computer science is a theoretical subject area devoid of the practical world, and all those implications attributed to computer science that are not provable are not under the purview of computer science.

- Software engineering is the study of the practical problems faced in developing large software systems.
- Software engineering is the study of the hardware-software interface.
- Computer science is the study of the development of systems software.
- Computer science is the study of hardware and/or software.

Software engineers say that computer science works in a void and has no appreciation for the "real world" of software development. Computer scientists say that software engineering presents means of development that have no sound theoretical principles.

In implementing Software Engineering Education, thought should be given to the intellectual maturity of the student. If the student has been provided a firm base in the theory of "why and why not," then the application of "how" will have meaning and relevance. The instruction in software engineering should provide understanding of how the theory can or should be applied and show how the theory is a useful tool in software engineering. [90], [82], [4]

Choice of Methodology: Does it Make a Difference?

Top down functional design. The system is designed from a functional viewpoint, starting with a high-level view and progressively refining this into a more detailed design; this methodology is exemplified by structured design and step-wise refinement.

Object-oriented design. The system is viewed as a collection of objects, rather than as functions, with messages passed from object to object. Each object has its own set of associated operations. Object-oriented design is based on the idea of information hiding.

Data driven design. This methodology suggests that the structure of a software system should reflect the structure of the data processed by that system. Therefore, the software design is derived from an analysis of the input and output system data. [90], [16], [99]

Advancement of Computer Education in the 90's and 2000+

We have a good start because our ideas are aimed in the right direction, but we do not have a good mechanism in place to properly follow the path in that direction. There is a need for a new mentality in applying systems design. When we move from small programs to larger programs and even systems of programs or computer systems, it will be critical to understand what is added to a system by the transitions across the system.

It is good to look at the number of graduates from computer science programs, but you should also question or at least analyze the quality and fiber of the graduate with respect to practical applications of his/her education and knowledge of the essence needed to project current technology onto new generations of computer systems and problems. Future experts must be able to assimilate to future technologies and to imagine the nature of computer systems exploiting those capabilities. What even are the new classes of problems?

We live in an environment that is so competitive that missing a single skill in preparation could be disastrous. Graduate computer science programs must be challenged and bolstered to produce those skills in their alumni. The graduates must be able to cut the fat as well as the cancer from projects. They must be able to change software design and implementation from an exercise in trial and error artistry to an applied engineering design according to scientific principles.

The motivation is the law of the contrapositive, the inevitable, and the decadence seen in an earlier great society. Can we afford cost overrun ad infinitum, loss of life and product failure, unreliability and a hopeless life of patches? Typical graduates may not have their designs subjected to needs to protect life or a nation's security. But my personal perspective sees space stations, transportation and life support systems reliant on secure, robust, and simple designs. Look to the nation to sustain itself, not govern to provide sustenance. By the same token, is supporting a company's livelihood through maintainability that borders on redesign?

Who or what are the culprits? Possible candidates include inadequate coding of a design representation, imprecise testing, and failing to recognize what is not understood. Applying artistic standards will not force scientific and engineering results, nor matches of end product to specification.

Maintenance of programs has been the single largest cost to the tax payer. This is largely, I contend, because there is no understanding of the purpose and relationships within a project beyond a few thousand lines of code.

Observations on Problems with Current Design

(These are tools to build the mentality.)

Let's relate this to the object-oriented model for networks and circuit design (i.e., fields and domains of protection and formal relations and ordered sets).

- Relate this to Ada object-oriented tools, separate compilation, and libraries.
- Relate this to Ada environments and mandated executable methodologies (not a panacea but a start).
- Study standards via frameworks and templates.
- Relate this to developing standards for enforcement of methodologies and the opponents and proponents of same. [16], [66], [49]

What are we talking about?

- Is it an art?
- Is it an engineering science?
- Is it mandatory, requiring certification, and if so, then what criteria prepares a graduate for certification?

More on Advancing Computer Education
into Modern and Future Times

That is all the history, and, like it or not, we are living in the past in computing systems and problem solution design and implementation. Our challenge as professional educators is to bring down the myth of the monolithic, expensive, powerful computer and replace it with a more powerful, more economical, more reliable, and above all, more manageable system of computers. A world concerned with more complex problems will require a "quantum" jump in information processing to meet management requirements. The computers can assist, but only insofar as they are recognized as sophisticated tools and as they are reformed and organized to meet specific needs for processing data. The need for standards will become clear as communications among the components of such a system grow. Data elements, communications protocols, high level languages and more — all must be defined, standardized and conformance insured if large and flexible systems are to prove viable and costs are to be held to acceptable levels. One concept must always govern planning — that it consider the future. Ignoring the future results in inadequate, outmoded systems continually in need of costly change and updating, and never quite in tune with the work requirements. Concomitantly, no innovation or standard should be rejected as too costly without careful evaluation of the "cost of not doing it." [52]

In order to survive today, we must not only use new tools and methods, but also there must be an arm of enforcement of application of the methods; this may be viewed as the locus of paths of the tool set and method set and the space of these paths is constrained, knowable, and decomposable. The natural laws of the space must derive all paths, given an instance of tool and method sets. [75]

Some design ideas are available:

- Top down design with stepwise refinement.
- Object-oriented design.
- Data driven design.

Some implementation and design background:

- The programming process.
- Problem solving viz-a-viz computers.
- Engineering methods.
- Systems design steps or phases.
- Management theory phases or steps.
- Life cycle steps and model.
- Formal logic steps.
- Empirical information about designs.
- Human psychological reasoning process.
- Laws of algebra from commutative, associative, distributive, and identity to deductive and inductive proofs and formal inferences and calculuses.
- What are the formal criteria for computer engineering or scientific certification today?

Some adjunct and interesting factorials:

- Applications to space time continuum.
- Steps of top down design.
- Steps of bottom up design.
- Steps of object oriented design.
- Steps of data driven design.
- Algorithm analysis; perhaps more important than ever. The canned (previously designed, built, compiled) tools must be analyzed algorithmically for applicability and integrity. One bad apple spoils the barrel. [16], [75], [60]

The Engineering Design Process

1. Problem formulation — the problem is defined or described in broad terms without detail.
2. Problem analysis — the problem definition is refined to supply essential detail.
3. Search — a set of potential solutions to the problem is gathered.
4. Decision — each of the potential solutions is evaluated and compared to the alternates until the best solution is obtained.

5. Specification — the chosen solution is described in detail.

6. Implementation — the finished product is constructed from the design.

The Human Problem Solving Process

The Systems Design Process

Given: Formal Requirements Definition

1. Structure the primary functions reflecting the user's requirements.

2. Allocate these functions to the hardware, software, firmware, and human elements. Iterate to step 1.

3. Iterate the design to include any secondary functions. Iterate to steps 1 and 2. Re: A System Design Specification is built from 1, 2 & 3.

4. Validate the overall system design against the requirements. Iterate to Formal Requirements Definition. [16], [75], [60]

Environmental Factors in Support of New Methodologies

1. Philosophy of logic.

2. Psychological sciences.

3. Management science.

4. Communication skills.

5. Tool set management and development.

    a. Qparser sys for parser generators and translation theory education.

    b. C++ , an object oriented language approach to C.

    c. Ada as a programming language.

    d. Ada as a mind set and methodology for software engineering education.

    e. Execution Pascal as an interactive entry level computer engineering education primer.

    f. Franz-Lisp and object oriented AI built with Ada. [4], [102], [49], [48]

Questions that Motivate the Need for
New Education Methods

Why can't big problems be understood from a pure refinement and non-interdependent model?

Why doesn't big problem solution's interdependency necessarily require new design or reinvention of the wheel? Might this require a special analysis of the old design or algorithm?

Can the methodology be translatable, compilable, optimizable, and representable in the mathematics of design?

What must students know to understand the problems of today and the future?

Some suppositions on this knowledge base:

- Must have a mindset based in formal logical reasoning.
- Must have deductive, premise, and formal calculus power.
- Must have at least an intuitive understanding of graph theory, set theory, and formal relationships.
- Must have significant expressive power personally (i.e., knowledge of formal languages, and how to express top down, functional, and object-oriented ideas).
- Must be attuned to abstract algebras to the extent to apply formal logic and relationships to abstract symbolic nomenclature.
- Must have concrete understanding and experience with the engineering methods of problem solving and systems design. [4]

Points on Abstractions of
Software Engineering Principles

My considerations here primarily are with two classes of programs: (1) programming locally, and (2) programming-in-the-large. Locally refers to foreknowledge of eventual use of each module and the details of each module being well-known to all other portions of the effort. In-the-large refers to programming where the size of the program is not easily conceivable by a single person and where a consideration must be given to enough independency in each module that no foreknowledge or detail of a module by a potential user is needed in order to have the module used in a larger scheme. Some factors affecting whether one programs locally or in-the-large follow:

- Structured programming is a byword today, but what is it and how does it impact our concern here?
- Structure may be thought of as a program constructed of relatively independent modules connected via some hierarchy with one or more of the modules being the controlling module for the entire hierarchy. Generally there is an implicit abstraction of the solution design in the structure.
- Some key terms here are *structure*, *programming parts*, and either closely or loosely coupled *connectivity* between parts. [75]

An interesting application of this idea of structure is in program development management, where the dilemma of work assignment units may be parallel with module development and the independence of modules may lead to more control by a small team over what their eventual product looks like rather than being hogtied by the described use of the module by someone at a different hierarchy in the design or programming management. [75], [5]

Structured design may be looked at in two areas: (1) decomposition of hierarchy, and (2) specification of connectivity within the hierarchy. Some of management's greatest concerns are for the suitability and susceptibility of programs or modules to changes, maintenance, and reusability. Advanced studies in computer science must center on better decomposition and better specification. This connectivity question is a formal one. Is it tied to flow of control or to the assumptions that one module understands with respect to another module? If, in fact, the latter, then these abstract assumptions may say little about the detail of the true purpose of a module. [16] What is the mechanism that can define the correct abstract set of assumptions? This lies in part or module specification. For what more should the design be than a statement on the general assumptions about the solution set of the problem?

Doing more in essence is doing less, i.e., when millions of dollars are spent by taxpayers for a product, we expect expandability, extensibility, flexibility, specifiableness, modifiability, and the ability to recognize errors optimally. So when our design is so restricted in the class of problems it may be applied to, we have been disserviced. The specification or the set of assumptions that are abstract to the details of a subsection or module are now described. These open the modules to generality and maintainability.

SEI-Software Engineering Institute

These comments will hopefully support via examples the bridging of the gap and the quieting of the crisis.

Important projects completed this year and last using a new mind set in design point to the validity of the use of object-oriented design and methodologies in future designs. MITRE Corporation, Martin Marietta, and Softech have completed significant software projects with some interesting results. Of note is that time spent up front on design and analysis using formal design tools centered on a programming methodology resulted in up to 25-30 percent reduction in debugging and testing on the projects. Not only was this surprising, but the additions up front were of the order of 10 percent, which pointed to less effort resulting in better output in shorter time. The software lifecycle can be modified. [102], [104], [52], [20]

Life-Cycle Representation:

```
Analysis---------------------------------------------------
Requirements Definition------------------------------
Design-------------------------------------------
Coding---------------------------------------
Testing--------------------------------
Installation----------------------------
Operation-----------------------
Maintenance---------------
```

Life-Cycle Impact:

= Analysis--Retraining or 1990's ++

=Requirements--1990's Graduates

=Design--1990's Junior Analysts or Retraining

= Coding--1990's Programmers Reay if Tools
and Standards are in Place

= Testing--1998 and Junior Analysts

= Installation--1990's

= Operational--1990 ++ Systems

= Maintenance--Minimal for 1990 Designs

Figure 1. Software Lifecycle Modification

It is not yet possible to say that lifecycle cost for these projects will be less, but the cost of putting a system in the field is shown to be less, and the time to installation is less. This seems to say that for each additional dollar spent up front, two to three dollars are saved in the testing and installation phase.

This would point to shortened development periods, and possibly to the overall life of a system being significantly lengthened prior to obsolescence due to cost of maintainability or no longer meeting mission.

Support Information for Developing
Advanced Computer Education

There is another picture of the status of education: 1980 — classes in third generation languages; 1985 — first classes in fourth generation languages and introduction to modern methodologies. Use of second generation object-oriented and artificial intelligence based languages.

Wide usage of modern tools such as interactive editing, window managers, breakpoint and interactive tracing compilation tools. Introduction to the use of total environment concept of programming. Use of PDL's that can be compiled and executed to even show flaws in abstract idea relationships. Government, industry, and academic interest in better, cheaper software. Organizational support of solving the problem-solving-inadequacy that exists in the product coming from our educational institutions, whether undergraduate, graduate, high school, or trade schools. Example organizations: AJPO through ACEET; STARS; Software Engineering Institute; and the ACM and IEEE.

DoD may take a look at its DODCI for a control group for education impact and parallel results with contractor groups. These groups have enough control and accessibility that a metric of the social and psychological impact of education and experience may be reliably formed. This may give a forecast for the future of affordable, reliable, maintainable design methodology. [90], [26] By the 1990's, the next generation of courses must be in place. The graduates today must receive retraining priority and must be motivated to utilize modern methodologies in design and development.

By the 21st Century, the managers and leaders and those conceiving new systems must be products of modern methodology training and mindset. Life cycle models must receive modern training and interest at all phases.

What are the Proposed Courses in Support of Advanced Computer Science Education?

At the core of advanced computer and problem solving methodology is a combination of in-depth courses embodying the ideas of formal logic theory, computer-aided interactive graphics and window management, non-functional artificial intelligence rooted in objects and knowledge-base, and modern language and environment tools centered around the Ada mindset. [90], [75], [4], [5]

- Real Time Processing Concerns with Ada, et al.
- Software Engineering Standards Application

- Window Management Design & Analysis
- Graph Theory Applications in Program Design Analysis
- Abstractions of Problem Space Objects
- Proving Correctness of Object & Operation Abstractions
- Exploiting Concurrency in Translation Design Concerns
- Total Computing Environment Design
- Syntax-Directed Context Sensitive Editor for Abstract Languages
- Interface Design with Artificial Intelligence and Class and Object-oriented Decision Analysis
- Algorithmic analysis with emphasis on building reusability criteria
- APSE and MAPSE design concepts
- Advanced Technical Programmer Re-education
- Advanced Technical Manager Re-education
- Collecting Knowledge-Base Objects from Nature & the Universe
- Psychology in Changing the Mindset of Problem Solution Designers
- The Dynamics of Using Pictorial Information Transfer in Education and Design (over 80% of learning occurs from visual stimuli).

Education for the Future of Software Engineering

Mary Shaw
Software Engineering Institute

Abstract. The discipline of software engineering is developing rapidly. Its practitioners must deal with an evolving collection of problems and with new technologies for dealing with those problems. Software engineering education must anticipate new problems and technologies, providing education in the enduring principles of the field in the context of the best current practice. Since changes in the discipline cannot be completely anticipated, software engineers must be able to assume responsibility for their own continuing professional development. This paper describes significant changes now taking place in the field of software engineering and proposes some goals and objectives for the professional education of software engineers.

Software engineering is concerned with finding practical solutions to computational problems. Over the next few years, software engineering will be required

- to respond to society's broadening needs and higher expectations for software
- to deal with constantly increasing expectations for software functionality and performance
- to gain intellectual control over software development and support.

The major challenges that arise from these requirements will be to broaden software engineering's traditional scope of attention and to increase the scale of systems that can be successfully developed and supported. This will require significant changes in the character of the problems that we work on and the methods that we use to solve these problems.

The demand for software is rising more rapidly than our ability to supply the desired capability. For example, Figure 1 uses code size to estimate software demand. The growth rate for this particular application, onboard software in manned spacecraft, is nearly 30% annually. The figure compares this demand growth with the growth of programmer productivity, which is only about 5% annually. We clearly need to find ways to increase not only the productivity of software engineers but also the rate at which their productivity grows. This problem is one of several software engineering problems aggravated by increasing system complexity. Software engineering education will play a significant role in solving these problems.

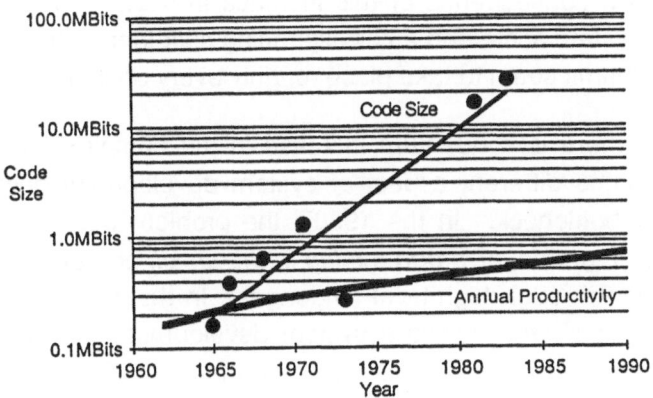

Figure 1. Relative Growth of Software Demand and Productivity

The argument of this paper is as follows. As system complexity increases, the essential character of the most critical problems of software engineering also changes. In order to cope with the complexity of large systems and the new kinds of problems that emerge, software engineering must move from an *ad hoc* basis to a technology-intensive basis rooted in sound models and theories. The principles we use and teach must transcend current practice; they must be codified and teachable. In some cases, such principles can be identified; in other cases we have some systematic understanding that is incompletely codified; in other cases we make do with rules of thumb while trying to develop sound models and theories. Software engineering education must prepare practitioners for future growth by teaching them principles based on sound models in the context of the best current practice.

Effects of Scale on Software Engineering

Software engineering has progressed from solving small problems to solving quite large ones. At each stage in this history, the attention of the software engineering community has been directed at some set of issues that can be understood as characteristic of the major problems of software development at that particular time. Each new generation of systems has been more ambitious than the previous, and new problems emerge as a consequence of this increase in scale. A significant increase in system scale and a corresponding shift in the character of the critical problems seem to take place roughly every decade.

Each time there is a quantum increase in the complexity of software systems, some different aspect of system development becomes the intellectual bottleneck. In the 1960's the problem was writing understandable programs, or *programming-in-the-small*, and the solution was implemented through high-level languages. In the 1970's the problem was organizing large software system development, and the solution was implemented through tools for *programming-in-the-large*. The significance of the distinction between programming-in-the-small and programming-in-the-large is that it is necessary to think about these two kinds of problems in essentially different ways; when the distinction was established, the attention of a significant fraction of the software engineering community was directed to that new problem. When a shift of bottleneck takes place, the problems encountered with smaller systems remain, but the new bottleneck forces the field to attend to a new set of problems in a fashion that may be essentially different from the way we thought about previous problems. The earlier, smaller problems don't disappear, however; they usually remain as subproblems in the larger systems.

In the decade since software engineering recognized programming-in-the-large as a significant issue, the complexity of software systems has grown by another leap, and another shift is now taking place. Software engineers must now deal with complex systems in which software is one of many components in a large heterogeneous system and in which the software is expected to serve as a surrogate for a human programmer, taking an active role in the development and control of software systems. We will describe those new modes of operation as *program-as-component* and *program-as-deputy*, respectively. This analysis is elaborated in "Beyond Programming in the Large: The Next Challenge for Software Engineering," Tech Memo SEI-86-TM-6, May 1986. [86]

Identification of these new modes recognizes a change in the character of the problems that depend on computational solutions as well as a change in the character of the software development and support process:

- They are not necessarily amenable to algorithmic solution.
- They involve judgmental elements such as selecting among competing, non-absolute preferences.
- They depend on problem-specific knowledge that must be consulted dynamically.
- They are so complex that solutions cannot be specified *a priori* but must be evolved through experience.
- They involve integration of a heterogeneous set of system components including hardware as well as software. They require graceful accommodation of unreliable data and other vagaries of physical systems.

The role of *program-as-component* arises in large heterogeneous systems. Such systems include programs in multiple languages for complex hardware systems; they may have mechanical constraints, produce noisy data, or impose real-time constraints on operation.

The role of *program-as-deputy* arises when large, creative portions of the program development process are delegated to software. This shift has been taking place gradually ever since the first symbolic assembler assigned addresses to variables. As time has passed, more and more expertise about various aspects of the software development process has been incorporated in programs which perform increasingly creative subtasks within the software development and management process.

These shifts reflect only the changes in the technology of software development and support. As system scale has increased, issues from several other areas have also become critical.

- *Professional Issues:* Software engineering will experience a significant personnel shortfall for at least the next 5-10 years. Attention to education, career paths, and professionalism will help to take up the slack.
- *Legal Issues:* Software is unlike either hard products or books. As a result, neither patent law nor copyright law is quite appropriate for software products and tools. Intellectual property law for software must deal with such issues as software protection, product liability, impediments to dissemination of new technology, and rights in technical data.
- *Economic Issues:* Costs of software development arise from many sources, and software consumes an increasing fraction of corporate resources. In addition, accounting rules for software influence corporate decisions about innovation. Software engineers often fail to appreciate cost components other than the ones directly associated with creating the software.
- *Managerial Issues:* Management concerns have interacted with software technology ever since we recognized the issues of programming-in-the-large. As systems grow larger, managerial issues expand to include improved costing and estimating techniques, the visibility into software development necessary for effective control, adequate performance measures for human organizations, and incentives and risk reduction measures to encourage more productive software technology.

Although these areas have not generally been covered in software engineering education, their role now requires attention.

The significance of these shifts is not so much the specific developments I have predicted, but the inevitability of some form of change. Progress in software engineering is a fact of life. Systems and tools will change continually, but more significantly the underlying paradigms will also change as increases in problem scale introduce new bottlenecks requiring essentially new techniques for resolution. As a result, our systems must include plans for change and accommodations for local inconsistency as changes take place. Software engineers must be educated to anticipate and accommodate regular change.

"Engineering" in Software Engineering

Engineering is the application of scientific and technical knowledge to the creation of effective systems that meet practical goals. Engineering disciplines have elements of both synthesis and analysis. In software engineering, synthesis includes design, programming, and integration; analysis includes requirement definition, evaluation, and measurement. Good engineering relies on a combination of underlying scientific principles, technical know-how and experience, and a pragmatic concern with effectiveness and utility. Although the field is gradually maturing, the description "software engineering" is still more an aspiration than an accomplishment.

Traditional methods of software development are *ad hoc* and labor-intensive. They will not be adequate to satisfy the increased demands on computing systems and the complexity of the resulting systems. Software engineering must move to a technology-intensive basis that draws on scientifically-based models and theories; it must be prepared to take advantage of advances in these areas as they become available. The education of software engineers is critical to this progress, for good ideas achieve practical utility only in the hands of people who use them wisely.

Over the past two decades a shift to methods based on scientific models has taken place in many aspects of programming-in-the-small. Algorithms and data structures were originally created in an *ad hoc* fashion, but regular use revealed patterns that could be organized systematically and in time provide a basis for formal theories. Some of the earliest formal models supported the analysis of algorithms. Our understanding of algorithms for certain problem domains is now quite well-structured, we can analyze the performance of specific algorithms, and we know theoretical limits on performance in many cases. Similarly, a theory to support abstract data types emerged during the 1970's. In the late 1960's computer scientists recognized the importance of good representations and their associated data structures. Refining this insight to a theory of abstract data types took about a decade; it required advances in formal specification, programming languages, verification, and programming methodology. Undergraduate computer science students should now routinely master algorithmic analysis and abstract data types; it is now reasonable (but not entirely realistic) to expect the material to be applied in routine practice.

Sound theories can also contribute significantly to our ability to construct software systems. For example, the compiler for a programming language is a medium-sized system with a structure that is now well understood. Whereas in the early 1960's the construction of a compiler was a significant achievement, compilers are now often constructed routinely. Good theoretical understanding of syntax developed in the 1960's led to effective techniques for constructing parsers in the 1970's, first manually and more recently automatically. Similarly, good theories for programming language semantics and type structures developed in the 1970's are now leading to automation of other stages of compiler construction.

Although programming-in-the-large has a somewhat shorter history, formal models are beginning to emerge for the information management problems in that domain. For example, configuration management and version control began on an *ad hoc* basis with simple tools for organized (and often massive) recompilation, but at least a few models of system configuration and remanufacture are guiding the construction of software tools. The theoretical basis not only shows how to manage dependency information to reconstruct a system correctly, it also supports more efficient strategies of system reconstruction by avoiding unnecessary steps (e.g., recompilation of modules in which the only changes were comments or which depend only on unchanged portions of modules that were changed).

These examples give the flavor of the progress toward sound foundations for software engineering. There are clearly many areas in which the models, theories, and methodologies are still primitive. However, the power of soundly based theories in at least a few areas offers encouragement for developing and refining theories in other areas.

In Search of Software Engineering Principles

A scientist or engineer instinctively attempts to formalize principles in the form of mathematical laws, and it would be convenient if software engineering could similarly be derived from a set of primitive equations. However, software engineering includes substantial social and organizational components — both behavioral and aesthetic — and it studies artificial constructs not constrained by the physical laws of materials. As a consequence, the models and theories of the field take many forms. We find good use for

- formal (mathematical) and informal theories
- structural and empirical models
- quantitative and qualitative evaluations
- synthetic and analytic principles
- algorithms and paradigms for design and human behavior
- strong and weak methods
- deep and shallow systems.

In general, the foundations of the field — the principles, models, and theories — should be systematic, codified, and abstracted from the examples where we learned them. These foundations should transcend changes of orders of magnitude in current technology, current problems, or current practice. It should be reasonably easy to teach these foundations to others.

At the current stage of software engineering's development, principles, models and theories are not yet available for all aspects of the discipline. Pragmatics lead us to develop and maintain software through a combination of principles and *ad hoc* techniques:

- principles that transcend current practice and current technology
- rules of thumb that guide current practice by codifying useful patterns
- methodologies that mechanize elements of current practice but do not generalize
- hacks

Good practice calls for drawing on techniques that lie as high on this list as possible.

Precise or detailed description of a technique does not make it a principle.   For example, the waterfall model for software development (Figure 2) is a methodology, or mechanization of current practice, and not a principle.

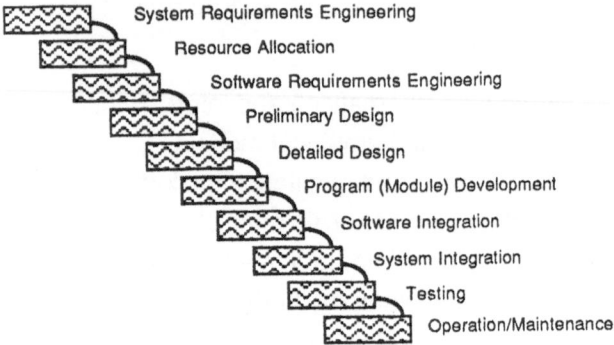

System Requirements Engineering
Resource Allocation
Software Requirements Engineering
Preliminary Design
Detailed Design
Program (Module) Development
Software Integration
System Integration
Testing
Operation/Maintenance

Figure 2. A Non-principle

Software engineering education should accommodate the current state of the field by presenting the strongest principles available in the context of the best current practice. Respect for the students and the state of the field require the material to be presented with honest assessments of the strengths and weaknesses of the techniques.   In order for the material to be useful when current practice is obsolete, the selection of material in a software engineering curriculum should favor those areas in which principles have developed; a good curriculum should refrain from simply teaching current practice in the absence of unifying principles.

The position papers for the SEI Education Workshop contained many exhortations about the need for principles, but few concrete examples. Discussions during the workshop brought out some more examples. I will survey some of the suggestions for the guiding ideas that are variously called principles, theories, models, rules, paradigms, laws and methods.

First, most of software engineering seems to share a few attributes. These are often implicit in attitudes and in selection of techniques rather than subjects of explicit discussion. These underlying principles show that software engineering is:

- *Reductionistic:* We believe that problems in software engineering can be decomposed into successively smaller subproblems and that the solutions to the subproblems can be recombined to obtain a solution to the larger problem. We believe that this accounts for the phenomena that we deal with and that no "vital spark" is required or lost in decomposition. We also generally believe in reproducibility of effect — that the same initial conditions and inputs always yield the same result — though this tends to break down in systems so large that the initial condition cannot be precisely specified.

- *Discrete:* The problems and artifacts of software engineering are discrete, rather than continuous. We don't deal with infinitesimals or limits. Although we sometimes model those effects, we do so with definite limits on accuracy. As a consequence, our reasoning relies on case analysis, induction, and abstraction rather than, for example, extrapolation and interpolation.

- *Non-universal:* We believe in the existence of knowledge extrinsic to software engineering. We do not believe that software engineering or computer science is a universal discipline in the sense that it must eventually account for all phenomena in the world. As a result we must deal with transition problems at the boundary of the field; these are often also the boundaries between discrete and continuous phenomena.

- *Incompletely quantifiable:* Although we try to treat software engineering as an engineering discipline and we use quantitative models and measures wherever possible, we recognize that aesthetic considerations must also be respected. This is particularly true of the design aspects of the field.

- *Computationally limited:* Software engineering is incompletely quantifiable not only because of aesthetic requirements but also because of fundamental incompleteness of the underlying mathematics. We have not only theorems about undecidability but also demonstrations of the intrinsic completeness of testing strategies.

Some approaches to problems appear consistently throughout software engineering but appear to be techniques that generally work rather than underlying principles that dictate what solutions must be. These articles of philosophy include:

- *Engineering discipline:* As noted above, calling the field "software engineering" is still more an aspiration than an achievement. Nevertheless, we find that it is worth while to apply soundly-based models and techniques wherever we can.

- *Abstraction:* Abstraction is suppression of detail. Good abstraction is suppression of detail that is, to the current audience, not significant. We use abstraction not only as an approach to managing the complexity of the systems that we develop but also as an approach to designing the interfaces to those systems. We believe that a computer system should allow its user to focus on the user's real problems rather than on the operation of the system.

- *Defect prevention:* We generally follow a strategy of defect prevention rather than of defect removal. This is an approach rooted in utility rather than in principle: it is most often less expensive and less nuisance to build systems correctly in the first place rather than debug them after the fact. However, this may not always be true; for example, the use of rule-based systems to develop prototypes by iteratively adding information about a complex application and testing the prototype seems to be appropriate in many cases.

- *Reusability:* Because of the creative effort involved, we believe that it is better to reuse system components than to build them from scratch. This is sometimes called the "buy-don't-build" philosophy. In fact, this is an observation about economics and utility rather than a universal truth. However, when we start designing with reuse in mind, we will in effect be constructing theories that explain small application domains; the theories will be expressed in whatever form the reusable code takes.

Some areas of software engineering rely extensively on formal theories. These tend to be the older areas in which our understanding of the material has had longer to evolve. Some of these well developed theories include formal syntax and semantics, various kinds of logics, the theory of computation, formal specification and verification, the theory of algorithms, and type theory. Programming languages are often based on these theories, and we now recognize a number of programming paradigms. The more traditional paradigms such as applicative or functional programming and imperative programming are being joined by object-oriented programming, message-based systems, constraint systems, and rule-based systems.

In other areas, only certain problems have been treated systematically for long enough to develop good models. These models are sometimes structural, as are the queuing-theoretic models for performance evaluation. In other cases the models are empirical, as are certain disk scheduling algorithms and cost estimation models. In the long run the structural models will best meet the test of surviving order-of-magnitude changes in technology or practice, but empirical models are welcome aids in the meanwhile.

Unfortunately, there are many areas of software engineering in which sound models or theories have not yet evolved. In these cases the best practice is *ad hoc*. We should be cautious about the role these practices play in software engineering education. On the one hand, they represent the best of current practice; on the other, they cannot be expected to be durable. Reasonable compromises may involve teaching the nature of the problems without dwelling on the details of the *ad hoc* solutions.

Goals and Objectives for Software Engineering Education

Software engineering is a part of computer science that draws heavily on mathematics, engineering, management, economics, communication, law, cognitive psychology, and design. It inherits a dilemma from computer science: changes in problems, technologies, and methods are an intrinsic part of the field, so the student and teacher are always aiming at a moving target. Since we are constantly assimilating new technologies, we are always on the leading edge of the learning curve for the current technology. This makes it critical for practicing engineers to deal comfortably with change.

Software engineers are educated in colleges and universities, in continuing education programs, and in in-house programs of individual companies. Although these programs reach rather different audiences, they address the same body of knowledge. As a result, a unified curriculum design may suffice to set agendas, but different organizations and presentation styles may be required for different audiences.

Whether software engineers learn this material at the beginning of their careers or afterward, they must be able to function immediately as professionals and to grow as the discipline evolves. Since software engineering is becoming a scientifically-based discipline, students must be educated in the fundamental principles not only of computer science but also of the other fields that contribute heavily to software engineering.

Following the Carnegie Plan for education [27, 78], we can state objectives for any software engineering curriculum, whether it be offered in academia or industry, whether it be a degree program or continuing education. We need a curriculum through which a student can acquire:

- A thorough and integrated understanding of the fundamental conceptual material of software engineering and the ability to apply this knowledge to the formulation and solution of real problems in software engineering.
- A genuine competence in the orderly ways of thinking which scientists and engineers have always used in reaching sound, creative conclusions; with this competence, the student will be able to make decisions in higher professional work and as a citizen.
- An ability to learn independently with scholarly orderliness, so that after graduation the student will be able to grow in wisdom and keep abreast of the changing knowledge and problems of his or her profession and the society in which he or she lives.
- A philosophical outlook, breadth of knowledge, and sense of values which will increase the student's understanding and enjoyment of life and enable each student to recognize and deal effectively with the human, economic, and social aspects of his or her professional problems.
- An ability to communicate ideas to others.

The focus of the curriculum should be on a *liberal professional education with emphasis on design and problem-solving skills*. Describing the education as "liberal" recognizes the importance of exposure to topics outside the student's specialty; at the graduate level this may be somewhat more narrowly directed at material related to software engineering than at the undergraduate level. Liberal education includes communication skills, both for understanding the work of others and for communicating one's own work. Describing the education as "professional" recognizes the legitimate motivations of students who value education because they can apply it rather than for pure intellectual enjoyment. The "design" component of the education recognizes the synthetic, creative aspect of the profession. "Problem-solving skills" refers to the ability to apply general concepts and methods from a variety of disciplines to all kinds of problems, abstract as well as practical, whose solutions require thought, insight, and creativity. Thus "problems" can range from the proof of a theorem to the design and construction of a specialized computer program and "skills" refers to creative intellectual ability, not merely the ability to perform repetitive routine actions.

A Word of Caution

The greatest danger to software engineering curriculum designers is lack of imagination. If we are too narrow, too shortsighted, or too low in our aspirations, we will deprive the field of the skills it needs to satisfy society's requirements for broader scope and larger scale in computer-based systems.

Acknowledgements

My understanding of software engineering education and the principles that support software engineering has come from many discussions with other computer scientists, especially my colleagues at Carnegie-Mellon. Particular insights in this paper came from discussions with Bill Wulf, Allen Newell, Nico Habermann, and Jim Horning. Jim Tomayko supplied data for the software demand figure. The discussion of software engineering principles evolved substantially during two long sessions with the Principles Working Group at the SEI Education Workshop.

Section II
Part 5

Bibliography

[1]   Aho, A.V., Kernighan, B.W. and Weinberger, P.J. *Awk - A Pattern Scanning and Processing Language: Programmer's Manual.* Computing Science Technological Report 118, AT&T Bell Laboratories, June 1985. 36 pp.

[2]   Ardis, M., Bouhana, J., Fairley, R., Gerhart, S., Martin, N. and McKeeman, W. *Core Course Documentation, Master's Degree Program in Software Engineering.* Technical Report TR-85-17, Wang Institute of Graduate Studies, 1985.

[3]   Baker, F.T. *Chief Programmer Team.* IBM Systems Journal, IBM, 1972.

[4]   Balkovich, E., Lerman, S. and Parmelee, R.P. "Computing in Higher Education: The Athena Experience." *ACM/IEEE-CS Joint Special Issue,* Volume 18, Number 11, November 1985.

[5]   Balzer, R. "The Role of Logic and AI in the Software Enterprise." *IEEE Software Engineering,* pp. 394, 1985.

[6]   Barbacci, M., Habermann, A.N. and Shaw M. "The Software Engineering Institute: Bridging Practice and Potential." *IEEE Software,* Volume 2, Number 6, November 1985.

[7]   Basili, Turner. "Iterative Enhancement." *IEEE Transactions on Software Engineering,* Volume 1, Number 4, pp. 390-396, December 1975.

[8]   Beizer, B. *Software System Test and Quality Assurance.* Van Nostrand Reinhold Co., 1984.

[9]   Ben-David, A., Ben-Porath, M., Loeb, J. and Rich, M. "An Industrial Software Engineering Retraining Course: Development Considerations and Lessons Learned." *IEEE Transactions on Software Engineering,* Volume SE-10, Number 1, pp. 748-755, November 1984.

[10]   Bentley, J.L. *Programming Pearls.* Addison-Wesley, 1986.

[11]   Boehm, B. *Software Engineering.* Technical Report TRW-SS-76-08, TRW Systems, October 1976.

[12]   Boehm, B. *Software Engineering Economics.* Prentice-Hall, Inc., 1981.

[13]   Boehm, B. "Software Technology in the 1990's: Using an Evolutionary Paradigm." *IEEE Computer,* Volume 16, Number 11, pp. 30-37, November 1983.

[14]   Boehm, B. "Prototyping vs. Specifying: A Multi-project
         Experiment." *Proceedings of the 7th International Conference on
         Software Engineering*, pp. 473-484. IEEE, March 1984.

[15]   Boehm, B.W. Notes on Requirement Analysis and Design.
         Data Processing Management Association Seminar.

[16]   Booch, Grady. *Software Engineering with Ada.*
         Benjamin/Cummings Pub. Co., 1983.

[17]   Bristol Polytech. *System Analysis Course.* Bristol Polytech
         School Catalog.

[18]   Brooks, F. *The Mythical Man-Month.* Addison-Wesley, 1975.

[19]   Brooks, R. E. "Using a Behavioral Theory of Program Com-
         prehension in Software Engineering." *Proceedings of the 3rd In-
         ternational Conference on Software Engieering*, pp. 196-201.
         IEEE Computer Society, May 1978.

[20]   Brooks, R.E. "Studying Programmer Behavior Experimentally:
         the Problems of Proper Methodology." *Communications of the
         ACM,* Volume 23, pp. 207-213, April 1980.

[21]   Busenberg, S.N. and Tam, W.C. "An Academic Program Provid-
         ing Realistic Training in Software Engineering." *Communications
         of the ACM,* Volume 22, Number 6, June 1979. Harvey Mudd
         College.

[22]   Cain, J.T., Langdon, G.G., Varanasi, M.R. *Model Program in
         Computer Science and Engineering.* Technical Report 4, IEEE
         Computer Society, April 1983.

[23]   Cameron, J.R. *JSP & JSD: The Jackson Approach to Software
         Development.* 1983.

[24]   Denning P.J. "A Discipline in Crisis." *Communications of the
         ACM,* Volume 24, Number 6, pp. 370-374, June 1981.

[25]   DeRemer, Frand and Kron, Hans H. "Programming-in-the-Large
         versus Programming-in-the-Small." *IEEE Transactions on
         Software Engineering,* Volume 2, Number 2, pp. 80-86, June
         1976.

[26]   SE of Computer. *The DoD STARS Program.* Vol. 16, #11.

[27]   Doherty, Robert E. *The Development of Professional Education.*
         Carnegie Press, Carnegie-Mellon University, 1950.

[28]   Fairley, R. "Toward Model Curricula in Software Engineering."
        SIGCSE Bulletin, Volume 10, Number 3, pp. 77-79, August
        1978.

[29]   Fairley, Richard. *Software Engineering Concepts.* McGraw-Hill,
        Inc., 1985.

[30]   Fairley, R.E. *The Role of Academe in Software Engineering
        Education.* Technical Report TR-85-19, Wang Institute of
        Graduate Studies, October 1985.

[31]   Feldman, S.I. "Make - A Program for Maintaining Computer
        Programs." *Software - Practice & Experience,* Volume 9, Num-
        ber 3, March 1975.

[32]   Feldman, J.A. and Sutherlin, W.R. "Rejuvenating Experimental
        Computer Science." *Communications of the ACM,* Volume 22,
        Number 9, pp. 497-502, September 1979.

[33]   Finniston, Montague Sir. *Engineering, Our Future.* Report of
        the Committee of Enquiry into the Engineering Profession Com-
        mand Paper 7794, HMSO, 1980.

[34]   Fjeldstad, R.K. and Hamlen, W.T. *Application Program Main-
        tenance Study: Report to our Respondents.* Technical Report,
        Proceedings of Guide 48, 1979.

[35]   Freedman, D.P. and Weinberg, G.M. *Handbook of Walkthrough,
        Inspections, and Technical Reviews.* Little-Brown, 1982.

[36]   Freeman, Peter and Newell, Allen. "A Model for Functional
        Reasoning in Design." *Proceedings of the 2nd International Joint
        Conference on Artificial Intelligence*, pp. 621-633. 1971.

[37]   Freeman, Peter. "Training Software Designers: Lessons from a
        Development Project." *Proceedings of the International Con-
        ference on National Planning for Informatics*, pp. 232-243. North
        Holland, 1975.

[38]   Freeman, Peter. "Realism, Style, and Design: Packing It Into a
        Constrained Course." *Proceedings of the ACM Symposium on
        Computer Science Education*, pp. 150-157. SIGCSE Bulletin
        8,1, ACM, 1976.

[39]   Freeman, Peter. "The Central Role of Design in Software
        Engineering." Freeman, Peter and Wasserman, Anthony
        I. (editors), *Interface Workshop on Software Engineering
        Education*, pp. 116-119. Springer-Verlag, Irvine, CA. July 1976.

[40]   Freeman, Peter, Wasserman, A.I. and Fairley, Richard
        E. "Essential Elements of Software Engineering Education."
        *Proceedings of the 2nd International Conference on Software
        Engineering,* pp. 116-122. 1976.

[41]   Freeman, Peter and Wasserman, A.I. "A Proposed Curriculum
        for Software Engineering Education." *Proceedings of the 3rd In-
        ternational Conference on Software Engineering,* pp. 52-62.
        1978.

[42]   Freeman, Peter. "The Central Role of Design in Software
        Engineering." *Software Engineering: Research Directions.*
        Academic Press, 1980, pages 121-132.

[43]   Freeman, H. and Lewis, P. (editors). *The Central Role of Design
        in Software Engineering: Implications for Research.* Academic
        Press, 1980.

[44]   Freeman, Peter. "Fundamentals of Design." *Software Design
        Techniques.* IEEE Press, 1983, pages 2-22.

[45]   Gardner, Howard. *The Mind's New Science: A History of the
        Cognitive Revolution.* Basic Books, 1985.

[46]   Garlan, D.B. and Miller, P.L. "GNOME: An Introductory Program-
        ming Environment Based on a Family of Structure Editors."
        *Proceedings ACM, SIGSOFT/SIGPLAN Software Engineering
        Symposium on Practical Software Development Enviroments.*
        ACM, April 1984.

[47]   Gill, T.A. *A Workable Approach to Software Engineering
        Documentation.* Technical Report TR-85-22, Wang Institute of
        Graduate Studies, December 1985.

[48]   Goldberg, A. and Robsen, A. *SMALLTALK-80: The Language
        and its Implementation.* Addison-Wesley, 1983.

[49]   Guttag, J. "Abstract Data Types and the Development of Data
        Structures." *CACM,* Volume 20, Number 6, pp. 369-404, 1977.

[50]   Hester, S.D., Parnas, D.L. and Utter, D.F. "Using Documentation
        as a Software Design Medium." *Bell System Technical Journal,*
        Volume 60, Number 8, pp. 1941-1977, October 1981.

[51]   Hoffman, A. "Survey of Software Engineering Courses." *SIGCSE
        Bulletin,* Volume 10, Number 3, pp. 80-83, August 1978.

[52]   Hopper, G.M., Admiral, USNR. "David and Goliath." *DODCI
        Selected Computer Articles,* 1983.

[53] Horning, J.J. and Wortman, D.B. "Software Hut: A Computer Program Engineering Project in the Form of a Game." *IEEE Transactions on Software Engineering,* Volume SE-3, Number 4, pp. 325-330, July 1977.

[54] Subcommittee on Software Engineering. *Draft Report on MSE-80: A Graduate Program In Software Engineering.* Technical Report, IEEE Computer Society Education Committee, May 1980.

[55] Jackson, M. *System Development.* Prentice-Hall, 1983.

[56] Jensen, R., Tonies, C. and Fletcher, W. "A Proposed 4-Year Software Engineering Curriculum." *SIGCSE Bulletin,* Volume 10, Number 3, pp. 84-92, August 1978.

[57] Jensen, R. and Tonies, C. *Software Engineering.* Prentice-Hall, Inc., 1979.

[58] Kant, E. "A Semester Course in Software Engineering." *ACM SIGSOFT Software Engineering Notes,* Volume 6, Number 4, August 1981.

[59] Kernighan, B.W. and Plauger, P.J. *Software Tools in Pascal.* Addison-Wesley, 1981.

[60] Knuth, D.E. "The Art of Computer Programming." *Fundamental Algorithms*, Volume 1. Addison-Wesley, 1973, pages 1-24. 2nd Edition.

[61] Koffman, E.B., Stemple, D. and Wardle, C.E. "Recommended Curriculum for CS2, 1984: A Report of the ACM Curriculum Task Force for CS2." *Communications of the ACM,* Volume 28, Number 8, August 1985.

[62] Leblang, D.B. and Chase, R.P., Jr. "Computer-Aided Software Engineering in a Distributed Workstation Environment." *Proceedings ACM, SIGSOFT/SIGPLAN Software Engineering Symposium on Practical Software Development Environments.* ACM, 1984.

[63] Lee, K.Y. "Status of Graduate Software Engineering Education." *Proceedings of the 1981 Annual Conference.* ACM, Los Angeles, California. 1981.

[64] Lee, K.Y. and Frankel, E.C. "Real-Life Software Projects as Software Engineering Laboratory Exercises." *ACM SIGSOFT Software Engineering Notes,* Volume 8, Number 3, July 1983. Seattle University.

[65]   Linderman, J.P. "Theory and Practice in the Construction of a
        Working Sort Routine." *AT&T Laboratories Technical Journal,*
        Volume 63, Number 8, pp. 1827-1843, 1984. part 2.

[66]   Liskov, B. and Zilles, S.N. "Specification Techniques for Data
        Abstractions." *IEEE Transactions on Software Engineering,*
        Volume SE-1, Number 1, March 1975.

[67]   Martin, N., Ligget, D. and Kirby, J. *The Wang Institute Software
        Environment.* Technical Report TR-85-05, Wang Institute of
        Graduate Studies, 1985.

[68]   McGill, J. "The Software Engineering Shortage: A Third Choice."
        IEEE Transactions on Software Engineering, Volume SE-10,
        Number 1, pp. 42-49, January 1984.

[69]   McIlroy, M.D. "Development of a Spelling List." *IEEE Trans-
        actions on Communications,* Volume COM-30, Number 1, pp.
        91-99, January 1982.

[70]   Myers, W. "An Assessment of the Competitiveness of the United
        States Software Industry." *IEEE Computer,* Volume 18, Number
        3, pp. 81-92, March 1985.

[71]   NATO Science Committee. *Software Engineering.* Conference
        Report. Garmisch, Germany, October 7-11, 1968 (January,
        1969).

[72]   Neisser, Ulric. "Chapter 11, A Cognitive Approach to Memory
        and Thought." *Cognitive Psychology.* Meredith Publishing, Co.,
        1967, pages 279-305.

[73]   Notkin, D.S. "The Gandalf Project." *The Jornal of Systems &
        Software,* Volume 5, Number 2, May 1985.

[74]   Osterweil, L.J. "Software Environment Research Directions for
        the Next Five Years." *IEEE Computer,* Volume 14, Number 4,
        pp. 35-43, 1981.

[75]   Parnas, D.L. "On the Criteria to be Used in Decomposing Sys-
        tems into Modules." *Communications of the ACM,* Volume 15,
        Number 12, pp. 1053-1058, December 1972.

[76]   Parnas, D.L. "Some Software Engineering Principles, from A
        Technique for Software Module Specification with Examples."
        CACM, Volume 15, Number 5, May 1972.

[77]   Parnas, D.L. and Clements, P.C. "A Rational Design Process:
        How and Why to Fake it." *Proc. Int. Joint Conf. on Theory and
        Practice of Software Development*, pp. 80-100. Springer-Verlag,
        March 1985.

[78]   Paul, F.W., Feucht, D.L., Jr., Teare, B.R., Neuman, D.P. and
        Tuma, D. "Analysis, Synthesis, and Evaluation - Adventures in
        Professional Engineering Problem Solving." *Proceedings Fifth
        Annual Frontiers in Education Conference,* pp. 244-251, Oc-
        tober 1975. IEEE and Amer. Soc. for Engr. Ed.

[79]   Perlman, G. *Shar, A Program In C.* Distributed on net.sources,
        January, 1985, Citing Gosling version of October 18, 1982.

[80]   Peters, Lawrence. *Software Design: Methods and Techniques.*
        Yourdon Press, 1981.

[81]   Pressman, Roger. *Software Engineering: A Practitioners Guide.*
        McGraw-Hill, Inc., 1982.

[82]   Redwine, S.T. and Riddle, W.E. "Software Technology
        Maturation." *Proceedings 8th International Conference on
        Software Engineering*, pp. 189-200. ACM, London, England.
        August 1985.

[83]   Riddle, W.E. and Williams, L.G. *Software Environments
        Workshop Report.* Technical Report TR-85-001, Rocky Moun-
        tain Institute of Software Engineering, December 1985.

[84]   Rochkind, M.J. "The Source Code Control System." *IEEE Trans-
        actions on Software Engineering,* Volume SE-1, Number 4,
        December 1975.

[85]   Shaw, M. (editor). *The Carnegie-Mellon Curriculum for Under-
        graduate Computer Science.* Springer-Verlag, 1985.

[86]   Shaw, M. *Beyond Programming-in-the-Large: The Next Chal-
        lenges for Software Engineering.* Technical Report SEI-86-
        TM-6, Software Engineering Institute, Carnegie-Mellon Univer-
        sity, May 1986.

[87]   Sheil, B.A. "The Psychological Study of Programming." *AMC
        Computing Surveys,* Volume 13, Number 1, pp. 101-120, March
        1981.

[88]   Simon, H.A. *Science of the Artificial.* MIT Press, 1969.

[89]   Simon, Herbert A. *The Sciences of the Artificial.* MIT Press,
        1981.

[90]   Sommerville, I. *Software Engineering.* Addison-Wesley Pub. Co., 1985.

[91]   Spicer, J.C. *A Spiral Appproach to Software Engineering Project Management Education.* Technical Report, Wang Institute of Graduate Studies, December 1983.

[92]   Stucki, L.G. and Peters, L. "A Software Engineering Graudate Curriculum." *Proceedings of the 1978 Annual ACM Conference,* pp. 63-67. ACM, 1978.

[93]   Teitelbaum, R. and Reps T. "The Cornell Program Synthesizer: A Syntax-Directed Programming Environment." *CACM,* Volume 24, Number 9, September 1981.

[94]   Teitelman, W. and Masinter, L. "The Interlisp Programming Environment." *Computer,* Volume 14, Number 4, April 1981.

[95]   Thayer, R.H. and Tozza, J.C. *Report on an Investigation to Determine a Set of Evaluation Criteria for Selecting Project Management Productivity Tools.* Technical Report, National Bureau of Standards, February 1985. Prepared by Software Management Consultants.

[96]   Tichy, W.F. "Design, Implementation and Evaluation of a Revision Control System." *Proc. 6th International Conference on Software Engineering,* pp. 58-67. IEEE Computer Society, September 1982.

[97]   Tichy, W. "RCS - A System for Version Control." *Software - Practice & Experience,* Volume 15, 1985.

[98]   Traub, J.F. "Quo Vademus: Computer Science in a Decade." *Communications of the ACM,* Volume 24, Number 6, pp. 351-369, June 1981.

[99]   U.S. Department of Defense. *Reference Manual for the Ada Programming Language, MIL 1815a.* 1983.

[100]   Wasserman, A.I. and Freeman, Peter. *Software Engineering Education: Needs and Objectives.* Springer-Verlag, 1976.

[101]   Wasserman, A.I. and Freeman, Peter. "Software Engineering Education: Status and Prospects." *Proceedings of the IEEE,* Volume 66, Number 8, pp. 886-892, August 1978.

[102]   Wegner, P. "Ada Education and Technology Transfer." *Ada Letters,* Volume 2, Number 2, 1982.

[103] Woffinden, Duard. lecture notes for EENG 593 Software Engineering, 1985. Air Force Institute of Technology, WPAFB, OH.

[104] Wolf, A.L., Clarke, L.A. and Wileden, J.C. "Ada-Based Support for Programming-in-the-Large." *IEEE Software,* Volume 2, Number 2, pp. 58-77, March 1985.

[105] Woodfield, S.N., Collofello, J.S. and Collofello, P.M. "Some Insights and Experiences in Teaching Team Project C.S." *Communications of the ACM,* 1983.

[106] Woodward, M.R. and Mander, K.C. "On Software Engineering Education: Experiences with the Software Hut Game." *IEEE Transactions on Software Engineering,* Volume SE-25, Number 1, February 1982.

[107] Worth, L. Personnel conversation with Professor Laurie Worth, University of Texas at Austin. December.

[108] Zave, P. "Let's Put More Emphasis on Prescriptive Methods." *Software Engineering Notes.* ACM, 1986.

[109] Zelkowitz, M.V., Yeh, R., Hamlet, G., Gannon, J.D. and Basili, V.R. *The Software Industry: A State of the Art Survey.* Technical Report, Department of Computer Science, University of Maryland, 1981.

[110] Zelkowitz, M., Yeh, R., Hamlet, R., Gannon, J. and Vasili, V. "Software Engineering Practices in the United States and Japan." *IEEE Computer,* June 1984.

Section III

Transcripts

Report of the Software Engineering Principles Working Group

This is the presentation made by A. Nico Habermann, Carnegie-Mellon University, summarizing the discussions of the working group on software engineering principles. This group was charged with determining the fundamental principles on which software engineering, and thus a curriculum, can be based.

The participants were: Gordon Bradley, Gary Ford, Susan Gerhardt, Bill Riddle, Mary Shaw, Ed Smith, and Nico Habermann, group leader.

The group was given the following questions to discuss:
1. *What are the fundamental principles of software engineering?*
2. *How have software engineering principles evolved?*
3. *How does one distinguish software engineering principles from computer science principles?*
4. *What are the non-computer science principles of software engineering? Do they include coordination, economics, communication, and human factors? Are there others?*
5. *Does software engineering have its own principles, or just a conglomerate of principles from other disciplines?*
6. *Is the software engineering profession eclectic or narrow?*
7. *What is the group's evaluation of the SEI's current curriculum proposal?*

Nico Habermann: We will report on our activities of today. We spent most of our time on two topics: methodology principles and the curriculum. Yesterday we discussed the list of questions. We added two questions, and this morning we addressed those.

The first item was that there may be other things that are standard practices or systematic methodologies that are in use today, that have not been reduced to principles yet, but that may in the future or now be a substitute for principles. We discussed in much more detail today the questions, "Is there any scientific methodology underlying software engineering that is more or less unique to software engineering that you don't find in other disciplines? How does software engineering distinguish itself, for instance, from mathematics or physics or other disciplines?"

SLIDE 1. GENERAL PRINCIPLES

- ANALYSIS OF EXISTING ARTIFACTS OR THEORIES
- COMBINATION OF DESIGN AND ANALYSIS
- DECOMPOSABILITY, REDUCIBILITY
- IMPOSSIBILITY OF ACCURATE REQUIREMENTS SPECIFICA-
TIONS
- ABSTRACTION
- LIMITS OF SCOPE AND SCALE
- DIVIDE AND CONQUER

SLIDE 2. PRINCIPLES OF PHILOSOPHY

- DEFECT PREVENTION VS. DEFECT REMOVAL
- SYSTEMATIC APPROACH VS. APPLICATION OF FORMALISM
- TESTING IS INTRINSICALLY INCOMPLETE
- COST EFFECTIVENESS IS REQUIRED OF ALL SOFTWARE
SYSTEMS

SLIDE 3. CONCRETE PRINCIPLES

- INFORMATION HIDING
- ITERATIVE NATURE OF SYSTEM DESIGN
- REPRODUCIBILITY OF DESIGN IDEAS AND DECISIONS
- OBJECT-ORIENTED PROGRAMMING
- DATA-DRIVEN DESIGN
- RULE-BASED SYSTEMS
- REUSABILITY
- VERIFICATION AND VALIDATION
- DEVELOPMENT UNDER INTELLECTUAL CONTROL

We came to the conclusion that, in addition to the principles that we discussed yesterday [Slides 1, 2, 3], we do see some principles that are fairly unique to software engineering, not entirely, but that one can see as a distinction between software engineering and several other disciplines. We have four of them [Slide 4].

SLIDE 4. PRINCIPLES OF METHODOLOGY

- REDUCTION PRINCIPLE
  - THE WHOLE = THE SUM OF THE PARTS (AND NOT MORE)
- DISCRETE NATURE OF THE SUBJECT OF SOFTWARE EN-GINEERING
  - CASE ANALYSIS
  - INDUCTION
  - ABSTRACTION
- THE EMBEDDED NATURE OF SOFTWARE
  - THE IMPACT OF CONTEXT, ENVIRONMENT, AND ENCLOSING SYSTEM
- QUANTIFIABLE MEASURES
  - DRIVER FOR DESIGN AND DEVELOPMENT
  - NOT EXCLUDING AESTHETICS

In the first place, we think that the field works with the reduction prin-ciple. That is the principle that says that it is possible to partition a problem in various ways, by refinement, abstraction, or other means; and that if you can indeed decompose the problem in such a way, then you can solve the separate parts. If you then put these together, you come up with a solution. We think that we are working with that prin-ciple in general; that we can do things like that, and that is in contrast to what the psychologists are saying. A psychologist will say the way that he goes about his discipline is that he will recognize and address certain parts (I would say even behavior), but then will come to the conclusion that by just summing all of those behaviors, he doesn't have a human being yet. There are still things that escape his analysis. There is always more to it. Just putting all the molecules together doesn't make the object. That is their philosophy, whereas we believe that we still work with the other ideas. Now maybe mathematicians have that idea, too, that they can decompose, put things together out of small units, and then come up with the whole. In this statement [Slide 4], we summarize that we believe that the whole is indeed equal to the sum of its parts. By putting things together, you don't get more than the parts.

The next one was that all the problems we are attacking, the way that we reasoned about them, and the way that we looked for solutions — we always are talking about discrete objects and the discrete way of approaching the solutions. We recognize a solution if we come past it in terms of discrete steps. With induction, for instance, we apply that principle, and we say that we can understand how something works if we are able to define the induction step and the initial state. If we think of things that have an undetermined or indefinite length, we still go back to this finite induction step in order to explain or prove the correctness of things. So we believe that that is one of our specific principles that we do not have in common with, for instance, physics, where they believe in a continuum. Maybe they also believe, in their hearts, in a discrete model. Nevertheless, they work as if things are continuous.

This continuity has an impact on the way that we do business and on what we do. That leads us to look for a case analysis of our problems and to inductive steps and abstraction. So, that is the second principle that we think is strongly present in the things that we do.

Another principle is that we recognize that our software products, and our software that we reason about and that we produce, are always functioning in a larger environment as part of a larger entity. It may be it is a system or is working in a context or in an environment. But that is again in contrast to physics, for instance. The physicists talk about the universe, and they apply laws that they may experiment with in the laboratory, but then they will extrapolate from what they see and make this avowed statement for the universe as a whole, whereas what we are saying is that we are much more restricted. We recognize that our product is going to function in the larger entity, about which we have only limited knowledge, and also in which we do not participate in the design. The context is often given to us and the properties of the context are given, and these properties have an impact on the product that we are supposed to produce. We always have to understand it and it comes in various forms to us, through the human aspect, or the economic aspect, maybe the functional aspect of the interaction with other systems. In all of these cases, we always have to take those into account. That is in contrast to mathematicians or physicists who have their universe in mind, where their solutions are valid for the entire domain that they are looking at.

Next we stated that some people take the attitude that what you cannot measure doesn't exist. Now, that is a very strong statement. People sometimes behave that way, that if you can't measure it, you should ignore it, discard it, or simply not take it into account. That is the second way of stating it. Sometimes people have a tendency to say, "Only that which I can measure is of value and all the other things are immaterial." Some of us feel that that is not the correct way of stating it. Although we agreed that it is a good idea to try to find ways to measure things and try to quantify the disciplines (it is a good objective), nevertheless, there are things that go beyond the quantifiable measures. In particular, we discussed the matter of taste and the way that you design software. Some people, as we all know, have a very strong perception of taste. What they do is look for the elegance in the solution, the beauty in the algorithm, and the lines of the program. We want to recognize the aesthetics as one of the factors that has an impact on the thing you do. So we rephrased it into this form [Slide 4] and said it is good to go after ways to quantify things and also to find new methods for quantification. But on the other hand, we do recognize the importance and the contribution of other factors. But to go for the quantifiable measures is a principle that is productive in this discipline. So those were the four principles that we added to the principles of yesterday.

Now, you may remember that we had the different categories yesterday. We had the principles of philosophy, the general principles, the topic principles, and the principles of methodology. We added to that list.

We looked at the curriculum. At first we tried to answer the following question. If you look at the curriculum, as proposed here, [Appendix B, MSE Curriculum] and then go through these topics step by step, can you indicate the principles that underlie a particular topic? After a discussion, we came to the conclusion that we were not doing it and we couldn't. It might have been possible if from the very beginning we had tried to come up with fairly concrete principles for each of the topics. But what we have done instead is come up with much higher level principles. We came to the conclusion that we could not identify principles underlying each topic. The reason for not being able to do it was we had uncomfortable feelings about the way that the curriculum is presented.

We have the following criticism. The presentation itself lacks the right organization in two ways. It lacks order and it lacks hierarchical decomposition. The way that it is right now, it is a flat structure of a number of topics, and it is not clear in which order these topics should be presented in the curriculum. We also think that the modules are not grouped together in a useful way. We would like to see how these modules fit together to form other units that are major components of the program. We also had a major objection to the packaging. We thought that these topics would not make sense in the form of short courses that could be presented in a limited amount of time.

There were some suggestions of how you judge these modules and what would be the kinds of things that can help you to design them. We came up with four criteria to judge whether you want to include something and how to structure it. The first is that if you've got a topic, then you need to find the relevant theory behind it. Maybe it is not very strong; maybe it is. You have to determine what the weight is going to be. The next criterion is what are the applicable methods that apply to the topic? What is there that can help you to make it practical, to apply it? The third one is what available techniques are there to support the topics that you propose? The last one is the assessment that applies to the former three, but also to the topic itself. In whatever you do, the most important thing is the scientific, analytic approach to it. Having gone through the topic, defined the substance of it, and found what the theory is behind it, then assess the value of it, the applicability of the methodology, the economic value, and so on.

SLIDE 5. BIASES IN PROPOSED CURRICULUM

- EMPHASIS ON FORMAL METHODS
- NEGLECT OF SYSTEMATIC PRACTICES
- PROCESS OF SOFTWARE ENGINEERING NOT ADEQUATELY COVERED
- LACK OF DISCERNIBLE CONCERN FOR COMPARATIVE EVALUATIONS; LAYING THE FOUNDATIONS FOR GRADUATES TO MAKE JUDGMENTS ABOUT FUTURE TECHNOLOGIES

Next, we observed in the way that the curriculum is described, there is a bias toward formal methods [Slide 5].

Some of us argue that this bias is, by itself, not a bad thing. It is actually good to look for formal methods. That by itself is not a criticism, but it has a side effect that may not be good. The side effect is that you neglect to observe that there are systematic techniques right now in place that substitute for the principles or the formalism. Some of those are valuable and therefore should be paid attention to.

Another specific criticism was that if you look at the list of topics, the process of software engineering itself is not strongly represented. That is a specific criticism.

We did come up with yet another category of principles. At the end of our discussion, we said, "Let's give it one more try, and see if we can come up with more specific principles for each of those topics." We don't have an exhaustive list, but we did recognize that it is possible to come up with such principles [Slide 6].

SLIDE 6. TOPIC AREA PRINCIPLES

- PRINCIPLE OF DESIGN: MAKE THE OBJECTIVES CLEAR
  - CUSTOMER SATISFACTION
  - OPTIMAL PERFORMANCE
  - MINIMUM CODE SIZE
  - RELIABILITY
- PRINCIPLE OF TESTING: VIEW IT AS VALIDATION, NOT VERIFICATION
- PRINCIPLE OF REQUIREMENTS: REQUIREMENTS ARE DEVELOPED THROUGH ITERATIVE INTERACTION BETWEEN DEVELOPER AND CLIENT

We asked questions like, "What would you say is the first thing to do when you talk about software design?" The answer is you have to make your objectives clear. What are the goals of the software product? Is it reliability? There are a number of possible answers to the question. The principle is that the first thing that you do when you start designing is to make the purpose and the objectives of that product clear.

Another principle is that testing by itself is not going to be satisfactory. Verification is different, but we do recognize that the focus of testing is validation, to see whether the kinds of things that you have in mind for the software indeed are there. That is the kind of a thing that you can test.

With respect to requirements, the principle is that requirements cannot be precise and accurate. That has certain consequences. If you adopt that principle, you know that you have to go through an iterative process between the client and producer to make the requirement more specific.

Our conclusion is that the curriculum design should go through a next round, and that the first things that should be done are determining the order in which topics will be presented, and the grouping of modules into clear entities. If we have that kind of an organization, I think that we can come back to the principle question.

One last thing: we think that we actually did a good job in coming up with the general principles, but that you cannot attach those to specific topics. Those principles should be the things that are always on the side in the matrix structure, while the specific topics are across the top. Those are the things you can always fall back to. That has an impact on everything that you teach and on all the topics.

Bill McKeeman: I have one concern that I expressed yesterday. I saw no attention being paid to the student. Curriculum is a state transition diagram on students. I don't think the state of the student, before and after, has been taken into account, either motivation or knowledge.

Nico Habermann: That is a good remark. We did not address that at all.

Dick Fairley: Yesterday someone raised the point that it may not be a good idea to try to modularize such a curriculum, because there is such a feeding and reinforcement of the various issues that we talked about. Did you address that point?

Mary Shaw: One of the things behind the conclusion is that there was a general feeling that the curriculum should be defined as an entity before it was broken out into modules. Then the conceptual skeleton on which the entire curriculum hangs would be clear and would be the supporter of the design of the curriculum as a whole. This should then show the way to breaking the material out into modules.

Susan Gerhart: I thought that we felt that we were missing the principle of modularization in the curriculum design. That did not come through to us at all.

Nico Habermann: We did not find the principle by which the designers came up with this particular set of modules.

Dave Wortman: We need the system model for the modules.

Ev Mills: My impression was that the modularization was partly in an attempt to make these topics both fit into this curriculum and be suitable for other types of short course presentations. I wonder if there is always a conflict when you try to do that. Have you talked about that potential problem?

Nico Habermann: We spent a lot of time on the packaging, and we came to the conclusion that that was not satisfactory. Our conclusions were that you should not try to do both at the same time. You should first come up with an overall design of what kind of structure the curriculum has, then order how things will happen, and then try to carve out things into smaller parts and make several packages that can be taught separately.

Ev Mills: I guess that your answer is the same. But I was thinking about this dual purpose of type of instruction, both within a regular degree program and also as a form of instruction for industry on a short course basis. There is a conflict there, which I think is going to cause problems.

Nico Habermann: Yes. We recognize the problem, but once again we propose that you first ignore these two issues and once you've got the structure, then address them separately. That was our advice.

Gordon Bradley: I guess we don't believe in reductionism for the curriculum. We think that the curriculum is more than the sum of the modules and that breaking it up and trying to teach it in industry may kill the object. It is not clear that you can take something you taught in two years, unified, and break it up into pieces and teach the same thing by teaching the pieces.

Ev Mills: I agree. That is what I was hoping that you would think.

Gordon Bradley: I don't know whether there was universal agreement on that.

Nico Habermann: It was actually nice for us to discover that. We had just been discussing this principle of reduction at length, and came to the conclusion that we believed in it. Then we applied it to the curriculum and came to the conclusion that we did not believe in it.

Norm Gibbs: Did you deliberate about what should be done in the case where companies have people that they would like to have reeducated, but that they are too valuable to release for long periods of time to have university experience? Did you really address their needs?

Nico Habermann: We did not address that. Is there anybody in the room who would like to discuss that question?

Dick Fairley: I would observe that perhaps we can't talk about education of industrial people, but only the training of industrial people in current techniques; education rightfully belongs somewhere else.

Nico Habermann: I don't believe that. I would like to hear Al's opinion on that.

Al Pietrasanta: I absolutely hope it is not true. I believe that we can continue to educate, in the full sense of the word, industrial people. I think that they need to have a level of experience to absorb the educational objectives of this program.

Dick Fairley: Let me clarify. In the context of what Norm said, that you can't release your people, I agree. If you can release the people and bring them to Thornwood [*IBM Corporate Technical Institutes*], you can educate them. But if a person cannot be released from the job and can only get there a few hours a week over a long period of time, then perhaps you can't achieve the educational objectives, but only training objectives.

Nico Habermann: I still don't believe that. I get educated by doing this, for instance, today and yesterday. I really get educated. There are some people who have good ideas that I have never thought of. I was not here particularly for training purposes. But I do think that if you have a certain level of understanding, then it is certainly possible within a short amount of time to get educated in some of this.

Mary Shaw: I do not really believe that the reductionistic arguments don't apply to the curriculum and that it is inevitable that you can only do training. I believe that the reductionistic position does not simply say that the sum is the whole of its parts, but also recognizes the rule by which those parts are recombined. And so, in the particular case of the education of professionals, the fact that the teaching is done in units rather than as a complete whole doesn't mean that it will fail to educate. It is necessary to be careful about establishing the context of each of these units, to make sure that the units are clear as to what they contain and how they relate to other units, and to invest energy and make sure that the combining of those units actually takes place, overcoming the difficulties that are enclosed by this fragmentation and the periodic presentations. But I don't believe that it is impossible.

Jim Tomayko: I'd like to make one general statement about principles in relation to software engineering. I notice that whenever we talk about this, there is a certain amount of awkwardness. And then, after you bang away at it a while, there is a certain amount of frustration at the other end. I have a little theory as to why I think this is happening. We have been following the model that if we go from good basic science, it leads to better engineering. When you look at the other kinds of sciences besides computer science, like biology and psychology, you've got scientists studying living things. If you have sciences like chemistry and physics, you've got scientists studying phenomena that are nonliving but they are natural. Then you have computer scientists, who are studying things that are neither living nor natural. I think that this is really an important distinction. We are studying an artifact that we made ourselves. I don't want to get into the "computer science isn't a science" debate because I don't care whether it is or not. I think for this discussion it doesn't matter. The point is maybe the way that we think about things relative to existing science and engineering doesn't work in this case because we are dealing with a phenomenon that is completely different.

Nico Habermann: In some sense, I think that what we discussed in our group denies that. You see a clear correspondence with other disciplines. Indeed, we also see clear distinctions. But we did not come to a conclusion that there is really something going on here that is entirely different from other things that have been done or are still being done in other disciplines. We recognize, for instance, that we have in common with the physicists the experimental nature of the way we go about our jobs. I believe what we do is analyze and make models. Instead of theories, we often make models beforehand and then analyze the adequacy of those models afterwards. We borrow from mathematics in the way that we form models. We have done that in the form of data abstraction and data encapsulation and so on. We have that in common with the mathematicians. You can see that there are lots of things where there is an overlap. But on the other hand, in the principles that I showed here [Slide 4] just now, we recognize that there are certain things that are more specific to software engineering than they are to other disciplines. And so, you also see the distinction. But I think that you put it too strongly, as if it were entirely different from other disciplines, which we believe is not the case.

Report of the Current Software Engineering Curricula Working Groups

This working group was split into two subgroups, one concentrating on the evaluation of existing curricula and the other trying to structure a prototypically *best* curriculum. These groups combined their findings for presentation.

Report of the Subgroup on Existing Curricula

This is the presentation made by Al Pietrasanta, IBM Corporation, summarizing the discussions of the subgroup on existing curricula. This subgroup was charged with examining the programs at various schools to see what lessons could contribute to the development of the SEI graduate curriculum.

The participants were: Dave Budgen, Bob Glass, Bill McKeeman, Walt Seward, Jim Tomayko, and Al Pietrasanta, subgroup leader.

The group was given the following questions to discuss:

1. *What are the educational prerequisites of a Master of Software Engineering degree program?*

2. *What are the experience prerequisites of a Master of Software Engineering degree program?*

3. *What are the similarities among the existing Master of Software Engineering programs? What are the differences among them?*

4. *What are the focus and content of the typical undergraduate software engineering project course? Of such a graduate-level course?*

5. *What are the strengths and weaknesses of the current Master of Software Engineering curricula?*

6. *Where do the staff of the current software engineering education programs come from?*

7. *What is the group's evaluation of the SEI's proposed curriculum?*

Al Pietrasanta: We have representation from the Wang Institute, Seattle University, the University of Stirling (Scotland), Texas Christian University, and the Air Force Institute of Technology. So, I would say that we have excellent representation from the universe of existing software engineering programs. The way that we looked at our charge was to try to investigate these existing programs and extract from them advice, counsel, direction and problems to feed into the SEI for its curriculum.

Now, in that context, yesterday I presented two of the subjects that we looked into — student prerequisites and faculty. And it appeared that they were two of the interesting ones to start with, because they both generated some comment in the meeting and after. As a result of that, we have revisited those two subjects for about an hour this morning. And I want to revisit them for you nearer the end of my presentation.

We spent some time on the question of the student project as part of the curriculum. There was absolutely no question that the project must be part of the curriculum. Project team size tends to be on the order of three to five individuals and the amount of time spent varies; but generally, I would say that it is a full year. In those cases that it was not a full year, the recommendation was that it become a full year. Wang actually conducts it in two separate parts. The Air Force would like it longer than theirs currently is, and Seattle and TCU tend to be a full year.

The Stirling program conducts its project outside the university. It, unlike the other programs, does not require industry experience for admission, so it tends to compensate for that by building in, to the extent possible, a pseudo experience level by having their students intern six months in industry.

Continuing to discuss the project component, we looked at some parameters relative to it. What is the purpose of it? There is general agreement that you want to build a working product. You've got to come out with something tangible at the end of this project activity. The problem with establishing a working product is: how big can you make it? Obviously, the larger, the better, the more complex, the better, but you are constrained in terms of time or people. Should you build that product as sort of stand-alone or can you possibly during the project have that product ultimately integrated into something larger, which is much closer to a real life experience?

You want the student to participate through a series of process steps, ideally all of the process steps (requirements, analysis, specification, design, code, test, integration, etc.) because that is the sort of live experience that you are trying to give them. Clearly the problem with that is trying to cover them all. Sometimes the project does not cover all of the process steps, but does a good job in covering some of them. There are pros and cons to that approach. So, don't think that this is revolutionary. The fact is the project is intended to be a microcosm of the real world; if you micro that microcosm too much, you lose sight of the real world; and yet, you are constrained by the number of people and the length of time available.

In addition to building a working product, in addition to going through process steps, we believe that measurements need to be taken of the work. We are talking about estimating the work to be done. We are talking about measuring against those estimates. We are talking about evaluating the data you collect against those measurements. And the parameters would be time, effort, quality measurements, etc., very valuable experience, obviously very real life experience, not only to do the work, but to measure what you are doing in order to improve what you are doing.

The interesting problem here is that it is difficult to estimate the project if everybody knows that it is going to be completed in thirteen weeks and it's going to take four people and you have already defined it that way. What is it that you are estimating? But the group believes that there are creative ways around that. There are ways to build in estimating techniques, there are ways to build in scheduling techniques, measurement techniques and quality control techniques into a project. And that is very valuable to do.

How do these different programs manage these projects? A variety of answers arose. Generally, however, a faculty member acts as the "manager." And it varies all the way from that faculty member being an active participant in the project, to the other extreme, where if a student walks into the faculty member's office and asks a question, he will answer it; but other than that, the faculty member has little involvement.

So, there seems to be a spectrum of faculty involvement under which a student may often be "a project leader." Sometimes throughout the whole project, other groups rotate the project leader assignment during the length of the project in order to convey that experience. The difficulty there, among others, is the active faculty manager. It is a tremendous time drain, in addition to whatever else the faculty member is doing.

The project ought to be tool rich. There ought to be a plethora of tools, in all of these various phases, that the project participants are able to play with and use, in fact must use, in order to complete the project. The problem is that it takes a lot of time for the students to learn the tools that they need in the project. There may be prerequisite conditions, that you've got to learn the tool, before you use the tool in the project. And there is no such thing as a standard tool kit. And so, we could not give you back, "This is the set of common tools a project ought to use," although I will share with you some lists that we have put together.

Finally, what do you want the student to get out of it? You want the student to be able to exercise judgment, technical judgment, during the course of product development, on tools, on techniques, and what you are trying to do, in this constrained period of time, is to build up that technical judgment capability.

Just one final point on the project, and that is, I asked the question, "So there is no standard tool kit so what do you use?" And under "Languages," the top three are C, Pascal, and Lisp, each with two votes. The next four are Ada, Prolog, Modula-2 and Awk, each with one vote. But I think you get a sense of the language level that is being used here, which I think looks good.

Now, to continue, consider management tools if we are going to do a project and manage the project, it would be nice to teach how you can 'configuration manage' such an activity. A couple of examples were RCS and SCCS. Other examples include specification tools, design tools, profilers, editors, performance analyzers, comparators, document preparation tools. And it supports the statement before; it makes the project tools rich. That is one of the benefits that students are getting out of it. There may not be a standard set, but choose state-of-the-art tools, acquaint them with the best of breed, if you possibly can.

Relative to the proposed SEI curriculum (see the Appendix), other than discuss the project, we did two things. One is we nitpicked the pages with all the modules, but I am not going over that because Jim Tomayko made notes on what we felt was right and wrong and overemphasized and underemphasized. But we made some general observations. Drawing from the experience of the existing programs, I was personally surprised to find out how high the percentage of the program is core material. I said I thought the core curriculum percentage was too high in the SEI program, which is stated as 33-50%. It turns out to be that existing programs have a required portion that is much higher than that. If you consider the core plus mandatory project, what percent of the total time is that? And it turned out to be something like 27 out of 36 units. There might be room for a couple of electives. In other words, virtually all of the program was predefined. That was true with Wang and TCU. The Air Force has a high percentage of required content. They have beyond the core some specialty tracks but the student must take one of a limited number of specialty tracks. And once again, the freedom of the electives is very limited.

This raises the question: if you require so much, what do you do with experienced students coming in the door who know the material? First of all, experience shows that this doesn't seem to be a big problem. Second of all, you've got some options. One is that you can give them an exam on the material. If they pass the exam, they don't have to take the course. Or perhaps even a better approach is they take the course, but you give them more advanced assignments and special assignments during the course, so that you keep them interested and you keep them at their level, which might be beyond some of the other students. So, that doesn't seem to be a problem, even with the heavy core course requirements.

The other question, sort of the reverse of the coin, is: what if the student walks in, not knowing some basic material? And there are examples of that that have come up. Some of the basic subjects were hardware architecture, software architecture, discrete math, data structures. Now, here is the either/or choice: You can throw that stuff into the master's program or you can set them as a requirement to enter the master's program. It seems to me that the sense I got out of my group, they were set as a requirement of entry, generally. And now, the student walks in and meets a lot of other qualifications, but may not have one or two of these subjects. You say "Go get them. Take a course and once you pass that course, not for credit in this program, then you qualify for this program." And that is being done.

We asked the question, "Is there a technical track and a management track?" The management courses in the SEI curriculum, do you mix those with technical ones or what do you do? There was a pretty uniform opinion from our group. You must have a set of technical management courses like project management, and you give them to all of the students. In other words, the ones who are not management today and may not ever be management, they take those project management courses. You do not make the distinction. Even though it's got the label of "management" on it, that material is so basic that all students must get it. So, leave it as part of the core and give it to everyone. Now, those who are in management or those who aspire to management may in fact take more of that material in specialty or elective courses.

I asked the question of tools in the project and I asked the question, "What about tool use in courses, not projects?" And I got a split vote here. Two of the five schools have heavy use of tools in courses. Three of the five have little use of tools in courses. Coincidentally, the two that use tools heavily are the non-university two (Wang and the Air Force). I am not sure if there is any correlation. The three who have little tool use built into the courses say there should be a lot more. So, the general recommendation is that to the extent possible, nonproject courses should have built into them the use of tools.

I asked the question on grading and I didn't get any revelations here. Everybody is grading on an A through F or 100 through 0 system, except, in some cases, the project may just be graded Pass/Fail.

Revisiting the question of faculty and students: Now, we are clearly recommending — and I want to reconfirm what I said yesterday — we are clearly recommending that the program should be oriented to people who have working experience and obviously, the program should have a faculty who has the qualifications to teach it.

Now, if you are going out and inserting this program into a university, you are probably going to head down the track of having the university develop the faculty, and the SEI may be giving some help to do that. But through on-the-job training, through the SEI courses and through the use of adjuncts coming in from industry (who can help out on some of the courses), the program can get off the ground and then gravitate to the point where it is self-sustaining and strong.

If the recommendation is not to have any experience — which we are not recommending — then we are saying that it is going to be a longer curriculum because, somehow or other, you have to build in a pseudo experience, which isn't going to be great. But somehow you've got to do that. We call that the "Stirling sandwich," thanks to Stirling University. They not only have the curriculum component, but they do intend, to the extent possible, to build in a surrogate of experience during the program. There is much more I could say about that, but I won't. So, I will stop right there. Thank you.

Report of the Subgroup on Best Curriculum

*This is the presentation made by Jon Bentley of AT&T Bell Laboratories, summarizing the discussions of the subgroup on best curriculum. This subgroup concentrated on identifying the best that can be done **now** to improve software engineering education.*

The participants were: Jim Collofello, Manny Lehman, Bill Richardson, George Rowland, Dick Thayer, Dave Wortman, and Jon Bentley, subgroup leader.

The group was given the following questions to discuss:

1. *What should be the focus and content of the typical under-granduate software engineering project course? Of such a graduate-level course?*
2. *At what in the curriculum should the project be scheduled? At what point in the software lifecycle should the project start?*
3. *Where should the staff of software engineering education programs come from?*
4. *What is the group's evaluation of SEI's proposed curriculum?*
5. *In a Master of Software Engineering curriculum, which topics should be in core courses, and which should be electives?*

Jon Bentley: We told you that we decided not to do the original questions in order, but instead look at the parameters, deciding the kind of curriculum which to have. Today we discussed the core curriculum, which included a number of issues that have already been raised. So, I am going to be able to proceed rather rapidly.

We have a number of general comments on the SEI curriculum. One thing that bothered several people is: are we concentrating too much on "how to go out"? One example is that at our school, our students go out immediately and go to work for Hughes. I believe that we do have to do a small amount of this, primarily to underlie, to illustrate, that it isn't the long-term education, but the principles.

Something else that bothered us, that bothered Manny Lehman a lot more than looking at the curricula, was the implicit dependence upon the waterfall model. You just hear water falling on almost every page of the SEI curriculum, and that traumatized him tremendously. I think that Jim Collofello especially could point out that in designing a curriculum you try to avoid getting too much into that.

Another point that we made on the curriculum is that, more than many curricula, this one must be a cohesive set of courses, where the points that you make in one course are not denied immediately in the next course. You should wait a course or two before you deny them. It is essential here, in every single example, to point out a technique and then use it in the next course. This is going to require both good course design and cohesive faculty.

One thing that I was very impressed about at Wang Institute, for instance, is that they make a point or at least make the appearance to a visitor, that they have a cohesive faculty that tries to reinforce these things and tries to illustrate these points. And that is absolutely essential here.

We discussed, to some degree, the background that we would assume. I think that we are fairly in agreement here. We assume there would be a B.S. in Computer Science, basically in the background. We talked about a few particular courses. We felt that you needed Probability and Statistics for certain things, logic, some economic background, a few particular B.S. courses that came up. We won't give those in general. We would like to see some listed in future editions of the curriculum. It would be very helpful to us in evaluating this.

I think that we were troubled, it is fair to say, at the dependence on modules, where right now, you assume that you have at least 30 or 40 modules that break nicely into 15 units or 15-hour pieces. It wasn't at all clear to us that that is the way the world is, because there are things here that are obviously a half a module or a few lectures here or a course.

We are a little bit dubious about whether you really can divide the world up quite that strongly. We are also dubious of the size of the core, as we just mentioned. First of all, we had to define the core. The core, of course, is what every right thinking software engineer must know. But we didn't have "right thinking" well defined. But once again, by "right thinking," it is clear what we mean.

There is also this issue in the core, that there is a spectrum between the required electives, and you must do at least one out of these four courses. So, it wasn't clear to us what things were required electives or somewhere in the middle. We were impressed that the current size of the core is only four courses. The implication that what every right thinking software engineer needs to know may be accomplished in thirteen modules, four university courses, or an easy semester is fairly impressive. You know, it's like, "You can go to school for a semester and be a software engineer." So, these are some of the issues that bothered us.

Before we go on from this, are there any comments from the people in the group, to elaborate on this?

From the floor: Were you in a different group from ours?

Jon Bentley: I was the one taking notes at the front. I didn't have a chance to listen. I just took notes.

We then went through the existing core (reproduced in the Appendix) and, judging by the number of detailed comments to Jim Collofello about this, on several of these we recommended fairly large changes. We suggested a number of things. I won't get into all of the details of these, but the introduction course, we felt, should be rewritten as an overview. In the interfaces course, we wanted to see more emphasis on the human/machine interface. We felt quite positive that this was an essential course to have. We would have reworked a number of courses. We felt that it was important to have a course emphasizing languages, both implementation languages, evaluation of Prolog versus other languages, as well as requirements languages. This was an essential concept. One of us particularly thought that there needs to be more emphasis on the software process. We then decided to combine a couple of the management courses in various ways.

When we came to additional material that we felt was missing from the core, the first thing we talked about was the notion of project experience. Yesterday, we mentioned that there were several other ways to get the corresponding experience: from exercises, individual and group projects, industrial experiences, previous experiences, case studies, and situations similar to teaching hospitals. We feel that in the core we don't want to legislate in too Draconian a fashion exactly what we want to do. There are possibly many paths to experience.

Additional classes we came up with, that we felt should be in the core, were formal methods in the core. Again, we felt that there were not enough formal methods in this. The title that Manny Lehman wanted to propose was "Calculus and Development." It is course 312 in the Imperial College curriculum.

I felt something very important was the notion of systems, architecture and design, a more technical course in how you build large systems. I thought that was very obviously missing, from at least the way that we read it. And it was quite essential to have this, an architecture of things.

Modern notions on systems engineering and ethical and legal issues were not prominent. Other things we weren't quite as sure about were the issues of — we wanted to say "data bases," but couldn't. We had to say "information repositories."

Mary Shaw: Why couldn't you say "data bases?"

Jon Bentley: I just take notes.

We also recommend an analysis course, where you combine these various things and there is an emphasis more on management. And since there was only one management course, we felt that there should be perhaps more management to the core. Those are our recommendations. I think that it is time to open it up now for any comments, especially from the group.

Bill McKeeman: Well, a very small thing. You have the technical communication and the human communication course there. I think our experience is that you have to have that fairly late, because until they have something they need to write about or need to present, it is hard to get them motivated to do it well. We found it better later in the curriculum, rather than early, which is where the present plan puts it.

Jon Bentley: Well, I think that one thing that we came up with here is that that is the kind of course that must be reinforced throughout the entire curriculum.   You can't have one course early on taught by a professional technical writer and then have everyone else ignore writing about things.   This is something that you have to have, writing reinforced and the speaking presentations reinforced, throughout the entire curriculum. This is especially something that no matter whether you put it first or last, it must be reinforced throughout.

Bill Wulf: Do you honestly believe that somebody who has gotten through high school and university programs and has been out in industry for a while, probably having to write some project plans and project reports, still can't write? I mean, is there any hope for this guy? (Laughter)

Jon Bentley: You and I eventually got PhD's, so there is some hope.

Dick Fairley: I wanted to ask a different question, and it's about the assumed background. We hit pretty hard on the necessary background, not only in Computer Science but in significant work in an application area. We were a little bit nebulous on exactly what application. Clearly, you need more than a Computer Science background to be a software engineer, in the view of our group.

Jon Bentley: Comments?

Dick Thayer: We agree. At that point in time, we didn't know what else to do. We weren't sure how to go beyond that particular point, at least not in the few hours available to us.

Jim Tomayko: I've got a two part question. Should we use the modules at all or would we be better off packaging the curriculum in already existing forms such as courses, or, if the modules are a good idea, are people comfortable with having them different sizes, different lengths?

Mary Shaw: The university semester course is not a sacred size, any more than anything else is a sacred size. The content of a module ought to dictate the size of the units, and within some fairly liberal tolerance the units ought to be sized to fit the content.

Dick Fairley: I think the objective of having modules is so that you can deliver it to people in industry. And what I have heard from people in industry is that 20 hours is about the most you can spare people. That is five half-days in a one or a two week period. So, if the objective is to deliver to industry, then I think that you are constrained by their viewpoint.

Jon Bentley: Well, this raises the important viewpoint that Fred Brooks made yesterday, having a curriculum design in context. But my personal opinion on this is that by trying to do one intergalactic curriculum that will be applicable on any planet that we might land on in the foreseeable future, we may do something that is optimal for that circumstance and viable at no place in particular. And I am quite worried at this point about these mere packaging issues, of modules versus not, that are driving a lot of things. As we went through here and designed our courses, it was clear that this is really two modules and this is really four modules. And it was a weird chunk to be defined. I think if you design it into the curriculum, you have to worry a lot about that.

Peter Freeman: I would agree basically with Mary Shaw's comments. I would observe also that, as in building systems, it sometimes is very useful to decompose the problem. And I think in terms of curriculum development that there is a good effect of driving the module level down, so that then the curriculum designer can focus on one small, well-defined set of material at a time. I think that that will strengthen the module. However, as in building systems, the overall architecture must be carefully fashioned and you must make sure that those modules can then be reintegrated to form a well-functioning, overall system.

Jim Tomayko: So, just to summarize, modules are okay and if they have to be different sizes, that's okay, too.

Jon Bentley: I think it depends upon a lot of the context in which the modules are to be taught.

Mary Shaw: I think that maybe the hour is the wrong measure. The point that you made about the dangers of trying to do simple packaging for very diverse audiences is a good one, but is one that textbook authors have confronted for years and years and years. And the solution that we have been using to cope with the situation is that the textbook author writes down a rendition of the material and the instructor interprets that material for the audience at hand. If we don't allow ourselves to be driven by the university size of the module and don't allow ourselves to be driven by any other arbitrary size of the module, but organize the material to suit its own content, then the number of hours dedicated to the teaching of that material can be allowed to be context dependent, unless we put some kind of artificial loading about how you describe something in the system. It may very well be the case that some body of material that is motivated very highly by five years of experience in the trenches can be taught in one long day in industry but would take a semester in a university. So, I think we need to be a little cautious about identifying any particular body of material by some simple number of hours that is independent of the audience that is consuming it.

Peter Freeman: Let me observe that there is a long tradition of separating curriculum, the content and the interdependencies, from its implementation or the actual program. My remembrance is that there was a good curriculum for information systems that was published in the Communications of the ACM in May 1972. The authors very carefully made the distinction between, "Here's our curriculum," and, "Now, here are some suggestions as to how this curriculum might be implemented in different contexts." And I would suggest that may be a good pattern for SEI to follow as well.

Nico Habermann: In reference to formalism, I was wondering whether you meant that, in terms of quantity, there weren't enough different formal methods explored in the curriculum or included in the curriculum, versus what we sensed was a tendency to emphasize more the formal approach, than say the systematic, or conventional approach. We thought, actually, it was good to go that way. But we wanted to make the observation that emphasizing one particular attitude or approach may lead to neglecting something else.

Jon Bentley: And furthermore I think academic institutions are quite prone to be like the old drunk who looked for his wallet under the street light, because that is where the light was, even though he lost it somewhere else. Mathematicians are prone to teach academic material. And then I think that you are right in pointing out the specific reason for that. I think that the primary advocate of this course is in fact Manny Lehman, who has left already. Would anyone else in the group care to stand up and defend it?

Bill Richardson: I think that the point that Manny was trying to make, and I will not pass judgment on it one way or the other, is that there needed to be a core introduction, an overview, if you will, of the formal methods, as opposed to immediately leaping into a particular formal method after a particular point.

Jon Bentley: As Manny talked about it, I thought of a course that Susan Gerhart taught at Wang. I don't know if you would care to comment upon that experience. Is it worthwhile to have formal methods gathered together in one course, or should they be scattered throughout the curriculum?

Susan Gerhart: Definitely scattering helps, having some kind of reinforcement, taking a topic from one context and looking at it another. I think that is very helpful.

Bill McKeeman: Christopher Strachey said, "No formalization without insight." Insight often doesn't come until you have something to apply it to. So lumping them together early is quite difficult.

Jon Bentley: I think it is important to illustrate and to have a balance between showing a formal method and the state-of-the-art in the industry. The thing that we addressed in our group was that people coming in after five years out in the real world have forgotten what the logical order is. It might help to have these things addressed cohesively, in one unit, to remind them.

Bill McKeeman: In our group we would call that "precore."

Jon Bentley: That might be an important place for precore.

Mary Shaw: I think this discussion is not quite putting its finger on the reason for including the formal materials in the curriculum. It seems to me that the dominant test for including material in a curriculum like this is that things you are teaching will transcend two or three orders of magnitude in technology improvement along whatever dimension today. The ideas that are most likely to endure under those changes tend to be the ones that are well-systematized; those are often formalized. So the motivation for including formal techniques in a curriculum is that those techniques have been codified in such a way that they are likely to be very durable and therefore of high value to the student.

Now, given that motivation, it doesn't bother me if there is a bias in the ultimate curriculum that favors formal methods, because I think they have higher value per unit time invested, considering that they have long-term payoff. But looking at it that way, it seems to me that they clearly need to be distributed throughout the curriculum to the points at which you discuss the problems to which they apply. If you isolate them in particular courses, that very structure denies their relevance to the problems to which they are very explicitly designed to apply.

Susan Gerhart: Let me give you an example of an informal method that I think contrasts with the formal method. You take a requirements or needs analysis kind of exercise, for example, a problem to determine what is the best possible approach to take to meet that need. That includes activities of interviewing users, collecting data in the organization, doing a lot of things that can be done systematically, of that nature, but which are not formal methods and certainly not the sort of thing that computer scientists feel comfortable with. That is an example of a kind of bias that is brought about by too much emphasis on formal methods, ignoring these things which are more than just communication skills.

Bill Richardson: I think our group discussed that point when we added analysis as one of the items, that it was a requirement, classical analysis, interviews and that sort of a thing.

Nico Habermann: I have two questions to Al Pietrasanta, because he hasn't had a chance yet. You listed tools among the things that are needed for the courses. What is right now available and how should we go about making things more easily available to this type of curriculum? Can we do that through contact with industry, for instance, or should it be that we create them in our own environments?

Al Pietrasanta: I got the sense from my group that it was going to be rather specialized and that a particular entity will create its own environment, create its set of tools. We have no agreement nor did we explore the point, much beyond saying it was not possible. That is, there is no "standard tool kit" and, therefore, there is no single set of recommendations which we would pass on and then encourage everybody to get that set.

There are several candidate tools under any category that you might mention. Our recommendation is to bring as many tools in as possible and get as many running as possible and expose the students to as many as possible. If there are half a dozen specification techniques, we recommended that there be a course in the comparative evaluation of specification techniques and the students ought to play with one at least. What's the one? Pick your own. Pick the one you're happy with. Pick the one you've used.

Dick Fairley: We have two full-time master's level employees at Wang Institute whose job is to support the faculty in providing tools for courses. And they are more than full-time jobs for those two people. Two people can't do an adequate job in finding tools, bringing them in, writing materials and getting them running. So you definitely need that kind of support.

The second point I'd like to make relates to SEI and it is that I think there is a great opportunity for SEI to either do directly or cause the development of "educational strength tools," simple tools that illustrate principles, but don't require a month or three weeks' learning time to figure out how to use them. Maybe they are PC-based; I'm not sure, but simple tools that illustrate principles without being of industrial strength.

Nico Habermann: My concern was actually to get access to real, live situations, because if you do it in this way, you will never have access to — let's say a large data base — and be able to extract any information from that or get in touch with a large software development project at IBM Federal Systems Division or places like that. In this way, I think you will always remain in the realm of the toys.

Al Pietrasanta: Well, toy is better than nontoy. I think subsetting but still forcing the student to get some hands on experience is good. And there was a discussion of PSLPSA that I happened to hear but didn't participate in. It is a pretty complicated tool. We have subsetted it. We have a very small, 30-word syntax of PSLPSA. You can get somebody to learn and use it rather quickly. You can apply it to some reasonable size problems, with educational benefit. You don't have to spend a year doing a requirements analysis or a specification with PSL to get the benefits out of it. I think you can do that for every tool. If some of these were packaged for tutorial benefit then that would be the best of all.

Mary Shaw: Most of the project descriptions that I have seen over the years have been for the development of projects in isolation. Has anyone thought about the feasibility of bringing up not just a tool but the data base associated with some real or simulated project, so that you start the project by saying, "Well, the scenario is that it is now month 37 and here is the situation, and you need to take the next step," so that there is all of this real data to work within?

Al Pietrasanta: At IBM, we have a library management tool. It is probably the biggest thing in the world. It is impossible for any one person to know. It stores all the modules and carries them through and tracks them and it stores a lot of planning and control and management data. And I have explored some of the work that the Japanese companies are doing. They have outstanding, integrated library management tools, spanning the whole development process, incredibly useful tools. It would be great if we could subset something like that, down to a tutorial level.

Mary Shaw: But including the data and not just the tools.

Al Pietrasanta: Yes. The technical flow of the modules, the flow of the data and the flow of management information, which is all integrated in some of these.

Bill McKeeman: There are at least two experiences that we had in existing curricula which address that. In the C Kit projects I run, the students move into a project that is partially completed and do a piece of it which must interface to the existing pieces. While they go through an entire development cycle there is an existing world within which they have to live.

Susan Gerhart: Another example is Walt Scacchi at the University of Southern California and his "system factory." He runs a project course with 35 students, they work on a 9-month basis, and they have thousands and thousands of lines of code that they are developing through these 9-month kinds of iterations.

Al Pietrasanta: Well, I think one of the senses I get out of this, in addition to SEI packaging some model curricula and curricula content, if SEI could package some tutorial aids and tool-use packages, that would be of immense benefit.

Nico Habermann: Al, you have a lot of experience in evaluating a curriculum. Has your group discussed that issue? I think that we should consider not only these items of curricula, but how it is going to be evaluated, whether it is effective or not.

Al Pietrasanta: We had our chart that said, "Goals of the curriculum and how to assess those goals," and we didn't get to it, I'm sorry to say. Does anyone in my group care to comment? Bill, how do you evaluate the Wang curriculum?

Bill McKeeman: One small point is we keep close track of our graduates to see how well they are doing with what they were given.

Al Pietrasanta: Just one, final comment. I believe this is in the area of advanced education rather than training. I think that advanced education is to prepare a person for career growth. And I find it very difficult to measure an education program that is going to prepare a person for future growth. You can track the students, but I believe it would be wrong to try and set measurements on the program or assess the program simply on the basis of immediate skills that the student walks out with. You may be orienting the program in the wrong direction by trying to put measurements that measure the wrong thing. That is a negative comment of the measurements.

Bill McKeeman: Your first of the day, I might say.

Report of the Future Software Engineering Curriculum Working Group

This is the presentation made by Dick Fairley, Wang Institute, summarizing the discussions of the working group on future software engineering curriculum. This working group was charged with the task of looking 10 years into the future of software engineering to examine the educational needs for the practitioners in the 1990's.

The participants were: Bruce Barnes, Vic Basili, Fred Brooks, James Comer, Peter Freeman, Norm Gibbs, Ev Mills, Bill Wulf and Dick Fairley, Group Leader.

The group was given the following questions to discuss:

1. *Will software engineering be a recognized engineering discipline?*
2. *Will software engineering education programs be tailored to suit local industry?*
3. *Will the profession develop specializations? If so, what might those specializations be?*
4. *Will software engineering be distinguishable from computer systems engineering?*
5. *Will advances in tools, workstations, and other technologies make software engineering fundamentally different 10 years from now?*
6. *What constitutes change in software engineering practice?*
7. *Can we expect a greater rate of change in the software engineering profession over the next 10 years than occurred over the past 10?*
8. *What specialty areas are emerging, and what levels of specialization are developing?*
9. *What is the group's evaluation of SEI's proposed curriculum?*

Dick Fairley: If you recall, yesterday the Future of Software Engineering Working Group started from Mary Shaw's slide [Slide 1] showing software demand exceeding capacity and discussed what has to happen to mitigate current trends. We observed that many of the words we are using at this meeting are the same words we used 10 years ago, but believe we have a more sophisticated and deeper understanding of the issues [Slide 2]. This may not be true, but it is the premise we will operate on. We tried to keep that as a guiding principle this morning.

SLIDE 1. SOFTWARE DEMAND EXCEEDS CAPACITY

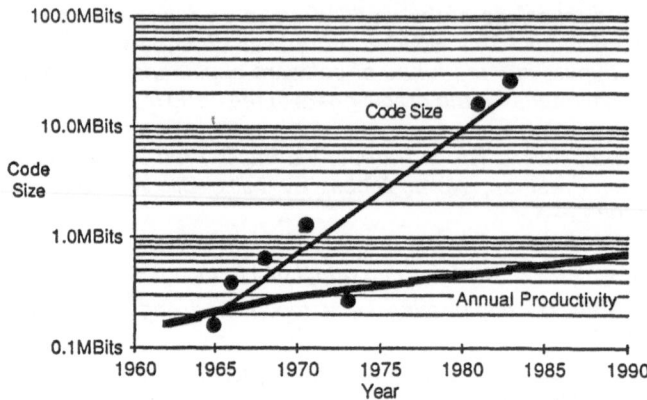

**ONBOARD CODE SIZE FOR MANNED SPACECRAFT
AND ANNUAL PROGRAMMER PRODUCTIVITY**

*DEMAND FOR QUALITY SOFTWARE RISES FASTER
THAN OUR ABILITY TO PRODUCE*

SLIDE 2. WHAT HAS TO HAPPEN TO MITIGATE
CURRENT TRENDS?

- REUSABILITY ON A GRAND SCALE
- SOME DEGREE OF AUTOMATION
  - INDIVIDUALS
  - TEAMS
- PACKAGING OF SOFTWARE
- CAPTURE EXPERTISE
  - MORE REPRESENTATIONS
  - AI
- SHIFT FROM LABOR INTENSIVE TO CAPITAL INTENSIVE THINKING
- ORDERS OF MAGNITUDE INCREASE IN COMPUTING POWER PER DOLLAR
- NARROW GAP BETWEEN THE BEST AND MEDIOCRE IN BOTH COMPANIES AND GROUPS
- DECREASE TECHNOLOGY ADOPTION TIME LAG
- PAY MORE ATTENTION TO
  - PROBLEM DOMAINS
  - APPLICATIONS AREAS
- MORE AND BETTER PARADIGMS AND SUPPORTING TOOLS
- CHANGES IN CONTRACTING PRACTICES AND DEVELOP- MENT PARADIGMS

- BETTER SUPPORT FOR COMMUNICATIONS AND COORDINA-
TION OF WORK ACTIVITIES
- BETTER MEASUREMENT

THE WORDS ARE THE SAME AS 10 YEARS AGO,
BUT THE SEMANTICS ARE DIFFERENT!

Our group talked yesterday about reusability as a key issue [Slides 3 and 4] and what kinds of implications there are for what people need to know to work within that environment. If capturing expertise becomes an important issue, then what do people need to know in that area? We have more work to do there and just didn't have enough time. It indicates a direction that the SEI might want to do some more thinking about. What is the effect of greatly increased computing power [Slide 5] and its curriculum implications? We didn't say.

SLIDE 3. WHO WILL TEACH THE CURRICULUM?

- NOT TRADITIONAL COMPUTER SCIENCE RESEARCH
DEPARTMENTS
- SPECIAL TRACKS IN THE MASTER'S OF COMPUTER SCIENCE
PROGRAMS
- INDUSTRY SUPPORTED UNIVERSITY INSTITUTES
- IN-PLANT DELIVERY
- NATIONAL TECHNICAL UNIVERSITY OR TV DELIVERY
- TAILORING TO LOCAL NEED BY NON-RESEARCH UNITS
- COMPUTER SCIENCE AND SOFTWARE ENGINEERING WILL
SPLIT
  - NOT WITHIN 10 YEARS
  - THE SPLIT WILL NOT BENEFIT COMPUTER SCIENCE OR
  SOFTWARE ENGINEERING

SLIDE 4. ASSUME CURRENT TRENDS HAVE MITIGATED

- REUSABILITY
  - TO SUPPORT, NEED MORE POWERFUL MODELS OF ABSTRACTION AND INSTANTIATION (NOT HANDBOOK)
  - BUILD NEW PRODUCTS BY MODIFYING EXISTING ONES
  - ROLE OF MODULE GENERATORS
    - BASED ON SPECIFICATIONS (?)
- CURRICULUM
  - ABSTRACTIONS
  - OBJECT-ORIENTED APPROACHES
  - SPECIFICATION-BASED PROGRAM GENERATORS
- CAPTURE EXPERTISE
  - KNOWLEDGE ENGINEERING
  - BROADLY CONSTRUED SYSTEMATIC APPROACHES TO DOMAIN ANALYSIS

SLIDE 5. EFFECT OF GREATLY INCREASED COMPUTING POWER

- WE SEE NO QUALITATIVE CHANGES IN HARDWARE SUCH AS HAPPENED AT XEROX PARC IN THE 1970'S
- DISAGREEMENT ON EFFECT OF LARGE SCALE, RAPID RESPONSE PROJECT DATABASES
- WILL WIDEBAND COMMUNICATION BE AVAILABLE HOME TO OFFICE IN 10 YEARS?
- NATURE OF SYSTEMS ASKED TO BUILD WILL CHANGE
- 10-FOLD INCREASE IN SCREEN SIZE WILL CHANGE THE NATURE OF TOOLS

The Future Software Engineering Curriculum Working Group started this morning with a rambling discussion before we found a theme to pursue. A quote from Bill Wulf kept us on track this morning: "Ten years is not very long." It is not after all, and maybe some things that we can see in 50 years probably won't happen in 10 years. We tried to keep that as a guiding principle this morning.

SLIDE 6. FUTURE UNDERGRADUATE EDUCATION

- UNDERGRADUATE (COULD BE EITHER WAY)
  - COMPUTER SCIENCE MAJOR
  - STRONG MINOR (8 COURSES) IN AN APPLICATION AREA
  - SENIOR YEAR SEQUENCE IN SOFTWARE ENGINEERING
- APPLICATIONS AREAS
  - CONTINUOUS SYSTEMS (BASED ON DIFFERENTIAL EQUATIONS)
  - FINANCIAL/BANKING
  - MEDICINE/BIONICS
  - SENSOR/AFFECTOR
  - SYSTEMS/SOFTWARE
  - TELECOMMUNICATIONS
  - CAD/CAM/CIM
  - DISCRETE MODELING

We talked a lot about what the division between undergraduate, Master's and PhD level work might look like in software engineering in 10 years. At the undergraduate level [Slide 6], we believe that there should be a computer science major with a strong minor in an application area, or it could be the other way around. It might be a major in an applications area with a strong minor in computer science or a dual major with some material in the senior year, specifically in software engineering. We thought that an internship is desirable, but probably impractical. We believe that as the field evolves, apprenticeship will be an important part of future software engineering curricula.

SLIDE 7. FUTURE MASTER'S SOFTWARE ENGINEERING EDUCATION

- MEDICAL DOCTOR MODEL
  - SYSTEMS BUILDERS
  - COMPLEXITY SPECIALISTS
  - COORDINATORS OF INTERDISCIPLINARY TEAMS
  - "APPLICATIONS" BACKGROUND — PERHAPS A SOFTWARE BACKGROUND
  - SYSTEMS ENGINEER OF THE FUTURE
- ENTRANCE REQUIREMENTS
  - COMPUTER SCIENCE BACKGROUND
  - APPLICATIONS AREA BACKGROUND
- INTERNSHIP/APPRENTICESHIP COMPONENT
- PRIOR EXPERIENCE
  - MAJORITY OF GROUP FELT NECESSARY
  - MINORITY OF GROUP FELT DETRIMENTAL

The question of prior work experience for entry to master's programs was debated [Slide 7]. The majority of us felt that some kind of experience is needed for a couple of reasons. First, to raise something more general, educators talk about mathematical maturity. There is also something called "software maturity." Another point is that having experienced people in class raises the level of discussion, the level of understanding, the speed with which you can cover material and the depth to which you can go. The minority position was that the argument against previous experience is analogous to the argument about why high school students should not learn Basic. There are so many bad habits to undo that it takes a lot of time and effort to instill good habits.

SLIDE 8. STRONG POSITIONS OF FUTURE WORKING GROUP

- SOFTWARE ENGINEER IS THE CRITICAL SYSTEM ENGINEER OF THE FUTURE!!
- SOFTWARE ENGINEERING IS NOT AND WILL NOT BE A SUB-DISCIPLINE OF COMPUTER SCIENCE!!
- SOFTWARE ENGINEERING WILL NOT MIGRATE TO THE UN-DERGRADUATE LEVEL!!
  - "WE DON'T TEACH SURGERY TO UNDERGRADUATES."

We thought that this slide [Slide 8] needed bold emphasis. The software engineer is the critical systems engineer of the future. Software engineering is not and will not be a subdiscipline of computer science, but a separate discipline. I hear some of you hissing.

We discussed, "Will software engineering migrate to the undergraduate level?" and concluded that it will not. You don't teach surgery to undergraduates even though they do dissect frogs to get some idea of what it might be like. They certainly don't perform open heart surgery! We don't see a lot of migration. Obviously there is a reinforcing and a cross-feeding. Many people now pay more attention to style, structure and modularity in the introductory programming courses than they did 10 or 15 years ago. So certainly there is some reinforcement in both directions. We don't see that software engineering, as we envision it, will have a large following at the undergraduate level.

SLIDE 9. TOPICS IN A FUTURE MSE CURRICULUM

- LOGICAL AND MATHEMATICAL FOUNDATIONS
  - FORMAL REASONING
  - ANALYSIS AND SYNTHESIS
  - ALTERNATIVE PARADIGMS
  - ABSTRACTION/VERIFICATION
  - SYSTEM PARAMETERS/PHYSICAL REALITIES
- CARBON BASED FOUNDATIONS (PETER FREEMAN)
  - ECONOMIC FACTS/MODELS/IMPACTS
  - PLANNING/TRACKING/COORDINATION
  - LEGAL/SOCIAL/POLITICAL ISSUES
- PRINCIPLES VS. TECHNIQUES
  - LONGEVITY OF INFORMATION CONTENT

We talked about what the topics might be in a future MSE curriculum [Slide 9], and we came up with three areas: logical and mathematical foundations, formal reasoning, analysis and synthesis (with "and" emphasized). Clearly more work needs to be done here, but we hope it points the way. Let's allow people to build things, design them and make mistakes. Alternative paradigms are important. It is not clear what role logic programming or AI workstations will play or how they will impact software engineers. But software engineers should have those models in mind and know more than just how to do something in Pascal or Ada.

The central role is the dual role of abstraction and verification. We grappled a while with how to characterize the things that people need to know about the architecture of systems, how machines operate and what the physical realities are of transfer rates to external storage devices, transmission rates over telecommunication lines, CPU speeds and things of that nature. Clearly, this is an area of knowledge that the software engineer needs to have.

The second area Peter Freeman termed for us "carbon-based foundations," in contrast to calling this "intellectual foundations" which we thought sounded a little snobbish. These are basically soft areas. People need to know economic facts, models and the economic impacts of the systems they are building. They need to know about planning, tracking and coordination. Increasingly, if we see the software engineer as the systems engineer, then they have to know about the legal, social and political issues involved with their systems.

We, like the other working groups, talked quite a bit about principles versus techniques and tried to address them in a couple of ways. One approach is to ask, "What is the longevity of the information content of the material being presented?" If you are talking about a particular design technique which seems to be a passing fad, it may not be worth spending a lot of time on. On the other hand, if there are fundamental principles embodied that will persist over time, then it's useful to use that technique to illustrate the principles. Another way in which we addressed this issue was to think about the idea of apprenticeship and the teaching hospital, where people can actually get involved in projects as part of the program.

SLIDE 10. ADDITIONAL CURRICULAR ISSUES

- SYSTEM BUILDING ISSUES
  - DESIGN (AT SOME LEVEL)
  - MANAGEMENT OF COMPONENTS
  - SCHEDULING OF BUILDS
  - MEASUREMENT OF QUALITY AND PROGRESS
  - MODIFIABILITY
- 2 YEAR PROGRAMS
- PROFESSIONAL CERTIFICATION
  - COMING IN 5 YEARS (?)
  - TIED TO TESTING EXPERIENCE AS WELL AS MSE CONTENT
- PHD IN SOFTWARE ENGINEERING
  - COMPUTER SCIENCE DEPARTMENTS FAIL TO ACCEPT SOFTWARE ENGINEERING DISSERTATIONS
  - FAILURE RETARDS PROGRESS IN SOFTWARE ENGINEERING
  - WILL FORCE A SPLIT BETWEEN COMPUTER SCIENCE AND SOFTWARE ENGINEERING

We identified a set of issues called "system building issues" [Slide 10]. The list is incomplete and needs more work. We said that design at some level will continue to be an important component of what software engineers do. What we have in mind is that in 10 years we may be writing executable specifications, and traditional design, as we know it, may disappear. The level of abstraction and the mechanism of expression may be different, but it is nevertheless design of artifacts. The management of components means, "How do you deal with systems with a thousand or ten thousand components? How do you put that together? How do you schedule builds releases? How do you measure quality and progress?" We are concerned with constant evolution and modifiability of systems. Obviously, this is an incomplete list.

We think that the MSE is a two year program. We didn't try to talk about packaging of modules or which module comes first or later, but rather concentrated more on the issues, as I have indicated.

We believe that professional certification is coming, like it or not. People speculated a two-year time frame, which is being driven by concerns for legal liability as much as anything else. Certification might be tied to some period of experience in the form of an examination after leaving the MSE program. C.P.A.'s, doctors and lawyers have professional certification which involves their initial training, some experience and then a competency examination which follows the experience. This is where we talked about the internship and said, "Wouldn't it be nice if these people went out under someone's guidance and worked for a year or two?" This appears unrealistic even for 10 years from now.

Our last observation was about PhD programs. The failure of computer science departments to accept software engineering topics for dissertations is currently retarding progress in software engineering and will, as much as anything, force the split between computer science and software engineering. Yesterday we presented a conclusion that there will be a split between computer science and software engineering in 10 or maybe 15 years. We don't know the exact time frame for that, but we were much influenced by Fred Brooks' analogy of what happened to chemistry and chemical engineering 60 years ago. We feel that computing is in much the same position, 60 years later, as what happened when the split between chemistry and chemical engineering occurred.

That is the end of the slides. We are open for comments and discussion.

Nico Habermann: I'm not so concerned about whether computer science and software engineering have split or not. Time will show. What does concern me is the statement that computer science departments fail to accept software engineering dissertations. Is there real evidence of that? I would say that CMU does a fairly honest job in trying to do justice to software engineering. If you look at the record of our PhD students, you can notice that we have had several good systems theses that may not have focused directly on software enginering topics, but have a large software engineering component to them.

Dick Fairley: Wang Institute has proposed a PhD program and one of the topics we have talked about is the dissertation areas for software engineers. We think that theoretical advances in the field are always welcomed. The building of an Emacs or a Scribe is also a legitimate software engineering dissertation activity. Conducting experimental studies, perhaps involving human subjects, or the compilation of significant case studies might be acceptable. There is a chicken and egg problem here. A lot of these kinds of ideas don't get proposed in computer science departments because of the nature of the faculty and the environment. It never occurs to people that these are legitimate kinds of things to do in the software field.

Bill Wulf: There are a couple of comments here. The first one is that in some sense, schools like Carnegie Mellon, Stanford and MIT probably can accept this kind of dissertation with somewhat more impunity than other schools that are in the process of trying to establish their reputations. You are right. We don't have a history of doing this sort of thing and we have a more traditional view of what constitutes a PhD thesis.

The second comment is that even at those three schools, I see an increasing trend not to accept a significant piece of systems work as a thesis. I think it is an unfortunate phenomenon but a phenomenon that is true. I can point to specific examples, but I don't think that it would help.

Nico Habermann: I do not agree with the second comment. I believe that we should fight this. We should not let it go. It is absolutely wrong. If I get requests from other places to support them for that type of thesis, I will do the best that I can to convince the dean or the university administration of the validity of this type of work. Universities in general and the people here who are representing these universities should do the same thing. There is no reason to let go so easily.

Peter Freeman: One of the strongest things, Nico, that the three to six top schools can do to help those of us in schools whose reputations are not quite as illustrious but are trying to improve them is to support us by writing a letter. It is even better when you continue to accept those kinds of theses so we don't need to have letters. All we need to convince our faculty is to say, "Hey, look, CMU is accepting theses like this," or, "Stanford is accepting theses like this." I don't know of the cases that Bill is thinking of, but if those schools are moving away from this, then it poses a real problem for us.

Bill McKeeman: The business of building an artifact — for example, the Golden Gate Bridge — is no thesis unless you find an advance of knowledge in it. That is the definition of a thesis. If the Carnegie Mellon students were pressed to take their wonderful artifact and find some advance of technology and call that their thesis, as opposed to the artifact itself, I would consider that a waste of their time. I would like us not to have to do that here.

The other thing that you people in the top universities can do to help is to hire people who write theses like that. I don't see that happening.

Nico Habermann: I would say point them out to us, because it is extremely difficult to find systems people to come to universities. We have a very hard time finding qualified systems people.

Susan Gerhart: Maybe an even better test would be when these dissertations, wherever they are produced, actually use some software engineering methods like technical reviews or Jackson Design or whatever, and you can report on the experiences as well as the artifact and the technology.

Dick Thayer: You've kind of answered the question already, Dick Fairley, in that if there are faculty in the school that are software engineers, they will take software engineering dissertations. If you don't have this kind of faculty, you are not going to get a software engineering dissertation. That is true of any field. It is a self-solving problem if you solve the faculty problem.

Dick Fairley: To some extent. If you are the single software engineer in a theoretical department, you are not going to get very far.

Dick Thayer: Then you move.

Gordon Bradley: Traditionally, one accreditation issue is the differentiation between the PhD and the Doctor of Engineering. The U.S. Naval Postgraduate School in Monterey has been examining one of its departments that offers PhDs and wants to simultaneously offer a Doctor of Engineering. The Doctor of Engineering course work is exactly the same. The Doctor of Engineering does not have to be an advance of knowledge but can represent a contribution to the state of the practice. If you want to offer such a degree you ought to call it a Doctor of Engineering.

There is quite an issue of whether we are prepared methodologically or ethically to do experiments on human subjects. The methodology of our field has not included the study of human beings. The ethical issues associated with experimentation with human beings are significant. You need to worry about that one a little more.

Dick Fairley: I think there are people in our field who are qualified and know how to deal with the ethical and methodological issues of human experiments. They would do more of this kind of thesis if it were more readily accepted.

Gordon Bradley: The reviews by psychologists of that literature have been critical of the methodologies.

Dick Fairley: That indicates we need to improve our methodology.

We have been through quite a discussion at Wang Institute about the Doctor of Engineering versus the PhD and how the student and society are better served. Should we have two programs? Should there be a single program? After a lot of discussion, we decided that the PhD is the appropriate degree. First, because we believe it is a legitimate use of the degree as it is used across many fields. Second, the student is better served. Industry and universities do not regard the Doctor of Engineering very well. It is not very well-received by either camp. It is regarded as sort of halfway to the PhD, but for some reason the student didn't get there. I don't think that the student is well-served and I am not sure that society is well served by the Doctor of Engineering degree. We decided that it will be a PhD program, and the shape of that degree is still taking form.

Gordon Bradley: Why won't you accept the definition of a PhD? When someone says you have a PhD, it means that you have made an advance of knowledge in the field. It would seem to me that you want the best of both. You want the title of PhD, but you don't want to accept the standard definition of a theoretical advance of knowledge in the field.

Dick Fairley: No. It is an advance of knowledge, but not necessarily a theoretical advance. Advance of knowledge is at the core of all of this.

Gordon Bradley: Multics generated three PhD theses at MIT. There is no problem if there is something unique about the exemplary artifacts.

Dick Fairley: I take exception to that. I think there is a problem in getting artifacts accepted that incorporate advances of knowledge in many computer science departments.

Gordon Bradley: I'm with Nico. I don't see the problem.

Nico Habermann: We should not give up and say, "Fine. Let it be."

Dick Fairley: Well, as one who fought that battle for 15 years I was ready to give up and go somewhere else.

Gordon Bradley: Well, the other question that I have is about basing a PhD program on top of a terminal Master's program. That seems to me to be a problem. If you run a terminal Master's program first and the student goes into a PhD, that almost is by definition a Doctor of Engineering.

Dick Fairley: There are some problems to be worked out there. The PhD requires course work beyond what we envision as the core of our Master's program. Additional course work beyond the Master's is required to get into the PhD Clearly, there are some interfacing problems.

Gordon Bradley: I taught at Yale. There a student could not continue on from the terminal Master's into the PhD program.

Mary Shaw: I support wholeheartedly the acceptance of engineering theses in which the primary work of the thesis is a piece of engineering. I thought I heard Bill McKeeman say that simply producing that work should be accepted as the thesis. I take exception to that. I don't believe that at the doctoral level, simple virtuoso performance is adequate for the granting of the degree. I believe that the degree needs to transmit knowledge in some way by exposing an interesting system structure or by exposing the insight that led to that system's structure. Somehow the combination of the artifact and the supporting materials must convey to the observer the advance of knowledge that lies in the system. I would not accept the virtuoso performance.

Bill McKeeman: Let me speak to that. The issue is what the evaluation resides on. If the exemplar artifact (and its utility) shows great scientific creativity and stands by itself, I do think that's enough. I don't think a student should be forced then to dig in and try to dig out something which will advance knowledge. I run into trouble with this because that is not the way a PhD is usually defined. I think an exemplary artifact, well done, showing creativity, is in fact acceptable.

Mary Shaw: I believe that it needs to be coupled with a display of the artifact that allows the observer to get the knowledge out of it.

Bill McKeeman: Absolutely. The presentation is critical.

Gordon Bradley: The methodology of the field does not have a part that includes aesthetics like an architectural program or a music program. We do not have as part of our methodology the aesthetics that will allow judgment to be made about whether something is good or bad.

Dick Fairley: Only those in a given field are qualified to judge what constitutes an advancement of knowledge in that field.

Gordon Bradley: I think that that is absolutely right.

Dick Fairley: The software engineering community can add the component of aesthetics to our evaluation.

Vic Basili: I just wanted to argue that I don't see any problem with those dissertation topics for a PhD in computer science. They have to be coupled. You don't go look at the exemplary artifact afterwards and say, "Is there something I can take out?" If you do it in the first place with some goal in mind, then you prove what you were trying to prove and you've shown it. If you make the thesis show these things, then this becomes a different process. It's like trying to accomplish something by using ideal engineering techniques and measures to evaluate and show that you have succeeded in doing what you did. It is then a dissertation topic.

Bill Wulf: Students are never going to believe that these are acceptable thesis topics unless they see that promotion and tenure decisions are made on exactly the same basis.

Gary Ford: You said two things that had implications for undergraduate education which I think are important to the SEI Project. Number one: You said something about the medical model and there being lots of people who support the software engineer, who aren't software engineers, but maybe software technologists. Is that a legitimate concern? Is there a place for it in undergraduate education?

Dick Fairley: We didn't address that issue. My personal reaction is that I am a little concerned about educating undergraduates as technologists.

Gary Ford: If they are not software engineers, what are they and what educational background do they have?

The second issue is that the set of futures you put up there seems to be larger than the current set of things we are talking about in the curriculum. Does that imply that this material replaces what is in the current curriculum or is some of it that is now Master's level software engineering going to be pushed down into an undergraduate program in 10 years?

Dick Fairley: Well, it may be pushed down or it may be that the technology will advance to the point that some of the issues we spend a lot of time worrying about now will no longer be as important. We will have other issues to worry about, but perhaps they will be at a higher level of abstraction and with more powerful tools. I am not sure that things are going to get pushed down to any great extent.

Joe Newcomer: I have a question related to Gary's first comment. There are a number of professions in which the number of professionals available to fill the need simply aren't there. Instead, you have a set of paraprofessionals. The legal, medical and librarian areas are ones that pop to mind instantly. They tend to have two year programs taught at junior colleges. It seems to me that we might be headed in that direction. I can't comment on whether that's a good or bad direction. I am simply observing that that trend is going to be there, as soon as we start having enough of a body of knowledge to be teaching paraprofessional software engineers.

Dick Fairley: I'm not prepared to say whether that is good or bad. But it would seem to be an obvious trend that as the field becomes better defined and specializations emerge, we will understand how to coordinate and work those specialties together.

Gordon Bradley: How do you deal with the issue that most people who are working with computers without a background in computer science have begun to declare themselves software engineers? If you pick up the newspaper there are lots of people hiring software engineers all over the country. We only graduate 100 and they are hiring 1,000 a year. There are 900 other people who have declared themselves software engineers. The term is going to be quickly debased.

Dick Fairley: A certification program might have a good effect.

From the Floor: But it may be too late. The horse may be out of the barn. It's almost too late for computer science.

Ed Smith: Well, you had barbers calling themselves dentists 40 or 50 years ago.

Dick Thayer: I teach software engineering at the undergraduate level. How can you argue that there is no software engineering at this level when electrical engineers are primarily undergraduates? There is always a level of education and information that is at the undergraduate level. We have a two semester senior-level sequence in software engineering as a capstone course for students getting an undergraduate degree in computer science. Certainly there is an important component that should be there. But this is a much larger discussion about educational philosophy than I am prepared to get into right now.

Al Pietrasanta: My comment is related to a couple concerning the trend toward technicians, because it is my belief that we are headed toward a dramatically different software development process than we have today. Hopefully that process will have less people involved to produce the same end result because we will have achieved a better productivity level. One way to get to that productivity level is by a more automated process than we have today. Most profoundly, I think the pattern of people involved in the process is going to change. Today, we have a dominant number of professionals, with relatively equal levels in salaries, supported by a minimal number of technicians. I think that mix is going to change into a single professional job of software engineer or systems engineer doing the truly creative work and management. That person is going to be supported with a collection of technicians, to keep the process running, keep the tools running, keep the measurements going, and keep the documentation coming out. In answer to the question, I think all those technicians we are talking about will come from an associate or two year program. For the mass of professionals we have today, there is a mass of programs. We are headed toward super-professionals and technicians. Our planning ought to address that radical departure in terms of personnel, planning and so forth.

Peter Freeman: How is that different from the super programmer concept?

Al Pietrasanta: I think that it is the super programmer carried to an nth degree across the entire project.

Dick Fairley: I'd certainly like to thank all of you for your participation in the workshop. It has been a valuable experience for me, for many of you, and for the SEI. I think the proceedings are going to be a valuable contribution to software engineering education.

Section IV

Appendix

Appendix 1

Proposed Curriculum for a
Master of Software Engineering (MSE)

Original Draft Prepared by James Collofello
Arizona State University
An Academic Affiliate of the SEI

Edited by James E. Tomayko
Software Engineering Institute

Editor's Note: This appendix contains the version of the proposed Master's in Software Engineering curriculum plan distributed to the conference participants in advance of the workshop. The approach to SEi curriculum development has been extensively revised based on the thoughts contained in the contributed papers and the results of discussions during the meeting.

Referees: Dan Burton, Clyde Chittister, Gary Ford, Norm Gibbs, Nico Habermann, Albert Johnson, John Manley, Dick Martin, Mary Shaw, Nelson Weiderman.

Preliminary Considerations

Defining the Product: What is a Software Engineer?

One goal of the Software Engineering Institute (SEI) is to help raise the quality of software engineering practice. A means of doing this is the creation of a model curriculum for the education of software engineers that would be adaptable to implementation in academia, industry, and the military. Designing such a curriculum is difficult because the product, "software engineers," and the techniques, "software engineering," are not well defined or understood. The SEI is making an attempt at achieving a better sense of what software engineering is, but the field is still far from staked out.[1] that summarizes past and current thought on the matter.) Still, some attributes of software engineers and software engineering can be stated to serve as a basis for beginning a curriculum design. These include the ability to:

---

[1]See articles by Albert Johnson, "Experts Disagree on Meaning of Software Engineering," *Bridge*, Vol. I, No. 1, June-July 1986 and "Software Engineering Combines Management and Technical Skills," *Bridge*, Vol I., No. 2, August-September 1986.

- Specify, design, code, test, and modify software systems utilizing state-of-the-art software engineering technology.
- Plan, organize, estimate costs, schedule, and track a software development or modification effort at the project leader level.
- Define and ensure software quality through the development and use of software metrics, standards, review procedures and configuration management approaches.
- Work with and/or manage computer science specialists, programmers, and other engineers in the development and modification of complex systems.
- Assess advances in software engineering, apply them to projects, and evaluate their effectiveness.
- Serve as a knowledgeable participant in system design activities involving allocation of functions to software versus other system components.

Science and Engineering in the Context of Software Development

An important distinction alluded to in the list of attributes is that between software science and software engineering. Computer science is a true "science of the artificial." It is the study of the nature of an artifact. Software aspects of computer science should be applicable to software engineering much like physics is applicable to mechanical engineering. Still, it remains unclear how science and engineering interact in software development. Although it is generally acknowledged that a purely computer science background is insufficient for immediate productivity as a software engineer (existing MSE programs at Seattle University and the Wang Institute require actual industry experience in addition to an appropriate undergraduate degree for admission), it is still an open question as to what parts of software science are best needed as a foundation of the education of software engineers. (Later versions of this curriculum will attempt to address this point in more detail.)

Education vs. Training

In order to develop a graduate curriculum in software engineering, it is necessary to differentiate between software engineering education and software engineering training and to determine the degree of each which is to be reflected in the curriculum.[2] The discipline can be divided into three interdependent layers:

- Principles and concepts for cost-effective development and modification of high quality software.
- Methodologies and techniques based on these principles and concepts.
- Tools supporting methodologies and techniques and how to use them.

Level 1 (Principles and Concepts of Software Engineering) represents that part of software engineering that is fundamental to the discipline. These principles and concepts, although still evolving, are relatively invariant and form a common thread through all of the various methodologies and techniques. An understanding and appreciation of these principles and concepts lies at the heart of software engineering education.

Level 2 (Methodologies and Techniques) represents that part of software engineering which actually provides the mechanisms for orderly software development and evolution in accordance with the software engineering principles and concepts. New methodologies and techniques are appearing at a rate faster than they can be effectively evaluated. This level can thus be viewed from both an educational and a training perspective. Step-by-step instruction of a contemporary methodology or technique is training. Yet a careful analysis of the strengths and weaknesses of current methodologies and techniques as well as guidelines and criteria for selecting appropriate methodologies and techniques for a particular application is educational.

Level 3 (Tools) represents that part of software engineering which automates methodologies or techniques. This is the most rapidly changing portion of the discipline. Instruction in current tool utilization

---

[2]The SEI has decided to concentrate on development of a master's level curriculum as a logical starting place. Plans include exploration of both undergraduate and doctoral-level curricula at a later date.

can be viewed as training, while an awareness of tool existence and capabilities, as well as principles of tool development, can be regarded as education.

A graduate level software engineering curriculum must focus heavily on educational issues rather than training issues. This implies a heavy concentration on levels 1 and 2 as described above. However, due to the practical nature of this program, some "hands on" experience with selected methodologies and tools must also be provided. This can most naturally be handled through a significant software development or modification project in which all candidates for the degree must participate. Representative state-of-the-art software tools must be available and easily accessible for utilization in the projects.

Design of the MSE Curriculum

Prerequisites

Deciding what requirements should be met for entrance into an MSE program is made difficult both because of the lack of an adequate definition of the product and a full understanding of the role of science. More difficulties are present because of the intent to offer the curriculum for education and training in industry. Many practicing programmers, software engineers, quality assurance personnel and project managers have sketchy or no academic background in computer science. By requiring industry experience for admission, Seattle and Wang try to recruit students with something in common. Seattle also makes available courses in basic computer science to assist students in acquiring sufficient knowledge to enter the core coursework. Those courses do not count toward the degree.

Arguments have been made within the SEI that the statement of prerequisites should be developed after rather than before the statement of the curriculum. That approach is accepted for this version, so no description of prerequisites is included. However, it is anticipated the the prerequisite structure will consist of scientific and mathematical components coupled with liberal arts skills related to software production and management, and an explicit position on the role of work experience vis-a-vis academic preparation. Diagnostic exams are one proposal for matching students to the proper level of the curriculum.

Structural Outline

Currently the curriculum is structured on a modular basis, each module roughly equivalent to one or two semester hours or one work week in an industrial setting.   Although some modules serve as prerequisites to others, they can be packaged in many different ways to satisfy the needs of DoD, industry, and educational institutions. For example, schools interested in forming traditional courses out of the modules could combine them and perhaps make better use of faculty expertise by assigning faculty by module rather than by course. Industrial organizations could schedule and space out modules relative to peak production periods and heavy vacation months. Although it is expected that some of the academic affiliates of the SEI will install the entire curriculum, other institutions and companies would use modules in existing training programs and courses, or in new offerings inspired by the availability of innovative materials.

Ideally, educational institutions would have an MSE degree program consisting of about 33 semester credits, of which 6 will be devoted to the project. An organization offering the MSE degree program will have to make available relevant electives in the areas of computer science, electrical engineering, and management science to support the program. Also, appropriate state-of-the-art software engineering tools must be available (perhaps through SEI via networks) to complement and support the MSE courses and projects.

The proposed MSE curriculum consists of four parts:

1. Software Engineering Core: modules which are deemed necessary for all software engineers regardless of their specialization. The bulk of the core consists of basic principles and concepts of software engineering. Due to the rapid changes in the practice of software engineering expected over the next decades, this is a true core in that it is the only part of the curriculum immune to the whims of technology. By concentrating on basic science and engineering principles, the graduates of the core can be expected to adapt to new environments more effectively than those taught in a technology-dominant curriculum.

2. Software Engineering Specialization: modules which build upon the core and add depth to a specialization area. Currently software engineers are most pervasively involved in technical and managerial positions. However, due to the nature of software development, premature specialization in either of these areas would be a mistake. For students who have a definite leaning in one direction or another, sufficient modules will exist to build on an area of interest and to later return for continuing education in other specializations. As presented here, a technical specialization enables a student to acquire more in depth knowledge of development and modification methodologies, techniques, and tools. The managerial specialization provides the additional project management information necessary to more effectively lead a software project.

3. Electives: those courses normally found in a graduate computer science program and, in addition, courses in management science, psychology, and electrical engineering which can provide additional depth to software engineering specialization areas. Computer science electives particularly relevant to software engineering include graphics, computing system architectures, operating systems, distributed computing, compiler construction, real-time system design, computer security and privacy, data base systems, communications, and expert systems.

4. Software Engineering Project: the project is normally expected to be of a one academic year duration and involve a significant software development and or modification effort involving teams of degree candidates. The project is the vehicle whereby students can apply their newly acquired software engineering skills. An individual student's tasks on the project should be mapped to correlate closely with their chosen specialization area. State-of-the art software engineering tools must also be available for students to utilize on the project. Projects should ideally be for the production of "real" software in that there is a customer requesting the product and that the product, if successfully developed, will be used. The SEI Education Division plans to issue a guide to the preparation of suitable projects as a service to prospective instructors. At what point the student should begin working on the project is still undetermined.

The proportion of the curriculum devoted to each segment of the design is impossible to determine until more complete module descriptions and a better understanding of objectives are developed. Roughly a third to nearly half of the curriculum will be core, about a fifth spent on the project, and the remainder used for closely related specialization modules and electives.

Module Descriptions

The SEI Education Division Graduate Curriculum Project will produce 40 to 50 modules. A **module** is a unit of the curriculum embodied by a document of 20 to 30 pages containing:

- Title
- Capsule description: a short (30 words) description of the content of the module, similar to a college catalog entry.
- Philosophy: a brief explanation of why the module exists and its relationship to other modules.
- Behavioral objectives: specific statements of measurable knowledge and skills students will obtain by completing the module.
- Prerequisites: defined in terms of other modules, or in terms of knowledge obtained in undergraduate coursework.
- Syllabus: a summary outline of the content.
- Detailed outline: details of the topics to be covered, indicating the level of coverage.
- Annotated bibliography: a bibliography of the most pertinent papers in the literature, annotated to indicate which papers cover which parts of the module material, which papers are surveys and which provide deeper coverage, and which papers are most readable by students.
- Textbooks: a list of textbooks that offer coverage of the module material. In many cases this will be an empty list until an SEI monograph targeted at the module is published.
- Teaching support: where appropriate, exercises or project suggestions to aid the instructor.

- Software support: where appropriate, brief descriptions of software products that can support the module, including suggestions for how they may be used.

Each of the modules in this section is identified with a prefix and a number. The prefixes are:

- **TECH**
- **MGMT**

The numbers have three digits xyz where x corresponds to the place of the course in the curriculum (1 = core, 2 = specialty), y corresponds to the topic within the prefix area concentration, and z corresponds to the course within the topic area. For example, **TECH 131 Software Generation** is a technical course in the core topic of software design and implementation concepts, and the first course in that topic.

Note that the curriculum is still in a primitive state of development, and that prerequisites, specific topics, and balance among modules can only be established after objectives are defined.

Core Modules

TECH100   **Overview of Software Engineering**

Presentation of the history of the development of software engineering, its *raison d'etre*, a description of the behaviors of a software engineer, purpose of the curriculum, and (where applicable) an introduction to the support tools and resources available at the teaching site.

TECH101   **Communication Techniques for Software Engineers**

Practice of writing and oral presentation techniques to prepare students for creating technical documents and reports used in software engineering, such as requirements specifications, user documentation, and design reviews. Emphasis on awareness of good communication principles that can be applied in the curriculum and on the job.

TECH111   **Software Interface Engineering**

The study of principles relating to interaction among computers and computers and humans. Concentra-

tion on human factors and the evaluation of interface technology directed at man/machine communication. Hardware/software interfaces between
computers in embedded systems and networks, as
well as interfaces to knowledge bases.

TECH121   **Software Requirements Engineering**

Survey of the techniques of software requirements
specification, including formal and informal methods
such as rapid prototyping, modeling, and simulation.
Defining performance and quality requirements.

TECH131   **Software Generation**

Principles and theories of software design, including
structuring, object orientation, data flow, filters,
pipes, reusability, and automatic code generation.

TECH132   **Implementation Considerations**

Techniques of implementing software designs within
the constraints of languages and environments,
such as special considerations when using languages without inherent structuring (assembly languages, COBOL) and methods for making best use
of languages designed for engineering (Ada^{TM3}).

TECH133   **Tool Building**

Concepts of tool construction and utilization. Survey
of general purpose tools and specification and construction of project-specific tools.

TECH141   **Software Correctness Assessment**

The analysis of correctness and safety issues in
various types of software systems, such as real-
time software, embedded software, expert systems,
networks, and data processing. Also, a survey of
approaches for reasoning about and certifying
software correctness, including testing, program
verification, walkthroughs/inspections, and simulation.

TECH151   **Engineering Software Evolution**

Study of the techniques of controlling the evolution
of software systems relating to the evaluation of the

---

[3]Ada is a registered trademark of the U. S. Department of Defense.

impact of proposed software changes, maintaining software integrity, and software configuration management techniques and tools.

TECH161 **Software Quality Factors**

Identification of software quality factors and metrics, ways of evaluating metrics, and data collection and analysis techniques.

MGMT111 **Project Management**

An introduction to the principles of software development project management, including overall development plans, software quality assurance plans, work breakdown structures, PERT charts, GANTT charts, life cycle models, unit development folders, and earned value concepts.

MGMT121 **Project Organizational Structures**

Methodology of organizing personnel for project development and evolution through study of human factors, chief programmer teams, matrix management, functional approaches, and organizational behavior.

MGMT131 **Principles of Cost Estimation and Scheduling**

Evolution of estimating economic factors of software development from mythical man month ideas to current cost estimation and scheduling techniques and tools.

Specialty Modules

TECH211 **Human Interface Design**

Assessment of user needs and capabilities, analysis of current approaches, and guidelines for selection of an appropriate interface.

TECH221 **Software Requirements Specification Models, Techniques and Tools**

Analysis of requirements specification models, techniques, and tools, evaluation of the strengths and weaknesses of approaches, and guidelines for selection of techniques.

TECH222   **Software Prototyping**

Study of prototyping as a specification tool and review of existing techniques.

TECH231   **Design Methodologies and Tools**

Design and utilization of reusable software, analysis of design methodologies and tools, and guidelines for selection of a methodology.

TECH232   **Design of High Reliability Systems**

Principles and techniques of fault-tolerant design in which fault tolerance is software-centered.

TECH233   **Engineering Software for Applications in Artificial Intelligence**

Analysis of special considerations in the development of software for knowledge-based systems, use of list processing and logic-oriented implementation languages, special development tools, and handling self-evolving systems.

TECH234   **Real-time System Development**

Engineering software for real-time and/or embedded systems, including sizing and timing constraints, redundancy management, hardware environments, and interaction with analog devices.

TECH235   **Firmware**

Special considerations in the development of firmware.

TECH241   **Principles of Testing**

Fundamental consideration of levels of testing, test plans, test management, documentation of test cases, black box/white box testing approaches, and unit testing.

TECH242   **Integration and System Testing**

Higher level construction of systems, integration strategies, integration test plans, testing real-time systems, testing embedded software, analysis of integration and system testing techniques and tools, and guidelines for selecting among approaches.

TECH243   **Program Verification**

Proof of correctness, limitations, and analysis of tools.

TECH244	**Software Review Technologies**

Walkthroughs, inspections, human factors, checklists, organization of review groups, documenting review results, automated review techniques.

TECH245	**Software Safety**

Specification of software safety requirements, generating safe systems, validation of software safety requirements.

TECH251	**Software Configuration Management Techniques and Tools**

Analysis of SCM techniques and tools, strengths and weaknesses of techniques and tools, guidelines for selection of techniques and tools.

TECH261	**Reliability Metrics**

Current reliability models, error seeding.

TECH262	**Maintainability Metrics**

Complexity metrics, modifiability metrics, testability metrics, maintainability assessment techniques.

TECH263	**Management Metrics**

Productivity metrics, cost metrics, scheduling metrics, size metrics.

MGMT211	**Software Engineering Economics**

Risk assessment, cost/benefit analysis, trade-off studies.

MGMT212	**Software Contracting**

Legal issues, cost estimating applicable to contracting, quality assurance applied to contracting, financial management process, life cycle of contracted software, legal issues relating to erroneous software.

MGMT221	**Management of Project Personnel**

Human factors, evaluations, motivation issues.

MGMT231	**Cost Estimation and Scheduling Techniques and Tools**

Analysis of approaches, survey of tools, guidelines for selection of approaches.

Appendix 2

Educational Needs of the Software Community

Gary Ford
Software Engineering Institute

Preface

The importance of education in an industrialized and democratic society is generally accepted. It is nearly impossible to identify specific aspects of a person's education that are responsible for particular contributions that that person makes to society; instead we simply agree that education is necessary.

Nevertheless, for many broad classes of activities, we can identify some of the necessary education and training. For example, most professional activities require a background including natural language skills (reading, writing) and quantitative skills (measurement, arithmetic). Specialized activities may require education in the arts, social sciences, or physical sciences.

In this paper we will examine the class of activities informally called *software development*, identify some education and training needed by persons who perform these activities, and then suggest ways to meet the education needs. The distinction between *education* and *training* is important. Education provides the fundamentals upon which training can be based. Training usually has a short-term, well defined goal, and may concentrate on the performance of a particular process. Education has longer term, less well defined goals, and must also include reasoning about processes rather than just performance. We will concentrate on education almost exclusively in this discussion.

The Shortage of Software Professionals

It is difficult to predict accurately the growth of the software industry and the growing need of skilled software professionals. However, several studies have been done that agree roughly on the growth of the industry. Together, they can help define the scope of the problem.

As an example, consider the software needed to support NASA's manned spaceflight programs. The growth of the size of the software, measured in object instructions, has grown from approximately one million for Project Mercury to 40 million for the Space Shuttle [see Stokes, 1970; Reifer, 1977]. This represents a growth rate of 20% to 25% per year. Similar growth has been seen in the onboard software in military avionics systems. One survey estimated a 24% annual increase in the total number of computers, indicating perhaps a comparable overall growth rate in software needs [see Phister, 1979].

Similar studies of software personnel indicate growth rates of 3% to 4% [see Dolatta, 1976; Morrisey and Wu, 1979]. Most large producers of software indicate that they are experiencing difficulty in hiring enough software personnel, although they cannot provide a precise measure of the shortfall.

The productivity of software producers is also increasing, but again, not at a rate comparable to the growth of the size of and need for software systems. The same studies cited above indicate a 3% to 6% growth rate in productivity. Extrapolation of these growth rates would indicate that sometime in the 1990s there will be such a shortage that many software products will simply not be produced, and the ones that are will be attempted with insufficient personnel, resulting in very low quality.

The ramifications of this problem for the Department of Defense software contractor community are serious. With the increasing reliance on computers and software in nearly all weapons systems, communications systems, and command operations, there is the potential that most new systems will not be able to be developed.

Education as Part of the Solution

The shortage of skilled software professionals cannot be solved by simply increasing the number of persons in the profession. The situation is analogous to the shortage of telephone operators early in this century. The growth in the number of telephones and the number of calls being made was known, so the growth in the number of operators needed to place those calls was predictable. The prediction indicated that within a few years, every man, woman, and child in the United States would have to be employed as a telephone operator. (A study of military aircraft avionics software led to a similar prediction: by 2015, every man, woman, and child in the United States will have to be writing avionics software.)

Obviously, not every person in the country became a telephone operator. Technology advanced fast enough to increase dramatically the productivity of each operator, to the current situation where technology allows automatic placing of almost all calls. A similar advance in software engineering technology is needed.

Most observers agree that because software development is a substantially more creative activity than placing a telephone call, the advances in technology that will have the most benefit are new techniques and methodologies that can be employed by software engineers, rather than new machines that do the jobs for the engineers. Education is the major path to the goal of developing and using this new technology.

Software engineering education has several objectives. The first two are directly related to the problems already discussed: education must produce more software engineers and must increase the productivity of the current practitioners. Two other objectives are to produce two kinds of professionals, one that can use the emerging technology, and another that can create the needed new technology. We believe that all of these objectives can be met by a coordinated set of educational efforts.

First, it is necessary to identify just what constitutes the body of knowledge we wish to call *software engineering*. Second, that material needs to be organized as a coherent curriculum, complete with all varieties of supporting educational materials. Third, colleges and universities must be helped in many ways, including faculty development, so that they may offer the curriculum; this will help increase the number of software engineers. Fourth, existing software professionals must be given the opportunity to receive this education also, since the majority of them do not have broad backgrounds in the current principles of the discipline. This will help increase the productivity of these professionals.

With the appropriate educational background, we believe software engineers will be able to adjust rapidly to the expected advances in software technology, thus achieving the maximum increases in productivity promised by that technology. Thus education is critical to preventing the threatened "software crisis."

A Graduate Curriculum in Software Engineering

The Education Division of the Software Engineering Institute has undertaken to define the content of a software engineering curriculum. It has been decided that we should base that curriculum on fundamental knowledge from other disciplines, primarily computer science, rather than starting from scratch. The amount of prerequisite material was sufficiently large to make it impractical to try to structure the software engineering curriculum at the undergraduate level.

Additionally, if the curriculum is to reach current software professionals, most of whom already have undergraduate degrees, a graduate program is likely to be perceived as more attractive and more valuable. Many universities currently offer graduate programs for professionals, and these have often been very successful.

These factors indicate to us that a professionally oriented master's degree program is likely to have the most significant impact on the educational needs of the software community. This program might be offered by some schools as a Master of Science in Software Engineering (MSSE), and by others as a Master of Software Engineering (MSE). However, we recognize that the content of the curriculum, rather than the diploma, is most important, and so the material should be made available to professionals through their companies as well as through universities.

The development of an entirely new curriculum is a difficult task. It requires an enormous investment of resources, including personnel, time, and money. Probably no one university has the resources to commit to such a project. On the other hand, the Education Division of the SEI has been charged with investigating all aspects of software engineering education, and has been given the resources to do whatever needs to be done. This includes not only the design of the curriculum, but the production of all kinds of supporting materials (textbooks, exercises, software, etc.) Furthermore, the SEI can take an active role in the faculty development needed to allow universities to offer the curriculum, and can serve as *the* principal software engineering education resource center.

The plan for the development of the curriculum and support materials is relatively easy to describe. We expect to do the following:

1. Identify the fundamental principles of software engineering.
2. Identify the current techniques, methodologies, and tools of software engineering.
3. Identify those aspects of software engineering theory and practice that are essential to all professionals (the core curriculum), and those aspects that are specialized areas of knowledge needed by only some software engineers. This latter category will include topics that are application domain specific, and topics pertinent to the activities of only certain members of a development team (such as advanced topics in project management or software quality assurance).
4. Organize the content of the curriculum into modules of appropriate size to allow packaging the curriculum for the varying needs of diverse audiences. Our current idea is that a module will require about 15 hours of student contact time. One module could be taught as a two day industry short course; three related modules could be taught as a university semester course.
5. Produce complete documentation of each module, including course outline and syllabus, reading list, textbook suggestions, and exercise suggestions.
6. Where necessary, cause the production of additional support material, including textbooks or monographs, educational software (specifically, tools to support a software engineering laboratory), and materials to help instructors provide large scale project experience to students.

Once the curriculum is designed, our plan is to provide all the support necessary to have it successfully inserted into universities and company education programs. This will focus primarily on faculty development, because the shortage of computer science and software engineering educators is acute. We expect to provide opportunities for existing faculty to learn the material of the curriculum in training workshops, and then they can take the curriculum and materials back to their home institutions. The resultant compounding effect will allow us to teach more software engineers than if we presented the material directly to the students.

Special Issues in Software Engineering Education

The graduate curriculum is the most important immediate step toward improved software engineering education, but it is not the only step. Software development projects require a variety of personnel, with a variety of skills. Examples are project managers (management skills), applications scientists and engineers (domain specific knowledge), and software engineers and software engineering technicians (various levels of software knowledge and experience). The educational backgrounds of these persons will vary considerably, although all will need some familiarity with computer systems and software systems.

To address these needs, it is envisioned that additional educational projects will be undertaken by the SEI. Among these are the development of specialized modules or courses for advanced students and practitioners. A doctoral program in software engineering will also be investigated.

However, the greatest number of software professionals will be needed at a lower level. As the discipline of software engineering matures, we expect that it will be easier to distinguish it from computer science, and thus it may become possible to develop an undergraduate curriculum in software engineering.

The need for such a curriculum is beginning to become evident. Many employers now comment that newly hired computer science graduates are not ready for immediate assignment to software development projects because of their inexperience with large projects, their lack of group programming skills, and a lack of understanding of management and business economics. Such comments should not be regarded as indictments of computer science curricula, but rather as an indication that employers really need software engineers rather than computer scientists. Just as employers have distinguished physicists from electrical engineers, and chemists from chemical engineers, when recruiting new college graduates, they will soon begin to distinguish computer scientists from software engineers.

One other special issue should be mentioned. The defense contractor community will be developing future software systems in the Ada™ language, and therefore there is a great need for software engineers capable of using this language. However, Ada is one tool among many that a software engineer must use. The foundations of software engineering, upon which Ada is based, are the domain of software engineering education, and are being addressed by the graduate curriculum project. The syntax and semantics of Ada, on the other hand, are training issues. The Technology Transition and Training Department of the SEI is involved with Ada insertion projects. However, the leaders in Ada training are the Ada Joint Program Office (AJPO), the Association for Computing Machinery (ACM) Special Interest Group on Ada (SIGAda), and the Ada JOVIAL Users' Group (AdaJUG). The SEI will not try to duplicate the efforts of these groups.

Summary

The apparent exponential growth of the size of software systems for both the Department of Defense and others needs to be matched by a similar growth in the number and productivity of software engineers. The most significant means of such a large productivity increase is the development of new technology to support software engineering. This technology is likely to take the form of techniques, methodologies, and associated software tools, and the use of this technology will require a substantial education effort.

The SEI Education Division has the resources to undertake this effort. Its major activities are the development of a graduate curriculum in software engineering, production of supporting materials, and the insertion of the curriculum into the educational community. The impact of this effort is expected to be apparent in the 1990s.

References

[1]   Dolotta, T.A. and others. *Data Processing in 1980-85.* John Wiley & Sons, New York, 1976.

[2]   Morrisey, J. and Wu, S.Y. "Software Engineering: An Economic Perspective." In *Proceedings, Fourth International Conference on Software Engineering.* IEEE Catalog, September, 1979.

[3]   Phister, M., Jr. *Data Processing Technology and Economics.* Digital Press, Bedford, MA, 1979.

[4]   Reifer, D.J. "Software Acquisition Planning for the DoD Space Transportation System (Space KShuttle)." In *Proceedings, AIAA/DPMA Third Software Management Conference.* Washington, D.C., 1977.

[5]   Stokes, J.C. "Managing the Developing of Large Software Systems: Apollo Real-tie Control Center." In *Proceedings, Wescon 70,* August, 1970.